SECOND EDITION

GOOGLE
HACKS™

Tara Calishain and Rael Dornfest

D1041074

O'REILLY®

Beijing · Cambridge · Farnham · Köln · Paris · Sebastopol · Taipei · Tokyo

Google Hacks™, Second Edition

by Tara Calishain and Rael Dornfest

Published by O'Reilly Media, Inc., 1005 Gravenstein Highway North, Sebastopol, CA 95472.

O'Reilly books may be purchased for educational, business, or sales promotional use. Online editions are also available for most titles (*safari.oreilly.com*). For more information, contact our corporate/institutional sales department: (800) 998-9938 or *corporate@oreilly.com*.

Editors:	Brian Sawyer	**Production Editor:**	Adam Witwer
	Rael Dornfest	**Cover Designer:**	Edie Freedman
Series Editor:	Rael Dornfest	**Interior Designer:**	Melanie Wang
Executive Editor:	Dale Dougherty		

Printing History:

February 2003:	First Edition.
December 2004:	Second Edition.

 This book uses RepKover™, a durable and flexible lay-flat binding.

ISBN: 0-596-00857-0

[I]

To our Grannies: Olivia and Miriam

Contents

Foreword

When the first edition of *Google Hacks* appeared, we were frankly a bit surprised that there was enough *hacking* going on to make up a whole book. No longer. People continue to discover more ways than we ever imagined to tweak, tone, and otherwise futz around with Google bits for myriad uses.

In the 18 months since *Google Hacks* first appeared, search has, if possible, only grown in importance. Not only is there more information than ever to be found—via email, computer hard drives, and newly digitized repositories of previously offline content—there is also a greater need to automate tasks and to locate that needle of information in a haystack that just will not stop growing.

We hope that you enjoy this new *Google Hacks* effort and continue to help us make the most of the world's information by making it universally accessible and useful.

—Craig Silverstein, Director of Technology, Google

Foreword to the First Edition

When we started Google, it was hard to predict how big it would become. That our search engine would someday serve as a catalyst for so many important web developments was a distant dream. We are honored by the growing interest in Google and offer many thanks to those who created this book—the largest and most comprehensive report on Google search technology that has yet to be published.

Search is an amazing field of study, because it offers infinite possibilities for how we might find and make information available to people. We join with the authors in encouraging readers to approach this book with a view toward discovering and creating new ways to search. Google's mission is to organize the world's information and make it universally accessible and useful, and we welcome any contribution you make toward achieving this goal.

Hacking is the creativity that fuels the Web. As software developers ourselves, we applaud this book for its adventurous spirit. We're adventurous, too, and were happy to discover that this book highlights many of the same experiments we conduct on our free time here at Google.

Google is constantly adapting its search algorithms to match the dynamic growth and changing nature of the Web. As you read, please keep in mind that the examples in this book are valid today but, as Google innovates and grows over time, may become obsolete. We encourage you to follow the latest developments and to participate in the ongoing discussions about search as facilitated by books such as this one.

Virtually every engineer at Google has used an O'Reilly publication to help them with their jobs. O'Reilly books are a staple of the Google engineering library, and we hope that *Google Hacks* will be as useful to others as the O'Reilly publications have been to Google.

With the largest collection of web documents in the world, Google is a reflection of the Web. The hacks in this book are not just about Google, they are also about unleashing the vast potential of the Web today and in the years to come. *Google Hacks* is a great resource for search enthusiasts, and we hope you enjoy it as much as we did.

Thanks,

—The Google Engineering Team
December 11, 2002
Mountain View, California

Credits

About the Authors

Tara Calishain is the editor of ResearchBuzz (*http://www.researchbuzz. com*), a weekly newsletter on Internet searching and online information resources. She's also a regular columnist for *Searcher* magazine. She's been writing about search engines and searching since 1996; her recent books include *Web Search Garage*.

Rael Dornfest is Chief Technology Officer at O'Reilly Media. He assesses, experiments, programs, fiddles, fidgets, and writes for the O'Reilly Network and various O'Reilly publications. Rael is Series Editor of the O'Reilly Hacks series (*http://hacks.oreilly.com*) and has edited, contributed to, and coauthored various O'Reilly books, including *Mac OS X Panther Hacks*, *Mac OS X Hacks*, the *Google Pocket Guide*, *Google: The Missing Manual*, *Essential Blogging*, and *Peer to Peer: Harnessing the Power of Disruptive Technologies*. He is also Program Chair for the O'Reilly Emerging Technology Conference (*http://conferences.oreilly. com/etech*). In his copious free time, Rael develops bits and bobs of freeware, particularly the Blosxom weblog application (*http://www.blosxom. com*), is Editor in Chief of MobileWhack (*http://www.mobilewhack.com*), and (more often than not) maintains his Raelity Bytes weblog (*http:// www.raelity.org*).

Contributors

The following people contributed their hacks, writing, and inspiration to this book:

- Tim Allwine is a Senior Software Engineer at O'Reilly Media. He develops software for the Market Research group—various spidering tools that collect data from disparate sites—and is involved in the development of web services at O'Reilly.

- DJ Adams (*http://www.pipetree.com/qmacro*) is an SAP hacker who pines for the days when he wrote job control language and S/370 assembler and got around central London on his skateboard. Currently, he is knee-deep in NetWeaver technologies and uses up spare brain cycles playing with REST, RDF, and Jabber. He wrote O'Reilly's *Programming Jabber: Extending XML Messaging* and cowrote *Google Pocket Guide*, also from O'Reilly. He lives in Europe with Sabine and Joseph.

- AvaQuest (*http://www.avaquest.com*) is a Massachusetts-based IT services firm that specializes in applying advanced information retrieval, categorization, and text mining technologies to solve real-world problems. GooglePeople and GoogleMovies, created by Ava-Quest consultants Nathan Treloar, Sally Kleinfeldt, and Peter Richards, came out of a web mining consulting project the team worked on in the summer of 2002, shortly after the Google Web API was announced.

- Paul Bausch (*http://www.onfocus.com*) is a freelance web developer and author living in Oregon. He was a cocreator of the Blogger weblog software and recently cowrote a book about weblogs called *We Blog: Publishing Online with Weblogs*. He believes (like Google) that "love" (75,700,000) will conquer "hate" (7,900,000).

- Erik Benson (*http://www.erikbenson.com*).

- Justin Blanton (*http://justinblanton.com*) has a B.S. in computer engineering and is currently attending law school in Silicon Valley, where he is focusing on intellectual property law and will likely practice both patent prosecution and litigation. Much of his "free time" is spent writing about various things on his web site, including Mac OS X, mobile phones and other gadgets, general tips and tricks for the Movable Type CMS, and life in general.

- CapeScience.com (*http://www.capescience.com*) is the development community for Cape Clear Software, a web services company. In addition to providing support for Cape Clear's products, Cape-Science makes all sorts of fun web services stuff, including live services, clients to other services, utilities, and other geekware.

- Antoni Chan (*http://www.alltooflat.com*) is one of the founders of All Too Flat, a bastion of quirky content, pranks, and geeky humor. The Google Mirror is a 2,500-line CGI script that was developed over the period of a year starting in October 2001. When not working on his web site, he enjoys playing music, bowling, and running after a Frisbee.

- Tanya Harvey Ciampi (*http://www.multilingual.ch*) grew up in Buckinghamshire, England, and went on to study in Zurich, where she obtained her diploma in translation. She now lives in Ticino, the Italian-speaking region of Switzerland, where she works as an English technical translator (from Italian, German, and French) and proofreader, and teaches translation and Internet search techniques based on her WWW Search Interfaces for Translators. In her free time, she enjoys fishing with her father on the west coast of Ireland, writing poems, and playing Celtic music.

- Peter Drayton (*http://www.razorsoft.net/weblog/*) is a program manager in the CLR team at Microsoft. Before joining Microsoft, he was an independent consultant, trainer for DevelopMentor, and author of *C# Essentials* and *C# in a Nutshell* (O'Reilly).

- Andrew Flegg (*http://www.bleb.org*) works for IBM in the U.K., having graduated from the University of Warwick a few years ago. He's currently the webmaster of Hursley Lab's intranet site. Most of his work (and fun) at the moment is taken up with Perl, Java, HTML, and CSS. Andrew is particularly keen on clean, reusable code, which always ends up saving time in the long run. He's written several open source projects, as well as a couple of commercial applications for RISC OS (as used in the Iyonix PC, the first desktop computer using an Intel XScale).

- Andrew Goodman (*http://www.page-zero.com*) is founder and principal of Page Zero Media, which helps clients perform better on paid search campaigns. He blogs his thoughts regularly as Editor-at-Large of Traffick.com, a contrarian's guide to search engines and portals. *Fortune Small Business*, *The Washington Post*, *New Media Age*, *The New York Times*, *Bloomberg Markets*, *Business Week*, *Reuters*, *The National Post*, *CBS Marketwatch*, *Forbes*, and numerous other business publications have sought his views on search advertising. He is author of *Winning Results with Google AdWords* (McGraw-Hill, late 2004). One of his favorite Google hacks is GooPoetry.

- Kevin Hemenway (*http://www.disobey.com*), better known as Morbus Iff, is the creator of disobey.com, which bills itself as "content for the discontented." Publisher, developer, and writer of more home cooking than you could ever imagine (like the popular open source syndicated reader AmphetaDesk, the best-kept gaming secret Gamegrene.com, the popular Ghost Sites and Nonsense Network, the giggle-inducing articles at the O'Reilly Network, a few pieces at

Apple's Internet Developer site, etc.), he's an ardent supporter of cloning merely so he can get more work done. He cooks with a Fry Pan of Intellect +2 and lives in Concord, New Hampshire.

- Mark Horrell (*http://www.markhorrell.com*) has worked in search engine optimization since 1996 when he joined Net Resources International, a publisher of industrial engineering web sites, where he conceived and developed the company's Internet marketing strategy. He left in 2002 and is now a freelance web developer based in London, U.K., specializing in search engine–friendly design.

- Judy Hourihan (*http://judy.hourihan.com*).

- Leland Johnson (*http://protoplasmic.org*) is currently a student at Illinois Institute of Technology. He tried learning Perl in 1999, then tried again and was successful in 2001, and now uses it for everything except his classes. When he's not busied by his classes, he updates his weblog, explores Chicago, and plays far too many video games.

- Steven Johnson (*http://www.stevenberlinjohnson.com/*) is the author of two books, *Emergence* and *Interface Culture*. He cocreated the sites FEED and Plastic.com, and now blogs regularly at *http://www.stevenberlinjohnson.com*. He writes the monthly "Emerging Technology" column for *Discover* magazine, and his work has appeared in many publications, including *The New York Times*, *Harper's*, *Wired*, and *The New Yorker*. He lives in Brooklyn, New York.

- Richard Jones (*http://richard.jones.name*) has spent the last four years working as a software engineer for Agent Oriented Software (*http://www.agent-software.com*). AOS develops a leading intelligent agent development platform known as JACK Intelligent Agents. Before AOS, he worked as a software engineer for Senate Software (a small search technology company), where he developed web page relevance heuristics. Before that, Richard was a cofounder of Earthmen Technology, which developed network intrusion detection technologies. At Earthman, he was responsible for a majority of the development, which included low-level TCP/IP networking code, Linux kernel hacking, and fast-pattern matching algorithms. He has two degrees, one in computer science and another in cognitive science, both from LaTrobe University (*http://www.latrobe.edu.au*). While in school, Richard majored in computer science, linguistics, and psychology, areas he retains a keen interest in. Richard is also a squash-playing Buddhist.

- Stuart Langridge (*http://www.kryogenix.org*) gets paid to hack on the Web during the day, and does it for free at night when he's not arguing about Buffy or Debian GNU/Linux. He's keen on web standards, Python, and strange things you can do with JavaScript, all of which can be seen at his web site and weblog. He's also slightly surprised that the Google Art Creator, which was an amusing little hack done in a day, is the most popular thing he's ever written and got him into a book.

- Beau Lebens (*http://www.dentedreality.com.au*) is a PHP web developer who believes that even complex systems can be made simple for an end user. Originally from Perth, Western Australia, he is currently working in Hawaii. He has released a number of projects on his web site, including webpad, the web-based text editor; Avant-Blog, a Palm/Pocket PC Blogging application; and the PHP Blogger API, which provides PHP developers with access to the Blogger API. Beau is a big believer in simpler, distributed technologies like Atom, REST, and RSS for the future of the Web.

- Philipp Lenssen (*http://blog.outer-court.com*) was born in 1977 and currently lives in Stuttgart, Germany. He's working as developer on the web sites of a popular German car maker. Previously, he spent 9 months living in Malaysia and prefers to eat very spicy. In his spare-time, Philipp is the author behind the daily Google Blogoscoped (a weblog covering Google, online research, and internet fun in general), trying to crack his head on how to tap the web consciousness.

- Mark Lyon (*http://marklyon.org*) is the creator of the Google GMail Loader. A former programmer for the U.S. Army Corps of Engineers, he gave up his aspirations of programming greatness after an unsuccessful interview at Google. He is now a law student at Mississippi College in Jackson, Mississippi, with plans to practice intellectual property and technology law. In his spare time, he writes novel but mediocre software in whatever language strikes his fancy.

- Paul Mutton (*http://www.jibble.org*) currently works for Netcraft in the U.K. He graduated with first-class honors in computer science, winning the IEE Institution Prize for being the best overall student in his department. He uses Google on a daily basis and Internet Relay Chat (IRC) to collaborate with fellow Ph.D. students in other countries. In his remaining spare time, he uses his Sun Certified Java Programmer skills to develop all sorts of open source software on his personal web site (*http://www.jibble.org*). Some of his research has culminated in the creation of the popular PieSpy application (*http://www.jibble.org/piespy*), which infers and visualizes social networks on IRC and even appeared on Slashdot once. He can normally be found jibbling around in *#jibble* and *#irchacks* on the freenode IRC network with the nickname Jibbler, or Paul on smaller networks.

- Mark Pilgrim (*http://diveintomark.org*) is the author of *Dive Into Python*, a free Python book for experienced programmers, and *Dive Into Accessibility*, a free book on web accessibility techniques. He works for MassLight, a Washington, D.C.–based training and web development company, where, unsurprisingly, he does training and web development. But he lives outside Raleigh, North Carolina, because it's warmer.

- Andrew Savikas works in the O'Reilly Tools Group, where he helps the production department turn manuscripts into O'Reilly books. Andrew is the author of *Word Hacks*, also published by O'Reilly. He developed and maintains the custom Word template and VBA macros used by all the O'Reilly authors who don't insist on writing in POD. Except for the ones who insist on writing in XML. Or Troff. Andrew also works with FrameMaker, FrameScript, InDesign, DocBook XML, Perl, Python, Ruby, and whatever else he finds lying around the office. He has a degree in communications from the University of Illinois at Urbana-Champaign, and lives in Boston with his wife Audrey, who loves to see her name in print.

- Chris Sells (*http://www.sellsbrothers.com*) is an independent consultant, speaker, and author specializing in distributed applications in .NET and COM. He's written several books and is currently working on *Windows Forms for C# and VB.NET Programmers* and *Mastering Visual Studio .NET*. In his free time, Chris hosts various conferences, directs the Genghis source-available project, plays with Rotor, and makes a pest of himself in general at Microsoft design reviews.

- Alex Shapiro (*http://www.touchgraph.com*) is the founder and CTO of TouchGraph LLC. Alex graduated from Columbia's computer science program in 2000, and spent his early career at a consulting company. After the stock-market bubble burst, he decided to spend time developing a network visualization product he had conceived. Through network visualization, Alex found that he could combine his interests in user interface design, graph theory, and sociology. After seeing a business demand for his technology, Alex founded TouchGraph LLC, which is slowly gathering a list of respected clients.

- Kevin Shay (*http://www.staggernation.com*) is a writer and web programmer who lives in Brooklyn, New York. His Google API scripts,

Movable Type plug-ins, and other work can be found at the soon-to-launch staggernation.com.

- Gary Stock (*http://www.googlewhack.com/stock.htm*) coined the term "Google whack" while he had intended to be doing research for UnBlinking (*http://www.unblinking.com*). When Gary writes for UnBlinking, he might better be focused on his role as CTO of the news clipping and briefing service Nexcerpt (*http://www.nexcerpt.com*). Gary works at Nexcerpt to get a break from stewardship of the unusual flora and fauna on the 160 acres of woods and wetland that he owns, which in turn keeps him from spending time with his wife (and Nexcerpt CEO) Julie, whom he married to offset his former all-consuming career as an above-top-secret computer spy, which he had entered to avoid permanently becoming a jazz arranger and pianist. Seriously.

- Aaron Swartz (*http://www.aaronsw.com*) is a teenage writer, coder, and hacker. He is a coauthor of the RSS 1.0 specification, a member of the W3C RDF Core Working Group, and metadata adviser to the Creative Commons. He's also the guy behind the Google Weblog (*http://google.blogspace.com*). He can be reached at *me@aaronsw.com*.

- Brett Tabke (*http://www.webmasterworld.com*) is the owner/operator of WebmasterWorld.com, the leading news and discussion site for web developers and search engine marketers. Tabke has been involved in computing since the late 1970s and is one of the Internet's foremost authorities on search engine optimization.

- Adam Trachtenberg (*http://www.trachtenberg.com*) is Manager of Technical Evangelism at eBay, where he preaches the gospel of the eBay platform to developers and businessmen around the globe. Before eBay, Adam cofounded and served as Vice President for Development at two companies, Student.Com and TVGrid.Com. At both firms, he led the front- and middle-end web site design and development. Adam began using PHP in 1997 and is the author of *Upgrading to PHP 5* and coauthor of *PHP Cookbook*, both published by O'Reilly Media. He lives in San Francisco and has a B.A. and M.B.A. from Columbia University

- Phillip M. Torrone is a feature columnist for *http://www.engadget.com* and contributing editor to *Popular Science*. Coauthor of *Flash Enabled: Design and Development for Mobile Devices*, Phillip has also contributed to numerous books and magazines on hardware hacking, cell phones, and PDAs. Phillip's latest work and more can be found at *http://www.flashenabled.com*.

- Matt Webb is an engineer and designer, splitting his working life between R&D with BBC Radio & Music Interactive and freelance projects (primarily in the social software world), most recently coauthoring *Mind Hacks* for O'Reilly. Online, he can be found at Interconnected (*http://interconnected.org/home*) and, in the real world, in London.

Acknowledgments

We would like to thank all those who contributed their ideas and code for Google hacks to this book. Many thanks to Nelson Minar and the rest of the Google Engineering Team, Nate Tyler, and everyone else at Google who provided ideas, suggestions, and answers—not to mention the Google Web API itself. And to Andy Lester and Justin Blanton, our technical editors along the way, goes much appreciation for their thorough nitpicking.

Tara

Everyone at O'Reilly has been great in helping pull this book together, but I wouldn't have gotten to participate in this book if it hadn't been for Tim Allwine, who first helped me with Perl programs a couple of years ago.

My family, especially my husband, has been great about tolerating my distraction as I sat around muttering to myself about variables and subroutines.

Even as this book was being written, I needed help understanding what Perl could and couldn't do. Kevin Hemenway was an excellent teacher, patiently explaining, providing examples, and when all else failed, pointing and laughing at my code.

Of course, most of this book wouldn't exist without the release of Google's API. A big thanks to Google for building a playground for us thousands of search-engine junkies. And just as big a thanks to the many contributors who so generously allowed their applications to appear in this book.

Finally, a big, big, he-gets-his-own-paragraph thanks to Rael Dornfest, who is a great coauthor/editor and a lot of fun to work with.

Rael

First and foremost, to Asha, Sam, and Mira—always my inspiration, joy, and best friends.

My extended family and friends, both local and virtual, who'd begun to wonder if they needed to send in a rescue party.

Brian Sawyer has, over the course of the last year, been my production liaison, coeditor, editor, "man Friday," and friend. Hat's off ;-) to Brian, and long may he stet.

I'd like to thank Dale Dougherty for bringing me in to work on the Hacks series; it's been a circle of wide circumference from *Google Hacks* to *Google Hacks*, Second Edition, and quite the journey of discovery. The O'Reilly editors, production, product management, and marketing staff are consummate professionals, hackers, and mensches. Extra special thanks goes out to my virtual cube-mate, Nat Torkington, to Laurie Petrycki for showing me the ropes, and Tim O'Reilly for his unfailing support and friendship.

Tara, it's been fabulous traveling this road with you, and I intend to make sure our paths keep on crossing at interesting intersections.

Karma points to Clay Shirky and Steven Johnson for egging me on to do more with the Google API than late-night fiddling. And, of course, a shout-out goes to the blogosphere population and folks in my Google neighborhood for their inspired prattling on APIs and all other things geek-worthy.

Preface

Search engines for large collections of data preceded the World Wide Web by decades. There were those massive library catalogs, hand-typed with painstaking precision on index cards and eventually, to varying degrees, automated. There were the large data collections of professional information companies such as Dialog and LexisNexis. Then there are the extant private, expensive medical, real estate, and legal search services.

Those data collections were not always easy to search, but with a little finesse and a lot of patience, it was always possible to search them thoroughly. Information was grouped according to established ontologies, the data preformatted according to particular guidelines.

Then came the Web.

Information on the Web—as anyone who has ever looked at half a dozen web pages knows—is not all formatted the same way. Nor is it necessarily accurate. Nor up to date. Nor spellchecked. Nonetheless, search engines cropped up, trying to make sense of the rapidly increasing index of information online. Eventually, special syntaxes were added for searching common parts of the average web page (such as title or URL). Search engines evolved rapidly, trying to encompass all the nuances of the billions of documents online, and they continue to evolve today.

Google™ threw its hat into the ring in 1998. The second incarnation of a search engine service known as BackRub, the name *Google* was a play on the word *googol*: a one followed by a hundred zeros. From the beginning, Google was different from the other major search engines online—AltaVista, Excite, HotBot, and others.

Was it the technology? Partially. The relevance of Google's search results was outstanding. But more than that, Google's focus and more human face made it stand out online.

With its friendly presentation and constantly expanding set of options, it's no surprise that Google continues to draw lots of fans. There are weblogs devoted to it. Search engine newsletters, such as ResearchBuzz, spend a lot of time covering Google. Legions of devoted fans spend a lot of time uncovering undocumented features, creating games (such as *Google whacking*), and even coining new words (such as *Googling*, the practice of checking out a prospective date or hire via Google's search engine.) People Google prospective employers and blind dates; goods and services; school reports and movie reviews; facts and fiction; fun and profit.

At the time of this writing, Google knows about more than eight billion web pages, over 880 million images, and 845 million Usenet messages and has just announced Google Print (*http://print.google.com*), bringing even the printed word to the Web.

In April 2002, Google reached out to its fan base by offering the Google API. The Google API gives programmers a way to access the Google search results with automated queries. While you can do all the searching, sifting, and sorting by hand, there's nothing like getting your computer to do it for you.

Google has changed the way people and computers alike approach the Web.

Why Google Hacks?

Hacks are generally considered to be "quick-and-dirty" solutions to programming problems or interesting techniques for getting a task done. But what does this kind of hacking have to do with Google?

Considering the size of the Google index, there are many times when you might want to do a particular kind of search but you get too many results for the search to be useful. Or you may want to do a search that the current Google interface does not support.

The idea of *Google Hacks* is not to give you some exhaustive manual of how every command in the Google syntax works (although we do give this more than a fair shake), but rather to show you some tricks for making the best use of a search, show off just what's possible when you automate your queries with a little programming know-how, and shine a light into some of the overlooked corners of Google's offerings. In other words, *hacks*.

How This Book Is Organized

The combination of Google's myriad services and over four billion pages of constantly shifting data can do strange things to your imagination and give you lots of new perspectives on how best to search. This book goes beyond the instruction page to the idea of *hacks*: tips, tricks, and techniques you can use to make your Google searching experience more fruitful, more fun, or (in a couple of cases) just more weird.

This book is divided into several chapters:

Chapter 1, *Web*

This chapter describes the fundamentals of how Google's search works. You'll find tips and tricks for Google's special syntax (think "special sauce"); specialty searches like the phonebook, calculator, package and stock tracking; the Google cache, related links, and more. Beyond a mere list of "this syntax means that," we'll take a look at how to eke every last bit of searching power out of each syntax—and how to mix and match for some truly monstrous searches.

Chapter 2, *Advanced Web*

Kick your newfound search expertise into high gear, automating your trawling, crawling, and recombination by hacking Google programmatically. You'll meander farther, dig deeper, and come up with results that you never would have found by letting your fingers do the walking and eyeballs the scanning.

Chapter 3, *Images*

Take a break from all that text crawling and immerse yourself in some of the millions of photographs, drawings, icons, and diagrams that Google Images has turned up in the process of crawling and indexing the Web.

Chapter 4, *News and Groups*

Catch up on the day's news and events as brought to you by Google News. Get involved in a group discussion on the Internet or start a Google Group of your own.

Chapter 5, *Add-Ons*

Go beyond the web browser, integrating Google into your toolbar, desktop, and word processor. Take advantage of some of the services built on Google. Search on the go via email or instant messenger, from your phone or PDA.

Chapter 6, *Gmail*

Google's Gmail™ isn't your average, ordinary web mail service. From its slick, interactive, real-application–like JavaScript-powered web interface to its gigabyte of storage space, there's more than enough to make you switch. And then there are the alternate uses you just won't believe until you try.

Chapter 7, *Ads*

Google's AdSense™ brings subtle, mostly text ads to your web site or weblog—no matter how large or how small. And AdWords™ breaks down the barrier to entry for getting your business or project found on the Net.

Chapter 8, *Webmastering*

If you're a web wrangler, you see Google from two sides: from the searcher side and from the side of someone who wants to get the best search ranking for a web site. In this chapter, you'll learn about Google's (in)famous PageRank™, how to clean up for a Google visit, and how to make sure that your pages aren't indexed by Google if you don't want them to be.

Chapter 9, *Programming Google*

This chapter introduces you to the wonders of the Google Application Programming Interface (API) underlying many of the hacks in this book. If you've ever been tempted to try your hand at programming, this is as good a place as any to find inspiration.

How to Use This Book

You can read this book from cover to cover if you like, but for the most part, each hack stands on its own. So feel free to browse, flipping around whatever sections interest you most. If you're a Perl newbie, you might want to try some of the easier hacks and then tackle the more extensive ones as you get more confident.

How to Run the Hacks

The programmatic hacks in this book run either on the command line (that's Terminal for Mac OS X folk, DOS command window for Windows users) or as CGI scripts—dynamic pages living on your web site, accessed through your web browser.

Command-Line Scripts

Running a hack on the command line invariably involves the following steps:

1. Type the program into a garden-variety text editor: Notepad on Windows, TextEdit on Mac OS X, vi or Emacs on Unix/Linux, or anything else of the sort. Save the file as directed—usually as *scriptname.pl* (the *pl* bit stands for Perl, the predominant programming language used in *Google Hacks*).

Alternatively, you can download the code for all of the hacks online at *http://www.oreilly.com/catalog/googlehks2*, a ZIP archive filled with individual scripts already saved as text files.

2. Get to the command line on your computer or remote server. In Mac OS X, launch the Terminal (Applications → Utilities → Terminal). In Windows, click the Start button, select Run..., type command, and hit the Enter/Return key on your keyboard. In Unix ... well, we'll just assume you know how to get to the command line.

3. Navigate to where you saved the script at hand. This varies from operating system to operating system, but usually involves something like cd ~/Desktop (that's your Desktop on the Mac).

4. Invoke the script by running the programming language's interpreter (e.g., Perl) and feeding it the script (e.g., *scriptname.pl*) like so:

```
$ perl scriptname.pl
```

Most often, you'll also need to pass along some parameters—your search query, the number of results you'd like, and so forth. Simply drop them in after the script name, enclosing them in quotes if they're more than one word or if they include an odd character or three:

```
$ perl scriptname.pl '"much ado about nothing" script' 10
```

The results of your script are almost always sent straight back to the command-line window in which you're working, like so:

```
$ perl scriptname.pl '"much ado about nothing" script' 10
1. "Amazon.com: Books: Much Ado About Nothing: Screenplay ..." [http://www.
amazon.com/exec/obidos/tg/detail/-/0393311112?v=glance]
2. "Much Ado About Nothing Script" [http://www.signal42.com/much_ado_about_
nothing_script.asp]
...
```

 The elllpsis (...) bit signifies that we've cut off the output for brevity's sake.

To stop output scrolling off your screen faster than you can read it, on most systems you can "pipe" (read: redirect) the output to a little program called more:

```
$ perl scriptname.pl | more
```

Hit the Enter/Return key on your keyboard to scroll through line by line, the space bar to leap through page by page.

You'll also sometimes want to direct output to a file for safekeeping, importing into your spreadsheet application, or displaying on your web site. This is as easy; refer to the code shown next.

```
$ perl scriptname.pl > output_filename.txt
```

And to pour some input into your script from a file, simply do the opposite:

```
$ perl scriptname.pl < input_filename.txt
```

Don't worry if you can't remember all of this; each hack has a "Running the Hack" section, and some even have a "The Results" section that shows you just how it's done.

CGI Scripts

CGI scripts—programs that run on your web site and produce pages dynamically—are a little more complicated if you're not used to them. While fundamentally they're the same sort of scripts as those run on the command line, they are more troublesome because setups vary so widely. You may be running your own server, your web site may be hosted on an Internet service provider's (ISP) server, your content may live on a corporate intranet server—or anything in between.

Since going through every possibility is beyond the scope of this (or any) book, you should check your ISP's knowledge base or call their technical support department, or ask your local system administrator for help.

Generally, though, the methodology is the same:

1. Type the program in to a garden-variety text editor: Notepad on Windows, TextEdit on Mac OS X, vi or Emacs on Unix/Linux, or anything else of the sort. Save the file as directed—usually as *scriptname.cgi* (the *cgi* bit reveals that you're dealing with a CGI—that's common gateway interface—script).

   Alternatively, you can download the code for all of the hacks online at *http://www.oreilly.com/catalog/googlehks2*, a ZIP archive filled with individual scripts already saved as text files.

2. Move the script over to wherever your web site lives. You should have some directory on a server somewhere in which all of your web pages (all those *.html* files) and images (ending in *.jpg*, *.gif*, etc.) live. Within this directory, you'll probably see something called a *cgi-bin* directory: this is where CGI scripts must usually live in order to be run rather than just displayed in your web browser when you visit them.

3. You usually need to bless CGI scripts as executable—to be run rather than displayed. Just how you do this depends on the operating system of your server. If you're on a Unix/Linux or Mac OS X system, this usually entails typing the following on the command line:

   ```
   $ chmod 755 scriptname.cgi
   ```

4. Now you should be able to point your web browser at the script and have it run as expected, behaving in a manner similar to that described in the "Running the Hack" section of the hack at hand.

Just what URL you use once again varies wildly. It should, however, look something like this: *http://www.your_domain.com/cgi-bin/scriptname.cgi*, where *your_domain.com* is your web site domain, *cgi-bin* refers to the directory in which your CGI scripts live, and *scriptname.cgi* is the script itself.

If you don't have a domain and are hosted at an ISP, the URL is more likely to look like this: *http://www.your_isp.com/~your_username/cgi-bin/scriptname.cgi*, where *your_isp.com* is your ISP's domain, *~your_username* is your username at the ISP, *cgi-bin* refers to the directory in which your CGI scripts live, and *scriptname.cgi* is the script itself.

If you come up with something called an "Internal Server Error" or see the error code 500, something's gone wrong somewhere in the process. At this point you can take a crack at debugging (read: shaking the bugs out) yourself or ask your ISP or system administrator for help. Debugging—especially CGI debugging—can be a little more than the average newbie can bear, but there is help in the form of a famous Frequently Asked Question (FAQ): "The Idiot's Guide to Solving Perl CGI Problems." Google for it and step through as directed.

Using the Google API

Be sure to consult Chapter 9 for an introduction to the Google API, how to sign up for a developer's key—you'll need one for many of the hacks in this book—and the basics of programming Google in a selection of languages to get you going.

Learning to Code

Fancy trying your hand at a spot of programming? O'Reilly's best-selling *Learning Perl* (*http://www.oreilly.com/catalog/lperl3*) by Randal L. Schwartz and Tom Phoenix provides a good start. Apply what you learn to understanding and using the hacks in this book, perhaps even taking on the "Hacking the Hack" sections to tweak and fiddle with the scripts. This is a useful way to get a little programming under your belt if you're a searching nut, since it's always a little easier to learn how to program when you have a task to accomplish and existing code to leaf through.

Where to Go for More

There's so much to Google that it's easy to miss minor tweaks and major new offerings alike. Pay a regular visit to the Google "More, more, more" page (*http://www.google.com/options*). Stay on top of all things Google by reading or subscribing to the Google blogs, unofficial (*http://google.blogspace.com*) and official (*http://www.google.com/googleblog*).

Ga-ga over Google? Pick up a Google-branded tchotchke—green lava lamp, double latte mug, t-shirt, backback, or book—at the official Google Store (*http://www.googlestore.com*).

Conventions

The following is a list of the typographical conventions used in this book:

Italic

> Used to indicate new terms, URLs, filenames, file extensions, directories, and program names, and to highlight comments in examples. For example, a path in the filesystem will appear as */Developer/Applications*.

`Constant width`

> Used to show code examples, commands and options, contents of files, or output from commands.

`Constant width bold`

> Used for emphasis and user input in code.

`Constant width italic`

> Used in examples and tables to show text that should be replaced with user-supplied values.

Color

> The second color is used to indicate a cross-reference within the text.

You should pay special attention to notes set apart from the text with the following icons:

> This is a tip, suggestion, or general note. It contains useful supplementary information about the topic at hand.

> This is a warning or note of caution.

The thermometer icons, found next to each hack, indicate the relative complexity of the hack:

beginner   moderate   expert

Using Code Examples

This book is here to help you get your job done. In general, you may use the code in this book in your programs and documentation. You do not need to contact us for permission unless you're reproducing a significant portion of the code. For example, writing a program that uses several chunks of code from this book does not require permission. Selling or distributing a CD-ROM of examples from O'Reilly books *does* require permission. Answering a question by citing this book and quoting example code does not require permission. Incorporating a significant amount of example code from this book into your product's documentation *does* require permission.

We appreciate, but do not require, attribution. An attribution usually includes the title, author, publisher, and ISBN. For example: "*Google Hacks, Second Edition,* by Tara Calishain and Rael Dornfest. Copyright 2004 O'Reilly Media, Inc., 0-596-00857-0."

If you feel your use of code examples falls outside fair use or the permission given above, feel free to contact us at *permissions@oreilly.com*.

Safari Enabled

 When you see a Safari® enabled icon on the cover of your favorite technology book that means the book is avaialbe online through the O'Reilly Network Safari Bookshelf.

Safari offers a solution that's better than e-Books. It's a virtual library that let's you easily search thousands of top tech books, cut and paste code samples, download chapters, and find quick answers when you nee the most accurate, current information. Try it free at *http://safari.oreilly.com*.

How to Contact Us

We have tested and verified the information in this book to the best of our ability, but you may find that features have changed (or even that we have made mistakes!). As a reader of this book, you can help us to improve future editions by sending us your feedback. Please let us know about any errors, inaccuracies, bugs, misleading or confusing statements, and typos that you find anywhere in this book.

Please also let us know what we can do to make this book more useful to you. We take your comments seriously and will try to incorporate reasonable suggestions into future editions. You can write to us at:

O'Reilly Media, Inc.
1005 Gravenstein Hwy N.
Sebastopol, CA 95472
(800) 998-9938 (in the U.S. or Canada)
(707) 829-0515 (international/local)
(707) 829-0104 (fax)

To ask technical questions or to comment on the book, send email to:

bookquestions@oreilly.com

The web site for *Google Hacks,* Second Edition, lists examples, errata, and plans for future editions. You can find this page at:

http://www.oreilly.com/catalog/googlehks2

For more information about this book and others, see the O'Reilly web site:

http://www.oreilly.com

Got a Hack?

To explore Hacks books online or to contribute a hack for future titles, visit:

http://hacks.oreilly.com

Web

Hacks 1–20

Google's front page is deceptively simple: a search form and a couple of buttons. Yet that basic interface—so alluring in its simplicity—belies the power of the Google engine underneath and the wealth of information at its disposal. If you use Google's search syntax to its fullest, the Web is your oyster.

Searching in Google doesn't have to be a case of just entering what you're looking for in the search box and hoping for the best. Google offers you many ways—via special syntax and search options—to refine your search criteria and help Google better understand what you're looking for. We'll dig into Google's powerful, all-but-undocumented special syntax and search options, and show how to use them to their fullest. We'll cover the basics of Google searching, wildcards, word limits, syntax for special cases, mixing syntax elements, advanced search techniques, and using specialized vocabularies, including slang and jargon.

Google Web Search Basics

Whenever you search for more than one keyword at a time, a search engine has a default strategy for handling and combining those keywords. Can those words appear individually anywhere in a page, or do they have to be right next to each other? Will the engine search for both keywords or for either keyword?

Phrase Searches

Google defaults to searching for occurrences of your specified keywords anywhere in the page, whether side-by-side or scattered throughout. To return results of pages containing specifically ordered words, enclose them in quotes, turning your keyword search into a *phrase search*, to use Google's terminology.

On entering a search for the keywords:

```
to be or not to be
```

Google will find matches where the keywords appear anywhere on the page. If you want Google to find you matches where the keywords appear together as a phrase, surround them with quotes, like this:

```
"to be or not to be"
```

Google will return matches only where those words appear together (not to mention explicitly including stop words such as "to" and "or"; see the section "Explicit Inclusion" a little later).

Phrase searches are also useful when you want to find a phrase but aren't quite sure of the exact wording. This is accomplished in combination with wildcards, explained later in the chapter in "Full-Word Wildcards."

Basic Boolean

Whether an engine searches for all keywords or any of them depends on what is called its *Boolean default*. Search engines can default to Boolean AND (searching for all keywords) or Boolean OR (searching for any keywords). Of course, even if a search engine defaults to searching for all keywords, you can usually give it a special command to instruct it to search for any keyword. Lacking specific instructions, the engine falls back on its default setting.

Google's Boolean default is AND, which means that, if you enter query words without modifiers, Google will search for all of your query words. For example, if you search for:

```
snowblower Honda "Green Bay"
```

Google will search for all the words. If you prefer to specify that any one word or phrase is acceptable, put an OR between each:

```
snowblower OR snowmobile OR "Green Bay"
```

 Make sure you capitalize the OR; a lowercase or won't work correctly.

If you particularly want one term along with one of two or more other terms, group them with parentheses, like so:

```
snowblower (snowmobile OR "Green Bay")
```

This query searches for the word "snowmobile" or phrase "Green Bay" along with the word "snowblower." A stand-in for OR, borrowed from the computer programming realm, is the | (pipe) character, as in:

```
snowblower (snowmobile | "Green Bay")
```

Negation

If you want to specify that a query item must *not* appear in your results, prepend a – (minus sign or dash):

```
snowblower snowmobile -"Green Bay"
```

This will search for pages that contain both the words "snowblower" *and* "snowmobile," but *not* the phrase "Green Bay."

Note that the – symbol must appear directly before the word or phrase that you don't want. If there's space between, as in the following query, it won't work as expected:

```
snowblower snowmobile - "Green Bay"
```

Do be sure, however, that there's a space *before* the – symbol.

Explicit Inclusion

On the whole, Google will search for all the keywords and phrases that you specify (with the exception of those you've specifically negated with –, of course). However, there are certain words that Google will ignore because they are considered too common to be of any use in the search. These words—"I," "a," "the," and "of," to name a few—are called *stop words*.

You can force Google to take a stop word into account by prepending a + (plus) character, as in:

```
+the king
```

Stop words that appear inside of phrase searches are not ignored. Searching for:

```
"the move" glam
```

will result in a more accurate list of matches than:

```
the move glam
```

simply because Google takes the word "the" into account in the first example but ignores it in the second.

Synonyms

Every so often you get the feeling that you're missing out on some useful results because the keyword or keywords you've chosen aren't the only way to express what you're looking for.

The Google synonym operator, the ~ (tilde) character, prepended to any number of keywords in your query, asks Google to include not only exact matches, but also what it thinks are synonyms for each of the keywords. Searching for:

```
~ape
```

turns up results for monkey, gorilla, chimpanzee, and others (both singular and plural forms) of the ape or related family as if you'd searched for:

```
monkey gorilla chimpanzee
```

and some you'd never have thought to include in your query.

Google figures out synonyms algorithmically, so you may well be surprised to find results around words that your garden-variety thesaurus would not have suggested. (Synonyms are bolded along with exact keyword matches on the results page, so they're easy to spot.)

Number Range

One of the more difficult things to convey in an Internet search query is a range—of dates, currency, size, weight, height, or any two arbitrary values.

The number range operator, .. (two periods), looks for results falling inside your specified numeric range.

Looking for that perfect pair of Prada pumps, size 5 or 6? Try this for size:

```
prada pumps size 5..6
```

Perhaps you're looking to spend $800 to $1,000 on a nice digital SLR camera; Google for:

```
slr digital camera 3..5 megapixel $800..1000
```

The one thing to remember is always to provide some clue as to the meaning of the range, e.g., $, size, megapixel, kg, and so forth.

You can also use the number range syntax with just one number, making it the minimum or maximum of your query. Do you want to find some land in Montana that's at least 500 acres? No problem:

```
acres Montana land 500..
```

On the other hand, you may want to make sure that raincoat you buy for your terrier doesn't cost more than $30. That's possible too:

```
raincoat dog ..$30
```

 Google normally does not recognize special characters like $ in the process of searching. But because the $ sign was necessary for the number feature, you can use it in all sorts of searches. Try the search "yard sale" bargains 10 and then "yard sale" bargains $10. Notice how the second search gives you far fewer results? That's because Google is matching $10 exactly.

Simple Searching and Feeling Lucky

The I'm Feeling Lucky™ button is a thing of beauty. Rather than giving you a list of search results from which to choose, you're whisked away to what Google believes is the most relevant page given your search (i.e., the first result in the list). Entering washington post and clicking the I'm Feeling Lucky button takes you directly to *http://www.washingtonpost.com*. Trying president will land you at *http://www.whitehouse.gov*.

Case Sensitivity

Some search engines are case sensitive; that is, they search for queries based on how the queries are capitalized. A search for "GEORGE WASHINGTON" on such a search engine would not find "George Washington," "george washington," or any other case combination.

Google is case insensitive. If you search for Three, three, THREE, even ThrEE, you get the same results.

Full-Word Wildcards

Some search engines support a technique called *stemming*. Stemming is adding a wildcard character—usually * (asterisk) but sometimes ? (question mark)—to part of your query, requesting the search engine return variants of that query using the wildcard as a placeholder for the rest of the word at hand. For example, moon* would find moons, moonlight, moonshot, etc.

Google doesn't support explicit stemming. It didn't used to support stemming at all, but now it implicitly stems for you. So, dietary will yield results for diet, diets, and other variations on the theme.

Google does offer a full-word wildcard. While you can't have a wildcard stand in for part of a word, you can insert a wildcard (Google's wildcard character is *) into a phrase and have the wildcard act as a substitute for one full word. Searching for "three * mice", therefore, finds three blind mice, three blue mice, three green mice, etc.

What good is the full-word wildcard? It's certainly not as useful as stemming, but then again, it's not as confusing to the beginner. One * is a stand-in for one word; two * signifies two words, and so on. The full-word wildcard comes in handy in the following situations:

- Avoiding the 10-word limit (see "The 10-Word Limit" next) on Google queries. You'll most frequently run into these examples when you're trying to find song lyrics or a quote. Plugging the phrase Fourscore and seven years ago, our fathers brought forth on this continent into Google will search only as far as the word "on"; everything thereafter is summarily ignored by Google.

- Checking the frequency of certain phrases and derivatives of phrases, such as: intitle:"methinks the * doth protest too much" and intitle: "the * of Seville" (intitle: is described later in "Special Syntax").

- Filling in the blanks on a fitful memory. Perhaps you remember only a short string of song lyrics; search using only what you remember rather than randomly reconstructed full lines.

Let's take as an example the disco anthem "Good Times" by Chic. Consider the following line: "You silly fool, you can't change your fate."

Perhaps you've heard that lyric, but you can't remember if the word "fool" is correct or if it's something else. If you're wrong (if the correct line is, for example, "You silly child, you can't change your fate"), your search will find no results and you'll come away with the sad conclusion that no one on the Internet has bothered to post lyrics to Chic songs.

The solution is to run the query with a wildcard in place of the unknown word, like so:

```
"You silly *, you can't change your fate"
```

You can use this technique for quotes, song lyrics, poetry, and more. You should be mindful, however, to include enough of the quote to find unique results. Searching for "you * fool" will glean you far too many irrelevant hits.

The 10-Word Limit

Unless you're fond of long, detailed queries, you might never have noticed that Google has a hard limit of 10 words—that's keywords and special syntaxes combined—ignoring anything beyond. While this has no real effect on casual Google users, search hounds quickly find that this limit rather cramps their style.

Favor Obscurity

By limiting your query to the more obscure of your keywords or phrase fragments, you'll hone results without squandering precious query words. Let's say you're interested in a phrase from Hamlet: "The lady doth protest too much, methinks." At first blush, you might simply paste the entire phrase into the query field. But that's 7 of your 10 allotted words right there, leaving no room for additional query words or search syntax.

The first thing to do is ditch the first couple of words; "The lady" is just too common a phrase. This leaves the 5 words "doth protest too much, methinks." Neither "methinks" nor "doth" are words that you might hear every day, providing a nice Shakespearean anchor for the phrase. That said, one or the other should suffice, leaving the query at an even 4 words with room to grow:

    "protest too much methinks"

or:

    "doth protest too much"

Either of these will provide, within the first five results, origins of the phrase and pointers to more information.

Unfortunately, this technique won't do you much good in the case of "Do as I say, not as I do," which doesn't provide much in the way of obscurity. Attempt clarification by adding something like quote origin English usage and you're stepping beyond the 10-word limit. One solution is described next.

Playing the Wildcard

Help comes in the form of Google's full-word wildcard, described earlier. It turns out that Google doesn't count wildcards toward the limit.

So, when you have more than 10 words, substitute a wildcard for common words, like so:

    "do as * say not as * do" quote origin English usage

Presto! Google runs the search without complaint, and you're in for some well-honed results.

 Common words such as "I," "a," "the," and "of" actually do no good in the first place. Called *stop words* they are ignored by Google entirely unless used in within a phrase. To force Google to take a stop word into account, prepend it with a + (plus) character, as in: +the.

Special Syntax

In addition to the basic AND, OR, and phrase searches, Google offers some rather extensive special syntax for narrowing your searches.

As a full-text search engine, Google indexes entire web pages instead of just titles and descriptions. Additional commands, called *special syntax* or *advanced operators*, let Google users search specific parts of web pages for specific types of information. This comes in handy when you're dealing with more than eight billion web pages and need every opportunity to narrow your search results. Specifying that your query words must appear only in the title or URL of a returned web page is a great way to have your results get very specific without making your keywords themselves too specific. Following are descriptions of the special syntax elements, ordered by common usage and function.

 Some of these syntax elements work well in combination. Others fare not quite as well. Still others do not work at all. For detailed discussion on what does and does not mix, see "Mixing Syntax," below.

intitle:

> intitle: restricts your search to the titles of web pages. The variation allintitle: finds pages wherein all the words specified appear in the title of the web page. Using allintitle: is basically the same as using the intitle: before each keyword.
>
> > intitle:"george bush"
> > allintitle:"money supply" economics
>
> You may wish to avoid the allintitle: variation, because it doesn't mix well with some of the other syntax elements.

intext:

> intext: searches only body text (i.e., ignores link text, URLs, and titles). While its uses are limited, it's perfect for finding query words that might be too common in URLs or link titles.
>
> > intext:"yahoo.com"
> > intext:html
>
> There's an allintext: variation, but again, this doesn't play well with others.

inanchor:

> inanchor: searches for text in a page's link anchors. A link anchor is the descriptive text of a link. For example, the link anchor in the HTML

code `<a href="http://www.oreilly.com">O'Reilly Media</a>` is "O'Reilly Media."

    `inanchor:"tom peters"`

As with other `in*:` syntax elements, there's an `allinanchor:` variation, which works in a similar way (i.e., all the keywords specified must appear in a page's link anchors).

`site:`

> `site:` allows you to narrow your search by either a site or a top-level domain. The AltaVista search engine, by contrast, has two syntax elements for this function (`host:` and `domain:`), but Google has only the one.
>
> `site:loc.gov`
> `site:thomas.loc.gov`
> `site:edu`
> `site:nc.us`
>
> Be aware that `site:` is no good for trying to search for a page that exists beneath the main or default site (i.e., in a subdirectory such as /~sam/ album/). For example, if you're looking for something below the main GeoCities site, you can't use `site:` to find all the pages in *http://www. geocities.com/Heartland/Meadows/6485/*; Google returns no results. Use `inurl:` instead.

`inurl:`

> `inurl:` restricts your search to the URLs of web pages. This syntax tends to work well for finding search and help pages, because they tend to be rather regular in composition. An `allinurl:` variation finds all the words listed in a URL but doesn't mix well with some other special syntax.
>
> `inurl:help`
> `allinurl:search help`
>
> You'll see that using the `inurl:` query instead of the `site:` query has one immediate advantage: you can use it to search subdirectories.

 While the `http://` prefix in a URL is ignored by Google when used with `site:`, search results come up short when including it in an `inurl:` query. Be sure to remove prefixes in any `inurl:` query for the best (read: any) results.

You can also use `inurl:` in combination with the `site:` syntax to draw out information on subdomains. For example, how many subdomains does *oreilly.com* really have? A quick query will help you figure that out:

    `site:oreilly.com -inurl:www.oreilly.com`

This query asks Google to list all pages from the *oreilly.com* domain, but leave out those pages which are from the common subdomain *www*, since you already know about that one.

link:

> link: returns a list of pages linking to the specified URL. Enter link: www.google.com and you'll get a list of pages that link to the Google home page, *www.google.com* (not anywhere in the google.com domain). Don't worry about including the *http://* bit; you don't need it and, indeed, Google appears to ignore it even if you do put it in. link: works just as well with "deep" URLs—*http://www.raelity.org/apps/blosxom/*, for instance—as with top-level URLs such as *raelity.org*.

cache:

> cache: finds a copy of the page that Google indexed even if that page is no longer available at its original URL or has since changed its content completely.

> cache:www.yahoo.com

> If Google returns a result that appears to have little to do with your query, you're almost sure to find what you're looking for in the latest cached version of the page at Google.

> The Google cache is particularly useful for retrieving a previous version of a page that changes often.

daterange:

> daterange: limits your search to a particular date or range of dates on which a page was indexed. It's important to note that a daterange: search has nothing to do with when a page was created, but when it was indexed by Google. So a page created on February 2 but not indexed by Google until April 11 would turn up in a daterange: search for April 11.

> "Geri Halliwell" "Spice Girls" daterange:2450958-2450968

> For an in-depth treatment of finding content either by the date it was created or when it was first noticed by Google, see "Search a Particular Date Range" [Hack #16].

filetype:

> filetype: searches the suffixes or filename extensions. These are usually, but not necessarily, different file types; filetype:htm and filetype: html will give you different result counts, even though they're the same file type. You can even search for different page generators—such as ASP, PHP, CGI, and so forth—presuming the site isn't hiding them behind redirection and proxying. Google indexes several different Microsoft formats, including PowerPoint (*.ppt*), Excel (*.xls*), and Word (*.doc*).

```
homeschooling filetype:pdf
"leading economic indicators" filetype:ppt
```

related:

> related:, as you might expect, finds pages that are related to the specified page. This is a good way to find categories of pages; a search for related:google.com returns a variety of search engines, including Lycos, Yahoo!, and Northern Light.
>
> ```
> related:www.yahoo.com
> related:www.cnn.com
> ```
>
> While an increasingly rare occurrence, you'll find that not all pages are related to other pages.

info:

> info: provides a page of links to more information about a specified URL. This information includes a link to the URL's cache, a list of pages that link to the URL, pages that are related to the URL, and pages that contain the URL.
>
> ```
> info:www.oreilly.com
> info:www.nytimes.com/technology
> ```
>
> Note that this information is dependent on whether Google has indexed the specified URL; if not, information will obviously be far more limited.

phonebook:

> phonebook:, as you might expect, looks up phone numbers.
>
> ```
> phonebook:John Doe CA
> phonebook:(510) 555-1212
> ```
>
> The phonebook is covered in detail in "Google Phonebook: Let Google's Fingers Do the Walking" [Hack #6].

Mixing Syntax

There was a time when you couldn't mix Google's special syntax elements; you were limited to one per query. Even as Google released ever more powerful special syntax elements, not being able to combine them for their composite power stunted many a search.

This has since changed. While there remain some syntax elements that you just can't mix, there are plenty to combine in clever and powerful ways. A thoughtful combination can do wonders to narrow a search.

How Not to Mix Syntax

There are some simple rules to follow when mixing syntax elements. These, for the most part, revolve around how *not* to mix.

- Don't mix syntax elements that will cancel each other out, such as:

  ```
  site:ucla.edu -inurl:ucla
  ```

  Here you're saying you want all results to come from *ucla.edu*, but that site results should not have the string "ucla" in the results. Obviously, that's not going to produce many URLs.

- Don't overuse single syntax elements, as in:

  ```
  site:com site:edu
  ```

  While you might think you're asking for results from either *.com* or *.edu* sites, what you're actually saying is that site results should come from both simultaneously. Obviously, a single result can come from only one domain. Take the example `perl site:edu site:com`. This search will get you exactly zero results. Why? Because a result page cannot come from a *.edu* domain and a *.com* domain at the same time. If you want results from *.edu* and *.com* domains only, rephrase your search like this:

  ```
  perl (site:edu | site:com)
  ```

  With the pipe character (|), you're specifying that you want results to come either from the *.edu* or the *.com* domain.

- Don't use `allinurl:` or `allintitle:` when mixing syntax. It takes a careful hand not to misuse these in a mixed search. Instead, stick to `inurl:` or `intitle:`. If you don't put `allinurl:` in exactly the right place, you'll create odd search results. Let's look at this example:

  ```
  allinurl:perl intitle:programming
  ```

  At first glance, it looks like you're searching for the string "perl" in the result URL and the word "programming" in the title. And you're right: this will work fine. But what happens if you move `allinurl:` to the right of the query?

  ```
  intitle:programming allinurl:perl
  ```

  This won't bring any results. Stick to `inurl:` and `intitle:`, which are much more forgiving of where you put them in a query.

  The same advice goes for `allintext:` and `allinanchor:`.

- Don't use so much syntax that you get too narrow, like:

  ```
  title:agriculture site:ucla.edu inurl:search
  ```

  You might find that it's too narrow to give you any useful results. If you're trying to find something so specific that you think you'll need a narrow query, start by building a little bit of the query at a time. Say you want to find plant databases at UCLA. Instead of starting with the query:

  ```
  title:plants site:ucla.edu inurl:database
  ```

Try something simpler:

```
databases plants site:ucla.edu
```

and then try adding syntax to keywords you've already established in your search results:

```
intitle:plants databases site:ucla.edu
```

or:

```
intitle:database plants site:ucla.edu
```

How to Mix Syntax

If you're trying to narrow down search results, the intitle: and site: syntax elements are your best bet.

Titles and sites. For example, say you want to get an idea of what databases are offered by the state of Texas. Run this search:

```
intitle:search intitle:records site:tx.us
```

You'll find something on the order of 30 very targeted results. And, of course, you can narrow down your search even more by adding keywords:

```
birth intitle:search intitle:records site:tx.us
```

It doesn't seem to matter whether you put plain keywords at the beginning or the end of the search query; I put them at the beginning because they're easier to keep up with.

The site: syntax, unlike site syntax on other search engines, allows you to get as general as a domain suffix (site:com) or as specific as a domain or subdomain (site:thomas.loc.gov). So if you're looking for records in El Paso, you can use this query:

```
intitle:records site:el-paso.tx.us
```

and you'll get approximately one result.

Title and URL. Sometimes you want to find a certain type of information, but you don't want to narrow by type. Instead, you want to narrow by theme of information (e.g., you want help or a search engine). That's when you need to search in the URL.

The inurl: syntax will search for a string in the URL but won't count finding it within a larger word. So, for example, if you search for inurl:research, Google will not find pages from *www.researchbuzz.com*, but it will find pages from *www.research-councils.ac.uk*.

Say you want to find information on neurosurgery, with an emphasis on learning or assistance. Try:

```
intitle:neurosurgery inurl:help
```

This returns a more manageable 880 or so results. The whole point is to get a number of results that finds what you need but isn't so large as to be overwhelming. If you find 880 results overwhelming, you can easily mix the site: syntax into the search and limit your results to universities:

```
intitle:neurosurgery inurl:help site:edu
```

Beware, however, of using too much special syntax. As mentioned earlier, you can quickly detail yourself into no results at all.

The Antisocial Syntax Elements

The antisocial syntax elements are the ones that won't mix and should be used individually for maximum effect. If you try to use them with other syntax elements, you won't get any results.

The syntax elements that request special information—stocks:, rphonebook:, bphonebook:, and phonebook: [Hack #6] are all antisocial. That is, you can't mix them and expect to get a reasonable result.

The other antisocial syntax is link:, which shows pages that have a link to a specified URL. Wouldn't it be great if you could specify what domains you want the pages to be from? Sorry, you can't. The link: syntax does not mix with anything else—not even plain old keywords.

For example, say you want to find out what pages link to O'Reilly Media, Inc., but you don't want to include pages from the *.edu* domain. The query link:www.oreilly.com -site:edu will not work because the link: syntax does not work in combination. Well, that's not quite correct; you will get results, but they'll be for the phrase "link:www.oreilly.com" from domains that are not *.edu.*

If you want to search for links and exclude the *.edu* domain, there's no single command that will absolutely work. This one's a good try, though:

```
inanchor:oreilly -inurl:oreilly -site:edu
```

This search looks for the word "oreilly" in *anchor text*, the text that's used to define links; excludes pages that contain "oreilly" in the *search result* (e.g., *oreilly.com*); and, finally, excludes those pages that come from the *.edu* domain.

But this type of search is nowhere near complete. It finds only those links to O'Reilly that include the string "oreilly": if someone creates a link such as <a href="http://perl.oreilly.com/">Camel Book</a>, it won't be found by the preceding query. Furthermore, there are other domains that contain the string "oreilly," and there may be domains that link to "oreilly" that contain the string "oreilly" but aren't *oreilly.com*. You could alter the string slightly, to omit the *oreilly.com* site itself but not other sites containing the string "oreilly":

```
inanchor:oreilly -site:oreilly.com -site:edu
```

However, you would still be including many O'Reilly sites—*XML.com* and *MacDevCenter.com*, for instance—that aren't at *oreilly.com*.

All the Possibilities

While it is possible to write down every syntax-mixing combination and briefly explain how they might be useful, there wouldn't be room for much else in this book.

Experiment. Experiment a lot. Constantly keep in mind that most of these syntax elements do not stand alone, and you can get more done by combining them than by using them individually

Depending on what kind of research you are doing, different patterns will emerge over time. For example, you may discover that focusing on only PDF documents (`filetype:pdf`) finds you the results you need. You may discover that you should concentrate on specific file types in specific domains (`filetype:ppt site:tompeters.com`). Mix up the syntax in as many ways as is relevant to your research and see what you get.

As with anything else, the more you use Google's special syntax, the more natural it will become to you. And Google is constantly adding more, much to the delight of regular web combers.

If, however, you want something more structured and visual than a single query line, Google's Advanced Search should fit the bill.

Advanced Search

Google's default simple search allows you to do quite a bit, but not everything. Google's Advanced Search page (*http://www.google.com/advanced_search?hl=en*), shown in Figure 1-1, provides more options, such as date search and filtering, with "fill in the blank" searching options for those who don't take naturally to memorizing special syntax.

Most of the options presented on this page are self-explanatory, but we'll take a quick look at the kinds of searches that would be more difficult using the single-text-field interface of a simple search.

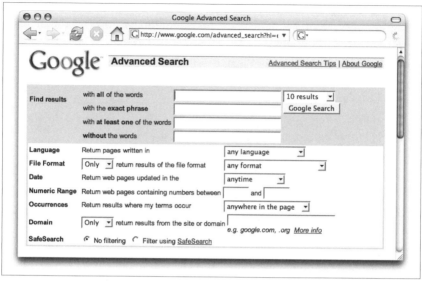

Figure 1-1. Google's Advanced Search page

Query Words

Because Google uses Boolean AND by default, it's sometimes hard to logically build out the nuances of a particular query. Using the text boxes at the top of the Advanced Search page, you can specify words that *must* appear—exact phrases, lists of words, at least one of which must appear—and words to be excluded.

Language

Using the Language pull-down menu, you can specify what language all returned pages must be in, from Arabic to Turkish.

File Format

The File Format option lets you include or exclude several different file formats, including Microsoft Word and Excel. There are a couple of Adobe formats (most notably PDF) and Rich Text Format as options here, too. This is where the Advanced Search is at its most limited; there are literally dozens of file formats that Google can search for, and this set of options represents only a small subset. To get at the others, use the filetype: special syntax described earlier in "Special Syntax."

Date

Date allows you to specify search results updated in the last three months, six months, or year. This date search is much more limited than the daterange: special syntax, which can give you results as narrow as one day, but Google stands behind the results generated using the Date option on the Advanced Search, while not officially sanctioning the use of the daterange: search.

Occurrences

Using the Occurrences pull-down menu, you can specify where the terms should occur. The options here, other than the default, generally reflect the allin*: syntax elements—in the title (allintitle:), text (allintext:), URL (allinurl:), and link anchors (allinanchor:) of the page.

Domain

The Domain feature is an interface to the site: syntax. It also allows negation, explained earlier, to explicitly *not* return results from a site or domain.

Safe Search

Google's Advanced Search further gives you the option to filter your results using SafeSearch. SafeSearch only filters sexually explicit content (as opposed to some filtering systems that filter pornography, hate material, gambling information, etc.). Please remember that machine filtering isn't 100% perfect.

Additional Google Properties

The rest of the page provides individual search forms for other Google properties, including a news search, a page-specific search, and links to some of Google's topic-specific searches. The news search and other topic-specific searches work independently of the main Advanced Search form at the top of the page.

The Advanced Search page is handy when you need to use its unique features or you need some help in putting together a complicated query. Its "fill-in-the-blank" interface will come in handy for the occasional searcher or someone who wants to get an advanced search exactly right. That said, it is limiting in other ways; it's difficult to use mixed syntax or build a single syntax search using OR. For example, there's no way to search for site:edu OR site:org using the Advanced Search. This search must be done from the Google search box.

Of course, there's another way you can alter the search results that Google gives you, and it doesn't involve the basic search input or the Advanced Search page. It's the preferences page, described in "Setting Preferences," later in this chapter.

Quick Links

If you're a Google regular, you've no doubt noticed those snippets of linked information proliferating near the top-left of the first results page (see Figure 1-2). Where once there was only a sponsored link or two between you and your results, now there are spelling suggestions, news headlines, stock quotes, and all other manner of bits and bobs of rather useful information.

Figure 1-2. Quick links augment search results with relevant, current, and local information

Google is going beyond Web search results to include relevant finds from its other properties and those of third parties. Here, briefly, is the current catalog of quick links:

Spelling
> One nice side effect of Google's listening to the Web is that it picks up a lot of words along the way. Some appear in the dictionary, while others haven't quite made their way into common parlance. Some are made up, while others are simply misspelled. Query Google for something that is commonly spelled another way, and it'll proffer some suggestions. "Consult the Dictionary" [Hack #9] delves further into the wonders of Google's spell checker.

Definitions
> TLAs (that's "three-letter acronyms") and geek speak abound. Rather than smiling knowingly when you've not a clue what someone just said, ask Google if it knows what your friend, boss, or medical professional is talking about. Prepend just about any word, obscure or garden-variety, with define (e.g., define happy) and the first item on your results page will in all probability be a definition pulled from one of any number of

Web dictionaries. Use define: (note the colon—e.g., define: osteichthyes) and you'll pull up a whole page full of definitions [Hack #10].

News Headlines

Google News (*http://news.google.com*; see Chapter 4) scrapes stories from (at present count) 4,500 news sources. Don't be surprised if there's something new and noteworthy related to your Google search.

Travel Information

Before you hop on that plane, Google your destination using the airport name (e.g., Los Angeles) or code (e.g., LAX) and the word airport. Click the "View conditions at [in this case] Los Angeles International (LAX), Los Angeles, California" link to visit the Federal Aviation Administration's (FAA) real-time airport status information. At the moment of this writing, LAX has no destination-specific delays, and both departures and arrivals are experiencing fewer than 15-minute gate hold and airborne delays, respectively.

Street Maps

If Google gleans something looking like a geographic location in your search query, it'll provide a link to Yahoo! and MapQuest maps of the area.

Google Local

Include the name of a city, state, or Zip Code anywhere in the U.S. or Canada in your search and Google Local (*http://local.google.com*) [Hack #7] just might suggest a local find. Google for indian food portland oregon and you'll find yourself tempted by the flavors of India House on SW Morrison Street or Wazwan on SW Fourth Street.

Google by Numbers, 1-2-3

You may remember a few important numbers from math class: pi or E or C, for instance. But numbers hold a very special place in Google's collective heart—after all, the name Google comes from *googol*, or 1.0×10^{100}. So it shouldn't come as a surprise that the geeks at Google have taught the search engine to pay attention to particular patterns of numbers, including anything that looks like a calculation (*http://www.google. com/help/features.html#calculator*) [Hack #47] or fits a special pattern usually found in particular reference numbers, including:

- UPS, FedEx, and U.S. Postal Service tracking numbers (e.g., 1Z9999W99999999999), linking to the package service's tracking page and filling in the number to get you going.
- Vehicle ID (VIN) numbers (e.g., AAAAA999A9AA99999).
- UPC codes (e.g., 073333531084) at *http://www.upcdatabase.com*.
- Telephone area codes (e.g., 510) at *http://www.whitepages.com*.

- Patent numbers (e.g., patent 4920273) in the U.S. Patent Database

- Federal Aviation Administration (FAA) airplane registration numbers (e.g., n199ua), particularly entertaining when you're waiting to board your plane, smartphone in hand [Hack #67]; look for it on the plane's tail.

- Federal Communications Commission (FCC) equipment ID numbers (e.g., fcc B4Z-34009-PIR).

Stock Quotes

Search for a stock symbol [Hack #8] and you'll be quick-linked to Yahoo! Finance.

Froogle Products

If Froogle (*http://froogle.google.com*) finds a product that seems to be what you're after, it'll link to "Product search results" and two or three offerings at sites like eBay, Golfsmith, Buy.com, and many more.

There are sure to be more quick links by the time you read this. To keep apprised of what's new, periodically visit the Google Web Search Features (*http://www.google.com/help/features.html*), or just keep Googling and see what appears.

Language Tools

In the early days of the Web, it seemed like most web pages were in English. But as more and more countries have come online, materials have become available in a variety of languages—including languages that don't originate with a particular country (such as Esperanto and Klingon).

Google offers several language tools, including one for translation and one for Google's interface. The interface option is much more extensive than the translation option, but the translation has a lot to offer.

The language tools are available by clicking the "Language Tools" link on the front page or by going to *http://www.google.com/language_tools?hl=en*.

Search Specific Languages or Countries

The first tool allows you to search for materials from a certain country and/ or in a certain language. This is an excellent way to narrow your searches; searching for French pages from Japan gives you far fewer results than searching for French pages from France. You can narrow the search further by searching for a slang word in another language. For example, search for the English slang word *bonce* on French pages from Japan.

Translate

The second tool on this page allows you to translate either a block of text or an entire web page from one language to another. Most of the translations are to and from English.

Machine translation is not nearly as good as human translation, so don't rely on this translation as either the basis of a search or as a completely accurate translation of the page you're looking at. Use it instead to give you the gist of whatever it translates.

You don't have to come to this page to use the translation tools. When you enter a search, you'll see that some search results that aren't in your language of choice (which you set via Google's preferences) have "[Translate this page]" next to their titles. Click on one of those and you'll be presented with a framed, translated version of the page. The Google frame, at the top, gives you the option of viewing the original version of the page, as well as returning to the results or viewing a copy suitable for printing.

Interface Language

The third tool lets you choose the interface language for Google, from Afrikaans to Welsh. Some of these languages are imaginary (Bork, bork, bork! and Elmer Fudd) but they do work.

> Be warned that if you set your language preference to Klingon, for example, you'll need to know Klingon to figure out how to set it back.
>
> As one of our *Google Hacks* readers, Jacek Artymiak, pointed out (*http://hacks.oreilly.com/pub/h/360*), if English is your native tongue, point your browser at *http://www.google.com/intl/en*. If you're not an English speaker but remember or care to guess at the language code (e.g., zu for Zulu), drop it in instead of en at the end of that URL. Further discussion revealed that simply suffixing the *http://www.google.com* URL with a period—*http://www.google.com.*—has the same delocalizing effect, reverting the interface to English.
>
> If you're really stuck, delete the Google cookie from your browser and reload the page; this should reset all preferences to the defaults.

How does Google manage to have so many interface languages when they have so few translation languages? The "Google in Your Language" program gathers volunteers from around the world to translate Google's interface. (You can get more information on that program at *http://www.google.com/intl/en/language.html*.)

Local Domain

Finally, the Language Tools page contains a list of region-specific Google home pages—over 100 of them, from Deutschland to the Pitcairn Islands.

Making the Most of Google's Language Tools

While you shouldn't rely on Google's translation tools to give you more than the gist of the meaning (since machine translation isn't that good), you can use translations to narrow your searches. I described the first method earlier: use unlikely combinations of languages and countries to narrow your results. The second way involves using the translator.

Select a word that matches your topic and use the translator to translate it into another language. (Google's translation tools work very well for single-word translations like this.) Now, search for that word in a country and language that don't match it. For example, you might search for the German word "Landstraße" (highway) on French pages in Canada. Of course, you'll have to be sure to use words that don't have English equivalents or you'll be overwhelmed with results.

Whew! By now it should be fairly clear that a simple interface such as the one Google has on its front page does not necessarily imply limited power. Still waters run deep indeed. Now that we have all of the tools, tips, and techniques under our belt to help us ask Google for what we want before it dives into the depths of web content, it's time to turn our attention to understanding what it brings back to the surface.

Anatomy of a Search Result

You'd think a list of search results would be pretty straightforward, wouldn't you—just a page title and a link, possibly a summary? Not so with Google. Google encompasses so many search properties and has so much data at its disposal that it fills every results page to the rafters. Within a typical search result you can find sponsored links, ads, links to stock quotes, page sizes, spelling suggestions, and more.

By knowing more of the nitty-gritty details of what's what in a search result, you'll be able to make some guesses ("Wow, this page that links to my page is very large; perhaps it's a link list") and correct roadblocks ("I can't find my search term on this page; I'll check the version Google has cached").

Let's use the word "flowers" to examine this anatomy. Figure 1-3 shows the result page for flowers.

Figure 1-3. Result page for "flowers"

First, you'll note at the top of the page is a selection of tabs, allowing you to repeat your search across other Google search categories besides web pages, including Google Groups **[Chapter 4]**, Google Images **[Chapter 3]**, and the Google Directory **[Hack #1]**. Beneath that you'll see a count for the number of results and how long the search took: about 48,000,000 results in 0.61 seconds (this will vary, sometimes by quite a bit).

Sometimes you'll see results/sites called out on colored backgrounds at the top or right of the results page (see Figure 1-3). These are called *sponsored links* (read: advertisements). Google has a policy of very clearly distinguishing ads and sticking to text-based advertising only rather than throwing flashing banners in your face like other sites do.

Beneath the sponsored links you sometimes see a category list. You'll see a category list only if you're searching for very general terms and your search consists of only one word. For example, if you searched for pinwheel flowers, Google wouldn't present the flowers category.

Other times you'll see news stories **[Chapter 4]** related to your query.

Why would you see category results? After all, Google is a full-text search engine, isn't it? It's because Google has taken the information from the Open Directory Project (*http://www.dmoz.org*) and crossed it with its own popularity rankings to make the Google Directory. When you see categories, you're seeing information from the Google Directory.

The first real (i.e., nonsponsored) result of the search for flowers is shown in Figure 1-4.

> **1-800-FLOWERS.COM, welcome to our store**
> 1-800-FLOWERS.COM, welcome to our store.
> www.1800flowers.com/ - 2k - Sep 26, 2004 - <u>Cached</u> - <u>Similar pages</u>

Figure 1-4. A typical search result

Let's break that down into chunks, shall we?

The top line of each result is the page title, hyperlinked to the original page.

The second line offers a brief extract from this site. Sometimes this is a description of the site or a selected sentence or two. Sometimes it's HTML mush. Google tends to use description metatags when they're available; it's rare when you can look at a Google search result and not have even a modicum of an idea what the site is all about.

The next line sports several informative bits of metadata. First, there's the URL; second, the size of the page (Google will have the page size available only if the page has been cached). There's a link to a cached version of the page if one is available. Finally, there's a link to find similar pages.

Why would you bother reading the search-result metadata? Why not simply visit the site and see if it has what you want?

If you've got a broadband connection and all the time in the world, you might not want to bother with checking out the metadata. But if you have a slower connection and time is at a premium, consider the search-result information.

First, check the page summary. Where does your keyword appear? Does it appear in the middle of a list of site names? Does it appear in a way that makes it clear that the context is not what you're looking for?

Check the size of the page if it's available. Is the page very large? Perhaps it's just a link list—a page full of hyperlinks, as the name suggests. Is it just 1 or 2 KB? It might be too small to find the level of detail that you're looking for.

If your aim is link lists, be on the lookout for pages larger than 20 KB and see "Browse the Google Directory" [Hack #1].

 Page size in Google results is never going to be more than 101 KB. That's because Google doesn't index more than 101 KB worth of a given web page.

Setting Preferences

Google's Preferences page, shown in Figure 1-5, provides a nice, easy way to set and save your searching preferences.

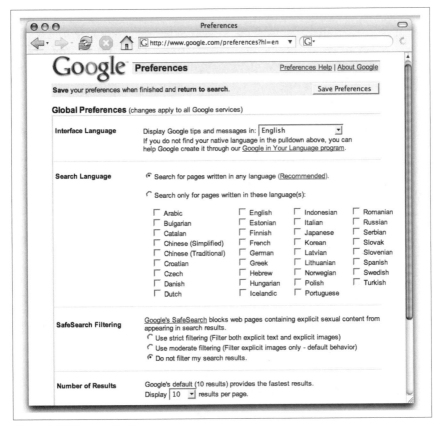

Figure 1-5. Google's Preferences page

Interface Language

You can set your Interface Language, affecting the language in which tips and messages are displayed. Language choices range from Afrikaans to Zulu, with plenty of odd options, including Bork, bork, bork! (the Swedish Chef), Elmer Fudd, and Pig Latin, thrown in for fun.

Search Language

Not to be confused with Interface Language, Search Language restricts what languages should be considered when searching Google's page index. The default is any language, but you could be interested only in web pages written in Chinese and Japanese, or French, German, and Spanish—the combination is up to you.

SafeSearch Filtering

Google's SafeSearch filtering affords you a method of avoiding search results that may offend your sensibilities. No filtering means you're offered anything in the Google index. Moderate filtering rules out explicit images, but not explicit language. Strict filtering filters both text and images. The default is moderate filtering.

Number of Results

By default, Google displays 10 results per page. For more results, click any of the "Result Page: 1 2 3..." links at the bottom of each result page, or simply click the "Next" link.

You can specify your preferred number of results per page (10, 20, 30, 50, or 100), along with whether you want results to open in the current window or a new browser window.

Settings for Researchers

For the purpose of research, it's best to have as many search results as possible on the page. Because it's all text, it doesn't take that much longer to load 100 results than it does to load 10. If you have a computer with a decent amount of memory, it's also good to have search results open in a new window; it'll keep you from losing your place and leave you a window with all the search results readily available.

If you can stand it, leave your filtering turned off, or at least limit the filtering to moderate instead of strict. Machine filtering is not perfect and, unfortunately, enabling it might mean that you'll miss something valuable. This is especially true when you're searching for a phrase that might be caught by a filter, such as "breast cancer."

Unless you're absolutely sure that you always want to do a search in one language, I'd advise against setting your language preferences on this page. Instead, alter language preferences as needed using the Google Language Tools ["Language Tools" earlier in this chapter].

Between the simple search, advanced search, and preferences, you've got all the tools necessary to build the Google query to suit your particular purposes.

 If you have cookies turned off in your browser, setting preferences in Google isn't going to do you much good. You'll have to reset them every time you open your browser. If you can't have cookies and you want to use the same preferences every time, consider making a customized search form.

Understanding Google URLs

If you're like most people, you usually pay little attention to the URLs in your browser's address bar as you surf from one site to the next. And you might choose to stick with this habit while searching Google. You ought to know, however, that a subtle alteration made to the URL that Google returns after a search can be an efficient method of tweaking your result set. In fact, there's at least one thing you can do by fiddling with (we like to call it *hacking*) the URL that you can do no other way, and there are quick tricks that might save you a trip back to the Advanced Search page.

Say you want to search for three blind mice. The URL of the page of results will vary depending on the preferences you've set, but it will look something like this:

```
http://www.google.com/search?num=100&hl=en&q=%22three+blind+mice%22
```

The query itself—q=%22three+blind+mice%22, %22 being a URL-encoded " (double quote)—is pretty obvious, but let's break down what those extra bits mean.

The num=100 refers to the number of search results to a page: 100 in this case. Google accepts any number from 1 to 100. Altering the value of num is a nice shortcut to altering the preferred size of your result set without having to meander over to the Advanced Search page and rerun your search.

Don't see the num= in your URL? Simply append it by clicking at the end of the URL in your browser's address bar and typing it in. To set the number of results per page to 20, for instance, you'd add &num=20.

You can add or alter any of the modifiers described here by appending them to the URL or changing their values—the part after the = (equals)—to something within the accepted range for the modifier in question. If you're adding a modifier, you'll need to use an & symbol (ampersand) too. Look at how the modifiers are joined together on URLs for other search results to see how it's done.

The `hl=en` means the language interface—the language in which you use Google, reflected in the home page, messages, and buttons—is in English. Google's Language Tools **["Language Tools" earlier in this chapter]** page provides a list of language choices. Run your mouse over each language choice and notice the change reflected in the URL; the URL for Pig Latin looks like this:

```
http://www.google.com/intl/xx-piglatin/
```

The language code is the bit between `intl/` and the last `/`—`xx-piglatin`, in this case. Apply that to the search URL at hand by altering the existing value of `hl`:

```
hl=xx-piglatin
```

What if you put multiple `hl` modifiers on a result URL? Google honors whichever one comes last, reading from left to right. While it makes for confusing URLs, this means that you can always resort to laziness and add an extra modifier at the end rather than editing what's already there, like so:

```
http://www.google.com/search?num=100&hl=en&q=%22three+blind+mice%22&hl=xx-
piglatin
```

There's one more modifier that, appended to your URL, may provide some useful modifications of your results:

`safe=off`

> Means the SafeSearch filter is off. The SafeSearch filter removes search results of a sexually explicit nature. `safe=on` means the SafeSearch filter is on.

Playing about with Google's URL may not seem like the most intuitive way to get results quickly, but it's much faster than reloading the Advanced Search form, and in one case (the "months old" modifier), it's the only way to get at a particular set of results.

Browse the Google Directory

Google has a searchable subject index in addition to its eight-billion-page
web search.

Google's Web Search indexes over eight billion pages, which means that it
isn't suitable for all searches. When you've got a search that you can't narrow down, like if you're looking for information on a person about whom
you know nothing, billions of pages will get very frustrating very quickly.

But you don't have to limit your searches to the Web. Google also has a
searchable subject index, the Google Directory, at *http://directory.google.
com*. Instead of indexing the entirety of billions of pages, the directory
describes sites instead, indexing about 1.5 million URLs. This makes it a
much better search for general topics.

Does Google spend time building a searchable subject index in addition to a
full-text index? No, Google bases its directory on the Open Directory Project
data at *http://dmoz.org/*. The collection of URLs at the Open Directory
Project is gathered and maintained by a group of volunteers, but Google
does add some of its own Googlish magic to it.

As you can see in Figure 1-6, the front of the site is organized into several
topics. To find what you're looking for, you can either do a keyword search,
or *drill down* through the hierarchies of subjects.

Beside most listings, a couple of which are shown in Figure 1-7, you'll see a
green bar. The green bar is an approximate indicator of the site's PageRank
in the Google search engine. (Not every listing in the Google Directory has a
corresponding PageRank in the Google web index.) Web sites are listed in
the default order of Google PageRank, but you also have the option to list
them in alphabetical order.

One thing you'll notice about the Google Directory is how the annotations
and other information varies between the categories. That's because the
information in the directory is maintained by a small army of thousands of
volunteers who are each responsible for one or more categories. For the
most part, annotation is pretty good.

Searching the Google Directory

Because the Google Directory is a far smaller collection of URLs, ideal for
more general searching, it does not have the various complicated special
syntaxes for searching that the web search does. However, there are a couple of special syntaxes that you should know about.

Figure 1-6. The Google Directory

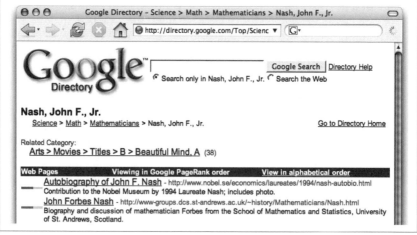

Figure 1-7. Individual listings under Science > Math > Mathematicians > Nash, John F., Jr.

intitle:
> Just like the Google web special syntax, intitle: restricts the query word search to the title of a page.

inurl:
> Restricts the query word search to the URL of a page.

When you're searching on Google's web index, your overwhelming concern is probably how to reduce your list of search results to something manageable. With that in mind, you might start with the narrowest possible search.

That's a reasonable strategy for the web index, but because you have a narrower pool of sites in the Google Directory, you want that search to be more general.

For example, say you were looking for information on author P. G. Wodehouse. A simple search on P. G. Wodehouse in Google's web index will get you over 86,000 results, possibly compelling you to immediately narrow down your search. But doing the same search in the Google Directory returns only 143 results. You might consider that a manageable number of results, or you might want to start carefully narrowing down your results further.

The Directory is also good for searching for events. A Google web search for "Korean War" will find you a million and a half results, while searching the Google Directory will find just over 2,830. This is a case where you will probably need to narrow down your search. Use general words indicating what kind of information you want—timeline, for example, or archives, or lesson plans. Don't narrow down your search with names or locations—that's not the best way to use the Google Directory.

HACK #2   Glean a Snapshot of Google in Time

Google Zeitgeist provides a weekly, monthly, and yearly overview of what the Web was interested in.

Turning to Google itself for a definition of *zeitgeist*, (define:zeitgeist), there's consensus that it refers to "the spirit of the times." And Google Zeitgeist (*http://www.google.com/press/zeitgeist.html*) is just that: a mirror that the Web (according to Google) holds up to us, providing a snapshot of the week, month, or year that was.

A typical weekly Google Zeitgeist (Figure 1-8) lists the top 10 gaining and declining queries and some hand-picked statistics (e.g., top Google News queries, popular sequels), fun facts (e.g., Tour de France versus Wimbledon), aggregate information gleaned about Googlers (e.g., operating systems, web browsers, languages), and any other trends that the Zeitgeist crew cares to delve into.

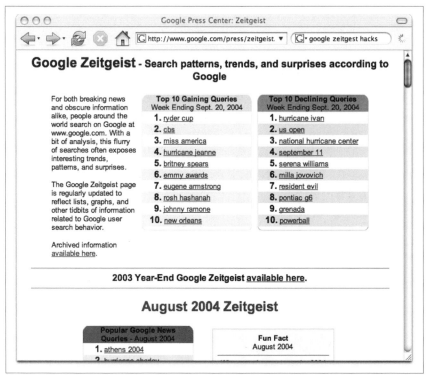

Figure 1-8. The week's top 10 gaining and declining queries

It takes only a few moments of visiting Google Zeitgeist before you're itching to go back a little further in time: the week your second child was born, the month of the Olympics, the year you graduated from high school. Click the "Archived information available here" link to browse the Google Zeitgeist Archive (Figure 1-9) of updates for every week, month, and year since January 2001.

Weekly Zeitgeist updates actually started in June 2001 at the same time the monthlies switched from PDF to HTML format.

The monthlies and year-ends provide more detail with trend graphs and also further break down searching by country, from Korea to Canada and points in between.

While Google Zeitgeist's statistics aren't earth shattering (e.g., "Searches for 'iraq' more than doubled on March 19, the date that Operation Iraqi

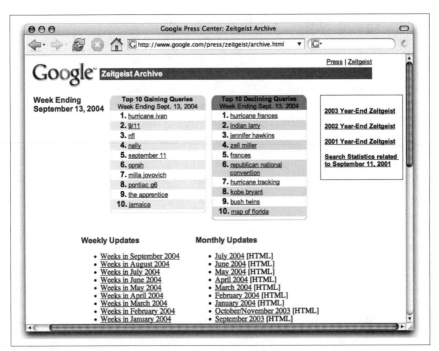

Figure 1-9. The Zeitgeist Archive holds weekly, monthly, and yearly updates from January 2001 to today

Freedom began"—imagine that!), it does provide you a snapshot of what the world in aggregate (55 billion searches in 2003) found interesting enough to look up.

See Also

- If Google Zeitgeist piques your interest, you might also try the Yahoo! Buzz Index (*http://buzz.yahoo.com*), a similar collection of statistics around popular Yahoo! Searches: the day's top movers (overall and by various Yahoo! categories), most viewed and emailed Yahoo! news items, and a market trend–like chart (click the "View Complete Chart..." link associated with any of the buzz listings on the front page) of leaders and movers, according to *buzz score* (*http://help.yahoo.com/ help/us/buzz/#buzz-04*).

Graph Google Results over Time

#3   Use Google as a trend watcher.

As of November 2004, Google's index contains a whopping eight billion pages and growing. And it doesn't just record pages; it's filled with news and events, commentary and discussion, changes and trends. You might think of Google as a mirror that we hold up to the Web that approximates how we define and represent ourselves and our world.

It should come as no surprise, then, that people spend an awful lot of time and energy watching Google results in an attempt to spot emerging topics and track trends. If you've been tapped to do this for your company, product, project, or service, G-Metrics (*http://g-metrics.com*) might be right up your alley. G-Metrics measures the occurrence of a keyword or set of keywords defined by you across time—complete with graphs.

Register with G-Metrics (registration requires only your name and email address) for a login key. Once logged in, you can set queries, alter, remove, or review your queries and the results they've captured. Figure 1-10 shows my current watchlist, each query sporting a result count and percentage change over time.

my watchlist

Date	Query Title	Lang.	Googlecount*	Change (%)		Options
2004/10/04	fred		7,030,000	+1.74		| del | rss |
2004/10/04	weblog site:uk		1,050,000	-9.48		| del | rss |
2004/10/04	weblog site:us		29,500	+8.46		| del | rss |
2004/10/04	weblog site:gov		521	-0.38		| del | rss |
2004/10/04			0	+0.00		| del | rss |

Figure 1-10. G-Metrics watchlist results

Click a query for a trend graph from the time you added the search, counts for the past seven days, and Google's current top 10 results for that query, as shown in Figure 1-11.

We also show you how to track result counts over time **[Hack #3]**, but G-Metrics takes this further, allowing you to monitor trends without a lot of legwork; your queries are "set it and forget it." You can even subscribe to an RSS feed of the results of any one of your queries. Sure, you could set up Google Alerts **[Hack #59]**, feed the numbers into a spreadsheet, and do the graphing yourself—but why?

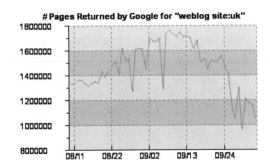

google query: weblog site:uk

Title: weblog site:uk   [add to my list]
Lang. restriction: none

7-day results

Date	Googlecount	Change (%)
2004/10/04	1,050,000	-9.48%
2004/10/03	1,160,000	-1.69%
2004/10/02	1,180,000	-2.48%
2004/10/01	1,210,000	+25.52%
2004/09/30	964,000	-25.85%
2004/09/29	1,300,000	+23.81%
2004/09/28	1,050,000	-8.70%
2004/09/27	1,150,000	-19.01%
2004/09/26	1,420,000	-3.40%
2004/09/25	1,470,000	-5.77%

top-10 results returned by google.com

Guardian Unlimited | **Weblog**
... This **weblog** is no longer being updated. Please go to Newsblog - Guardian

Figure 1-11. G-Metrics trend graphing and details for a particular query

Visualize Google Results

#4   The TouchGraph Google Browser is the perfect Google complement for those who appreciate visual displays of information.

Some people are born text crawlers. They can retrieve the mostly text resources of the Internet and browse them happily for hours. But others are more visually oriented and find that the flat text results of the Internet leave something to be desired, especially when it comes to search results.

If you're the type who appreciates visual displays of information, you're bound to like the TouchGraph Google Browser (*http://www.touchgraph. com/TGGoogleBrowser.html*). This Java applet allows you to start with the pages that are similar to one URL, and then expand outward to pages that are similar to the first set of pages, on and on, until you have a giant map of *nodes* (a.k.a. URLs) on your screen.

The TouchGraph Google Browser was created by Alex Shapiro (*http://www. touchgraph.com/*).

Note that what you're finding here are URLs that are similar to another URL. You aren't doing a keyword search, and you're not using the link: syntax. You're searching by Google's measure of similarity.

Starting to Browse

Start your journey by entering a URL on the TouchGraph home page and clicking the "Graph It" link. Your browser will launch the TouchGraph Java applet, covering your window with a large mass of linked nodes, as shown in Figure 1-12.

> You'll need a web browser capable of running Java applets. If Java support in your preferred browser comes in the form of a plug-in, your browser should have the smarts to launch a plug-in locator/downloader and walk you through the installation process.

If you're easily entertained like me, you might amuse yourself for a while just by clicking and dragging the nodes around. But there's more to do than that.

Expanding Your View

Hold your mouse over one of items in the group of pages. You'll notice that a little box with an H pops up. Click on that and you'll get a box of information about that particular node, as shown in Figure 1-13.

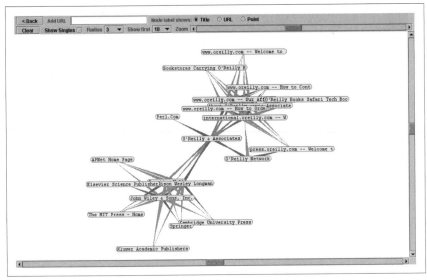

Figure 1-12. Mass of linked nodes generated by TouchGraph

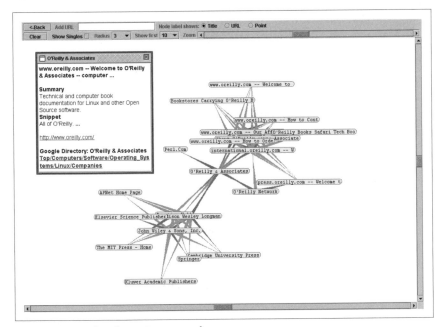

Figure 1-13. Node information pop-up box

The box of information contains title, snippet, and URL—pretty much everything you'd get from a regular search result. Click on the URL in the box to open that URL's web page itself in another browser window.

Not interested in visiting web pages just yet? Want to do some more search visualization? Double-click on one of the nodes. TouchGraph uses the API to request from Google pages similar to the URL of the node you double-clicked. Keep double-clicking at will; when no more pages are available, a green C will appear when you put your mouse over the node (no more than 30 results are available for each node). If you do it often enough, you'll end up with a whole screen full of nodes with lines denoting their relationship to one another, as Figure 1-14 shows.

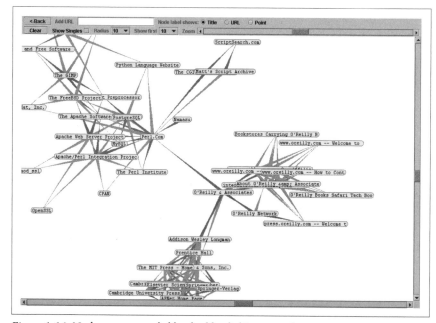

Figure 1-14. Node mass expanded by double-clicking on nodes

Visualization Options

Once you've generated similarity page listings for a few different sites, you'll find yourself with a pretty crowded page. TouchGraph has a few options to change the look of what you're viewing.

For each node, you can show page title, page URL, or *point* (the first two letters of the title). If you're just browsing page relationships, the title's probably best. However, if you've been working with the applet for a while and have mapped out a plethora of nodes, the point or URL options can save some space. The URL option removes the *www* and *.com* from the URL, leaving the other domain suffixes. For example, *www.perl.com* will show as *perl*, while *www.perl.org* shows as *perl.org*.

Speaking of saving space, there's a zoom slider on the upper-right side of the applet window. When you've generated several distinct groups of nodes, zooming out allows you to see the different groupings more clearly. However, it also becomes difficult to see relationships between the nodes in the different groups.

TouchGraph offers the option to view the *singles*, the nodes in a group that have a relationship with only one other node. This option is off by default; check the Show Singles checkbox to turn it on. I find it's better to leave them out; they crowd the page and make it difficult to establish and explore separate groups of nodes.

The Radius setting specifies how many nodes will show around the node you've clicked on. A radius of 1 will show all nodes directly linked to the node you've clicked, a radius of 2 will show all nodes directly linked to the node you've clicked as well as all nodes directly linked to those nodes, and so on. The higher the radius, the more crowded things get. The groupings do, however, tend to settle themselves into nice little discernable clumps, as shown in Figure 1-15.

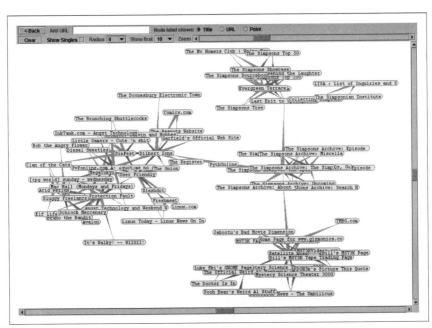

Figure 1-15. Node mass with Radius set to 4

A drop-down menu beside the Radius setting specifies how many search results (i.e., how many connections) are shown. A setting of 10 is, in my experience, optimal.

Making the Most of These Visualizations

Yes, it's cool. Yes, it's unusual. And yes, it's fun dragging those little nodes around. But what exactly is the TouchGraph good for?

TouchGraph does two rather useful things. First, it allows you to see at a glance the similarity relationship between large groups of URLs. You can't do this with several flat results to similar URL queries. Second, if you do some exploration you can sometimes get a list of companies in the same industry or area. This comes in handy when you're researching a particular industry or topic. It'll take some exploration, though, so keep trying.

H A C K
#5

Check Your Spelling

Google sometimes takes the liberty of "correcting" what it perceives is a spelling error in your query.

If you've ever used other Internet search engines, you'll have experienced what I call *stupid spellcheck*. That's when you enter a proper noun and the search engine suggests a completely ludicrous query ("Elvish Parsley" for "Elvis Presley"). Google's quite a bit smarter than that.

When Google thinks it can spell individual words or complete phrases in your search query better than you can, it'll suggest a "better" search, hyper-linking it directly to a query. For example, if you search for hydrecefallus, Google will ask if you meant hydrocephalus, as shown in Figure 1-16.

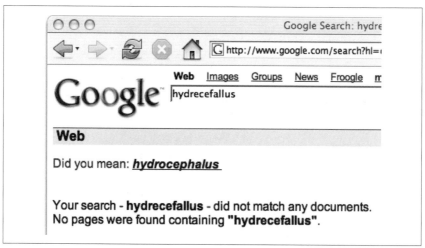

Figure 1-16. Google offers spelling suggestions when it thinks it knows better

Suggestions aside, Google will assume that you know of what you speak and return your requested results, provided that your query gleaned results.

If your query found no results for the spellings you provided and Google believes it knows better, it will automatically run a new search of its own suggestions. Thus, a search for hydrecefallus finding (hopefully) no results will spark a Google-initiated search for hydrocephalus.

Given the sheer number of pages on the Web and the odds that at least one of the people proffering a page on the subject you're after either can't spell or can't type, I don't see these automatically generated searches based on Google's suggestions coming up that often these days.

For instance, because two web pages cite this hack as it first appeared in the previous edition of this title, the hydrecefallus example is blown. And I couldn't find another misspelling that both came up short on results and for which Google had any suggestions.

On the other hand—at least for now—a search for spodding oil texas turns up only 4 results, while the same search with correct spelling ("spudding"), spudding oil texas, returns 708.

Mind you, Google does not arbitrarily come up with its suggestions, but builds them based on its own database of words and phrases found while indexing the Web. If you search for nonsense like garafghafdghasdg, you'll get no results and be offered no suggestions.

This is a lovely side effect and a quick and easy way to check the relative frequency of spellings. Query for a particular spelling, making note of the number of results. Then click on Google's suggested spelling and note the number of results. It's surprising how close the counts are sometimes, indicating an oft-misspelled word or phrase.

Embrace Misspellings

Don't make the mistake of automatically dismissing the proffered results from a misspelled word, particularly a proper name. I've been a fan of cartoonist Bill Mauldin for years now, but I repeatedly misspell his name as "Bill Maudlin." And judging from a quick Google search, I'm not the only one. There is no law stating that every page must be spellchecked before it goes online, so it's often worth taking a look at results despite misspellings.

As an experiment, try searching for two misspelled words on a related topic, like ventriculostomy hydrocephalis. What kind of information did you get? Could the information you got, if any, be grouped into a particular online *genre*?

At the time of this writing, the search for ventriculostomy hydrocephalis gets only 10 results. The content here is generally from people dealing with various neurosurgical problems. Again, there is no law that states that all web materials have to be spellchecked.

Use this to your advantage as a researcher. When you're looking for layman accounts of illness and injury, the content you desire might actually be more often misspelled than not. On the other hand, when looking for highly technical information or references from credible sources, filtering out misspelled queries will bring you closer to the information you seek.

HACK #6 Google Phonebook: Let Google's Fingers Do the Walking

Google makes an excellent phonebook, even to the extent of doing reverse lookups.

Google combines residential and business phone number information and its own excellent interface to offer a phonebook lookup that provides listings for businesses and residences in the United States. However, the search offers three different syntaxes, different levels of information provide different results, the syntaxes are finicky, and Google doesn't provide documentation.

The Three Syntaxes

Google offers three ways to search its phonebook:

phonebook
> Searches the entire Google phonebook

rphonebook
> Searches residential listings only

bphonebook
> Searches business listings only

> The result page for phonebook: lookups lists only five results, residential and business combined. The more specific rphonebook: and bphonebook: searches provide up to 30 results per page. For a better chance of finding what you're looking for, use the appropriate targeted lookup.

Using the Syntaxes

Using a standard phonebook requires knowing quite a bit of information about what you're looking for: first name, last name, city, and state.

Google's phonebook requires no more than last name and state to get it started. Casting a wide net for all the Smiths in California is as simple as:

```
phonebook:smith ca
```

Try giving 411 a whirl with that request! Figure 1-17 shows the results of the query.

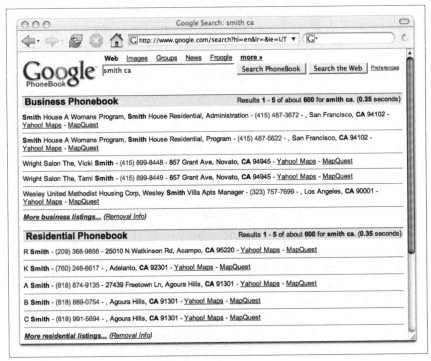

Figure 1-17. A phonebook: result page

Notice that, while intuition might tell you that there are thousands of Smiths in California, the Google phonebook says that there are only 600. Just as Google's regular search engine maxes out at 1,000 results, its phonebook maxes out at 600. Fair enough. Try narrowing down your search by adding a first name, city, or both:

```
phonebook:john smith los angeles ca
```

At the time of this writing, the Google phonebook found 2 business and 20 residential listings for John Smith in Los Angeles, California.

Caveats

The phonebook syntaxes are powerful and useful, but they can be difficult to use if you don't remember a few things about how they work.

The syntaxes are case sensitive. Searching for phonebook:john doe ca works, while Phonebook:john doe ca (notice the capital P) doesn't.

Wildcards don't work. Then again, they're not needed, since the Google phonebook does all the wildcarding for you. For example, if you want to find shops in New York with "Coffee" in the title, don't bother trying to envision every permutation of "Coffee Shop," "Coffee House," and so on. Just search for bphonebook:coffee new york ny and you'll get a list of any business in New York whose name contains the word "coffee."

Exclusions don't work. Perhaps you want to find coffee shops that aren't Starbucks. You might think phonebook:coffee -starbucks new york ny would do the trick. After all, you're searching for coffee and not Starbucks, right? Unfortunately not; Google thinks you're looking for both the words "coffee" and "starbucks," yielding just the opposite of what you were hoping for: everything Starbucks in NYC.

OR *doesn't always work.* You might start wondering if Google's phonebook accepts OR lookups. You then might experiment, trying to find all the coffee shops in Rhode Island or Hawaii: bphonebook:coffee (ri | hi). Unfortunately that doesn't work; the only listings you'll get are for coffee shops in Hawaii. That's because Google doesn't appear to see the (ri | hi) as a state code, but rather as another element of the search. So if you reversed your search above, and searched for coffee (hi | ri), Google would find listings that contained the string "coffee" and either the strings "hi" or "ri." So you'll find Hi-Tide Coffee (in Massachusetts) and several coffee shops in Rhode Island. It's neater to use OR in the middle of your query, and then specify your state at the end. For example, if you want to find coffee shops that sell either donuts or bagels, this query works fine: bphonebook:coffee (donuts | bagels) ma. That finds stores that contain the word "coffee" and either the word "donuts" or the word "bagels" in Massachusetts. The bottom line: you can use an OR query on the store or resident name, but not on the location.

 Try some phonebook lookups that you couldn't do by dialing 411. For example, try searching by last name and area code, or last name and Zip Code! Google's phone book lookup is very accommodating.

Reverse Phonebook Lookup

All three phonebook syntaxes support reverse lookup, though it's probably best to use the general phonebook: syntax to avoid not finding what you're looking for due to its residential or business classification.

To do a reverse search, just enter the phone number with area code. Lookups without area code won't work.

```
phonebook:(707) 827-7000
```

(This is the phone number of O'Reilly world headquarters in Sebastopol, California, USA.)

Note that reverse lookups on Google are a hit-or-miss proposition and don't always produce results. If you're not having any luck, consider using a more dedicated phonebook site such as WhitePages.com (*http://www.whitepages. com/*).

Finding Phonebooks Using Google

While Google's phonebook is a good starting point, its usefulness is limited. If you're looking for a phone number at a university or other large institution, while you won't find the number in Google, you certainly can find the appropriate phonebook, if it's online.

If you're looking for a university phonebook, try this simple search first: inurl:phone site:*university.edu*, replacing *university.edu* with the domain of the university you're looking for. For example, to find the online phonebook of the University of North Carolina at Chapel Hill, you'd search for:

```
inurl:phone site:unc.edu
```

If that doesn't work, there are several variations you can try, again substituting your preferred university's domain for *unc.edu*:

```
title:"phone book" site:unc.edu
(phonebook | "phone book") lookup faculty staff site:unc.edu
inurl:help (phonebook | "phone book") site:unc.edu
```

If you're looking for several university phonebooks, try the same search with the more generic site:edu rather than a specific university's domain. There are also web sites that list university phonebooks, one of which is the Phonebook Gateway Server Lookup (*http://www.uiuc.edu/cgi-bin/ph/lookup*), with over 330 phonebooks.

Think Global, Google Local

HACK #7

Take web searching to the streets—your street, in fact. Google Local narrows down all those zillions of results to those within range of a particular city, state, or postal code.

While the Web and Google have taught us to think global when it comes to looking for information, web searches often fail in the simple task of finding things in our own backyards. Sure, the island of Celebes is the home to Sulawesi Kalossi, but where can I find the finest cup of Sulawesi coffee within walking distance? And even more importantly: do they have free wireless Internet access?

That's not to say that Google isn't paying attention to any mention of locale in your queries. If you were, let's say, to search for scooters san francisco, you would notice a set of local San Francisco finds ["Quick Links" earlier in this chapter] at the top of the results page. As you can see in Figure 1-18, Google also provides addresses, phone numbers, and mileage (from the center of San Francisco, presumably).

Figure 1-18. Local find sometimes appear as "magic links" at the top of the results page

Google combines its index with data gleaned from the Yellow Pages to zero in on local results that very often prove interesting and useful.

This data is so interesting, in fact, that Google has taken the service beyond that sprinkling of magic links, launching Google Local (*http://local.google. com*), a location-aware frontend to the Google search engine. The Google Local home page (Figure 1-19) looks very much like what you're used to from Google, the only real difference being that there are two search boxes instead of just the one: What and Where. In the What box, you type your search query as usual. In the Where box, you can localize your search by providing a city (by itself, if the city is unambiguously well-known—e.g., San Francisco or New York, not Rome or Concord) and a state name or Zip Code.

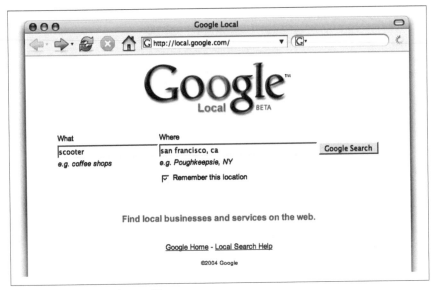

Figure 1-19. The Google Local home page

 Before you get too excited about finding that perfect coffee shop on the island of Celebes, you should know that Google Local searches the United States and Canada only. Don't get too used to that limitation, though: Google is planning on expanding.

Before you click the Google Search button, notice that a "Remember this location" checkbox is checked by default so that the next time you visit, Google will fill in your preferred locale for you.

 You can change the Where at any time and, as long as that "Remember this location" checkbox is checked, Google will remember for next time. If, for some reason, you'd like to clear the Where completely, just point your browser at *http://local.google.com/local?sl=1*.

My query for scooters san francisco turned up a nice collection of scooter shops, service centers, and other motorcycle- and scooter-focused results in and around San Francisco, as shown in Figure 1-20. Notice that each of the results is assigned a letter (e.g., San Francisco Scooter Centre is "A") associated with a pin in the map of the area to the right. Each result, as with the magic links, has associated address, phone number, and mileage information; there's also a link to driving directions over at MapQuest.com.

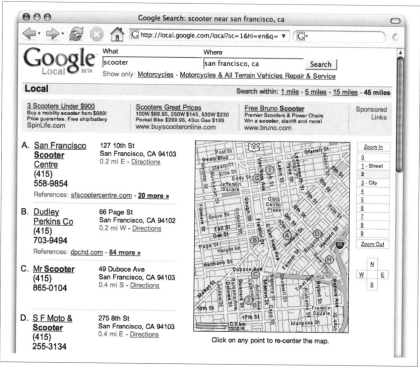

Figure 1-20. Google Local results

You can further constrain the search using the "Search within: 1 mile – 5 miles – 15 miles – 45 miles" links in the Google Local toolbar or by dropping down into one of the "Show only" categories listed beneath the query fields at the top of the page.

Click one of the results and you're taken not to the site itself (in fact, the business or service may not even *have* a web site ... shocking, I know!), but to further detail. If the business or service does indeed have a web presence, it's likely to be the first of the references listed. But this isn't necessarily so; for instance, while *sfscootercentre.com* is indeed the online home of the San Francisco Scooter Centre, San Francisco Moto & Scooter doesn't live at *scooter.com* (as is shown in one of the two results for the scooter shop), but at *sfmoto.com*.

As you can see in Figure 1-21, the map zeros in on only that one result and Google appends References to the bottom of the page. These are sites that refer to (and I don't just mean link to) the search result that you're focused on.

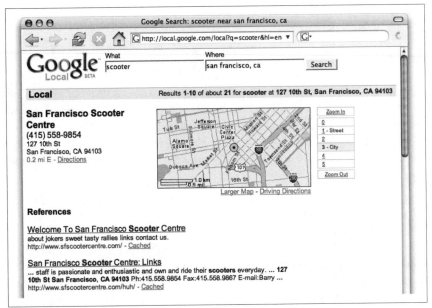

Figure 1-21. A typical Google Local result, complete with map and references

 You can pan around by clicking anywhere on any map to pull that bit into the center or clicking the N, S, E, W links to the right of the map. Zoom using the Zoom In or Zoom Out links or jump directly to a particular scale (e.g., Street or City) by clicking any link on the zoom numbered scale. Click the Larger Map link at the bottom of any map for a more detailed view of the area or Driving Directions to find your way there, no matter where you are.

While Google Local is still in beta at the time of this writing, it certainly seems to have promise. About the only thing missing at this point is the ability to narrow a locale to the area around a particular address rather than just city or Zip Code.

See Also

- Yahoo! Local (*http://local.yahoo.com*) actually goes even more local than Google Local, supporting full addresses rather than just city, state, and Zip Code.

HACK #8 Track Stocks

A well-crafted Google query will usually net you company information beyond those provided by traditional stock services.

Among the pantheon of lesser-known Google syntaxes is `stocks:`. Searching for `stocks:symbol`, where *symbol* represents the stock you're looking for, will redirect you to Yahoo! Finance (*http://finance.yahoo.com/*) for details. The Yahoo! page is actually framed by Google; off to the top-left is the Google logo, along with links to Quicken, Fool.com, MSN MoneyCentral, and other financial sites.

Feed Google a bum `stock:` query and you'll still find yourself at Yahoo! Finance, usually staring at a quote for stock that you've never heard of or a "Stock Not Found" page. Of course, you can use this to your advantage. Enter `stocks:` followed by the name of a company you're looking for (e.g., `stocks:friendly`). If the company's name is more than one word, choose the most unique word. Run your query and you'll arrive at the Yahoo! Finance stock lookup page shown in Figure 1-22.

Notice the Look Up button; click it and you'll be offered a list of companies that match "friendly" in some way. From there you can get the stock information that you want (assuming the company you wanted is on the list).

Beyond Google for Basic Stock Information

Google isn't particularly set up for basic stock research. You'll have to do your initial groundwork elsewhere, returning to Google armed with a better understanding of what you're looking for. I recommend going straight to Yahoo! Finance (*http://finance.yahoo.com*) to quickly look up stocks by symbol or company name. There you'll find all the basics: quotes, company profiles, charts, and recent news. For more in-depth coverage, I heartily recommend Hoovers (*http://www.hoovers.com*). Some of the information is free. For more depth, you'll have to pay a subscription fee.

More Stock Research with Google

Try searching Google for:

```
"Tootsie Roll"
```

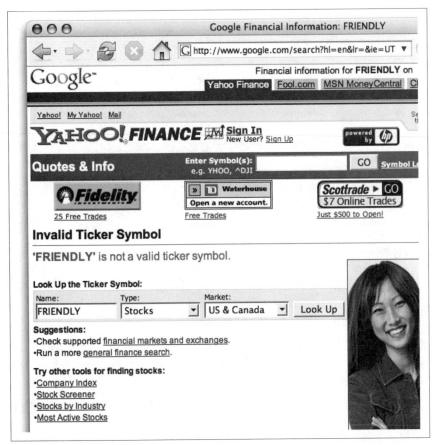

Figure 1-22. Yahoo! Finance stock lookup page

Now add the stock symbol, TR, to your query:

    "Tootsie Roll" TR

Aha! Instantly the search results shift to financial information. Now, add the name of the CEO:

    "Tootsie Roll" TR "Melvin Gordon"

You'll end up with a nice, small, targeted list of results, as shown in Figure 1-23.

Stock symbols are great "fingerprints" for Internet research. They're consistent, they often appear along with the company name, and they're usually enough to narrow down your search results to relevant information.

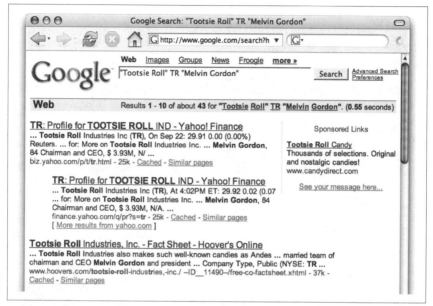

Figure 1-23. Using a stock symbol to limit results

There are also several words and phrases that you can use to narrow down your search for company-related information. Replacing *company* with the name of the company you're looking for, try these:

- For press releases: "*company* announced", "*company* announces", "*company* reported"

- For financial information: *company* "quarterly report", *company* SEC, *company* financials, *company* "p/e ratio"

- For location information: *company* parking airport location—doesn't always work but sometimes works amazingly well

HACK #9   Consult the Dictionary

Google, in addition to its own spellchecking index, provides hooks into Dictionary.com.

Google's spellchecking [Hack #5] is built on its own word and phrase database, gleaned while indexing web pages. Thus, it provides suggestions for lesser-known proper names, phrases, common sentence constructs, etc. Google also offers a definition service powered by Dictionary.com (*http:// www.dictionary.com*). Such definitions, coming from a credible source and augmented by various specialty indexes, can be more limited.

Run a search. On the results page, you'll notice the phrase "Searched the web for [query words]." If the query words would appear in a dictionary, they will be hyperlinked to a dictionary definition. Identified phrases will be linked as a phrase; for example, the query `"jolly roger"` will allow you to look up the phrase "jolly roger." On the other hand, the phrase `"computer legal"` will allow you to look up the separate words "computer" and "legal."

The definition search will sometimes fail on obscure words, very new words, slang, and technical vocabularies (otherwise known as *jargon*). If you search for a word's meaning and Google can't help you, try enlisting the services of a meta-search dictionary, like OneLook (*http://www.onelook.com/*), which indexes over six million words from over 1,000 dictionaries. If that doesn't work, try Google again with one of the following tricks, *queryword* being the word you want to find:

- If you're searching for several words—you're reading a technical manual, for example—search for them at the same time. Sometimes you'll find a glossary this way. For example, maybe you're reading a book about marketing, and you don't know many of the words. If you search for `storyboard stet SAU`, you'll get only a few search results, and they'll all be glossaries.

- Try searching for your word and the word glossary, say, `stet glossary`. Be sure to use an unusual word; you may not know what a "spread" is in the context of marketing but searching for `spread glossary` will get you over two million results for many different kinds of glossaries. See "Use Google Tools for Translators" **[Hack #20]** for language translation.

- Try searching for the phrase *queryword* `means` or the words `What does` *queryword* `mean?`.

- If you're searching for a medical or a technical item, narrow your search to educational (*.edu*) sites. If you want a contextual definition for using equine acupuncture and how it might be used to treat laminitis, try `"equine acupuncture" laminitis`.

- `site:edu` will give you a brief list of results. Furthermore, you'll avoid book lists and online stores, which is handy if you're seeking information and don't necessarily want to purchase anything. If you're searching for slang, try narrowing your search to sites like Geocities and Tripod and see what happens. Sometimes young people post fan sites and other informal cultural collections on free places like Geocities, and using these, you can find many examples of slang in context instead of dry lists of definitions. There are an amazing number of glossaries on Geocities; search for `glossary site:geocities.com`, and see for yourself.

Google's connection with Dictionary.com means that simple definition checking is fast and easy. But even more obscure words can be quickly found if you apply a little creative thinking.

Look Up Definitions

Do you find yourself smiling knowingly when your boss mentions that well-known business principle that you've never heard of? Overwhelmed with "geek speak"? Chances are Google's heard it mentioned—and possibly even defined—somewhere before.

Most specialized vocabularies remain, for the most part, fairly static; words don't suddenly change their meaning all that often. Not so with technical and computer-related jargon. It seems like every 12 seconds someone comes up with a new buzzword or term relating to computers or the Internet, and then 12 minutes later it becomes obsolete or means something completely different—often more than one thing at a time. Maybe it's not that bad. It just feels that way.

Google can help you in two ways, by helping you look up words and by helping you figure out what words you don't know but need to know.

Google Definitions

Before you assume you're going to be in for a lot of Googling, try the define search syntax mentioned in the "Quick Links" section earlier in this chapter. Simply prepend the definition you're after with the special syntax keyword define, like so:

```
define google
define julienne
define 42
```

Google tells us that these are defined as "most important spidering search engine," "cut a vegetable into long thin matchsticks," and "being two more than forty," thanks to to Juice New Media's Search Engine Glossary, The Youth Online Club, and WordNet at Princeton, respectively.

Click the associated "Definition in context" link to visit the page from which the definition was drawn.

Click the "Web definitions for..." link or prefix the word you're defining with define: (note the addition of a colon) in the first place, and you'll net a full page of definitions drawn from all manner of places. For instance, define:TLA finds turns up oodles of definitions (all about the same, mind you), as shown in Figure 1-24.

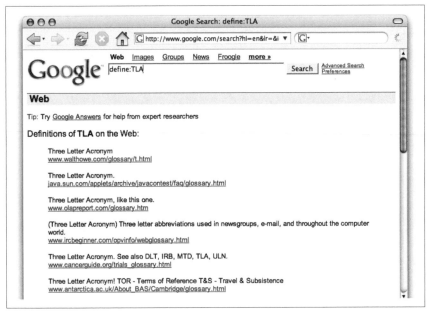

Figure 1-24. A page chock-full of definitions for TLA

 The define word syntax is still subject to spelling suggestions, so you don't have to worry too much about misspelling. The define:word form, however, doesn't perform a web
search at all and so will return no results or spelling suggestions whatsoever if it finds no definitions to offer you.

If all that didn't turn up anything useful, move on to Google Web Search
proper.

Slang

We have distinctive speech patterns that are shaped by our educations, our
families, and our location. Further, we may use another set of words based
on our occupation. When a teenager says something is "phat," that's
slang—a specialized vocabulary used by a particular group. When a copy-
writer scribbles "stet" on an ad, that's not slang, but it's still specialized
vocabulary or jargon used by a certain group—in this case, the advertising
industry.

Being aware of these specialty words can make all the difference when it
comes to searching. Adding specialized words to your search query—

whether slang or industry jargon—can really change the slant of your search results.

Slang gives you one more way to break up your search engine results into geographically distinct areas. There's some geographical blurriness when you use slang to narrow your search engine results, but it's amazing how well it works. For example, search Google for football. Now search for football bloke. Totally different results set, isn't it? Now search for football bloke bonce. Now you're into soccer narratives.

Of course, this is not to say that everyone in England automatically uses the word "bloke" any more than everyone in the southern U.S. automatically uses the word "y'all." But adding well-chosen bits of slang (which will take some experimentation) will give a whole different tenor to your search results and may point you in unexpected directions. You can find slang from the following resources:

The Probert Encyclopedia—Slang (http://www.probertencyclopaedia.com/slang.htm)
> This site is browseable by first letter or searchable by keyword. (Note that the keyword search covers the entire *Probert Encyclopedia*; slang results are near the bottom.) Slang is from all over the world. It's often cross-linked, especially drug slang. As with most slang dictionaries, this site contains material that might offend.

A Dictionary of Slang (http://www.peevish.co.uk/slang/)
> This site focuses on slang heard in the United Kingdom, which means slang from other places as well. It's browseable by letter or via a search engine. Words from outside the U.K. are marked with their place of origin in brackets. Definitions also indicate typical usage: humorous, vulgar, derogatory, etc.

Surfing for Slang (http://www.spraakservice.net/slangportal)
> Of course, each area in the world has its own slang. This site has a good meta-list of English and Scandinavian slang resources.

Start out by searching Google for your query without the slang. Check the results and decide where they're falling short. Are they not specific enough? Are they not located in the right geographical area? Are they not covering the right demographic—teenagers, for example?

Introduce one slang word at a time. For example, for a search for "football," add the word "bonce" and check the results. If they're not narrowed down enough, add the word "bloke." Add one word at a time until you get the results that you want. Using slang is an inexact science, so you'll have to do some experimenting.

Here are some things to be careful of when using slang in your searches:

- Try many different slang words.
- Don't use slang words that are generally considered offensive, except as a last resort. Your results will be skewed.
- Be careful when using teenage slang, which changes constantly.
- Try searching for slang when using Google Groups. Slang crops up often in conversation.
- Minimize your searches for slang when searching for more formal sources, such as newspaper stories.
- Don't use slang phrases if you can help it; in my experience, slang changes too much to be consistently searchable. Stick to established words.

Industrial Slang

Specialized vocabularies are those used in particular subject areas and industries. The medical and legal fields are good examples of specialized vocabularies, although there are many others.

When you need to tip your search to the more technical, the more specialized, and the more in-depth, think of a specialized vocabulary. For example, do a Google search for heartburn. Now do a search for heartburn GERD. Now do a search for heartburn GERD "gastric acid". You'll see each of them is very different.

With some fields, finding specialized vocabulary resources will be a snap. But with others, it's not that easy. As a jumping-off point, try the Glossarist site at *http://www.glossarist.com*, which is a searchable subject index of about 6,000 different glossaries covering dozens of different topics. There are also several other large online resources covering certain specific vocabularies. These resources include:

The On-Line Medical Dictionary (http://cancerweb.ncl.ac.uk/omd/)
This dictionary contains vocabulary relating to biochemistry, cell biology, chemistry, medicine, molecular biology, physics, plant biology, radiobiology, science, and technology, and currently has over 46,000 listings.

You can browse the dictionary by letter or search it by word. Sometimes you can search for a word that you know (bruise) and find another term that might be more common in medical terminology (contusion). You can also browse the dictionary by subject. Bear in mind that this dictionary is in the U.K. and some spellings may be slightly different for American users (e.g., "tumour" versus "tumor").

MedTerms.com (http://www.medterms.com/)

MedTerms.com has far fewer definitions (around 15,000), but it also has extensive articles from MedicineNet. If you're starting from absolute square one with your research and you need some basic information and vocabulary to get started, search MedicineNet for your term (bruise works well) and then move to MedTerms.com to search for specific words.

Law.com's legal dictionary (http://dictionary.law.com/lookup2.asp)

Law.com's legal dictionary is excellent because you can search either words or definitions; you can browse, too. For example, you can search definitions for the word inheritance and get a list of all the entries that contain the word "inheritance." This is an easy way to get to the words "muniment of title" without knowing the path.

As with slang, add specialized vocabulary slowly—one word at a time—and anticipate that it will narrow down your search results very quickly. For example, take the word "spudding," often used in association with oil drilling. Searching for spudding by itself finds only about 4,300 results on Google. Adding Texas knocks it down to 581 results, and this is still a very general search! Add specialized vocabulary very carefully or you'll narrow down your search results to the point where you can't find what you want.

Researching Terminology with Google

First things first: for heaven's sake, please don't just plug the abbreviation into the query box! For example, searching for XSLT will net you over two million results. While combing through the sites that Google turns up may eventually lead you to a definition, there's simply more to life than that. Instead, add "stands +for" to the query if it's an abbreviation or acronym. "XSLT stands +for" returns around 194 results, and the third is a tutorial glossary. If you're still getting too many results ("XML stands +for" gives you almost 3,000 results) try adding beginners or newbie to the query. "XML stands +for" beginners brings in 227 results, the third being "XML for beginners."

If you're still not getting the results you want, try "What is X?" or "X +is short +for" or X beginners FAQ, where X is the acronym or term. These should be regarded as second-tier methods, because most sites don't tend to use phrases such as "What is X?" on their pages, "X is short for" is uncommon language usage, and X might be so new (or so obscure) that it doesn't yet have a FAQ entry. Then again, your mileage may vary and it's worth a shot; there's a lot of terminology out there.

If you have hardware- or software-specific terminology—as opposed to hardware- or software-related—try the word or phrase along with anything you might know about its usage. For example, as a Perl module, Dyna-Loader is software-specific terminology. That much known, simply give the two words a spin:

```
DynaLoader Perl
```

If the results you're finding are too advanced, assuming you already know what a DynaLoader is, start playing with the words beginners, newbie, and the like to bring you closer to information for beginners:

```
DynaLoader Perl Beginners
```

If you still can't find the word in Google, there are a few possible causes: perhaps it's slang specific to your area, your coworkers are playing with your mind, you heard it wrong (or there was a typo on the printout that you got), or it's very, very new.

Where to Go When It's Not on Google

Despite your best efforts, you're not finding good explanations of the terminology on Google. There are a few other sites that might have what you're looking for:

Whatis (http://whatis.techtarget.com)
  A searchable subject index of computer terminology, from software to telecom. This is especially useful if you've got a hardware- or software-specific word because the definitions are divided up into categories. You can also browse alphabetically. Annotations are good and are often cross-indexed.

Webopedia (http://www.pcwebopaedia.com/)
  Searchable by keyword or browseable by category. This site also has a list of the newest entries on the front page so that you can check for new words.

Netlingo (http://www.netlingo.com/framesindex.html)
  This is more Internet oriented. This site shows up with a frame on the left containing the words, with the definitions on the right. It includes lots of cross-referencing and really old slang.

Tech Encyclopedia (http://www.techweb.com/encyclopedia/)
  Features definitions and information on over 20,000 words. The top 10 terms searched for are listed so that you can see if everyone else is as

confused as you are. Though entries had before-the-listing and after-the-listing lists of words, I saw only moderate cross-referencing.

Geek terminology proliferates almost as quickly as web pages. Don't worry too much about deliberately keeping up—it's just about impossible. Instead, use Google as a "ready reference" resource for definitions.

Search Article Archives

HACK #11

Google serves as a handy searchable archive for back issues of online publications.

Not all sites have their own search engines, and even the ones that do are sometimes difficult to use. Complicated or incomplete search engines are more pain than gain when attempting to search through archives of published articles. If you follow a couple of rules, Google is handy for finding back issues of published resources.

The trick is to use a common phrase to find the information you're looking for. Let's use *The New York Times* as an example.

Articles from the NYT

Your first intuition when searching for previously published articles from *NYTimes.com* might be to simply use `site:nytimes.com` in your Google query. For example, if I wanted to find articles on George Bush, why not use:

```
"george bush" site:nytimes.com
```

This will indeed find you all articles mentioning George Bush published on *NYTimes.com*. What it won't find is all the articles produced by *The New York Times* but republished elsewhere.

> While doing research, keep credibility firmly in mind. If you're doing casual research, maybe you don't need to double-check a story to make sure that it actually comes from *The New York Times*, but if you're researching a term paper, double-check the veracity of every article you find that isn't actually on *The New York Times* site.

What you actually want is a clear identifier, no matter the site of origin, that an article comes from *The New York Times*. Copyright disclaimers are perfect for the job. A *New York Times* copyright notice typically reads:

```
Copyright 2004 The New York Times Company
```

Of course, this would only find articles from 2004. A simple workaround is to replace the year with a Google full-word wildcard ["Full-Word Wildcards" earlier in this chapter]:

```
Copyright * The New York Times Company
```

Let's try that George Bush search again, this time using the snippet of copyright disclaimer instead of the `site:` restriction:

```
"Copyright * The New York Times Company" "George Bush"
```

At the time of this writing, you get over six times as many results for this search as for the earlier attempt.

Magazine Articles

Copyright disclaimers are also useful for finding magazine articles. For example, *Scientific American*'s typical copyright disclaimer looks like this:

```
Scientific American, Inc. All rights reserved.
```

(The date appears before the disclaimer, so I just dropped it to avoid having to bother with wildcards.)

Using that disclaimer as a quote-delimited phrase along with a search word—hologram, for example—yields the Google query:

```
hologram "Scientific American, Inc. All rights reserved."
```

At the time of this writing, you'll get 31 results, which seems like a small number for a general query like hologram. When you get fewer results than you'd expect, fall back on using the `site:` syntax to go back to the originating site itself.

```
hologram site:sciam.com
```

In this example, you'll find several results that you can grab from Google's cache but are no longer available on the *Scientific American* site.

Most publications that I've come across have some kind of common text string that you can use when searching Google for its archives. Usually it's a copyright disclaimer and most often it's at the bottom of a page. Use Google to search for that string and whatever query words you're interested in, and if that doesn't work, fall back on searching for the query string and domain name.

Find Directories of Information

Use Google to find directories, link lists, and other collections of information.

Sometimes you're more interested in large information collections than scouring for specific bits and bobs. Using Google, there are a couple of different ways of finding directories, link lists, and other information collections. The first way makes use of Google's full-word wildcards ["**Full-Word Wildards**" earlier in this chapter] and the intitle: ["**Special Syntax**" earlier in this chapter]. The second is judicious use of particular keywords.

Title Tags and Wildcards

Pick something you'd like to find collections of information about. We'll use "trees" as our example. The first thing we'll look for is any page with the words "directory" and "trees" in its title. In fact, we'll build in a little buffering for words that might appear between the two using a couple of full-word wildcards (* characters). The resultant query looks something like this:

    intitle:"directory * * trees"

This query will find "directories of evergreen trees," "South African trees," and of course "directories containing simply trees."

What if you wanted to take things up a notch, taxonomically speaking, and find directories of botanical information? You'd use a combination of intitle: and keywords, like so:

    botany intitle:"directory of"

And you'd get almost 1,000 results. Changing the tenor of the information might be a matter of restricting results to those coming from academic institutions. Appending an edu site specification brings you to:

    botany intitle:"directory of" site:edu

This gets you around 150 results, a mixture of resource directories, and, unsurprisingly, directories of university professors.

Mixing these syntaxes works rather well when you're searching for something that might also be an offline print resource. For example:

    cars intitle:"encyclopedia of"

This query pulls in results from Amazon.com and other sites selling car encyclopedias. Filter out some of the more obvious book finds by tweaking the query slightly:

    cars intitle:"encyclopedia of" -site:amazon.com
    -inurl:book -inurl:products

The query specifies that search results should not come from Amazon.com and should not have the word "products" or "book" in the URL, which eliminates a fair amount of online stores. Play with this query by changing the word "cars" to whatever you'd like for some interesting finds.

> Of course there are lots of sites selling books online, but when it comes to injecting "noise" into results when you're trying to find online resources and research-oriented information, Amazon.com is the biggest offender. If you're actually looking for books, try +site:amazon.com instead.

If mixing syntaxes doesn't do the trick for the resources you want, there are some clever keyword combinations that might just do the trick.

Finding Searchable Subject Indexes with Google

There are a few major searchable subject indexes and myriad minor ones that deal with a particular topic or idea. You can find the smaller subject indexes by customizing a few generic searches. "what's new" "what's cool" directory, while gleaning a few false results, is a great way of finding searchable subject indexes. directory "gossamer threads" new is an interesting one. Gossamer Threads is the creator of a popular link directory program. This is a good way to find searchable subject indexes without too many false hits. directory "what's new" categories cool doesn't work particularly well, because the word "directory" is not a very reliable search term, but you will pull in some things with this query that you might otherwise have missed.

Let's put a few of these into practice:

```
"what's new" "what's cool" directory phylum
"what's new" "what's cool" directory carburetor
"what's new" "what's cool" directory "investigative journalism"
"what's new" directory categories gardening
directory "gossamer threads" new sailboats
directory "what's new" categories cool "basset hounds"
```

The real trick is to use a more general word, but make it unique enough that it applies mostly to your topic and not to many other topics.

Take acupuncture, for instance. Start narrowing it down by topic: what kind of acupuncture? For people or animals? If for people, what kind of conditions are being treated? If for animals, what kind of animals? Maybe you should be searching for "cat acupuncture", or maybe you should be searching for acupuncture arthritis. If this first round doesn't narrow down search results enough for you, keep going. Are you looking for education or treatment? You can skew results one way or the other by using the site:

syntax. So maybe you want "cat acupuncture" site:com or arthritis acupuncture site:edu. Just by taking a few steps to narrow things down, you can get a reasonable number of search results focused around your topic.

Seek Out Weblog Commentary

Build queries to search only recent commentary appearing in weblogs.

There was a time when you needed to find current commentary, you didn't turn to a full-text search engine like Google. You searched Usenet, combed mailing lists, or searched through current news sites like CNN.com and hoped for the best.

But as search engines have evolved, they've been able to index pages more quickly than once every few weeks. In fact, Google tunes its engine to more readily index sites with a high information churn rate. At the same time, a phenomenon called the *weblog* (*http://www.oreilly.com/catalog/essblogging/*) has arisen: an online site keeps a running commentary and associated links, updated daily—and indeed, even more often in many cases. Google indexes many of these sites on an accelerated schedule. If you know how to find them, you can build a query that searches just these sites for recent commentary.

Finding Weblogs

When weblogs first appeared on the Internet, they were generally updated manually or by using homemade programs. Thus, there were no standard words you could add to a search engine to find them. Now, however, many weblogs are created using either specialized software packages (lsuch as Movable Type, *http://www.movabletype.org*, or Radio Userland, *http://radio.userland.com*) or as web services (such as Blogger, *http://www.blogger.com/*). These programs and services are more easily found online with some clever use of special syntaxes or magic words.

For hosted weblogs, the site: syntax makes things easy. Blogger weblogs hosted at blog*spot (*http://www.blogspot.com*) can be found using site:blogspot.com. Even though Radio Userland is a software program able to post its weblogs to any web server, you can find the majority of Radio Userland weblogs at the Radio Userland community server (*http://radio.weblogs.com*) using site:radio.weblogs.com.

Finding weblogs powered by weblog software and hosted elsewhere is more problematic; Movable Type weblogs, for example, can be found all over the Internet. However, most of them sport a "powered by movable type" link of some sort; searching for the phrase "powered by movable type" will, therefore, find many of them.

It comes down to magic words typically found on weblog pages, shout-outs, if you will, to the software or hosting sites. The following is a list of some of these packages and services and the magic words used to find them in Google:

Blogger
"powered by blogger" or site:blogspot.com

Blosxom
"powered by blosxom"

Greymatter
"powered by greymatter"

Geeklog
"powered by geeklog"

Manila
"a manila site" or site:editthispage.com

Pitas (a service)
site:pitas.com

pMachine
"powered by pmachine"

uJournal (a service)
site:ujournal.org

LiveJournal (a service)
site:livejournal.com

Radio Userland
intitle:"radio weblog" or site:radio.weblogs.com

WordPress
"powered by wordpress"

Using These "Magic Words"

Because you can't have more than 10 words in a Google query, there's no way to build a query that includes every conceivable weblog's magic words. It's best to experiment with the various words, and see which weblogs have the materials you're interested in.

First of all, realize that weblogs are usually informal commentary and you'll have to keep an eye out for misspelled words, names, etc. Generally, it's better to search by event than by name, if possible. For example, if you were looking for commentary on a potential strike, the phrase "baseball strike" would be a better search, initially, than a search for the name of the Commissioner of Major League Baseball, Bud Selig.

You can also try to search for a word or phrase relevant to the event. For example, for a baseball strike you could try searching for "baseball strike" "red sox" (or "baseball strike" bosox). If you're searching for information on a wildfire and wondering if anyone had been arrested for arson, try wildfire arrested and, if that doesn't work, wildfire arrested arson.

 Why not search for arson to begin with? Because it's not certain that a weblog commentator would use the word "arson." Instead, he might just refer to someone being arrested for setting the fire. "Arrested" in this case is a more certain word than "arson."

HACK #14   Cover Your Bases

Try all possible combinations of your search keywords at once.

You've got a set of query words but are not sure that they're the right set; you certainly don't want to miss any results by picking the wrong combination of keywords, including or excluding the wrong word. But the thought of typing in a dozen-plus permutations of keywords has your carpal tunnel flaring up in horror.

Search Grid (*http://blog.outer-court.com/search-grid*) lets you explore a wide range of Google search results by automatically searching for the various possible combinations of your keywords.

There are two versions of Search Grid. The older version features a grid that you fill with search words that you want to combine. You might, for example, put catsup, mustard, and pickles on the x-axis and relish, onions, and tomatoes on the y-axis, as shown in Figure 1-25.

Search Grid combines the results—relish catsup, relish mustard, relish pickles, onions catsup, onions mustard, onions pickles, etc.—and provides you with the first result of each possible combination, shown in Figure 1-26.

Note that you're not getting anything but the first result; this is not the tool to use if you want a very in-depth search of each query. Instead, it's meant to give you a *bird's-eye* view of the how the different combinations of search words impact the query.

There's a new version of Search Grid that's been integrated into a web tool called FindForward (*http://www.findforward.com/?t=grid*), which gives you screenshots of some Google search results. That one requires less typing. Just enter two to five words for which you want to check possible

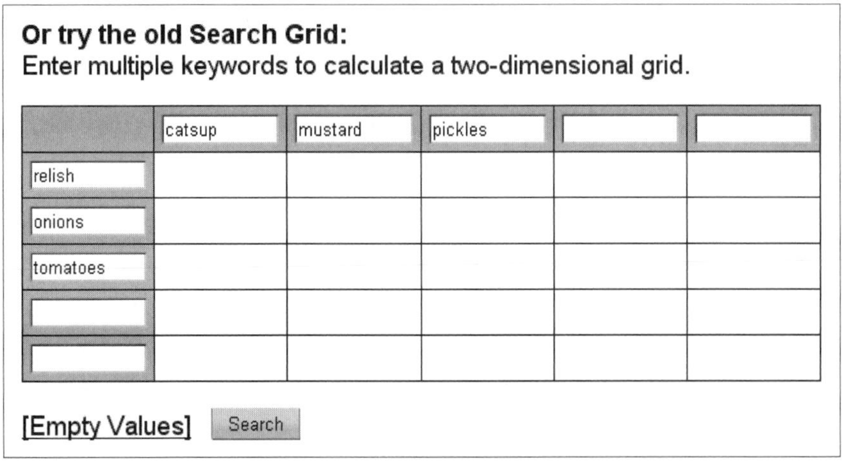

Or try the old Search Grid:
Enter multiple keywords to calculate a two-dimensional grid.

	catsup	mustard	pickles		
relish					
onions					
tomatoes					

[Empty Values]   Search

Figure 1-25. Search Grid populated with keywords to combine

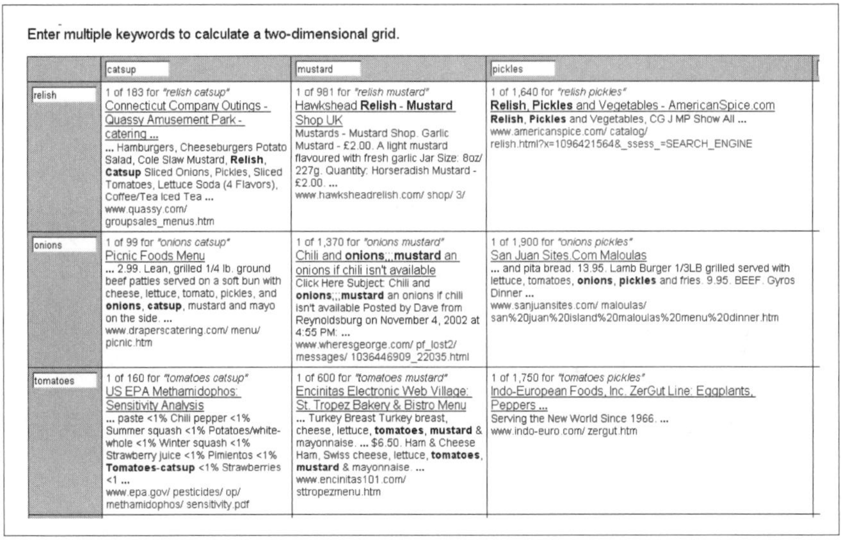

Enter multiple keywords to calculate a two-dimensional grid.

	catsup	mustard	pickles
relish	1 of 183 for *"relish catsup"* Connecticut Company Outings - Quassy Amusement Park - catering ... ... Hamburgers, Cheeseburgers Potato Salad, Cole Slaw Mustard, **Relish**, **Catsup** Sliced Onions, Pickles, Sliced Tomatoes, Lettuce Soda (4 Flavors), Coffee/Tea Iced Tea ... www.quassy.com/ groupsales_menus.htm	1 of 981 for *"relish mustard"* Hawkshead **Relish - Mustard** Shop UK Mustards - Mustard Shop. Garlic Mustard - £2.00. A light mustard flavoured with fresh garlic Jar Size: 8oz/ 227g. Quantity: Horseradish Mustard - £2.00. ... www.hawksheadrelish.com/ shop/ 3/	1 of 1,640 for *"relish pickles"* Relish, Pickles and Vegetables - AmericanSpice.com **Relish, Pickles** and Vegetables, CG J MP Show All ... www.americanspice.com/ catalog/ relish.html?x=10964215648_ssess_=SEARCH_ENGINE
onions	1 of 99 for *"onions catsup"* Picnic Foods Menu ... 2.99. Lean, grilled 1/4 lb. ground beef patties served on a soft bun with cheese, lettuce, tomato, pickles, and **onions, catsup**, mustard and mayo on the side. ... www.draperscatering.com/ menu/ picnic.htm	1 of 1,370 for *"onions mustard"* Chili and **onions,, mustard** an onions if chili isn't available Click Here Subject: Chili and **onions;,,mustard** an onions if chili isn't available Posted by Dave from Reynoldsburg on November 4, 2002 at 4:55 PM. ... www.wheresgeorge.com/ pf_lost2/ messages/ 1036446909_22035.html	1 of 1,900 for *"onions pickles"* San Juan Sites Com Maloulas ... and pita bread. 13.95. Lamb Burger 1/3LB grilled served with lettuce, tomatoes, **onions, pickles** and fries. 9.95. BEEF. Gyros Dinner ... www.sanjuansites.com/ maloulas/ san%20juan%20island%20maloulas%20menu%20dinner.htm
tomatoes	1 of 160 for *"tomatoes catsup"* US EPA Methamidophos: Sensitivity Analysis ... paste <1% Chili pepper <1% Summer squash <1% Potatoes/white-whole <1% Winter squash <1% Strawberry juice <1% Pimientos <1% **Tomatoes-catsup** <1% Strawberries <1 ... www.epa.gov/ pesticides/ op/ methamidophos/ sensitivity.pdf	1 of 600 for *"tomatoes mustard"* Encinitas Electronic Web Village: St. Tropez Bakery & Bistro Menu ... Turkey Breast Turkey breast, cheese, lettuce, **tomatoes, mustard** & mayonnaise. ... $6.50. Ham & Cheese Ham, Swiss cheese, lettuce, **tomatoes**, **mustard** & mayonnaise. ... www.encinitas101.com/ sttropezmenu.htm	1 of 1,750 for *"tomatoes pickles"* Indo-European Foods, Inc. ZerGut Line: Eggplants, Peppers ... Serving the New World Since 1966. ... www.indo-euro.com/ zergut.htm

Figure 1-26. The first result of several different searches, all in one grid

permutations. You'll get a large grid of search results, with screenshots available for some of the pages, as shown in Figure 1-27.

Note that this grid will search each of your keywords individually (one square for mustard, one for pickles, one for relish) and will search every possible combination of two words (pickles relish, pickles mustard, mustard relish, etc.), but it won't search for three- and four-word permutations. In other words, this tool won't find every single last possible permutation of your search. Again, it's an *overview* that gives you an idea of how different

Figure 1-27. Google search results—now with screenshots!

word combinations can affect your search, and it is not meant to be exhaustive.

Use this hack when you want to get a sense of how different queries are going to affect your search, when you're not sure about what set of search words will work best for you, and when you want to experiment with expanding your search without having to type several sets of keywords over and over again.

See Also

- It's hard to believe, but when it comes to building queries, word order matters. If you're interested in permuting just one query at a time, see "Permute a Query" **[Hack #28]**.

HACK Repetition Matters
#15
Repetition matters when it comes to keywords weighting your queries.

Using keywords multiple times can have an impact on the types and number of results you get.

Don't believe me? Try searching for internet. At the time of this writing, the home page for Microsoft's Internet Explorer browser is the first result. Now try searching for internet internet. At the time of this writing, the Internet Society (ISOC) pops to the top. Experiment with this using other words, putting additional query words in if you want to. You'll see that multiple query words can have an impact on how the search results are ordered and in the number of results returned.

How Does This Work?

Google doesn't talk about this on their web site, so this hack is the result of some conjecture and much experimentation.

First, enter a word one time. Let's use clothes as an example, which returns 51,800,000 results, the top being a site called The Emperor's New Clothes. Now, add another clothes to the query (i.e., clothes clothes). The number of results drops dramatically to 14,700,000, and the first result is for Traditional Korean Clothing, The Emperor's New Clothes is no longer in the top 10, and some new finds move their way up into the first few results.

Why stop now? Try clothes clothes clothes. Traditional Korean Clothing stays on top and The Emperor's New Clothes is still not found in the top 10.

A Theory

Here's a theory: Google searches for as many matches for each word or phrase you specify, stopping when it can't find any more. So clothes clothes returns pages with two occurrences of the word "clothes." clothes clothes clothes returns the same results, because Google can't do any better than two occurrences of "clothes" in any one page.

So What?

Because Google discards nonmatching multiple instances of the same query word, you can use this search as a weighting system for your searches. For example, say you were interested in pipe systems for the gas industry, but you're more interested in the impact that the pipe systems were having on the gas industry (and less so in companies that happen to sell piping systems for the gas industry).

Search for "pipe systems" gas. Now query for "pipe systems" gas gas. You'll notice that the focus of your results changes slightly. Now try "pipe systems" pipe pipe gas gas. Note how the focus slants back the other way.

Based on observations, here are a few guidelines for using multiple iterations of the same query term:

- Multiple iterations of product names or nouns seem to favor shopping sites. This is especially true if the name or noun is plural (e.g., scooters).

- Just because you're not getting different results for the second or third iteration doesn't mean you won't get different results for the fourth or fifth iteration (e.g., successive occurrences of baseball).

- Remember that Google has a limit of 10 words per query, so relegate repetition to only those situations where you can spare the query room [Hack #29].

HACK #16   Search a Particular Date Range

An undocumented but powerful feature of Google's search is the ability to search within a particular date range.

Before delving into the actual use of date range searching, there are a few things you should understand. The first is this: a date range search has nothing to do with the creation date of the content and everything to do with the indexing date of the content. If I create a page on March 8, 1999, and Google doesn't get around to indexing it until May 22, 2002, for the purposes of a date range search, the date in question is May 22, 2002.

The second thing is that Google can index pages several times, and each time it does so the date on it changes. So don't count on a date range search staying consistent from day to day. The daterange: timestamp can change when a page is indexed more than once. Whether it does change depends on whether the content of the page has changed.

Third, Google doesn't "stand behind" the results of a search done using the date range syntaxes. So if you get a weird result, you can't complain to them. Google would rather you use the date range options on their Advanced Search page, but that page allows you to restrict your options only to the last three months, six months, or year.

The daterange: Syntax

Why would you want to search by daterange:? There are several reasons:

- It narrows down your search results to fresher content. Google might find some obscure, out-of-the-way page and index it only once. Two years later, this obscure, never-updated page is still turning up in your search results. Limiting your search to a more recent date range will result in only the most current of matches.

- It helps you dodge current events. Say John Doe sets a world record for eating hot dogs and immediately afterward rescues a baby from a burning building. Less than a week after that happens, Google's search results are going to be filled with John Doe. If you're searching for information on (another) John Doe, babies, or burning buildings, you'll scarcely be able to get rid of him.

However, you can avoid Mr. Doe's exploits by setting the date range syntax to before the hot dog contest. This also works well for avoiding recent, heavily covered news events, such as a crime spree or a forest fire, and annual events of at least national importance such as national elections or the Olympics.

- It allows you to compare results over a period of time; for example, if you want to search for occurrences of "Mac OS X" and "Windows XP" over a period of time. Of course, a count like this isn't foolproof; indexing dates change over time. But generally it works well enough that you can spot trends.

Using the daterange: syntax is as simple as:

```
daterange:startdate-enddate
```

The catch is that the date must be expressed as a Julian date (read the sidebar, "Understanding Julian Dates") So, for example, July 8, 2002, is Julian date 2452463.5 and May 22, 1968, is 2439998.5. Furthermore, Google isn't fond of decimals in its daterange: queries; use only integers: 2452463 or 2452464 (depending on whether you prefer to round up or down) in the previous example.

You can use the daterange: syntax with most other Google special syntaxes, with the exception of the link: syntax, which doesn't mix well ["Mixing Syntaxes" earlier in this chapter] with other special syntax and other magic words (e.g., stocks: and phonebook:).

daterange: does wonders for narrowing your search results. Let's look at a couple of examples. Geri Halliwell left the Spice Girls around May 27, 1998. If you wanted to get a lot of information about the breakup, you could try doing a date search in a 10-day window—say, May 25 to June 4. That query would look like this:

```
"Geri Halliwell" "Spice Girls" daterange:2450958-2450968
```

At the time of this writing, you'll get about 16 results, including several news stories about the breakup. If you wanted to find less formal sources, search for Geri or Ginger Spice instead of Geri Halliwell.

That example's a bit on the silly side, but you get the idea. Any event that you can clearly divide into before and after dates—an event, a death, an overwhelming change in circumstances—can be reflected in a date range search.

Understanding Julian Dates

While date-based searching is fantastically useful, date-based searching with Julian dates is annoying at best—for a human, anyway.

A Julian date is just one number. It's not broken up into month, day, and year. It's the number of days that have passed since January 1, 4713 B.C. Unlike Gregorian days (those on the calendar you and I use every day), which begin at midnight, Julian days begin at noon, making them useful for astronomers.

While problematic for humans, they're rather handy for computer programming, because to change dates you simply have to add and subtract from one number and not worry about month and year changes, not to mention leap years and the differing number of days in each month. Google's daterange: special syntax element employs Julian dates.

If things weren't confusing enough, there is actually another date format that is *also* known as a Julian date format, a five-digit number, *yyddd*, where the first two digits represent the most significant digits of the year and the last three represent the day of the year, where the value is between 1 and 365 (or 366 in a leap year). Google's daterange: syntax doesn't support the *yyddd* format.

There are plenty of places you can convert Julian dates online. There are a couple of nice converters at the U.S. Naval Observatory Astronomical Applications Department (*http://aa.usno.navy.mil/data/docs/JulianDate.html*) and Mauro Orlandini's home page (*http://www.tesre.bo.cnr.it/~mauro/JD/*), the latter converting either Julian to Gregorian or vice versa.

More Julian dates and online computers can be found via a Google search for julian date (*http://www.google.com/search?q=julian+date*).

You can also use an individual event's date to change the results of a larger search. For example, former ImClone CEO Sam Waksal was arrested on June 12, 2002. You don't have to search for the name Sam Waksal to get a very narrow set of results for June 13, 2002:

```
imclone daterange:2452439-2452439
```

Similarly, if you search for imclone before the date of 2452439, you'll get very different results. As an interesting exercise, try a search that reflects the arrest, but date it a few days before the actual arrest:

```
imclone investigated daterange:2452000-2452435
```

This is a good way to find information or analysis that predates the actual event, but that provides background that might help explain the event itself.

(Unless you use the date range search, usually this kind of information is buried underneath news of the event itself.)

If you'd prefer to perform Google date range searches without all this nonsense about Julian date formats, use the FaganFinder Google interface (*http:// www.faganfinder.com/engines/google.shtml*), an alternative to the Google Advanced Search page, sporting daterange: searching via a Gregorian (read: familiar) date pull-down menu. In Figure 1-28, we're using the FaganFinder on our Spice Girls breakup example.

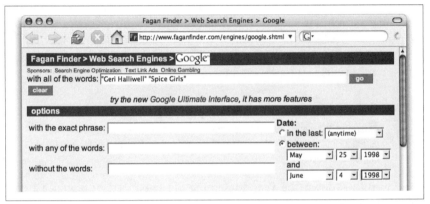

Figure 1-28. The FaganFinder Google interface with Gregorian-based date range searching

So that takes care of date range searching according to when Google ran across the content you're after, but what about narrowing your search results based on content creation date?

Searching by Content Creation Date

Searching for materials based on content creation is difficult. There's no standard date format (score one for Julian dates), many people don't date their pages anyway, some pages don't contain date information in their header, and still other content management systems routinely stamp pages with today's date, confusing things still further.

I can offer few suggestions for searching by content creation date. Try adding a string of common date formats to your query. If you wanted something from May 2003, for example, you could try appending:

("May * 2003" | "May 2003" | 05/03 | 05/*/03)

A query like that uses up most of your 10-word limit, however, so it's best to be judicious, perhaps by cycling through these formats one a time. If any one of these is giving you too many results, try restricting your search to the title tag of the page.

If you're feeling really lucky, you can search for a full date, such as May 9, 2003. Your decision then is whether you want to search for the date in the format above or as one of many variations: 9 May 2003, 9/5/2003, 9 May 03, and so forth. Exact-date searching will severely limit your results and should be used only as a last-ditch option.

When using date range searching, you'll have to be flexible in your thinking, more general in your search than you otherwise would be (because the date range search will narrow your results substantially), and persistent in your queries, because different dates and date ranges will yield very different results. That said, you'll be rewarded with smaller result sets focused on very specific events and topics in time.

HACK #17 Calculate Google Centuryshare

Determine the year in which Elvis achieved the height of his fame, over what period disco took hold of your nightlife, and when fuel economy actually mattered to anyone.

Looking to pin down the year something big happened or watch a trend unfold gradually over time? FindForward (*http://www.findforward.com*)—nee the Google Centuryshare Calculator (*http://blog.outer-court.com/centuryshare*)—employs some of the same logic as the Google Mindshare Calculator **[Hack #34]** to determine the weight of a search query across a 50-year period.

Let's say, for example, we search for Chernobyl, site of a terrible nuclear power plant accident in April 1986. Enter the search term—in this case, chernobyl—in FindForward's search box and choose a range of years from the pull-down menu to the right. Given that my choices were 1900–1950 or 1950–2000 and the fact that I know I was alive when it happened, I chose 1950–2000. Click Find and the engine will chew on your query for a bit, it's backend feeding a steady stream of queries to Google via the Google API **[Chapter 9]**. Figure 1-29 clearly shows that the Web knows a little something about Chernobyl and the year 1986.

So, how does the Centuryshare algorithm work?

Centuryshare tries to find natural peaks for ideas in particular years by searching the Web via Google. For every year, the number of the year is combined with the search query: to find out when Elvis Presley was at the height of his fame, the engine searches for Elvis Presley 1950, Elvis

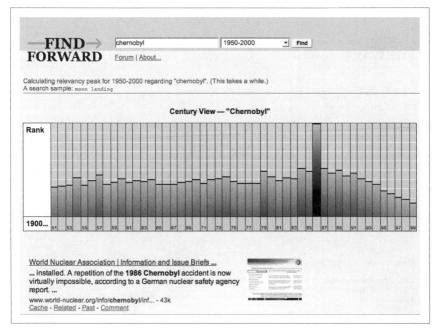

Figure 1-29. The Centuryshare Calculator clearly shows something important happened at Chernobyl in 1986

Presley 1951, Elvis Presley 1952, and so on, keeping track of the returned result count along the way.

But a simple count of results isn't quite enough. There is an additional transformation of these numbers that needs to be done in order for the result to be meaningful. Mention of various years occur in much larger quantity online: 1900, 1910, and 1920 occur more frequently, as do the years in the late part of the twentieth century—the boom of the Web.

So the Centuryshare calculator also gleans result count for each year by itself, without any additional search query (i.e., Google for 1950, 1951, 1952, etc.)

Those base numbers in hand, the engine then calculates a percentage based on the *result count of year and search query* relative to *year by itself, without search query*.

These result count percentages are normalized for display purposes and returned to you as a nice bar graph of results by year.

Compare the Chernobyl results in Figure 1-29 with those for the gentle rise and fall of disco in Figure 1-30.

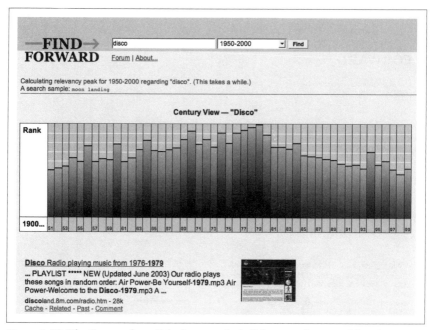

Figure 1-30. The Centuryshare Calculator on the bell (bottomed) curve of disco's reign

FindForward sports a host of other search features (*http://findforward.com/about/*), including Amazon.com, IRC logs, weblogs, assorted files people leave lying about on the Web, people (famous and not), and things. For instance, you can ask a question such as "When was Albert Einstein born?" and FindForward will trawl the Web, figure it out (or something close enough for horseshoes), and provide a link to the source, as shown in Figure 1-31).

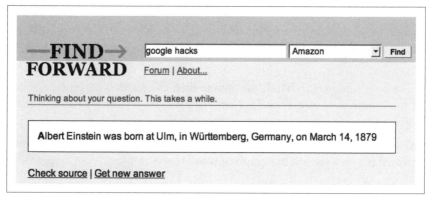

Figure 1-31. Ask a decent question…

Check the source out for yourself by clicking the "Check source" link or find another by clicking "Find new answer."

—Philipp Lenssen

 H A C K
#18
Hack Your Own Google Search Form
Build your own personal, task-specific Google search form.

If you want to do a simple search with Google, you don't need anything but the standard Simple Search form (the Google home page). But if you want to craft specific Google searches that you'll be using on a regular basis or providing for others, you can simply put together your own personalized search form.

Start with your garden-variety Google search form; something like this will do nicely:

```
<!-- Search Google -->
<form method="get" action="http://www.google.com/search">
<input type="text" name="q" size=31 maxlength=255 value="">
<input type="submit" name="sa" value="Search Google">
</form>
<!-- Search Google -->
```

This is a very simple search form. It takes your query and sends it directly to Google, adding nothing to it. But you can embed some variables to alter your search as needed. You can do this in two ways: via hidden variables or by adding more input to your form.

Hidden Variables

As long as you know how to identify a search option in Google, you can add it to your search form via a hidden variable. The fact that it's hidden just means that form users will not be able to alter it. They won't even be able to see it unless they take a look at the source code. Let's take a look at a few examples.

 While it's perfectly legal HTML to put your hidden variables anywhere between the opening and closing <form> tags, it's rather tidy and useful to keep them all together after all the visible form fields.

File Type
As the name suggests, file type specifies filtering your results by a particular file type (e.g., Word *.doc*, Adobe *.pdf*, PowerPoint *.ppt*, plain text *.txt*).

Add a PowerPoint file type filter, for example, to your search form, like so:

```
<input type="hidden" name="as_filetype" value="PPT">
```

Site Search

Narrows your search to specific sites. While a suffix like *.com* will work just fine, something more fine-grained like the *example.com* domain is probably better suited:

```
<input type="hidden" name="as_sitesearch" value="example.com">
```

URL Component

Specifies a particular path component to look for in URLs. This can include a domain name but doesn't have to. The following tries to tease out documentation in your result set:

```
<input type="hidden" name="hq" value="inurl:docs">
```

Date Range

Narrows your search to pages indexed within the stated number of months. Acceptable values are between 1 and 12. Restricting our results to items indexed only within the last seven months is just a matter of adding:

```
<input type="hidden" name="as_qdr" value="m7">
```

Number of Results

Indicates the number of results that you'd like appearing on each page, specified as a value of num between 1 and 100; the following asks for 50 per page:

```
<input type="hidden" name="num" value="50">
```

What would you use this for? If you're regularly looking for an easy way to create a search engine that finds certain file types in a certain place, this works really well. If this is a one-time search, you can always just hack the results URL **["Understanding Google URLs" earlier in this chapter]**, tacking the variables and their associated values on to the URL of the results page.

Mixing Hidden File Types: An Example

The site tompeters.com (*http://www.tompeters.com*) contains several Power-Point (*.ppt*) files. If you want to find just the PowerPoint files on their site, you'd have to figure out how their site search engine works or pester them into adding a file type search option. But you can put together your own search form that finds PowerPoint presentations on the tompeters.com site.

Even though you're creating a handy search form this way, you're still resting on the assumption that Google's indexed most or all of the site that you're searching. Until you know otherwise, assume that any search results Google gives you are incomplete.

Your form looks something like:

```
<!-- Search Google for tompeters.com PowerPoints -->
<form method="get" action="http://www.google.com/search">
<input type="text" name="q" size=31 maxlength=255 value="">
<input type="submit" name="sa" value="Search Google">
<input type="hidden" name="as_filetype" value="ppt">
<input type="hidden" name="as_sitesearch" value="tompeters.com">
<input type="hidden" name="num" value="100">
</form>
<!-- Search Google for tompeters.com PowerPoints -->
```

Using hidden variables is handy when you want to search for one particular thing all the time. But if you want to be flexible in what you're searching for, creating an alternate form is the way to go.

Creating Your Own Google Form

Some variables best stay hidden; however, for other options, you can let your form users be much more flexible.

Let's go back to the previous example. You want to let your users search for PowerPoint files, but you also want them to be able to search for Excel files and Microsoft Word files. In addition, you want them to be able to search tompeters.com, the State of California, or the Library of Congress. There are obviously various ways to do this user-interface–wise; this example uses a couple of simple pull-down menus:

```
<!-- Custom Google Search Form-->
<form method="get" action="http://www.google.com/search">
<input type="text" name="q" size=31 maxlength=255 value="">
<br />
Search for file type:
<select name="as_filetype">
<option value="ppt">PowerPoint</option>
<option value="xls">Excel</option>
<option value="doc">Word</option>
</select>
<br />
Search site:
<select name="as_sitesearch">
```

```
<option value="tompeters.com">TomPeters.com</option>
<option value="state.ca.us">State of California</option>
<option value="loc.gov">The Library of Congress</option>
</select>
<input type="hidden" name="num" value="100">
<input type="submit" value="Search Google">
</form>
<!-- Custom Google Search Form-->
```

FaganFinder (*http://www.faganfinder.com/engines/google.shtml*) is a wonderful example of a thoroughly customized form.

HACK #19   Go Beyond Google's Advanced Search

Soople augments the functionality of Google Advanced Search with comprehensive yet easy-to-use forms for every Google occasion.

Google may have started as a simple search engine, but it got past that a long time ago. Now it offers calculators, converters, number ranges, dictionaries, stock symbol search, and UPS package tracking. That wealth of offerings makes it a great handy reference tool, but who can remember all those search syntaxes?

Well, pour yourself a nice hot bowl of Soople (*http://www.soople.com*) and perform advanced searches with ease. Soople provides several dozen search interfaces, each geared toward a particular Google search feature or property (see Figure 1-32). By providing you with prefabricated yet flexible specialized search forms, Soople helps you concentrate on your reference task and not on building syntax.

The Soople main page opens with 13 different specialty interfaces, allowing you to filter for particular file types, break out searches by language, hunt down images, news, and definitions, and more. And it doesn't stop there. At the top of the page are five tabs: calculators, translation tools, phone and location lookups, and a Superfilter. All of Soople's results appear in regular Google results pages; there's no use of the Web API here, just custom search forms pointing at Google proper.

As an example of just how detailed Soople gets, the calculator page is actually 10 different forms covering different mathematical functions—from trigonometric functions to conversion to finding percentages and roots.

See Also

- Soople takes building custom search forms to an extreme (and very useful) conclusion; see "Hack Your Own Google Search Form" [Hack #18] for more inspiration.

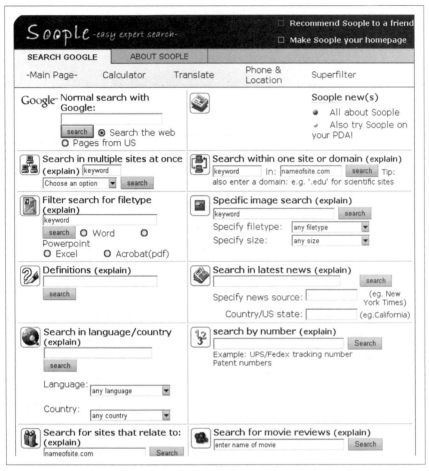

Figure 1-32. Soople's dozens of interfaces, aimed at just the Google search you're after

- Check out "Build a Custom Date Range Search Form" **[Hack #48]** for specialty forms with a narrow focus.

HACK #20 Use Google Tools for Translators

Create a customized search form for language translation.

If you do a lot of the same kind of research every day, you might find that a customized search form makes your job easier. If you spend enough time on it, you may find that it's elaborate enough that other people may find it useful as well.

WWW Search Interfaces for Translators (*http://www.multilingual.ch/search_interfaces.htm*) offers four amazing tools for finding material of use to translators. Created by Tanya Harvey Ciampi from Switzerland, the tools are available in AltaVista and Google flavors. A user-defined query term is combined with a set of specific search criteria to narrow down the search to yield highly relevant results.

The first tool, shown in Figure 1-33, finds glossaries. The pull-down menu finds synonyms of the word "glossary" in various parts of a search result (title, URL, or anywhere). For example, imagine having to seek out numerous specialized computer dictionaries before finding one containing a definition of the term "firewall." This glossary search tool spares you the work by setting a clear condition: "Find a glossary that contains my term!"

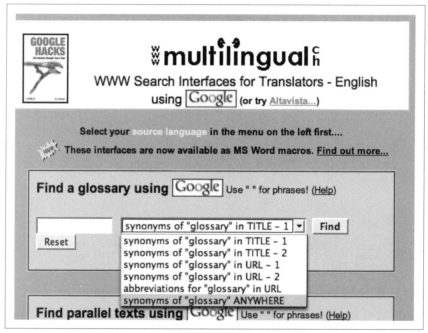

Figure 1-33. Digging into Google's trove of glossaries

If you're getting too many results for the glossary word you searched for, try searching for it in the title of the results instead, for example, intitle: firewall rather than firewall.

The second tool, shown in Figure 1-34, finds "parallel texts," identical pages in two or more languages, useful for multilingual terminology research.

Finding pages in two or more languages is not easy; one of the few places to do it easily is with Canadian government pages, which are available in

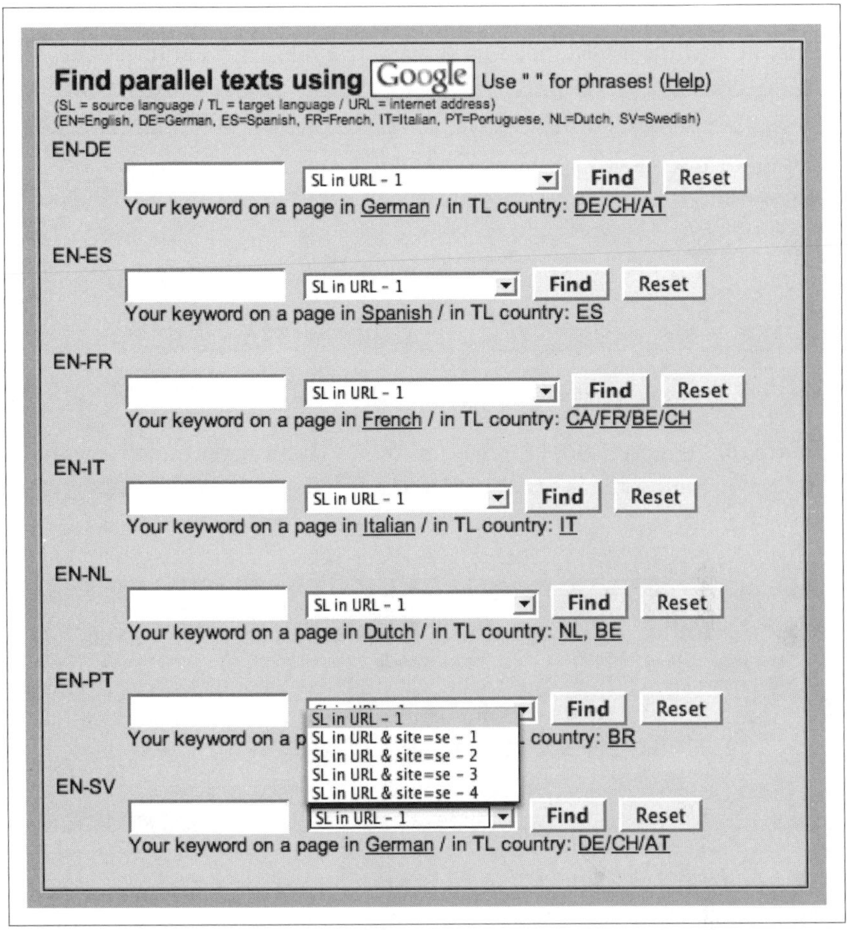

Find parallel texts using Google **Use " " for phrases! (Help)**

(SL = source language / TL = target language / URL = internet address)
(EN=English, DE=German, ES=Spanish, FR=French, IT=Italian, PT=Portuguese, NL=Dutch, SV=Swedish)

EN-DE

| | SL in URL – 1 ▼ | **Find** | Reset |

Your keyword on a page in <u>German</u> / in TL country: <u>DE/CH/AT</u>

EN-ES

| | SL in URL – 1 ▼ | **Find** | Reset |

Your keyword on a page in <u>Spanish</u> / in TL country: <u>ES</u>

EN-FR

| | SL in URL – 1 ▼ | **Find** | Reset |

Your keyword on a page in <u>French</u> / in TL country: <u>CA/FR/BE/CH</u>

EN-IT

| | SL in URL – 1 ▼ | **Find** | Reset |

Your keyword on a page in <u>Italian</u> / in TL country: <u>IT</u>

EN-NL

| | SL in URL – 1 ▼ | **Find** | Reset |

Your keyword on a page in <u>Dutch</u> / in TL country: <u>NL, BE</u>

EN-PT

| | SL in URL – 1 ▼ | **Find** | Reset |

Your keyword on a p | SL in URL – 1 | country: <u>BR</u>
SL in URL & site=se – 1
SL in URL & site=se – 2
SL in URL & site=se – 3
EN-SV | SL in URL & site=se – 4

| | SL in URL – 1 ▼ | **Find** | Reset |

Your keyword on a page in <u>German</u> / in TL country: <u>DE/CH/AT</u>

Figure 1-34. Matching parallel texts

French and English. This tool provides several different search combinations between SL (source language) and TL (target language).

The first set of searches defaults to Google, though you can search AltaVista instead, if you prefer. It provides several language sets (English-German, English-Spanish, English-French, etc.) and gives you options for searching in each one (SL in URL, link to TL, page in TL country, etc.).

The second set of searches also offers several language sets and several ways to search them (three different ways to search for the source language in the URL, keyword on the page in the target language, etc.). In some cases, this tool also lets you specify the country for the target language (for example, French could be a target language in Canada, France, or Switzerland).

The third tool, shown in Figure 1-35, finds variations on the word "abbreviations" in the title or URL of a search result to find lists of abbreviations.

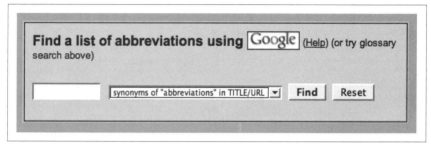

Figure 1-35. Finding abbreviations—make that abbv., or is it abbrev.?

A fourth tool (Figure 1-36) searches for idioms (I can never quite remember: is it "feed a cold, starve a fever" or "feed a fever, starve a cold"?), proverbs, and slang.

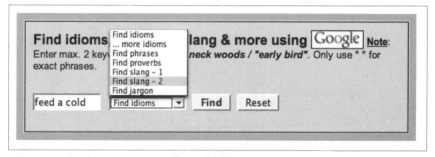

Figure 1-36. Finding idioms, proverbs, and slang

These search tools are available in several languages and do a lot of work for translators; in fact, they pull out so much information that you might think they'd require the Google API. But they don't; the query is generated on the client side and then passed to Google.

It's accomplished quite elegantly. First, take a look at the source code for the form and see if you notice anything. Here's a hint: pay attention to the form element names. Notice that this hack integrates search synonyms without having to use the Google API or any kind of CGI. Everything's done via the form.

```
<!-- Initializing the form and opening a Google search
in a new window -->
<form method="GET" target="_blank"
action="http://www.google.com/search">

<!-- Taking the keyword search specified by the user -->
```

```
<input type="text" name="q" size="12">
<select name="q" size="1">

<!-- This is the cool stuff. These options provide several
different modifiers designed to catch glossaries
in Google. -->
<option selected value="intitle:dictionary OR intitle:glossary
OR intitle:lexicon OR intitle:definitions">
synonyms of "glossary" in TITLE - 1</option>
<option value="intitle:terminology OR intitle:vocabulary
OR intitle:definition OR intitle:jargon">
synonyms of "glossary" in TITLE - 2</option>
<option value="inurl:dictionary OR inurl:glossary OR inurl:lexicon
OR inurl:definitions">
synonyms of "glossary" in URL - 1</option>
<option value="inurl:terminology OR inurl:vocabulary
OR inurl:definition
OR inurl:jargon">synonyms of "glossary" in URL - 2</option>
<option value="inurl:dict OR inurl:gloss OR inurl:glos
OR inurl:dic">
abbreviations for "glossary" in URL</option>
<option value="dictionary OR glossary OR lexicon
OR definitions">synonyms of "glossary" ANYWHERE</option>
</select>

<!-- Ending the submission form. -->
<input type="submit" value="Find">
<input type="reset" value="Reset" name="B2">
</form>
```

The magic at work here is to be found in the following two lines:

```
<input type="text" name="q" size="12">
<select name="q" size="1">
```

Notice that both the query text field and glossary pop-up menu are named the same thing: name="q". When the form is submitted to Google, the values of both fields are effectively combined and treated as one query. So entering a query of dentistry and selecting synonyms of "glossary" in TITLE - 1 from the pop-up menu result in a combined Google query of:

```
dentistry intitle:dictionary OR intitle:glossary OR intitle:lexicon OR
intitle:definitions
```

Hacking the Hack

This hack uses customized Google forms as an interface for translators, but you could use this idea for just about anything. Do you need to find legal statutes? Financial materials? Information from a particular vertical market? Anything that has its own specialized vocabulary that you can add to a form can be channeled into a hack like this. What kind of interface would you design?

## CHAPTER TWO

Advanced Web
Hacks 21–49

If you've just arrived from Chapter 1 and think that you have more than enough information to Google yourself silly, hold on to your hat. Now you'll put into high gear all that you've learned about the ins and outs of Googling.

In this chapter you'll meander your Google neighborhood, range farther across the Web, dig deeper into individual sites, twist and recombine your queries, squeeze the last drop of results out of every search, and even go beyond the bounds of Google's index—all without wearing out your fingers.

Because you'll get your computer to do the lion's share of the work for you.

This chapter hacks Google programmatically. Through bite-sized programs, we'll introduce you to the kind of trawling, crawling, and recombination that's possible with just a few lines of code. And it's all possible thanks to something called the Google API—that's Application Programming Interface, or Google for computers.

In April 2002, Google announced an alternate interface to the friendly search box you see on Google.com. They opened up their index to anyone with a little programming know-how and a reasonable amount of patience. Initially, this wasn't much to write home about. Some of the earliest applications simply Googled and incorporated the results into a web page—so-called Google boxes [Hack #22]. But as more people experimented with the API, the variety of applications grew from the marginally interesting to the seriously useful. And so was born the book that you're holding in your hands.

This chapter and the rest of this book contain hacks that take advantage of this alternate interface. Some simply automate the sorts of tasks that might take you forever and a day to do by hand. Others run automatically to keep tabs on searches—and results—of interest to you. And still others provide a bird's-eye view of your results in context, which is just not possible by eyeballing any number of results pages.

Assumptions

These hacks do assume a little more than an adventurous spirit and a researcher's tenacity. We assume that you already have some programming background or are willing to learn the basics as you go along. In fact, we've been happy to hear about so many readers picking up and learning a little programming through the hacks in the previous edition of this book; learning to program is so much easier if you have a particular task in mind.

You'll need to type in (or download) programs or scripts and run them from the command line (that's Terminal in Mac OS X or the DOS command window in Windows). Some are run as CGI scripts, bits of dynamic content running on your web site and talked to through your web browser. For more information on running hacks on the command line and as CGI scripts in your browser, see "How to Run the Hacks" in the Preface.

Almost all of the hacks are written in Perl (*http://www.perl.com*), with a few Python (*http://www.python.org*), PHP (*http://www.php.net*), Java (*http://java.sun.com*), and .NET (*http://www.microsoft.com/net*) programs sprinkled throughout. To run a particular hack, you'll need the appropriate language to be available on your computer. Since instruction on installing and using these languages is beyond the scope of this book, you should start with a visit to the language's home page and might consider picking up a copy of one of O'Reilly's fine selection of books (*http://www.oreilly.com*). *Learning Perl* by Randal L. Schwartz and Tom Phoenix (O'Reilly) will be particularly useful.

Most of the hacks use the Google API. For an introduction to the programmatic side of Google, a detailed walkthrough of the Google API, and examples of programming Google using Perl, Python, PHP, Java, and .NET, turn to Chapter 9.

There are also a few hacks that involve *spidering* or *screen scraping*—which is essentially using your program to read a site's web pages and extract salient information—to get to data that are either not available through the Google API or on another site entirely. If spidering appeals to you, you might also check out *Spidering Hacks* by Kevin Hemenway and Tara Calishain (O'Reilly).

Like a Version

HACK
#21

Gather a list of what Google thinks are synonyms for a keyword you provide.

The Google ~ synonym operator ["Special Syntax" in Chapter 1] widens your search criteria to include not only the specific keywords in your search, but also words Google has found to be synonyms of, or at least in some way related to, your query words. So while, for example, food facts may only match a handful of pages of interest to you, ~food ~facts seeks out nutrition information, cooking trivia, and more. And finding these synonyms is an entertaining and potentially useful exercise in and of itself. Here's one way...

Let's say we're looking for all the synonyms for the word "car." First, we search Google for ~car to find all the pages that contain a synonym for "car" In its search results, Google highlights synonyms in **bold**, just as it highlights regular keyword matches. Scanning the results (the second page is shown in Figure 2-1) for ~car finds car, cars, motor, auto, BMW, and other synonyms in boldface.

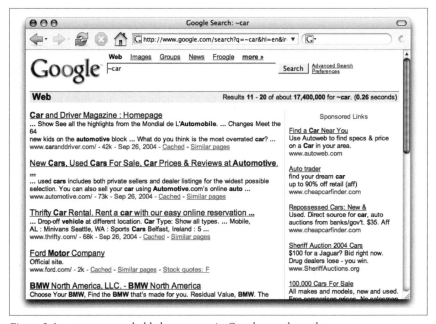

Figure 2-1. ~car turns up bolded synonyms in Google search results

Now let's focus on the synonyms rather than our original keyword, "car." We'll do so by excluding the word "car" from our query, like so: ~car -car. This saves us from having to wade through page after page of matches for the word "car."

Once again, we scan the search results for new synonyms. (I ran across automotive, racing, vehicle, and motor.)

Make a note of any new bolded synonyms and subtract them from the query (e.g., ~car –car –automotive –racing –vehicle –motor) until you hit Google's 10-word limit ["The 10-Word Limit" in Chapter 1], after which Google starts ignoring any additional words that you tack on.

In the end, you'll have compiled a goodly list of synonyms, some of which you'd not have found in your typical thesaurus thanks to Google's algorithmic approach to synonyms.

The Code

If you think this all sounds a little tedious and more in the job description of a computer program, you'd be right. Here's a short Python script to do all the iteration for you. It takes in a starting word and spits out a list of synonyms that it accrues along the way.

> You'll need the PyGoogle [Hack #98] library to provide an interface to the Google API.

```python
#!/usr/bin/python
# Available at http://www.aaronsw.com/2002/synonyms.py
import re
import google # get at http://pygoogle.sourceforge.net/
sb = re.compile('<b>(.*?)</b>', re.DOTALL)
def stripBolds(text, syns):
  for t in sb.findall(text):
    t = t.lower().encode('utf-8')
    if t != '...' and t not in syns: syns.append(t)
  return syns
def findSynonyms(q):
  if ' ' in q: raise ValueError, "query must be one word"
  query = "~" + q
  syns = []

  while (len(query.split(' ')) <= 10):
    for result in google.doGoogleSearch(query).results:
      syns = stripBolds(result.snippet, syns)

    added = False
    for syn in syns:
      if syn in query: continue
      query += " -" + syn
      added = True
      break
```

```
            if not added: break # nothing left

    return syns
if __name__ == "__main__":
  import sys
  if len(sys.argv) != 2:
    print "Usage: python " + sys.argv[0] + " query"
  else:
    print findSynonyms(sys.argv[1])
```

Save the code as *synonyms.py*.

Running the Hack

Call the script on the command line **["How to Run the Hacks" in the Preface]**, passing it a starting word to get it going, like so:

```
% python synonyms.py car
```

The Results

You'll get back a list of synonyms like these:

```
['auto', 'cars', 'car', 'vehicle', 'automotive', 'bmw', 'motor', 'racing',
'van', 'toyota']
```

—Aaron Swartz

Capture Google Results in a Google Box
Add a little box of Google results to any page in your web site.

A *Google box* is a small HTML snippet that shows Google search results for whatever you're searching for. You might wish to display on your web page a box of pages similar to yours, pages that link to yours, or the top hits for a search that might be of interest to your readers.

Google boxes as a concept—the idea of taking a shortened version of Google results and integrating them into a web page or some other place—are not new. In fact, they're on their way to becoming ubiquitous when it comes to weblog and content management software. The Google box is easy to implement and was one of the first examples of Google API usage. As such, it enjoys the position of *proto-application*: a lot of developers whip up a Google box just to see if they can. Do a Google search for `Google Box` to see some other examples of Google boxes for different languages and applications.

What goes in a Google box, anyway? Why would anybody want to integrate them into a web page?

It depends on the page. Putting a Google box that searches for your name onto a weblog provides a bit of an ego boost and can give a little more information about you without seeming like bragging (yeah, right). If you have a topic-specific page, set up a Google box that searches for the topic (the more specific, the better the results). And if you've got a general news-type page, consider adding a Google box for the news topic. Google boxes can go pretty much anywhere, with Google updating its index often enough that the content of a Google box stays fresh.

The Code

Here's a classic piece of Perl code to produce a Google box as a regular text file filled with garden-variety HTML code, suitable for incorporating into any web page.

```perl
#!/usr/local/bin/perl
# google_box.pl
# A classic Google box implementation.
# Usage: perl google_box.pl <query> <# results>

# Your Google API developer's key.
my $google_key='insert key here';

# Location of the GoogleSearch WSDL file.
my $google_wdsl = "./GoogleSearch.wsdl";

use strict;

use SOAP::Lite;

# Bring in those command-line arguments.
@ARGV == 2
  or die "Usage: perl googlebox.pl <query> <# results>\n";
my($query, $maxResults) = @ARGV;
$maxResults = 10 if ($maxResults < 1 or $maxResults > 10);

# Create a new SOAP::Lite instance, feeding it GoogleSearch.wsdl.
my $google_search = SOAP::Lite->service("file:$google_wdsl");

# Query Google.
my $results = $google_search ->
  doGoogleSearch(
    $google_key, $query, 0, $maxResults, "false", "",
    "false", "", "latin1", "latin1"
  );

# No results?
@{$results->{resultElements}} or die "no results";

print join "\n",
```

```
map( {
  qq{<a href="$_->{URL}">} .
  ($_->{title} || $_->{URL}) .
  qq{</a> <br />}
} @{$results->{resultElements}} );
```

Save the code to a file called *google_box.pl*. Be sure to replace *insert key here* in the seventh line with your personal Google API key.

Running the Hack

This Google box takes two bits of information on the command line ["How to Run the Hacks" in the Preface]: the query you want to run and maximum number of results you'd prefer (up to 10). If you don't provide the number of results, the Google box will default to 10. Run it as follows:

```
% perl google_box.pl "query" # of results
```

where *query* is the search query you'd like to run against Google and *# of results* is the maximum number of results you want it to return.

This will print the results to the screen. To save them to a text file for inclusion in your web pages, specify the name of a file to save the results to, like so:

```
% perl google_box.pl "query" # of results > google_box.html
```

You can leave out specifying *# of results* and the script will default to 10 results in your Google box.

The Results

Here's a sample Google box for "camel book", referring to O'Reilly's popular *Programming Perl* title:

```
<a href="http://www.oreilly.com/catalog/pperl2/">oreilly.com --
Online Catalog:Programming Perl, 2nd Edition</a> <br />
<a href="http://www.oreilly.com/catalog/pperl3/">oreilly.com --
Online Catalog:Programming Perl, 3rd Edition</a> <br />
<a href="http://www.oreilly.com/catalog/pperl2/noframes.html">Programming
Perl, 2nd Edition</a> <br />
<a href="http://www.tuxedo.org/~esr/jargon/html/entry/Camel-Book.html">Camel
Book</a> <br />
<a href="http://www.cise.ufl.edu/perl/camel.html">The Camel Book<a> <br />
```

Integrating a Google Box

When you incorporate a Google box into your web page, you'll have two considerations: refreshing the content of the box regularly and integrating the content into your web page. For refreshing the content of the box, you'll need to run regularly the program using something like cron under Unix or the Windows Scheduler.

To include the content on your web page, Server Side Includes (SSI) is always rather effective. With SSI, including a Google box takes little more than something like this:

```
<!-- #include virtual="./google_box.html" -->
```

For more information on using Server Side Includes, check out the NCSA SSI Tutorial (*http://hoohoo.ncsa.uiuc.edu/docs/ tutorials/includes.html*), or search Google for Server Side Includes Tutorial.

Google boxes are a nice addition to your web pages, whether you run a weblog or a news site. But for many Google box searches, the search results won't change that often, especially for more common search words.

Making the Google Box Timely

As you might remember, Google has a daterange: search syntax available. This version of the Google box takes advantage of the daterange: [Hack #16] syntax, allowing you to specify how many days back you want your query to run. If you don't provide a number, the default is 1, and there's no maximum. I wouldn't go back much further than a month or so. The fewer days back you go, the more often the results in the Google box will change.

You'll need the *Julian::Day* module to get this hack rolling (*http://search.cpan.org/search?query=time%3A%3Ajulianday*).

The code. The code is essentially identical to that of the classic Google box, save the additional bits to accept and deal with a date range on the command line and build a daterange: query, called out in bold:

```
#!/usr/local/bin/perl
# timebox.pl
# A time-specific Google box.
# Usage: perl timebox.pl <query> <# results> <# days back>

# Your Google API developer's key.
my $google_key='insert key here';

# Location of the GoogleSearch WSDL file.
my $google_wdsl = "./GoogleSearch.wsdl";
```

```
use strict;

use SOAP::Lite;
use Time::JulianDay;

# Bring in those command-line arguments.
@ARGV == 2
    or die "Usage: perl timebox.pl <query> <# results> <# days back>\n";
my($query, $maxResults, $daysBack) = @ARGV;
$maxResults = 10 if ($maxResults < 1 or $maxResults > 10);
$daysBack = 1 if $daysBack <= 0;

# Figure out when yesterday was in Julian days
my $yesterday = int local_julian_day(time) - $daysBack;

# Create a new SOAP::Lite instance, feeding it GoogleSearch.wsdl.
my $google_search = SOAP::Lite->service("file:$google_wdsl");

# Query Google.
my $results = $google_search ->
  doGoogleSearch(
    $google_key, "$query daterange:$yesterday-$yesterday", 0,
    $maxResults, "false", "",  "false", "", "latin1", "latin1"
  );

# No results?
@{$results->{resultElements}} or die "no results";

print join "\n",
  map( {
    qq{<a href="$_->{URL}">} .
    ($_->{title} || $_->{URL}) .
    qq{</a> <br />}
  } @{$results->{resultElements}} );
```

Save the code to a text file named *timebox.pl*. And, again, don't forget to replace *insert key here* with your Google API key.

Running the hack. You'll have to provide three bits of information on the command line: the query you want to run, the maximum number of results you'd prefer (up to 10), and the number of days back that Google should consider:

```
% perl timebox.pl "query" # of results # days back
```

Replace *query* with your search query, *# of results* with the number of results you'd like (up to 10), and *# days back* with the number of days back you'd like to search for results.

Again, to send the results to a text file rather than the screen, call the script like this:

```
% perl timebox.pl "query" # of results # days back > google_box.html
```

You can leave out specifying *# of results* and *# days back* and the script will default to 10 results and one day back, respectively.

The results. Here's a sample Google box for the top five "google hacks" results (this book included, hopefully), indexed the day before the time of this writing:

```
% perl timebox.pl "google hacks" 5 1
<a href="http://isbn.nu/0596004478">Google Hacks</a> <br />
<a href="http://isbn.nu/0596004478/shipsort">Google Hacks</a> <br />
<a href="http://isbn.nu/0596004478/amazonca">Amazon.ca: Google Hacks</a>
<br />
<a href="http://www.oreilly.de/catalog/googlehks/">Google Hacks</a> <br />
<a href="http://www.oreilly.de/catalog/googlehks/author.html">Google Hacks
</a> <br />
```

Hacking the hack. Perhaps you'd like your Google box to reflect "this day in 1999." No problem for this slightly tweaked version of the Timely Google box (changes highlighted in bold):

```
#!/usr/local/bin/perl
# timebox_thisday.pl
# A Google box for this day in <year>
# Usage: perl timebox.pl <query> <# results> [year]

# Your Google API developer's key.
my $google_key='insert key here';

# Location of the GoogleSearch WSDL file.
my $google_wdsl = "./GoogleSearch.wsdl";

use strict;

use SOAP::Lite;
use Time::JulianDay;

my @now = localtime(time);

# Bring in those command-line arguments.
@ARGV == 2
or die "Usage: perl timebox.pl <query> <# results> [year]\n";
 my($query, $maxResults, $year) = @ARGV;
$maxResults = 10 if ($maxResults < 1 or $maxResults > 10);
$year =~ /^\d{4}$/ or $year = 1999;

# Figure out when this day in the specified year is.
my $then = int julian_day($year, $now[4], $now[3]);

# Create a new SOAP::Lite instance, feeding it GoogleSearch.wsdl.
```

```
my $google_search = SOAP::Lite->service("file:$google_wdsl");

# Query Google.
my $results = $google_search ->
  doGoogleSearch(
    $google_key, "$query daterange:$then-$then", 0,
    $maxResults, "false", "",  "false", "", "latin1", "latin1"
  );

# No results?
@{$results->{resultElements}} or die "no results";

print join "\n",
  "$query on this day in $year<p />",
  map( {
    qq{<a href="$_->{URL}">} .
    ($_->{title} || $_->{URL}) .
    qq{</a> <br />}
  } @{$results->{resultElements}} );
```

The results. The hacked version of timely Google box runs just like the first version, except that you specify the maximum number of results and a year. Going back further than 1999 doesn't yield particularly useful results given that Google came online in 1998.

Let's take a peek at how Netscape was doing in 1999:

```
% perl timebox_thisday.pl "netscape" 5 1999
netscape on this day in 1999:<p />
<a href="http://www.showgate.com/aol.html">WINSOCK.DLL and NETSCAPE Info for
AOL Members</a> <br />
<a href="http://www.univie.ac.at/comment/99-3/993_23.orig.html">Comment 99/3
- Netscape Communicator</a> <br />
<a href="http://www.ac-nancy-metz.fr/services/docint/netscape.htm">NETSCAPE.
</a> <br />
<a href="http://www.ac-nancy-metz.fr/services/docint/Messeng1.htm">Le
Courrier électronique avec Netscape Messenger</a> <br />
<a href="http://www.airnews.net/anews_ns.htm">Setting up Netscape 2.0 for
Airnews Proxy News</a> <br />
```

HACK #23 Build Google Directory URLs

Use ODP category information to build URLs for the Google Directory.

The Google Directory (*http://directory.google.com*) overlays the Open Directory Project (ODP or DMOZ, *http://www.dmoz.org*) ontology onto the Google core index. The result is a Yahoo!-like directory hierarchy of search results and their associated categories with the added magic of Google's popularity algorithms.

The ODP opens its entire database of listings to anybody—provided you're willing to download a 283 MB file (and that's compressed!). While you're probably not interested in all the individual listings, you might want particular ODP categories, or you may be interested in watching new listings flowing into certain categories.

Unfortunately, the ODP does not offer a way to search by keyword sites added within a recent time period. So instead of searching for recently added sites, the best way to get new site information from the ODP is to monitor categories.

Because the Google Directory builds its directory based on the ODP information, you can use the ODP category hierarchy information to generate Google Directory URLs. This hack searches the ODP category hierarchy information for keywords that you specify, and then builds Google Directory URLs and checks to make sure that they're active.

You'll need to download the category hierarchy information from the ODP to get this hack to work. The compressed file containing this information is available from *http://dmoz.org/rdf.html*, and the specific file is here: *http://dmoz.org/rdf/structure.rdf.u8.gz*. Before using it, you must uncompress it with a decompression application specific to your operating system. In the Unix environment, the command looks something like this:

```
% gunzip structure.rdf.u8.gz
```

 Bear in mind that the full category hierarchy is over 35 MB. If you just want to experiment with the structure, you can get an excerpt from *http://dmoz.org/rdf/structure.example.txt*. This version is a plain text file and does not require uncompressing.

The Code

Save the following code to a text file called *google_dir.pl*:

```perl
#!/usr/bin/perl
# google_dir.pl
# Uses ODP category information to build URLs into the Google Directory.
# Usage: perl google_dir.pl "keywords" < structure.rdf.u8

use strict;

use LWP::Simple;

# Turn off output buffering.
$|++;

my $directory_url = "http://directory.google.com";
```

```
@ARGV == 1
  or die qq{usage: perl google_dir.pl "{query}" < structure.rdf.u8\n};

# Grab those command-line specified keywords and build a regular expression.
my $keywords = shift @ARGV;
$keywords =~ s!\s+!\|!g;

# A place to store topics.
my %topics;

# Loop through the DMOZ category file, printing matching results.
while (<>) {
  /"(Top\/.*$keywords.*)"/i and !$topics{$1}++
    and print "$directory_url/$1\n";
}
```

Running the Hack

Run the script from the command line ["How to Run the Hacks" in the Preface], along with a query and the piped-in contents of the DMOZ category file:

```
% perl googledir.pl "keywords" < structure.rdf.u8
```

Replace *keywords* with the particular keywords that you're after.

If you're using the shorter category excerpt *structure.example.txt*, use this:

```
% perl googledir.pl "keywords" < structure.example.txt
```

The Results

Feeding the keyword mosaic into this hack would look something like this:

```
% perl googledir.pl "mosaic" < structure.rdf.u8
http://directory.google.com/Top/Arts/Crafts/Mosaics
http://directory.google.com/Top/Arts/Crafts/Mosaics/Glass
http://directory.google.com/Top/Arts/Crafts/Mosaics/Ceramic_and_Broken_China
http://directory.google.com/Top/Arts/Crafts/Mosaics/Associations_and_
Directories
http://directory.google.com/Top/Arts/Crafts/Mosaics/Stone
http://directory.google.com/Top/Shopping/Crafts/Mosaics
http://directory.google.com/Top/Shopping/Crafts/Supplies/Mosaics
...
```

Hacking the Hack

There isn't much hacking that you can do to this hack; it's designed to take ODP data, create Google URLs, and verify those URLs. How well you can get this to work for you really depends on the types of search words that you choose.

Choose words that are more general. If you're interested in a particular state in the U.S., for example, choose the name of the state and major cities, but don't choose the name of a very small town or of the governor. Choose the name of a company but not of its CFO. A good rule of thumb is to choose the keywords that you might find as entry names in an encyclopedia or almanac. You can easily imagine finding a company name as an encyclopedia entry, but it's a rare CFO who could achieve the same.

Find Recipes

Let the Google API transform those random ingredients in your fridge into a wonderful dinner.

Google can help you find news, catalogs, discussions, web pages, and so much more—and it can also help you figure out what to have for dinner tonight!

This hack uses the Google API to help you transform those random ingredients in your fridge into a wonderful dinner. Well, you do have to do some of the work. But it all starts with this hack.

The Code

This hack comes with a built-in form that calls the query and the recipe type, so there's no need to set up a separate form:

```perl
#!/usr/local/bin/perl
# goocook.cgi
# Finding recipes with google.
# goocook.cgi is called as a CGI with form input.

# Your Google API developer's key
my $google_key='insert key here';

# Location of the GoogleSearch WSDL file.
my $google_wdsl = "./GoogleSearch.wsdl";

use SOAP::Lite;
use CGI qw/:standard/;

my %recipe_types = (
    "General"          => "site:allrecipes.com | site:cooking.com | site:
epicurious.com | site:recipesource.com",
    "Vegetarian/Vegan" => "site:fatfree.com | inurl:veganmania | inurl:
vegetarianrecipe | inurl:veggiefiles",
    "Wordwide Cuisine" => "site:Britannia.org | inurl:thegutsygourmet |
inurl:simpleinternet | inurl:soupsong"
);
```

```
print
  header( ),
  start_html("GooCook"),
  h1("GooCook"),
  start_form(-method=>'GET'),
  'Ingredients: ', textfield(-name=>'ingredients'),
  br( ),
  'Recipe Type: ', popup_menu(-name=>'recipe_type',
    -values=>[keys %recipe_types], -default=>'General'),
  br( ),
  submit(-name=>'submit', -value=>"Get Cookin'!"),
  submit(-name=>'reset', -value=>"Start Over"),
  end_form( ), p( );

if (param('ingredients')) {
  my $google_search = SOAP::Lite->service("file:$google_wdsl");
  my $results = $google_search ->
    doGoogleSearch(
      $google_key,
      param('ingredients') . " " . $recipe_types{param('recipe_type')},
      0, 10, "false", "",  "false", "", "latin1", "latin1"
    );

  @{$results->{'resultElements'}} or print "None";
  foreach (@{$results->{'resultElements'}}) {
    print p(
      b($_->{title}||'no title'), br( ),
      a({href=>$_->{URL}}), br( ),
      i($_->{snippet}||'no snippet')
    );
  }
}

print end_html( );
```

Save the code as a CGI script **["How to Run the Scripts" in the Preface]** named *goocook. cgi* in your web site's *cgi-bin* directory.

Running the Hack

This hack runs as a CGI script, producing a dynamic web page alongside the rest of the pages in your web site. Since just where you place and how you run CGI scripts varies from server to server and ISP to ISP, you're best left to ask your administrator or provider for help.

Once the script is in place, call it by pointing your Web browser at *goocook. cgi*, fill in the ingredients you have on hand, select a recipe type, and hit the "Get Cookin'!" button.

Hacking the Hack

Of course, the most obvious way to hack this hack is to add new recipe options to it. That involves first finding new recipe sites, and then adding them to the hack.

Adding new recipe sites entails finding the domains that you want to search. Use the cooking section of the Google Directory to find recipes, starting here: *http://directory.google.com/Top/Home/Cooking/Recipe_Collections/*.

Next, find what you want and build it into a query supplement like the one in the form, surrounded by parentheses with each item separated by a |. Remember, using the `site:` syntax means that you'll be searching for an entire domain, so if you find a great recipe site at *http://www.geocities.com/reallygreat/food/recipes/*, don't use the `site:` syntax to search it; use the `inurl:` search instead (`inurl:geocities.com/reallygreat/food/recipes`). Just remember that an addition like this counts heavily against your 10-word query limit.

Let's look at an example. The cookbook section of the Google Directory has a seafood section with several sites. Let's pull out five sites and turn them into a constraint on our query:

```
(site:simplyseafood.com | site:baycooking.com | site:coastangler.com | site:
welovefish.com | site:sea-ex.com)
```

Next, test the query constraints live in Google by adding a query (in this case, `salmon`) and running it as a search:

```
salmon (site:simplyseafood.com | site:baycooking.com | site:coastangler.com
| site:welovefish.com | site:sea-ex.com)
```

Run a few different queries with a few different query words (salmon, scallops, whatever) and make sure that you're getting a decent number of results. Once you're confident that you have a good selection of recipes, you'll need to add this new option to the hack:

```
my %recipe_types = (
  "General"            => "site:allrecipes.com | site:cooking.com | site:
epicurious.com | site:recipesource.com",
  "Vegetarian/Vegan"   => "site:fatfree.com | inurl:veganmania | inurl:
vegetarianrecipe | inurl:veggiefiles",
  "Wordwide Cuisine" => "site:Britannia.org | inurl:thegutsygourmet |
inurl:simpleinternet | inurl:soupsong"
);
```

Simply add the name you want to call the option (a `=>`) and the search string. Make sure you add it before the closing parenthesis and semicolon. Your code should look something like the code shown next.

```
my %recipe_types = (
    "General"              => "site:allrecipes.com | site:cooking.com | site:
epicurious.com | site:recipesource.com",
    "Vegetarian/Vegan"  => "site:fatfree.com | inurl:veganmania | inurl:
vegetarianrecipe | inurl:veggiefiles",
    "Wordwide Cuisine" => "site:Britannia.org | inurl:thegutsygourmet |
inurl:simpleinternet | inurl:soupsong"
    "Seafood" => "site:simplyseafood.com | site:baycooking.com | site:
coastangler.com | site:welovefish.com | site:sea-ex.com"

);
```

You can add as many search sets to the hack as you want. You may want to add Chinese Cooking, Desserts, Soups, Salads, or any number of other options.

—*Tara Calishain and Judy Hourihan*

HACK #25 Track Result Counts over Time

Query Google for each day of a specified date range, counting the number of results at each time index.

Sometimes the results of a search aren't of as much interest as knowing the number thereof. How popular is a particular keyword? How many times is so-and-so mentioned? How do differing phrases or spellings stack up against each other?

You may also wish to track the popularity of a term over time to watch its ups and downs, spot trends, and notice tipping points. Combining the Google API and daterange: **[Hack #16]** syntax is just the ticket.

This hack queries Google for each day over a specified date range, counting the number of results for each day. This leads to a list of numbers that you could enter into Excel and chart, for example.

There are a couple of caveats before diving right into the code. First, the average keyword will tend to show more results over time as Google ads more pages to its index. Second, Google doesn't stand behind its date range search; results shouldn't be taken as gospel.

This hack requires the *Time::JulianDay* (*http://search.cpan. org/search?query=Time%3A%3AJulianDay*) Perl module.

The Code

Save the following code as a file named *goocount.pl*:

```perl
#!/usr/local/bin/perl
# goocount.pl
# Runs the specified query for every day between the specified
# start and end dates, returning date and count as CSV.
# Usage: goocount.pl query="{query}" start={date} end={date}\n}
# where dates are of the format: yyyy-mm-dd, e.g. 2002-12-31

# Your Google API developer's key.
my $google_key='insert key here';

# Location of the GoogleSearch WSDL file.
my $google_wdsl = "./GoogleSearch.wsdl";

use SOAP::Lite;
use Time::JulianDay;
use CGI qw/:standard/;

# For checking date validity.
my $date_regex = '(\d{4})-(\d{1,2})-(\d{1,2})';

# Make sure all arguments are passed correctly.
( param('query') and param('start') =~ /^(?:$date_regex)?$/
  and param('end') =~ /^(?:$date_regex)?$/ ) or
  die qq{usage: goocount.pl query="{query}" start={date} end={date}\n};

# Julian date manipulation.
my $query = param('query');
my $yesterday_julian = int local_julian_day(time) - 1;
my $start_julian = (param('start') =~ /$date_regex/)
  ? julian_day($1,$2,$3) : $yesterday_julian;
my $end_julian = (param('end') =~ /$date_regex/)
  ? julian_day($1,$2,$3) : $yesterday_julian;

# Create a new Google SOAP request.
my $google_search = SOAP::Lite->service("file:$google_wdsl");

print qq{"date","count"\n};

# Iterate over each of the Julian dates for your query.
foreach my $julian ($start_julian..$end_julian) {
  $full_query = "$query daterange:$julian-$julian";
  # Query Google
  my $result = $google_search ->
    doGoogleSearch(
      $google_key, $full_query, 0, 10, "false", "",  "false",
      "", "latin1", "latin1"
    );

  # Output
  print
    '""',
    sprintf("%04d-%02d-%02d", inverse_julian_day($julian)),
```

```
          qq{","$result->{estimatedTotalResultsCount}"\n};
     }
```

Be sure to replace *insert key here* with your Google API key.

Running the Hack

Run the script from the command line **["How to Run the Hacks" in the Preface]**, specifying a query, start, and end dates.

Perhaps you'd like to see track mentions of the latest Macintosh operating system (code name "Panther") leading up to, on, and after its launch (October 24, 2003). The following invocation sends its results to a comma-separated (CSV) file for easy import into Excel or a database:

```
% perl goocount.pl query="OS X Panther" \
start=2003-10-20 end=2003-10-28 > count.csv
```

Leaving off the > and CSV filename sends the results to the screen for your perusal:

```
% perl goocount.pl query="OS X Panther" \
start=2003-10-20 end=2003-10-28
```

If you want to track results over time, you could run the script every day (using cron under Unix or the scheduler under Windows), with no date specified, to get the information for that day's date. Just use >> filename.csv to append to the filename instead of writing over it. Or you could get the results emailed to you for your daily reading pleasure.

The Results

Here's that search for Panther, the new Macintosh operating system:

```
% perl goocount.pl query="OS X Panther" \
start=2003-10-20 end=2003-10-28
"date","count"
"2003-10-20","28"
"2003-10-21","39"
"2003-10-22","68"
"2003-10-23","48"
"2003-10-24","98"
"2003-10-25","40"
"2003-10-26","56"
"2003-10-27","79"
"2003-10-28","130"
```

Notice the expected spike in new finds on release day, October 24th.

Working with These Results

If you have a fairly short list, it's easy to just look at the results and see if there are any spikes or particular items of interest about the result counts. But if you have a long list or you want a visual overview of the results, it's easy to use these numbers to create a graph in Excel or your favorite spreadsheet program.

Simply save the results to a file, and then open the file in Excel and use the chart wizard to create a graph. You'll have to do some tweaking but just generating the chart provides an interesting overview, as shown in Figure 2-2.

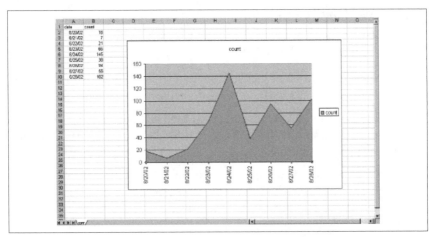

Figure 2-2. An Excel graph tracking mentions of Mac OS X Panther

Hacking the Hack

You can render the results as a web page by altering the code ever so slightly (changes are in bold) and directing the output to an HTML file (>> filename.html):

```
...
print
  header( ),
  start_html("GooCount: $query"),
  start_table({-border=>undef}, caption("GooCount:$query")),
  Tr([ th(['Date', 'Count']) ]);

foreach my $julian ($start_julian..$end_julian) {
  $full_query = "$query daterange:$julian-$julian";
  my $result = $google_search ->
    doGoogleSearch(
      $google_key, $full_query, 0, 10, "false", "", "false",
```

```
      "", "latin1", "latin1"
    );

  print
    Tr([ td([
      sprintf("%04d-%02d-%02d", inverse_julian_day($julian)),
      $result->{estimatedTotalResultsCount}
    ]) ]);
}

print
  end_table( ),
  end_html;
```

Feel Really Lucky

HACK
#26

Take the domain in which the first result of a query appears and do more
searching within that domain.

Does Google make you feel lucky? How lucky? Sometimes as lucky as the
top result is, more results from the same domain are just as much so.

This hack performs two Google queries. It first saves the domain of the top
result of the first search is saved. Then it runs the second query, searching
only the saved domain for results.

Take, for example, Grace Hopper, famous both as a computer programmer
and as the person who coined the term *computer bug*. If you were to run a
search with "Grace Hopper" as the primary search and overlay a search for
COBOL on the domain of the first result returned, you'd find the following
three links at the top of the results page:

```
GHC - 2004
http://www.gracehopper.org/ghc_press_factsheet1.html
... Website: www.gracehopper.org ... and on making machines understand
ordinary language instructions led ultimately to the development of the
business language COBOL. ...
GHC - 2004
http://www.gracehopper.org/ghc_press_factsheet.html
... Website: www.gracehopper.org ... and on making machines understand
ordinary language instructions led ultimately to the development of the
business language COBOL. ...
GHC2002
http://www.gracehopper.org/gmh2002/resources.html
... uspers-h/g-hoppr.htm. Whitman College: http://people.whitman.edu/
~pitterk/class/cobol.html. Yale University (The Ada Project): http ...
```

You could also do a primary search for a person ("Stan Laurel") and a sec-
ondary search for another person ("Oliver Hardy"). Or search for a person,
followed by their corporate affiliation.

Don't try doing a link: search with this hack. The link: special syntax doesn't work with any other special syntaxes, and this hack relies upon inurl:.

The Code

Save the code as *goolucky.cgi*, a CGI script on your web server ["How to Run the Hacks" in the Preface] or that of your Internet service provider.

```perl
#!/usr/local/bin/perl
# goolucky.cgi
# Gleans the domain from the first (read: top) result returned, allows
# you to overlay another query, and returns the results, and so on...
# goolucky.cgi is called as a CGI with form input.

# Your Google API developer's key.
my $google_key='insert key here';

# Location of the GoogleSearch WSDL file.
my $google_wdsl = "./GoogleSearch.wsdl";

use strict;

use SOAP::Lite;
use CGI qw/:standard/;

# Create a new SOAP instance.
my $google_search = SOAP::Lite->service("file:$google_wdsl");

# If this is the second time around, glean the domain.
my $query_domain = param('domain') ? "inurl:" . param('domain') : '';
my $results = $google_search ->
  doGoogleSearch(
    $google_key, param('query') . " $query_domain", 0, 10,
    "false", "", "false", "", "latin1", "latin1"
  );

# Set domain to the results of the previous query.
param('domain', $results->{'resultElements'}->[0]->{'URL'});
param('domain', param('domain') =~ m#://(.*?)/#);

print
  header( ),
  start_html("I'm Feeling VERY Lucky"),
  h1("I'm Feeling VERY Lucky"),
  start_form( ),
  'Query: ', textfield(-name=>'query',
  -default=>'"Grace Hopper"'),
  '   ',
  'Domain: ', textfield(-name=>'domain'),
  '   ',
```

```
    submit(-name=>'submit', -value=>'Search'),
    p( ),
    'Results:';

foreach (@{$results->{'resultElements'}}) {
  print p(
    b($_->{title}), br( ),
    a({href=>$_->{URL}}, $_->{URL}), br( ),
    i($_->{snippet})
  );
}

print
  end_form( ),
  end_html( );
```

Replace *insert key here* with your Google API key.

Running the Hack

Point your web browser at the CGI script, *goolucky.cgi*. The script pops up a form in which you should enter a query and a domain within which to search; hit the Search button when you're ready to run your query.

Hacking the Hack

You can also run this hack so that it only uses one query. For example, do a search with Query A, and the search grabs the domain from the first result. Then run another search, again using Query A, but restrict your results to the domain that was grabbed in the first search. This is handy when you're trying to get information on one set of keywords, instead of trying to link two different concepts. Figure 2-3 illustrates the I'm Feeling VERY Lucky search.

Get Random Results (on Purpose)
#27   Surfing random pages can turn up some brilliant finds.

Why would any researcher worth her salt be interested in random pages? While surfing random pages isn't what one might call a focused search, you'd be surprised at some of the brilliant finds that you'd never have come across otherwise. I've loved random page generators associated with search engines ever since discovering Random Yahoo! Link (*http://random.yahoo. com/bin/ryl*, although no longer working at the time of this writing). It made me think that creating such a thing to work with the Google API might prove interesting, useful even.

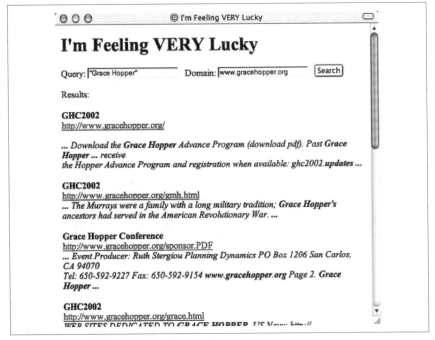

Figure 2-3. *I'm Feeling VERY Lucky search*

The Code

This code searches for a random number between 0 and 99999 (yes, you can search for 0 with Google) in addition to a modifier pulled from the @modifiers array. To generate the random page, you don't, strictly speaking, need something from the modifer array. However, it helps make the page selection even more random.

With the combination of a number between 0 and 99999 and a modifier from the @modifiers array, Google will get a list of search results, and from that list you'll get a "random" page. You could go higher with the numbers if you wanted, but I wasn't sure that this hack would consistently find numbers higher than 99999. (Zip Codes are five digits, so I knew a five-digit search would find results more often than not.)

Save the code as a CGI script named *goorandom.cgi*. The only change you need to make is to replace *insert key here* with your Google API key.

```perl
#!/usr/local/bin/perl
# goorandom.cgi
# Creates a random Google query and redirects the browser to
# the top/first result.
# goorandom.cgi is called as a CGI without any form input
```

```perl
# Your Google API developer's key.
my $google_key='insert key here';

# Location of the GoogleSearch WSDL file.
my $google_wdsl = "./GoogleSearch.wsdl";

use strict;

use SOAP::Lite;

# A list of search modifiers to be randomly chosen amongst for
# inclusion in the query.
my @modifiers = ( "-site:com", "-site:edu", "-site:net",
                  "-site:org", "-site:uk", "-filetype:pdf", );

# Picking a random number and modifier combination.
my $random_number   = int( rand(99999) );
my $random_modifier = $modifiers[int( rand( scalar(@modifiers) ) )];

# Create a new SOAP object.
my $google_search   = SOAP::Lite->service("file:$google_wdsl");

# Query Google.
my $results = $google_search ->
  doGoogleSearch(
    $google_key, "$random_number $random_modifier",
    0, 1, "false", "",  "false", "", "latin1", "latin1"
  );

# redirect the browser to the URL of the top/first result
print "Location: $results->{resultElements}->[0]->{URL}\n\n";
```

Running the Hack

This hack runs as a CGI script ["How to Run the Hacks" in the Preface]. Point your web browser at *goorandom.cgi*.

Hacking the Hack

There are a couple of ways to hack this hack.

Modifying the modifiers. You'll notice each modifier in the @modifier array is preceded by a negative (which means "exclude this"). You can, of course, add anything you wish, but it's highly recommended that you keep to the negative theme; including something like "computers" in the list gives you a chance—a slight chance, but a chance nevertheless—of coming up with no search results at all. The hack randomly excludes domains; here are a few more possibilities:

```
-intitle:queryword
-inurl:www
-inurl:queryword
-internet
-yahoo
-intitle:the
```

If you want to, you could create modifiers that use OR (|) instead of nega-
tives, and then slant them to a particular topic. For example, you could create an array with a medical slant that looks like this:

```
(medicine | treatment | therapy)
(cancer | chemotherapy | drug)
(symptoms | "side effects")
(medical | research | hospital)
(inurl:edu | inurl:gov )
```

Using the OR modifier does not guarantee finding a search result like using a
negative does, so don't narrow your possible results by restricting your
search to the page's title or URL.

Adding a touch more randomness. The hack, as it stands, always picks the
first result. While it's already highly unlikely that you'll ever see the same
random page twice, you can achieve a touch more randomness by choosing
a random returned result. Take a gander at the actual search itself in the
hack's code:

```
my $results = $google_search ->
  doGoogleSearch(
    $google_key, "$random_number $random_modifier",
    0, 1, "false", "",  "false", "", "latin1", "latin1"
  );
```

You see that 0 at the beginning of the fourth line? That's the offset: the number of the first result to return. Change that number to anything between 0
and 999, and you'll shift the results returned by that number—assuming, of
course, that the number you choose is smaller than the number of results for
the query at hand. For the sake of just about guaranteeing a result, it's probably best to stick to numbers between 0 and 10. How about randomizing the
offset? Simply alter the code as follows (changes in bold):

```
...
# picking a random number, modifier, and offset combination
my $random_number   = int( rand(99999) );
my $random_modifier = $modifiers[int( rand( scalar(@modifiers) ) )];
my $random_offset = int( rand(10) );
...
my $results = $google_search ->
  doGoogleSearch(
    $google_key, "$random_number $random_modifier",
    $random_offset, 1, "false", "",  "false", "", "latin1", "latin1"
```

```
    );

    ...
```

HACK #28 Permute a Query

Run all permutations of query keywords and phrases to squeeze the last drop of results from the Google index.

Google, ah, Google. Search engine of over eight billion pages and zillions of possible results. If you're a search engine geek like I am, few things are more entertaining than trying various tweaks with your Google search to see what exactly makes a difference to the results.

It's amazing what makes a difference. For example, you wouldn't think that word order would make much of an impact, but it does. In fact, buried in Google's documentation is the admission that the word order of a query will impact search results.

While that's an interesting thought, who has time to generate and run every possible iteration of a multiword query? Google API to the rescue! This hack takes a query of up to four keywords or "quoted phrases" (as well as supporting special syntaxes) and runs all possible permutations, showing result counts by permutation and the top results for each permutation.

The Code

Save the following code as a CGI script ["How to Run the Hacks" in the Preface] named *order_matters.cgi* in your web site's *cgi-bin* directory. As you type in the script, be sure to replace *insert key here* with your Google API key.

You'll need to have the *Algorithm::Permute* Perl module for this program to work correctly (*http://search.cpan.org/ search?query=algorithm%3A%3Apermute&mode=all*).

```perl
#!/usr/local/bin/perl
# order_matters.cgi
# Queries Google for every possible permutation of up to 4 query keywords,
# returning result counts by permutation and top results across
permutations.
# order_matters.cgi is called as a CGI with form input

# Your Google API developer's key.
my $google_key='insert key here';

# Location of the GoogleSearch WSDL file.
my $google_wdsl = "./GoogleSearch.wsdl";
```

```
use strict;

use SOAP::Lite;
use CGI qw/:standard *table/;
use Algorithm::Permute;

print
  header( ),
  start_html("Order Matters"),
  h1("Order Matters"),
  start_form(-method=>'GET'),
  'Query:   ', textfield(-name=>'query'),
  '   ',
  submit(-name=>'submit', -value=>'Search'), br( ),
  '<font size="-2" color="green">Enter up to 4 query keywords or "quoted
phrases"</font>',
  end_form( ), p( );

if (param('query')) {

  # Glean keywords.
  my @keywords = grep !/^\s*$/,  split /([+-]?".+?")|\s+/, param('query');

  scalar @keywords > 4 and
  print('<font color="red">Only 4 query keywords or phrases allowed.</font>
'), last;

  my $google_search = SOAP::Lite->service("file:$google_wdsl");

  print
  start_table({-cellpadding=>'10', -border=>'1'}),
  Tr([th({-colspan=>'2'}, ['Result Counts by Permutation' ])]),
  Tr([th({-align=>'left'}, ['Query', 'Count'])]);

  my $results = {}; # keep track of what we've seen across queries

  # Iterate over every possible permutation.
  my $p = new Algorithm::Permute( \@keywords );
  while (my $query = join(' ', $p->next)) {

    # Query Google.
    my $r = $google_search ->
    doGoogleSearch(
      $google_key,
      $query,
      0, 10, "false", "",  "false", "", "latin1", "latin1"
    );
      print Tr([td({-align=>'left'}, [$query, $r->
{'estimatedTotalResultsCount'}] )]);
    @{$r->{'resultElements'}} or next;

    # Assign a rank.
    my $rank = 10;
```

```
    foreach (@{$r->{'resultElements'}}) {
      $results->{$_->__CON_L_BRACKETCON_R_BRACKET__} = {
        title => $_->{title},
        snippet => $_->{snippet},
        seen => ($results->{$_->{URL}}->{seen}) + $rank
      };
      $rank--;
    }
  }

  print
    end_table( ), p( ),
    start_table({-cellpadding=>'10', -border=>'1'}),
    Tr([th({-colspan=>'2'}, ['Top Results across Permutations' ])]),
    Tr([th({-align=>'left'}, ['Score', 'Result'])]);

  foreach ( sort { $results->{$b}->{seen} <=> $results->{$a}->{seen} } keys
  %$results ) {
    print Tr(td([
      $results->{$_}->{seen},
      b($results->{$_}->{title}||'no title') . br( ) .
      a({href=>$_}, $_) . br( ) .
      i($results->{$_}->{snippet}||'no snippet')
    ]));
  }

    print end_table( ),
  }
  print end_html( );
```

Running the Hack

Point your web browser at the CGI script *order_matters.cgi* on your web server. Enter the query you want to check (up to four words or phrases). The script will first search for every possible combination of the search words and phrases, as shown in Figure 2-4.

The script will then display the top 10 search results across all permutations of the query, as shown in Figure 2-5.

At first blush, this hack looks like a novelty with few practical applications. But if you're a regular researcher or a web wrangler, you might find it of interest.

If you're a regular researcher—that is, there are certain topics that you research on a regular basis—you might want to spend some time with this hack and see if you can detect a pattern in how your regular search terms are impacted by changing word order. You might need to revise your searching so that certain words always come first or last in your query.

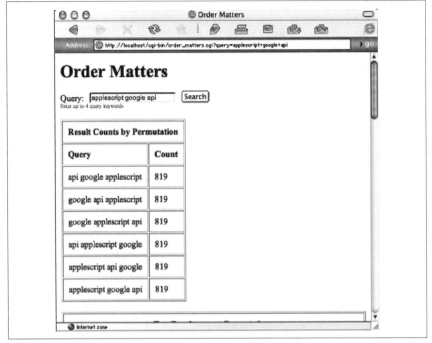

Figure 2-4. Permutations for applescript google api

If you're a web wrangler, you need to know where your page appears in Google's search results. If your page loses a lot of ranking ground because of a shift in a query arrangement, maybe you want to add some more words to your text or shift your existing text.

HACK Weight a Query Keyword

#29

Add more weight to a particular keyword in your Google search query for more targeted results.

As we've mentioned before, Google will provide different results based on how many times a search word is used in a query **[Hack #15]**.

Part of this is assumed to be because Google tries to search your query in order, giving higher relevance to words that appear in the same order in a page as they do in your query. (In other words, when you search for baseball baseball, Google tries to find, and assigns more weight to, pages that have the phrase "baseball baseball" in them, even if you don't use quotes in your search.)

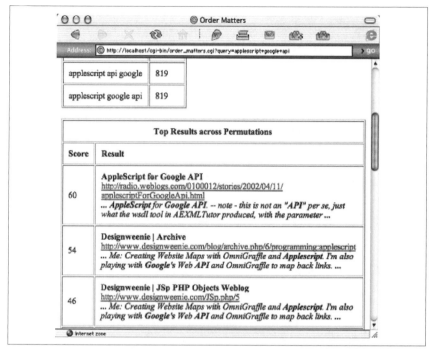

Figure 2-5. Top results for permutations of applescript google api

Google also seems to look for multiple iterations of the same word in your result pages. So when you search for baseball baseball baseball, Google looks for the word baseball three times in your result pages.

This is a nifty and little-known search trick when you want to emphasize a particular word in your search, but typing in the same word several times is a drag. This hack automates the process for you, adding weight to the keyword of your choice and sending you on to Google for results.

The Code

Save the following code as a CGI script **["How to Run the Hacks" in the Preface]** named *sinker.cgi* in your web site's *cgi-bin* directory.

> This script doesn't require the Google API! Instead, it directly opens a Google search result URL.

```
#!/usr/local/bin/perl
# sinker.cgi
# Weight a specific keyword in a Google query.
```

```
use strict;

use CGI qw{:standard};

# Display the query form if both a query and sinker are not provided.
unless (param('query') and param('sinker')) {
  print
    header( ),
    start_html("Search Sinker"),
    h1("Search Sinker"),
    start_form(-method=>'GET'),
    'Query: ', textfield(-name=>'query'), p( ),
    'Sinker (word to weight): ', textfield(-name=>'sinker'), p( ),
    submit(-name=>'submit', -value=>'Search'), p( ),
    "You will be taken straight to a Google results page. Be sure to look in
the Google query box at the top of the page to see how your query turned
out.",
    end_form( ), p( );
}
else {
  # Normalize the sinker and prefix with a space.
  my($sinker) = param('sinker') =~ /^\s*(.+)\s*$/;
  $sinker = " $sinker";

  # Build the Google query URL.
  my $query = param('query') . $sinker x ( 10 - (scalar split / /,
param('query')) );

  # Webify the query.
  $query =~ s/([^a-zA-Z0-9 ])/"%".sprintf("%2.2x", unpack("C", ($1)))/eg;
  $query =~ tr/ /+/;

  # Redirect the browser to Google, sinker search in tow
  print redirect("http://www.google.com/search?num=100&q=$query");
}
```

Running the Hack

Point your browser at the *sinker.cgi* script on your web server. In the form, enter any query in the Query field and the word you want to emphasize in the Sinker field and click the Search button. You'll be redirected to a Google results page chock-full of up to 100 results.

Be sure to take a gander at how your query turned out in the Google search box at the top of the results page. If, for instance, you queried for "Moises Alou" with a sinker of baseball, the resulting query sent on to Google would look like this:

    "Moises Alou" baseball baseball baseball baseball baseball baseball baseball
    baseball

Restrict Searches to Top-Level Results

HACK #30   Separate out search results by the depth at which they appear in a site.

Google's a mighty big haystack in which to find the needle you seek. And there's more, so much more: some experts believe that Google and its ilk index only a bare fraction of the pages available on the Web.

Because the Web's growing all the time, researchers have to come up with lots of different tricks to narrow down search results. Tricks and—thanks to the Google API—tools. This hack separates out search results appearing at the top level of a domain from those beneath.

Why would you want to do this?

- Clear away clutter when searching for proper names. If you're searching for general information about a proper name, this is one way to clear out mentions in news stories, etc. For example, the name of a political leader such as Tony Blair might be mentioned in a story without any substantive information about the man himself. But if you limited your results to only those pages on the top level of a domain, you would avoid most of those *mention hits*.

- Find patterns in the association of highly ranked domains and certain keywords.

- Narrow search results to only those bits that sites deem important enough to have in their virtual foyers.

- Skip past subsites, such as home pages created by J. Random User on his service provider's web server.

The Code

Save the code as a CGI script **["How to Run the Hacks" in the Preface]** named *gootop.cgi*:

```
#!/usr/local/bin/perl
# gootop.cgi
# Separates out top-level and sub-level results.
# gootop.cgi is called as a CGI with form input.

# Your Google API developer's key.
my $google_key='insert key here';

# Location of the GoogleSearch WSDL file.
my $google_wdsl = "./GoogleSearch.wsdl";

# Number of times to loop, retrieving 10 results at a time.
my $loops = 10;

use strict;
```

```
use SOAP::Lite;
use CGI qw/:standard *table/;

print
  header( ),
  start_html("GooTop"),
  h1("GooTop"),
  start_form(-method=>'GET'),
  'Query: ', textfield(-name=>'query'),
  '   ',
  submit(-name=>'submit', -value=>'Search'),
  end_form( ), p( );

my $google_search = SOAP::Lite->service("file:$google_wdsl");

if (param('query')) {
  my $list = { 'toplevel' => [], 'sublevel' => [] };

  for (my $offset = 0; $offset <= $loops*10; $offset += 10) {
    my $results = $google_search ->
      doGoogleSearch(
        $google_key, param('query'), $offset,
        10, "false", "",  "false", "", "latin1", "latin1"
      );

    foreach (@{$results->{'resultElements'}}) {
      push @{
        $list->{ $_->{URL} =~ m!://[^/]+/?$!
        ? 'toplevel' : 'sublevel' }
      },
      p(
        b($_->{title}||'no title'), br( ),
        a({href=>$_->{URL}}, $_->{URL}), br( ),
        i($_->{snippet}||'no snippet')
      );
    }
  }

  print
    h2('Top-Level Results'),
    join("\n", @{$list->{toplevel}}),
    h2('Sub-Level Results'),
    join("\n", @{$list->{sublevel}});
}

print end_html;
```

Gleaning a decent number of top-level domain results means throwing out quite a bit. It's for this reason that this script runs the specified query a number of times, as specified by my $loops = 10;, each loop picking up 10 results, some subset being top-level. To alter the number of loops per query, simply change the value of $loops. Realize that each invocation of the script burns through $loops number of queries, so be sparing and don't bump that number up to anything ridiculous; even 100 will eat through a daily allotment in just 10 invocations.

The heart of the script, and what differentiates it from your average Google API Perl script [Hack #92], lies in the code that follows.

```
push @{
   $list->{ $_->{URL} =~ m!://[^/]+/?$!
   ? 'toplevel' : 'sublevel' }
}
```

What that jumble of characters is scanning for is :// (as in http://) followed by anything other than a / (slash), thereby sifting between top-level finds (e.g., *http://www.berkeley.edu/welcome.html*) and sublevel results (e.g., *http://www.berkeley.edu/students/john_doe/my_dog.html*). If you're Perl savvy, you may have noticed the trailing /?$; this allows for the eventuality that a top-level URL ends with a slash (e.g., *http://www.berkeley.edu/*), as is often true.

Running the Hack

This hack runs as a CGI script. Figure 2-6 shows the results of a search for non-gmo (Genetically Modified Organisms, that is).

Figure 2-6. GooTop search for non-gmo

Hacking the Hack

There are a couple of ways to hack this hack.

More depth. Perhaps your interests lie in just how deep results are within a site or sites. A minor adjustment or two to the code and you have results grouped by depth:

```perl
#!/usr/bin/perl

# gootop.cgi
# Separates out top level and sub-level results
# gootop.cgi is called as a CGI with form input.

# Your Google API developer's key.
my $google_key='insert key here';

# Location of the GoogleSearch WSDL file.
my $google_wdsl = "./GoogleSearch.wsdl";

# Number of times to loop, retrieving 10 results at a time.
my $loops = 1;

use strict;

use lib qw!/home/rael/lib/perl!; #FIXME
use SOAP::Lite;
use CGI qw/:standard *table/;

print
  header(),
  start_html("GooTop"),
  h1("GooTop"),
  start_form(-method=>'GET'),
  'Query: ', textfield(-name=>'query'),
  '   ',
  submit(-name=>'submit', -value=>'Search'),
  end_form(), p();

my $google_search  = SOAP::Lite->service("file:$google_wdsl");

if (param('query')) {
  my @list = ();

  for (my $offset = 0; $offset <= $loops*10; $offset += 10) {
    my $results = $google_search ->
      doGoogleSearch(
        $google_key, param('query'), $offset,
        10, "false", "",  "false", "", "latin1", "latin1"
      );

    foreach (@{$results->{'resultElements'}}) {
      push @{ $list[scalar ( split(/\//, $_->{URL} . ' ') - 3 ) ] },
```

```
            p(
              b($_->{title}||'no title'), br(),
              a({href=>$_->{URL}}, $_->{URL}), br(),
              i($_->{snippet}||'no snippet')
              );
        }

    }

    for my $level (1..$#list) {
        print h2("Level: $level");
        ref $list[$level] eq 'ARRAY' and print join "\n", @{$list[$level]};
    }
}

print end_html;
```

Figure 2-7 shows that non-gmo search again using the depth hack.

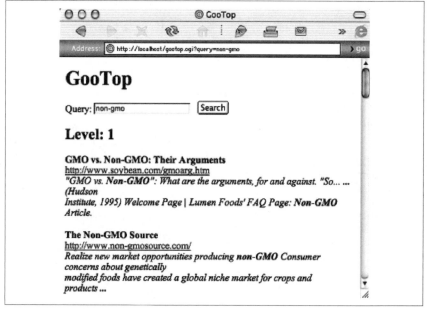

Figure 2-7. GooTop non-gmo search using depth hack

Query tips. Along with the aforementioned code hacking, here are a few query tips to use with this hack:

- Consider feeding the script a `daterange:` [Hack #16] query to further narrow results.

- Keep your searches specific, but not too much so for fear of turning up no top-level results. Instead of cats, for example, use "burmese cats", but don't try "burmese breeders" feeding.

- Try the link: syntax ["Special Syntax" in Chapter 1]. This is a nice use of a syntax otherwise not allowed in combination ["Mixing Syntaxes" in Chapter 1] with any others.

- On occasion, intitle: works nicely with this hack. Try your query without special syntaxes first, though, and work your way up, making sure you're getting results after each change.

Search for Special Characters

#31 Search for the tilde and other special characters in URLs.

Google can find lots of different things, but at the time of this writing, it can't find special characters—except for $, recently added for use in number range searches ["Google Web Search Basics" and "Number Range" in Chapter 1]. That's a shame, because special characters can come in handy. The tilde (~), for example, denotes personal web pages.

This hack takes a query from a form, pulls results from Google, and filters the results for the presence of several different special characters in the URL, including the tilde.

Why would you want to do this? By altering this hack slightly (see the "Hacking the Hack" section), you could restrict your searches to just pages with a tilde in the URL, an easy way to find personal pages. Maybe you're looking for dynamically generated pages with a question mark (?) in the URL; you can't find these using Google by itself, but you can with this hack. And, of course, you can turn the hack inside-out and not return results containing ~, ?, or other special characters. In fact, this code is more of a beginning than an end unto itself: you can tweak it in several different ways to do several different things.

The Code

Save this code to a text file called *aunt_tilde.cgi*. Replace *insert key here* with your Google API key.

```
#!/usr/local/bin/perl
# aunt_tilde.pl
# Finding special characters in Google result URLs.

# Your Google API developer's key.
my $google_key='insert key here';
```

```perl
# Number of times to loop, retrieving 10 results at a time.
my $loops = 10;

# Location of the GoogleSearch WSDL file.
my $google_wdsl = "./GoogleSearch.wsdl";

use strict;

use CGI qw/:standard/;
use SOAP::Lite;

print
  header( ),
  start_html("Aunt Tilde"),
  h1("Aunt Tilde"),
  start_form(-method=>'GET'),
  'Query: ', textfield(-name=>'query'),
  br( ),
  'Characters to find: ',
  checkbox_group(
    -name=>'characters',
    -values=>[qw/ ~ @ ? ! /],
    -defaults=>[qw/ ~ /]
  ),
  br( ),
  submit(-name=>'submit', -value=>'Search'),
  end_form( ), p( );

if (param('query')) {

  # Create a regular expression to match preferred special characters.
  my $special_regex = '[\\' . join('\\', param('characters')) . ']';

  my $google_search  = SOAP::Lite->service("file:$google_wdsl");

  for (my $offset = 0; $offset <= $loops*10; $offset += 10) {
    my $results = $google_search ->
      doGoogleSearch(
        $google_key, param('query'), $offset, 10, "false", "",  "false",
        "", "latin1", "latin1"
      );

    last unless @{$results->{resultElements}};

    foreach my $result (@{$results->{'resultElements'}}) {

      # Output only matched URLs, highlighting special characters in red
      my $url = $result->{URL};
      $url =~ s!($special_regex)!<font color="red">$1</font>!g and
        print
          p(
            b(a({href=>$result->{URL}},$result->{title}||'no title')), br(
),
```

```
            $url, br(  ),
            i($result->{snippet}||'no snippet')
        );
    }
}

    print end_html;
}
```

Running the Hack

Point your browser at the *aunt_tilde.cgi* CGI script, type a search query into the Query field, click the checkboxes next to the special characters you're after, and click the Search button.

Hacking the Hack

There are a couple of interesting ways to change this hack.

Choosing special characters. You can easily alter the list of special characters that you're interested in by changing one line in the script:

```
-values=>[qw/ ~ @ ? ! /],
```

Simply add or remove special characters from the space-delimited list between the / (forward slash) characters. If, for example, you want to add & (ampersands) and z (why not?), while dropping ? (question marks), that line of code should be:

```
-values=>[qw/ ~ @ ! & z /],
```

Don't forget those spaces between characters in the list.

Excluding special characters. You can just as easily decide to exclude URLs that contain your special characters as include them. Simply change the =~ (read: does match) in this line:

```
$url  =~ s!($special_regex)!<font color="red">$1</font>!g and
```

to !~ (read: does *not* match), leaving:

```
$url  !~ s!($special_regex)!<font color="red">$1</font>!g and
```

Now, any result containing the specific characters will *not* show up.

Dig Deeper into Sites

#32   Dig deeper into the hierarchies of web sites matching your search criteria.

One of Google's big strengths is that it can find your search term instantly and with great precision. But sometimes you're not interested so much in one definitive result as in lots of diverse results; maybe you even want some that are a bit more on the obscure side.

One method I've found rather useful is to ignore all results shallower than a particular level in a site's directory hierarchy. You avoid all the clutter of finds on home pages and go for subject matter otherwise hidden away in the depths of a site's structure. While content comes and goes, ebbs and flows from a site's main focus, it tends to gather in more permanent locales, categorized and archived, like with like.

This script asks for a query along with a preferred depth, above which results are thrown out. Specify a depth of four and your results will come only from *http://example.com/a/b/c/d*, not */a*, */a/b/*, or */a/b/c*.

Because you're already limiting the kinds of results that you see, it's best to use more common words for what you're looking for. Obscure query terms can often return absolutely no results.

> The default number of loops, retrieving 10 items apiece, is set to 50. This is to assure that you glean some decent number of results because many will be tossed. You can, of course, alter this number, but bear in mind that you're using that number of your daily quota of 1,000 Google API queries per developer's key.

The Code

Save this code as *deep_blue_g.cgi*, a CGI script ["How to Run the Hacks" in the Preface] on your web server. As you type it in, replace *insert key here* with your Google API key.

```
#!/usr/local/bin/perl
# deep_blue_g.cgi
# Limiting search results to a particular depth in a web
# site's hierarchy.
# deep_blue_g.cgi is called as a CGI with form input.

# Your Google API developer's key.
my $google_key='insert key here';

# Location of the GoogleSearch WSDL file.
my $google_wdsl = "./GoogleSearch.wsdl";
```

```
# Number of times to loop, retrieving 10 results at a time.
my $loops = 10;

use SOAP::Lite;
use CGI qw/:standard *table/;

print
  header( ),
  start_html("Fishing in the Deep Blue G"),
  h1("Fishing in the Deep Blue G"),
  start_form(-method=>'GET'),
  'Query: ', textfield(-name=>'query'),
  br( ),
  'Depth: ', textfield(-name=>'depth', -default=>4),
  br( ),
  submit(-name=>'submit', -value=>'Search'),
  end_form( ), p( );

# Make sure a query and numeric depth are provided.
if (param('query') and param('depth') =~ /\d+/) {

  # Create a new SOAP object.
  my $google_search = SOAP::Lite->service("file:$google_wdsl");

  for (my $offset = 0; $offset <= $loops*10; $offset += 10) {
    my $results = $google_search ->
      doGoogleSearch(
        $google_key, param('query'), $offset, 10, "false", "",  "false",
        "", "latin1", "latin1"
      );

    last unless @{$results->{resultElements}};

    foreach my $result (@{$results->{'resultElements'}}) {

      # Determine depth.
      my $url = $result->{URL};
      $url =~ s!^\w+://|/$!!g;

      # Output only those deep enough.
      ( split(/\//, $url) - 1) >= param('depth') and
        print
          p(
            b(a({href=>$result->{URL}},$result->{title}||'no title')), br(
),
            $result->{URL}, br( ),
            i($result->{snippet}||'no snippet')
          );
    }
  }

  print end_html;
}
```

Running the Hack

This hack runs as a CGI script. Point your browser at *deep_blue_g.cgi*, fill out the query and depth fields, and click the Submit button.

Figure 2-8 shows a query for "Jacques Cousteau", restricting results to a depth of six; that's six levels down from the site's home page. You'll notice some pretty long URLs in there.

Figure 2-8. A search for "Jacques Cousteau", restricting results to six levels down

Hacking the Hack

Perhaps you're interested in just the opposite of what this hack provides: you want only results from higher up in a site's hierarchy. Hacking this hack is simple enough: swap in a < (less than) symbol instead of the > (greater than) in the following line:

```
( split(/\//, $url) - 1) <= param('depth') and
```

Summarize Results by Domain

#33 Get an overview of the sorts of domains (educational, commercial, foreign, and so forth) found in the results of a Google query.

You want to know about a topic, so you do a search. But what do you have? A list of pages. You can't get a good idea of the types of pages these are without taking a close look at the list of sites.

This hack is an attempt to get a *snapshot* of the types of sites that result from a query. It does this by taking a *suffix census*, a count of the different domains that appear in search results.

This is most ideal for running link: queries, providing a good idea of what kinds of domains (commercial, educational, military, foreign, etc.) are linking to a particular page.

You could also run it to see where technical terms, slang terms, and unusual words are turning up. Which pages mention a particular singer more often? Or a political figure? Does the word "democrat" come up more often on *.com* or *.edu* sites?

Of course, this snapshot doesn't provide a complete inventory, but as overviews go, it's rather interesting.

The Code

Save the code as *suffixcensus.cgi*, a CGI script ["How to Run the Hacks" in the Preface] on your web server:

```
#!/usr/local/bin/perl
# suffixcensus.cgi
# Generates a snapshot of the kinds of sites responding to a
# query. The suffix is the .com, .net, or .uk part.
# suffixcensus.cgi is called as a CGI with form input.

# Your Google API developer's key.
my $google_key='insert key here';

# Location of the GoogleSearch WSDL file.
my $google_wdsl = "./GoogleSearch.wsdl";

# Number of times to loop, retrieving 10 results at a time.
my $loops = 10;

use SOAP::Lite;
use CGI qw/:standard *table/;

print
  header( ),
```

```
        start_html("SuffixCensus"),
        h1("SuffixCensus"),
        start_form(-method=>'GET'),
        'Query: ', textfield(-name=>'query'),
        '   ',
        submit(-name=>'submit', -value=>'Search'),
        end_form( ), p( );

    if (param('query')) {
        my $google_search  = SOAP::Lite->service("file:$google_wdsl");
        my %suffixes;

        for (my $offset = 0; $offset <= $loops*10; $offset += 10) {

            my $results = $google_search ->
              doGoogleSearch(
                $google_key, param('query'), $offset, 10, "false", "",  "false",
                "", "latin1", "latin1"
              );

            last unless @{$results->{resultElements}};

            map { $suffixes{ ($_->{URL} =~ m#://.+?\.(\w{2,4})/#)[0] }++ }
              @{$results->{resultElements}};
        }

        print
          h2('Results: '), p( ),
          start_table({cellpadding => 5, cellspacing => 0, border => 1}),
          map( { Tr(td(uc $_),td($suffixes{$_})) } sort keys %suffixes ),
          end_table( );
    }

    print end_html( );
```

Be sure to replace *insert key here* with your Google API key.

Running the Hack

This hack runs as a CGI script. Point your browser at *suffixcensus.cgi* to run it.

The Results

Searching for the prevalence of "soda pop" by suffix finds, as one might expect, the most mention on *.com*s, as shown in Figure 2-9.

Hacking the Hack

There are a couple of ways to hack this hack.

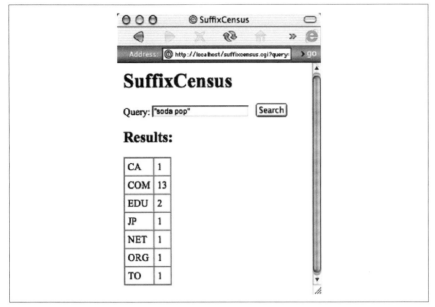

Figure 2-9. Prevalence of "soda pop" by suffix

Going back for more. This script, by default, visits Google 10 times, grabbing the top 100 (or fewer, if there aren't as many) results. To increase or decrease the number of visits, simply change the value of the $loops variable at the top of the script. Bear in mind, however, that making $loops = 50 might net you 500 results, but you're also eating quickly into your daily allotment of 1,000 Google API queries.

Returning comma-separated output. It's rather simple to adjust this script to run from the command line and return a comma-separated output suitable for Excel or your average database. Remove the starting HTML, form, and ending HTML output, and alter the code that prints out the results. In the end, you come to something like this (changes in bold):

```
#!/usr/local/bin/perl
# suffixcensus_csv.pl
# Generates a snapshot of the kinds of sites responding to a
# query. The suffix is the .com, .net, or .uk part.
# Usage: perl suffixcensus_csv.pl query="your query" > results.csv

# Your Google API developer's key.
my $google_key='insert key';

# Location of the GoogleSearch WSDL file.
my $google_wdsl = "./GoogleSearch.wsdl";
```

```
# Number of times to loop, retrieving 10 results at a time.
my $loops = 1;

use SOAP::Lite;
use CGI qw/:standard/;

param('query')
  or die qq{usage: suffixcensus_csv.pl query="{query}" [> results.csv]\n};

print qq{"suffix","count"\n};

my $google_search  = SOAP::Lite->service("file:$google_wdsl");

my %suffixes;

for (my $offset = 0; $offset <= $loops*10; $offset += 10) {

  my $results = $google_search ->
    doGoogleSearch(
      $google_key, param('query'), $offset, 10, "false", "",  "false",
      "", "latin1", "latin1"
    );

  last unless @{$results->{resultElements}};

  map { $suffixes{ ($_->{URL} =~ m#://.+?\.(\w{2,4})/#)[0] }++ }
    @{$results->{resultElements}};
}

print map { qq{"$_", "$suffixes{$_}"\n} } sort keys %suffixes;
```

Invoke the script from the command line like so:

```
$ perl suffixcensus_csv.pl query="query" > results.csv
```

Searching for mentions of "colddrink," the South African version of "soda pop," sending the output straight to the screen rather than a *results.csv* file, looks like this:

```
$ perl suffixcensus_csv.pl query="colddrink"
"suffix","count"
"com", "12"
"info", "1"
"net", "1"
"za", "6"
```

Measure Google Mindshare

Measure Google Mindshare

#34 Measure the Google mindshare of a particular person within a query domain.

Based on an idea by author Steven Johnson (*http://www.stevenberlinjohnson. com*), this hack determines the Google *mindshare* of a person within a particular set of Google queried keywords. What's Willy Wonka's Google mindshare of "Willy"? What percentage of "weatherman" does Al Roker hold? Who has the greater "The Beatles" Google mindshare, Ringo Starr or Paul McCartney? More importantly, what Google mindshare of your industry does your company own?

Google mindshare is calculated as follows. Determine the size of the result set for a keyword or phrase. Determine the result set size for that query along with a particular person. Divide the second by the first and multiply by 100, yielding percent Google mindshare. For example: A query for Willy yields about 2,760,000 results. "Willy Wonka" +Willy finds 133,000. We can conclude—however unscientifically—that Willy Wonka holds roughly a 5% ((133,000 / 2,760,000) x 100 = ~ 4.82) Google mindshare of "Willy."

Sure, it's a little silly, but there's probably a grain of truth in it somewhere.

The Code

Save the following code as a CGI script **["How to Run the Hacks" in the Preface]** called *google_mindshare.cgi* in your web site's *cgi-bin* directory.

```perl
#!/usr/local/bin/perl
# google_mindshare.cgi
# This implementation by Rael Dornfest,
# http://www.raelity.org/lang/perl/google/googleshare/
# Based on an idea by Steven Johnson,
# http://www.stevenberlinjohnson.com/movabletype/archives/000009.html

# Your Google API developer's key.
my $google_key='insert key here';

# Location of the GoogleSearch WSDL file.
my $google_wdsl = "./GoogleSearch.wsdl";

use SOAP::Lite;
use CGI qw/:standard *table/;

print
  header( ),
  start_html("Googleshare Calculator"),
  h1("Googleshare Calculator"),
  start_form(-method=>'GET'),
  'Query: ', br( ), textfield(-name=>'query'),
  p( ),
```

```
        'Person: ',br( ), textfield(-name=>'person'),
        p( ),
        submit(-name=>'submit', -value=>'Calculate'),
        end_form( ), p( );

    if (param('query') and param('person')) {
        my $google_search = SOAP::Lite->service("file:$google_wdsl");

        # Query Google for they keyword, keywords, or phrase.
        my $results = $google_search ->
            doGoogleSearch(
                $google_key, '"'.param('query').'"', 0, 1, "false", "", "false",
                "", "latin1", "latin1"
            );

        # Save the results for the Query.
        my $query_count = $results->{estimatedTotalResultsCount};

        my $results = $google_search ->
            doGoogleSearch(
                $google_key, '+"'.param('query').'" +"'.param('person').'"', 0, 1,
                "false", "", "false", "", "latin1", "latin1"
            );
        # Save the results for the Query AND Person.
        my $query_person_count = $results->{estimatedTotalResultsCount};

        print
            p(
                b(sprintf "%s has a %.2f%% googleshare of %s",
                    param('person'),
                    ($query_person_count / $query_count * 100),
                    '"'.param('query').'"'
                )
            )
    }

    print end_html( );
```

Running the Hack

Visit the CGI script in your browser. Enter a query and a person. The name doesn't necessarily have to be a person's full name. It can be a company, location, just about any proper noun, or anything, actually. Click the Calculate button and enjoy. Figure 2-10 shows the Willy Wonka example.

Fun Hack Uses

You can't do too many practical things with this hack, but you can have a lot of fun with it. Playing *unlikely percentages* is fun; see if you can find a name/word combo that gets a higher percentage than other percentages that

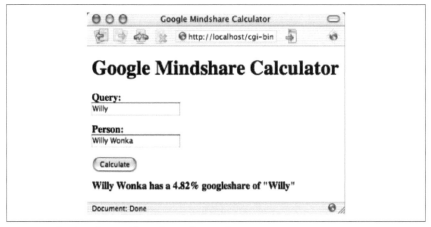

Figure 2-10. Google mindshare for Willy Wonka

you would consider more likely. Here are the answers to the questions posted at the beginning of this hack, and more:

- Willy Wonka has a 4.82% Google mindshare of "Willy."
- Al Roker has a 2.47% Google mindshare of "weatherman."
- Ringo Starr has a 1.55% Google mindshare of "The Beatles."
- Paul McCartney has a 6.95% Google mindshare of "The Beatles."
- Red Hat has a 5.08% Google mindshare of "Linux."
- Microsoft has a 6.87% Google mindshare of "Linux."

 HACK

#35 ## SafeSearch Certify URLs

Feed URLs into Google's SafeSearch to determine whether they point at questionable content.

Only three things in life are certain: death, taxes, and accidentally visiting a once family-safe web site that now contains text and images that would make a horse blush.

As you probably know if you've ever put up a web site, domain names are registered for finite lengths of time. Sometimes registrations accidentally expire; sometimes businesses fold and allow the registrations to expire; sometimes other companies take them over.

Other companies might just want the domain name, some companies want the traffic that the defunct site generated, and in a few cases, the new owners of the domain name try to hold it hostage, offering to sell it back to the original owners for a great deal of money. (This doesn't work as well as it used to because of the dearth of Internet companies that actually have a great deal of money.)

When a site isn't what it once was, that's no big deal. When it's not what it once was and is now X-rated, that's a bigger deal. When it's not what it once was, is now X-rated, and is on the link list of a site you run, that's a really big deal.

But how to keep up with all the links? You can visit each link periodically to determine if it's still okay, you can wait for hysterical emails from site visitors, or you can just not worry about it. Or you can put the Google API to work.

This program lets you check a list of URLs in Google's SafeSearch mode. If they appear in the SafeSearch mode, they're probably okay. If they don't appear, they're either not in Google's index or not "safe" enough to pass through Google's filter. The program then checks the URLs missing from a SafeSearch with a nonfiltered search. If they do not appear in a nonfiltered search, they're labeled as unindexed. If they do appear in a nonfiltered search, they're labeled as "suspect."

Danger, Will Robinson!

While Google's SafeSearch filter is good, it's not infallible. (I have yet to see an automated filtering system that is infallible.) So if you run a list of URLs through this hack and they all show up in a SafeSearch query, don't take that as a guarantee that they're all completely inoffensive. Take it merely as a pretty good indication that they are. If you want absolute assurance, you're going to have to visit every link personally and frequently.

 Here's a fun idea if you need an Internet-related research project. Take 500 or so domain names at random and run this program on the list once a week for several months, saving the results to a file each time. It'd be interesting to see how many domains/URLs end up being filtered out of SafeSearch over time.

The Code

Save the following Perl source code as a text file named *suspect.pl*:

```
#!/usr/local/bin/perl
# suspect.pl
# Feed URLs to a Google SafeSearch. If inurl: returns results, the
# URL probably isn't questionable content. If inurl: returns no
# results, either it points at questionable content or isn't in
# the Google index at all.
```

```perl
# Your Google API developer's key.
my $google_key = 'put your key here';

# Location of the GoogleSearch WSDL file.
my $google_wdsl = "./GoogleSearch.wsdl";

use strict;

use SOAP::Lite;

$|++; # turn off buffering

my $google_search = SOAP::Lite->service("file:$google_wdsl");

# CSV header
print qq{"url","safe/suspect/unindexed","title"\n};

while (my $url = <>) {
  chomp $url;
  $url =~ s!^\w+?://!!;
  $url =~ s!^www\.!!;

  # SafeSearch
  my $results = $google_search ->
      doGoogleSearch(
      $google_key, "inurl:$url", 0, 10, "false", "",  "true",
      "", "latin1", "latin1"
    );

  print qq{"$url",};

  if (grep /$url/, map { $_->{URL} } @{$results->{resultElements}}) {
    print qq{"safe"\n};
  }
  else {
    # unSafeSearch
    my $results = $google_search ->
        doGoogleSearch(
        $google_key, "inurl:$url", 0, 10, "false", "",  "false",
        "", "latin1", "latin1"
      );

    # Unsafe or Unindexed?
    print (
      (scalar grep /$url/, map { $_->{URL} } @{$results->{resultElements}})
        ? qq{"suspect"\n}
        : qq{"unindexed"\n}
      );
  }
}
```

Running the Hack

To run the hack, you'll need a text file that contains the URLs that you want
to check, one line per URL. For example:

```
http://www.oreilly.com/catalog/essblogging/
http://www.xxxxxxxxxx.com/preview/home.htm
hipporhinostricow.com
```

The program runs from the command line **["How to Run the Hacks" in the Preface]**.
Enter the name of the script, a less-than sign, and the name of the text file
that contains the URLs that you want to check. The program will return
results that look like this:

```
% perl suspect.pl < urls.txt
"url","safe/suspect/unindexed"
"oreilly.com/catalog/essblogging/","safe"
"xxxxxxxxxx.com/preview/home.htm","suspect"
"hipporhinostricow.com","unindexed"
```

The first item is the URL being checked, and the second is it's probable
safety rating as follows:

safe
> The URL appeared in a Google SafeSearch for the URL.

suspect
> The URL did not appear in a Google SafeSearch but did in an unfiltered
> search.

unindexed
> The URL appeared in neither a SafeSearch nor unfiltered search.

You can redirect output from the script to a file for import into a spreadsheet or database:

```
% perl suspect.pl < urls.txt > urls.csv
```

Hacking the Hack

You can use this hack interactively, feeding it URLs one at a time. Invoke
the script with perl suspect.pl, but don't feed it a text file of URLs to
check. Enter a URL and hit the return key on your keyboard. The script will
reply in the same manner that it does when fed multiple URLs. This is
handy when you just need to spot-check a couple of URLs on the command
line. When you're ready to quit, break out of the script using Ctrl-D under
Unix or Ctrl-Break on a Windows command line.

Here's a transcript of an interactive session with *suspect.pl*:

```
% perl suspect.pl
"url","safe/suspect/unindexed","title"
```

```
http://www.oreilly.com/catalog/essblogging/
"oreilly.com/catalog/essblogging/","safe"
http://www.xxxxxxxxxx.com/preview/home.htm
"xxxxxxxxxx.com/preview/home.htm","suspect"
hipporhinostricow.com
"hipporhinostricow.com","unindexed"
^d
%
```

HACK #36 Search Google Topics

Run queries against some of the available Google API specialty topics.

Google doesn't talk about it much, but it does make specialty web searches available. And I'm not just talking about searches limited to a certain domain. I'm talking about searches that are devoted to a particular topic (*http://www.google.com/options/specialsearches.html*). The Google API makes four of these searches available: the U.S. Government, Linux, BSD, and Macintosh.

In this hack, we'll look at a program that takes a query from a form and provides a count of that query in each specialty topic, as well as a count of results for each topic. This program runs via a form.

Why Topic Search?

Why would you want to topic search? Because Google currently indexes over eight billion pages. If you try to do more than very specific searches, you might find yourself with far too many results. If you narrow down your search by topic, you can get good results without having to exactly zero in on your search.

You can also use it to do some decidedly unscientific research. Which topic contains more iterations of the phrase "open source"? Which contains the most pages from *.edu* (educational) domains? Which topic, Macintosh or FreeBSD, has more on user interfaces? Which topic holds the most for Monty Python fans?

The Code

Save the following code as a CGI script ["How to Run the Hacks" in the Preface] named *gootopic.cgi* in the *cgi-bin* directory on your web server:

```perl
#!/usr/local/bin/perl
# gootopic.cgi
# Queries across Google Topics (and All of Google), returning
# number of results and top result for each topic.
# gootopic.cgi is called as a CGI with form input
```

```
# Your Google API developer's key.
my $google_key='insert key here';

# Location of the GoogleSearch WSDL file.
my $google_wdsl = "./GoogleSearch.wsdl";

# Google Topics
my %topics = (
  ''       => 'All of Google',
  unclesam => 'U.S. Government',
  linux    => 'Linux',
  mac      => 'Macintosh',
  bsd      => 'FreeBSD'
);

use strict;

use SOAP::Lite;
use CGI qw/:standard *table/;

# Display the query form.
print
  header( ),
  start_html("GooTopic"),
  h1("GooTopic"),
  start_form(-method=>'GET'),
  'Query: ', textfield(-name=>'query'), '   ',
  submit(-name=>'submit', -value=>'Search'),
  end_form( ), p( );

my $google_search = SOAP::Lite->service("file:$google_wdsl");

# Perform the queries, one for each topic area.
if (param('query')) {
  print
    start_table({-cellpadding=>'10', -border=>'1'}),
    Tr([th({-align=>'left'}, ['Topic', 'Count', 'Top Result'])]);

  foreach my $topic (keys %topics) {

    my $results = $google_search ->
      doGoogleSearch(
        $google_key, param('query'), 0, 10, "false", $topic,  "false",
        "", "latin1", "latin1"
      );

    my $result_count = $results->{'estimatedTotalResultsCount'};

    my $top_result = 'no results';

    if ( $result_count ) {
      my $t = @{$results->{'resultElements'}}[0];
```

```
    $top_result =
      b($t->{title}||'no title') . br(  ) .
      a({href=>$t->{URL}, $t->{URL}}) . br() .
      i($t->{snippet}||'no snippet');
  }

  # Output
  print Tr([ td([
    $topics{$topic},
    $result_count,
    $top_result
    ])
  ]);
  }

  print
    end_table( ),
  }

print end_html( );
```

Be sure to replace *insert key here* with your Google API key.

Running the Hack

Point your web browser at *gootopic.cgi*.

Provide a query and the script will search for your query in each special topic area, providing you with an overall ("All of Google") count, topic area count, and the top result for each. Figure 2-11 shows a sample run for "user interface", with Macintosh (surprisingly) not coming out on top.

Search Ideas

Trying to figure out how many pages each topic finds for particular top-level domains (e.g., *.com*, *.edu*, *.uk*) is rather interesting. You can query for inurl: *xx* site:*xx*, where *xx* is the top-level domain you're interested in. For example, inurl:va site:va searches for any of the Vatican's pages in the various topics; there aren't any. inurl:mil site:mil finds an overwhelming number of results in the U.S. Government special topic—no surprise there.

If you are in the mood for a party game, try to find the weirdest possible searches that appear in all the special topics.

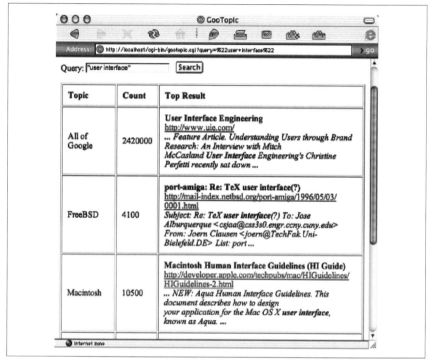

Figure 2-11. *Topic search for "user interface"*

 ## Find the Largest Page

#37

We all know about Feeling Lucky with Google. But how about Feeling Large?

Google sorts your search results by PageRank. Certainly makes sense. Sometimes, however, you may have a substantially different focus in mind and want things ordered in some other manner. Recency is one that comes to mind. Size is another.

In the same manner that Google's "I'm Feeling Lucky" button redirects you to the search result with the highest PageRank, this hack sends you directly to the largest (in kilobytes).

 This hack works rather nicely in combination with repetition [Hack #15].

The Code

Save the following code as a CGI script ["How to Run the Hacks" in the Preface] named *goolarge.cgi* in your web server's *cgi-bin* directory. Be sure to replace *insert key here* with your Google API key.

```perl
#!/usr/local/bin/perl
# goolarge.cgi
# A take-off on "I'm Feeling Lucky," redirects the browser to the largest
# (size in K) document found in the first n results.  n is set by number
# of loops x 10 results per.
# goolarge.cgi is called as a CGI with form input

# Your Google API developer's key.
my $google_key='insert key here';

# Location of the GoogleSearch WSDL file.
my $google_wdsl = "./GoogleSearch.wsdl";

# Number of times to loop, retrieving 10 results at a time.
my $loops = 10;

use strict;

use SOAP::Lite;
use CGI qw/:standard/;

# Display the query form.
unless (param('query')) {
  print
    header( ),
    start_html("GooLarge"),
    h1("GooLarge"),
    start_form(-method=>'GET'),
    'Query: ', textfield(-name=>'query'),
    '   ',
    submit(-name=>'submit', -value=>"I'm Feeling Large"),
    end_form( ), p( );
}

# Run the query.
else {
  my $google_search  = SOAP::Lite->service("file:$google_wdsl");
  my($largest_size, $largest_url);

  for (my $offset = 0; $offset <= $loops*10; $offset += 10) {

    my $results = $google_search ->
      doGoogleSearch(
        $google_key, param('query'), $offset,
        10, "false", "",  "false", "", "latin1", "latin1"
      );

    @{$results->{'resultElements'}} or print p('No results'), last;

    # Keep track of the largest size and its associated URL.
    foreach (@{$results->{'resultElements'}}) {
      substr($_ ->{cachedSize}, 0, -1) > $largest_size and
        ($largest_size, $largest_url) =
```

```
                    (substr($_->{cachedSize}, 0, -1), $_->{URL});
        }
    }

    # Redirect the browser to the largest result.
    print redirect $largest_url;
}
```

Running the Hack

Point your web browser at the *goolarge.cgi* CGI script. Enter a query and click the "I'm Feeling Large" button. You'll be transported directly to the largest page matching your query—within the first specified number of results (the default is 100 results: 10 loops of 10 results apiece), that is.

Usage Examples

Perhaps you're looking for bibliographic information of a famous person. You might find that a regular Google search doesn't net you any more than a mention on a plethora of content-light web pages. Running the same query through this hack sometimes turns up pages with extensive bibliographies.

Maybe you're looking for information about a state. Try queries for the state name along with related information, such as motto, capitol, or state bird.

Hacking the Hack

This hack isn't so much hacked as tweaked. By changing the value assigned to the $loops variable in my $loops = 10;, you can alter the number of results that the script checks before redirecting you to the largest result. Remember, the maximum number of results is the number of loops multiplied by 10 results per loop. The default of 10 considers the top 100 results. A $loops value of 5 would consider only the top 50; 20, the top 200; and so forth.

Perform Proximity Searches

GAPS performs a proximity check between two words.

Sometimes it would be advantageous to search both forward and backward. For example, if you're doing genealogy research, you might find your uncle John Smith as both "John Smith" or "Smith John." Similarly, some pages might include John's middle initial—"John Q Smith" or "Smith John Q."

If all you're after is query permutations, "Permute a Query" [Hack #28] might do the trick.

You might also need to find concepts that exist near each other but don't make up a phrase. For example, you might want to learn about keeping squirrels out of your bird feeder. Various attempts to create a phrase based on this idea might not work, but just searching for several words might not find specific enough results.

GAPS, created by Kevin Shay, allows you to run searches both forward and backward and within a certain number of spaces of each other. GAPS stands for Google API Proximity Search, and that's exactly what this application is: a way to search for topics within a few words of each other without having to run several queries in a row. The program runs the queries and automatically organizes the results.

You enter two terms (there is an option to add more terms that will not be searched for in proximity) and specify how far apart you want them (1, 2, or 3 words). You can specify that the words be found only in the order you request (wordA, wordB) or in either order (wordA, wordB, and wordB, wordA). You can specify how many results you want and in what order they appear (sorted by title, URL, ranking, and proximity).

Search results are formatted much like regular Google results, only a distance ranking is included beside each title. The distance ranking, between one and three, specifies how far apart the two query words were on the page. Figure 2-12 shows a GAPS search for google and hacks within two words of one another, order intact.

Click the distance rating link to pass the generated query on to Google directly.

Making the Most of GAPS

GAPS works best when you have words on the same page that are ambiguously or not at all related to one another. For example, if you're looking for information on Google and search engine optimization (SEO), you might find that searching for the words Google and SEO doesn't find the results that you want, while using GAPS to search for the words Google and SEO within three words of each other finds material focused much more on search engine optimization for Google.

GAPS also works well when you're searching for information about two famous people who might often appear on the same page, though not

Figure 2-12. GAPS search for "google" and "hacks" within two words of one another

necessarily in proximity to each other. For example, you might want information on Bill Clinton and Alan Greenspan, but might find that you're getting too many pages that happen to list the two of them. By searching for their names in proximity to each other, you'll get better results.

Finally, you might find GAPS useful in medical research. Many times your search results will include *index pages* that list several symptoms. However, including symptoms or other medical terms within a few words of each other can help you find more relevant results. Note that this technique will take some experimentation. Many pages about medical conditions contain long lists of symptoms and effects, and there's no reason that one symptom might be within a few words of another.

The Code

The GAPS source code is rather lengthy, so we're not making it available here. You can, however, get it online at *http://www.staggernation.com/gaps/ readme.html.*

See Also

If you like GAPS, you might want to try a couple of other scripts from Staggernation:

GAWSH (http://www.staggernation.com/gawsh)
Stands for Google API Web Search by Host. This program allows you to enter a query and get a list of domains that contain information on that query. If you click on the triangle beside any domain name, you'll get a list of pages in that domain that match your query. This program uses DHTML, which means that it'll only work with Internet Explorer or Mozilla/Netscape.

GARBO (http://www.staggernation.com/garbo)
Stands for Google API Relation Browsing Outliner. Like GAWSH, this program uses DHTML, so it'll work only with Mozilla/Netscape and Internet Explorer. When you enter a URL, GARBO will do a search for either pages that link to the URL you specify or pages related to that URL. Run a search and you'll get a list of URLs with triangles beside them. If you click on a triangle, you'll get a list of pages that either link to the URL you chose or are related to the URL you chose, depending on what you chose in the initial query.

HACK #39 Meander Your Google Neighborhood

Google Neighborhood attempts to detangle the Web by building a "neighborhood" of sites around a URL.

It's called the World Wide Web, not the World Wide Straight Line. Sites link to other sites, building a *web* of sites. And what a tangled web we weave.

Google Neighborhood by the Python-wise Mark Pilgrim (*http://diveintomark.org*) attempts to detangle some small portion of the Web by using the Google API to find sites related to a URL that you provide, scraping the links on the sites returned and building a "neighborhood" of sites that link both the original URL and each other.

If you'd like to give this hack a whirl without having to run it yourself, there's a live version available at *http://diveintomark.org/archives/2002/06/04/who_are_the_people_in_your_neighborhood*. The source code (included in the following section) for Google Neighborhood is available for download from *http://diveintomark.org/projects/misc/neighbor.py.txt*.

The Code

Google Neighborhood is written in the Python (*http://www.python.org*) programming language. Your system will need to have Python installed for you to run this hack.

```
"""Blogroll finder and aggregator"""
```

```
__author__ = "Mark Pilgrim (f8dy@diveintomark.org)"
__copyright__ = "Copyright 2002, Mark Pilgrim"
__license__ = "Python"

try:
    import timeoutsocket # http://www.timo-tasi.org/python/timeoutsocket.py
    timeoutsocket.setDefaultSocketTimeout(10)
except:
    pass
import urllib, urlparse, os, time, operator, sys, pickle, re, cgi, time
from sgmllib import SGMLParser
from threading import *

BUFFERSIZE = 1024
IGNOREEXTS = ('.xml', '.opml', '.rss', '.rdf', '.pdf', '.doc')
INCLUDEEXTS = ('', '.html', '.htm', '.shtml', '.php', '.asp', '.jsp')
IGNOREDOMAINS = ('cgi.alexa.com', 'adserver1.backbeatmedia.com', 'ask.
slashdot.org', 'freshmeat.net', 'readroom.ipl.org', 'amazon.com', 'ringsurf.
com')

def prettyURL(url):
    protocol, domain, path, params, query, fragment = urlparse.urlparse(url)
    if path == '/':
        path = ''
    return urlparse.urlunparse(('', domain, path, '', '', '')).replace('//',
'')

def simplifyURL(url):
    url = url.replace('www.', '')
    url = url.replace('/coming.html', '/')
    protocol, domain, path, params, query, fragment = urlparse.urlparse(url)
    if path == '':
        url = url + '/'
    return url

class MinimalURLOpener(urllib.FancyURLopener):
    def __init__(self, *args):
        apply(urllib.FancyURLopener.__init__, (self,) + args)
        self.addheaders = [('User-agent', '')]
    def http_error_401(self, url, fp, errcode, errmsg, headers, data=None):
        pass

class BlogrollParser(SGMLParser):
    def __init__(self, url):
        SGMLParser.__init__(self)
        self.url = url
        self.reset()

    def reset(self):
        SGMLParser.reset(self)
        self.possible = []
        self.blogroll = []
        self.ina = 0
```

```
    def _goodlink(self, href):
        protocol, domain, path, params, query, fragment = urlparse.
urlparse(href)
        if protocol.lower() <> 'http': return 0
        if self.url.find(domain) <> -1: return 0
        if domain in IGNOREDOMAINS: return 0
        if domain.find(':5335') <> -1: return 0
        if domain.find('.google') <> -1: return 0
        if fragment: return 0
        shortpath, ext = os.path.splitext(path)
        ext = ext.lower()
        if ext in INCLUDEEXTS: return 1
        if ext.lower() in IGNOREEXTS: return 0
        # more rules here?
        return 1

    def _confirmpossibles(self):
        if len(self.possible) >= 4:
            for url in self.possible:
                if url not in self.blogroll:
                    self.blogroll.append(url)
        self.possible = []

    def start_a(self, attrs):
        self.ina = 1
        hreflist = [e[1] for e in attrs if e[0]=='href']
        if not hreflist: return
        href = simplifyURL(hreflist[0])
        if self._goodlink(href):
            self.possible.append(href)

    def end_a(self):
        self.ina = 0

    def handle_data(self, data):
        if self.ina: return
        if data.strip():
            self._confirmpossibles()

    def end_html(self, attrs):
        self.confirmpossibles()

def getRadioBlogroll(url):
    try:
        usock = MinimalURLOpener().open('%s/gems/mySubscriptions.opml' %
url)
        opmlSource = usock.read()
        usock.close()
    except:
        return []
    if opmlSource.find('<opml') == -1: return []
    radioBlogroll = []
```

```
        start = 0
        while 1:
            p = opmlSource.find('htmlUrl="', start)
            if p == -1: break
            refurl = opmlSource[p:p+100].split('"')[1]
            radioBlogroll.append(refurl)
            start = p + len(refurl) + 10
        return radioBlogroll

def getBlogroll(url):
    if url[:7] <> 'http://':
        url = 'http://' + url
    radioBlogroll = getRadioBlogroll(url)
    if radioBlogroll:
        return radioBlogroll
    parser = BlogrollParser(url)
    try:
        usock = MinimalURLOpener().open(url)
        htmlSource = usock.read()
        usock.close()
    except:
        return []
    parser.feed(htmlSource)
    return parser.blogroll

class BlogrollThread(Thread):
    def __init__(self, master, url):
        Thread.__init__(self)
        self.master = master
        self.url = url

    def run(self):
        self.master.callback(self.url, getBlogroll(self.url))

class BlogrollThreadMaster:
    def __init__(self, url, recurse):
        self.blogrollDict = {}
        self.done = 0
        if type(url)==type(''):
            blogroll = getBlogroll(url)
        else:
            blogroll = url
        self.run(blogroll, recurse)

    def callback(self, url, blogroll):
        if not self.done:
            self.blogrollDict[url] = blogroll

    def run(self, blogroll, recurse):
        start = 0
        end = 5
        while 1:
            threads = []
```

```
            for url in blogroll[start:end]:
                if not self.blogrollDict.has_key(url):
                    t = BlogrollThread(self, url)
                    threads.append(t)
            for t in threads:
                t.start()
                time.sleep(0.000001)
            for t in threads:
                time.sleep(0.000001)
                t.join(10)
            start += 5
            end += 5
            if start > len(blogroll): break
        if recurse > 1:
            masterlist = reduce(operator.add, self.blogrollDict.values())
            newlist = [url for url in masterlist if not self.blogrollDict.
has_key(url)]
            self.run(newlist, recurse - 1)
        else:
            self.done = 1

def sortBlogrollData(blogrollDict):
    sortD = {}
    for blogroll in blogrollDict.values():
        for url in blogroll:
            sortD[url] = sortD.setdefault(url, 0) + 1
    sortI = [(v, k) for k, v in sortD.items()]
    sortI.sort()
    sortI.reverse()
    return sortI

def trimdata(sortI, cutoff):
    return [(c, url) for c, url in sortI if c >= cutoff]

def getRelated(url):
    import google
    results = []
    start = 0
    for i in range(3):
        data = google.doGoogleSearch('related:%s' % url, start)
        results.extend([oneResult.URL for oneResult in data.results])
        start += 10
        if len(data.results) < 10: break
    return results

def getNeighborhood(baseURL):
    relatedList = getRelated(baseURL)
    blogrollDict = BlogrollThreadMaster(relatedList, 1).blogrollDict
    neighborhood = sortBlogrollData(blogrollDict)
    neighborhood = trimdata(neighborhood, 2)
    neighborhood = [(c,url, prettyURL(url)) for c,url in neighborhood]
    return neighborhood
```

```
def render_html(baseURL, data):
    output = []
    output.append("""
<table class="socialnetwork" summary="neighborhood for %s">
<caption>Neighborhood for %s</caption>
<thead>
<tr>
<th scope="col">Name</th>
<th scope="col">Links</th>
<th shope="col">Explore</th>
</tr>
</thead>
<tbody>""" % (cgi.escape(prettyURL(baseURL)), cgi.
escape(prettyURL(baseURL))))
    for c, url, title in data:
        output.append("""<tr><td><a href="%s">%s</a></td><td>%s</td><td><a
href="%s">explore</a></td></tr>""" % (url, title, c, 'http://diveintomark.
org/cgi-bin/neighborhood.cgi?url=%s' % cgi.escape(url)))
    output.append("""
</tbody>
</table>""")
    return "".join(output)

def render_rss(baseURL, data):
    title = prettyURL(baseURL)
    channeltitle = "%s neighborhood" % title
    localtime = time.strftime('%Y-%m-%dT%H:%M:%S-05:00', time.localtime())
    output = []
    output.append("""<?xml version="1.0"?>
<rdf:RDF xmlns="http://purl.org/rss/1.0/"
xmlns:rdf="http://www.w3.org/1999/02/22-rdf-syntax-ns#" xmlns:dc="http://
purl.org/dc/elements/1.1/" xmlns:sy="http://purl.org/rss/1.0/modules/
syndication/" xmlns:admin="http://webns.net/mvcb/">

<channel rdf:about="%(baseURL)s">
<title>%(channeltitle)s</title>
<link>%(baseURL)s</link>
<description>Sites in the virtual neighborhood of %(title)s</description>
<language>en-us</language>
<lastBuildDate>%(localtime)s</lastBuildDate>
<pubDate>%(localtime)s</pubDate>
<admin:generatorAgent rdf:resource="http://divintomark.org/cgi-bin/
neighborhood.cgi/?v=1.1" />
<admin:errorReportsTo rdf:resource="mailto:f8dy@diveintomark.org"/>
<sy:updatePeriod>weekly</sy:updatePeriod>
<sy:updateFrequency>1</sy:updateFrequency>
<sy:updateBase>2000-01-01T12:00+00:00</sy:updateBase>
<items>
<rdf:Seq>
""" % locals())
    ##"""
    for c, url, title in data:
        output.append("""<rdf:li rdf:resource="%s" />
```

```
""" % url)
    output.append("""</rdf:Seq>
</items>
</channel>
""")
    for c, url, title in data:
        output.append("""<item rdf:about="%(url)s">
<title>%(title)s</title>
<link>%(url)s</link>
<description>%(c)s links</description>
</item>
""" % locals())
    output.append("""</rdf:RDF>""")
    return "".join(output)

if __name__ == '__main__':
    print render_html(getNeighborhood(sys.argv[1]))
```

You'll also need an HTML form to call the *neighborhood.cgi* script. Here's a simple one:

```
<form action="/cgi-bin/neighborhood.cgi" method="get">
URL: <input name="url" type="text" />
<br />
Output as: <input name="fl" type="radio" value="html" checked="true" /> HTML
<input name="fl" type="radio" value="rss" checked="true" /> RSS
<br />
<input type="submit" value="Meander" />
</form>
```

Save the form as *neighborhood.html*, being sure to alter the action= to point at the location in which you installed the CGI script ["How to Run the Scripts" in the Preface].

Running the Hack

Point your browser at the location of the form you saved just a moment ago. Provide it with the URL that you're interested in using as the center, select HTML or RSS output, and hit the Meander button.

Figure 2-13 shows a representation of Rael's (*raelity.org*'s, to be precise) Google Neighborhood. Clicking on any of the links on the left transports you to the URL shown. More interestingly, the "explore" link shifts your point of view, centering the neighborhood on the associated URL. You can thus meander a neighborhood to your heart's content; don't be surprised, especially in the blogging world, if you keep coming across the same links. Speaking of links, the number listed beneath the "Links" heading represents the number of links the associated site has to the currently focused site.

Figure 2-13. raelity.org's Google Neighborhood

Hacking the Hack

If you want to hack this hack, concentrate your efforts on a small block of code, specifying what file extensions you want to include and exclude, as well as what domains you want to exclude when calculating your neighborhoods:

```
IGNOREEXTS = ('.xml', '.opml', '.rss', '.rdf', '.pdf', '.doc')
INCLUDEEXTS = ('', '.html', '.htm', '.shtml', '.php', '.asp', '.jsp')
IGNOREDOMAINS = ('cgi.alexa.com', 'adserver1.backbeatmedia.com', 'ask.
slashdot.org','freshmeat.net', 'readroom.ipl.org', 'amazon.com',
'ringsurf.com')
```

Noticing/ignoring file extensions. The way the hack is currently written, the neighborhood is built around pretty standard files. However, you could create a neighborhood of sites served by PHP (*http://www.php.net*), including only URLs with a PHP (*.php*) extension. Or perhaps your interest lies in Word documents and PDF files. You'd alter the code as follows:

```
IGNOREEXTS = ('.xml', '.opml', '.rss', '.rdf', '.html', '.htm', '.shtml',
'.php', '.asp', '.jsp')
INCLUDEEXTS = ('', '.pdf', '.doc')
```

Ignoring domains. Sometimes, when building a neighborhood, you might notice that the same links are popping up again and again. They're not really part of the neighborhood but tend to be places that the web pages making up your neighborhood often link to. For example, most Blogger-based weblogs include a link to *http://www.blogger.com* as a matter of course.

Exclude domains that hold no interest to you by adding them to the IGNOREDOMAINS list:

```
IGNOREDOMAINS = ('cgi.alexa.com', 'adserver1.backbeatmedia.com',
'ask.slashdot.org', 'freshmeat.net', 'readroom.ipl.org', 'amazon.com',
'ringsurf.com', 'blogger.com')
```

Run a Google Popularity Contest

Put two terms, spelling variations, animals, vegetables, or minerals head to head in a Google-based popularity contest.

Which is the most popular word? Which spelling is more commonly used? Who gets more mentions, Fred or Ethel Mertz? These and other equally critical questions are answered by Google Smackdown (*http://www.onfocus.com/googlesmack/down.asp*).

Google Smackdown was written by Paul Bausch (*http://www.onfocus.com/*).

Why would you want to compare search counts? Sometimes finding out which terms appear more often can help you develop your queries better. Why use a particular word if it gets almost no results? Comparing misspellings can provide leads on hard-to-find terms or phrases. And sometimes it's just fun to run a popularity contest.

If you're just searching for keywords, Google Smackdown is very simple. Enter one word in each query box, a Google Web API developer's key **[Chapter 9]** if you have one, and click the "throw down!" button. Smackdown will return the winner and approximate count of each search.

If you're planning to use a special syntax, you'll have to be more careful. Unfortunately, the link: syntax doesn't work. Interestingly, phonebook: does; do more people named Smith or Jones live in Boston, MA?

To use any special syntaxes, enclose the query in quotes: "intitle:windows".

The next tip is a little backwards. If you want to specify a phrase, do not use quotes; Smackdown, by default, searches for a phrase. If you want to search for the two words on one page but not necessarily as a phrase (jolly *and* roger versus "jolly roger"), do use quotes. The reason the special syntaxes and phrases work this way is because the program automatically encloses phrases in quotes, and if you add quotes, you're sending a double quoted query to Google (""Google""). When Google runs into a double quote like that, it just strips out all the quotes.

> If you'd like to try a Google Smackdown without having to run it yourself, there's a live version available at: *http://www. onfocus.com/googlesmack/down.asp.*

The Code

Google Smackdown is written for ASP pages running under the Windows operating system and Microsoft Internet Information Server (IIS):

```
<%
'-----------------------------------------------------------
' Set the global variable strGoogleKey.
'-----------------------------------------------------------
Dim strGoogleKey
strGoogleKey = "you rkey goes here. "
'-----------------------------------------------------------
' The function GetResult() is the heart of Google Smackdown.
' It queries Google with a given word or phrase and returns
' the estimated total search results for that word or phrase.
' By running this function twice with the two words the user
' enters into the form, we have our Smackdown.
'-----------------------------------------------------------
Function GetResult(term)
    '-----------------------------------------------------------
    ' Set the variable the contains the SOAP request. A SOAP
    ' software package will generate a similar request to this
    ' one behind the scenes, but the query for this application
    ' is very simple so it can be set "by hand."
    '-----------------------------------------------------------
strRequest = "<?xml version='1.0' encoding='UTF-8'?>" & Chr(13) & Chr(10) &
Chr(13) & Chr(10)
    strRequest = strRequest & "<SOAP-ENV:Envelope xmlns:SOAP-ENV=""http://schemas.
xmlsoap.org/soap/envelope/"" xmlns:xsi=""http://www.w3.org/1999/XMLSchema-
instance"" xmlns:xsd=""http://www.w3.org/1999/XMLSchema"">" & Chr(13) & Chr(10)
    strRequest = strRequest & " <SOAP-ENV:Body>" & Chr(13) & Chr(10)
    strRequest = strRequest & " <ns1:doGoogleSearch xmlns:ns1=""urn:GoogleSearch""
SOAP-ENV:encodingStyle=""http://schemas.xmlsoap.org/soap/encoding/"">" &
Chr(13) & Chr(10)
    strRequest = strRequest & "  <key xsi:type=""xsd:string"">" & strGoogleKey &
"</key>" & Chr(13) & Chr(10)
```

```
strRequest = strRequest & "   <q xsi:type=""xsd:string"">""" & term & """</q>"
& Chr(13) & Chr(10)
strRequest = strRequest & "   <start xsi:type=""xsd:int"">0</start>" & Chr(13)
& Chr(10)
strRequest = strRequest & "   <maxResults xsi:type=""xsd:int"">1</maxResults>"
& Chr(13) & Chr(10)
strRequest = strRequest & "   <filter xsi:type=""xsd:boolean"">true</filter>" &
Chr(13) & Chr(10)
strRequest = strRequest & "   <restrict xsi:type=""xsd:string""></restrict>" &
Chr(13) & Chr(10)
strRequest = strRequest & "   <safeSearch xsi:type=""xsd:boolean"">false</
safeSearch>" & Chr(13) & Chr(10)
strRequest = strRequest & "   <lr xsi:type=""xsd:string""></lr>" & Chr(13) &
Chr(10)
strRequest = strRequest & "   <ie xsi:type=""xsd:string"">latin1</ie>" &
Chr(13) & Chr(10)
strRequest = strRequest & "   <oe xsi:type=""xsd:string"">latin1</oe>" &
Chr(13) & Chr(10)
strRequest = strRequest & " </ns1:doGoogleSearch>" & Chr(13) & Chr(10)
strRequest = strRequest & " </SOAP-ENV:Body>" & Chr(13) & Chr(10)
strRequest = strRequest & "</SOAP-ENV:Envelope>" & Chr(13) & Chr(10)
'-----------------------------------------------------------
' The variable strRequest is now set to the SOAP request.
' Now it's sent to Google via HTTP using the Microsoft
' ServerXMLHTTP component.
'
' Create the object...
'-----------------------------------------------------------
Set xmlhttp = Server.CreateObject("MSXML2.ServerXMLHTTP")

'-----------------------------------------------------------
' Set the variable strURL equal to the URL for Google Web
' Services.
'-----------------------------------------------------------
strURL = "http://api.google.com/search/beta2"

'-----------------------------------------------------------
' Set the object to open the specified URL as an HTTP POST.
'-----------------------------------------------------------
xmlhttp.Open "POST", strURL, false

'-----------------------------------------------------------
' Set the Content-Type header for the request equal to
' "text/xml" so the server knows we're sending XML.
'-----------------------------------------------------------
xmlhttp.setRequestHeader "Content-Type", "text/xml"

'-----------------------------------------------------------
' Send the XML request created earlier to Google via HTTP.
'-----------------------------------------------------------
xmlhttp.Send(strRequest)

'-----------------------------------------------------------
' Set the object AllItems equal to the XML that Google sends
```

```
' back.
'------------------------------------------------------------
Set AllItems = xmlhttp.responseXML


'------------------------------------------------------------
' If the parser hit an error--usually due to malformed XML,
' write the error reason to the user. And stop the script.
' Google doesn't send malformed XML, so this code shouldn't
' run.
'------------------------------------------------------------
If AllItems.parseError.ErrorCode <> 0 Then
 response.write "Error: " & AllItems.parseError.reason
 response.end
End If


'------------------------------------------------------------
' Release the ServerXMLHTTP object now that it's no longer
' needed--to free the memory space it was using.
'------------------------------------------------------------
Set xmlhttp = Nothing


'------------------------------------------------------------
' Look for <faultstring> element in the XML the google has
' returned. If it exists, Google is letting us know that
' something has gone wrong with the request.
'------------------------------------------------------------
Set oError = AllItems.selectNodes("//faultstring")
If oError.length > 0 Then
 Set oErrorText = AllItems.selectSingleNode("//faultstring")
 GetResult = "Error: " & oErrorText.text
 Exit Function
End If


'------------------------------------------------------------
' This is what we're after: the <estimatedTotalResultsCount>
' element in the XML that Google has returned.
'------------------------------------------------------------
Set oTotal = AllItems.selectSingleNode("//estimatedTotalResultsCount")
GetResult = oTotal.text
Set oTotal = Nothing

End Function
'------------------------------------------------------------
' Begin the HTML page. This portion of the page is the same
' for both the initial form and results.
'------------------------------------------------------------
%>
<!DOCTYPE HTML PUBLIC "-//W3C//DTD HTML 4.0 Transitional//EN">
<html>
<head>
 <title>Google Smackdown</title>
 <meta http-equiv="Content-Type" content="text/html; charset=utf-8">
 <script language="JavaScript">
 // This client-side JavaScript function validates user input.
```

```
// If the form fields are empty when the user clicks "submit"
// this will stop the submit action, and prompt the user to
// enter some information.
function checkForm( ) {
 var f = document.frmGSmack
 if ((f.text1.value == '') || (f.text1.value == ' ')) {
  alert('Please enter the first word or phrase.')
  return false;
 }
 if ((f.text2.value == '') || (f.text2.value == ' ')) {
  alert('Please enter the second word or phrase.')
  return false;
 }
 return true;
 }
</script>
</head>
<body>
<h1>Google Smackdown</h1>
```

This queries Google via its API and receives the estimated total results for each word or phrase.

```
<%
'-----------------------------------------------------------
' If the form request items "text1" and "text2" are not
' empty, then the form has been submitted to this page.
'
' It's time to call the GetResult( ) function and see which
' word or phrase wins the Smackdown.
'-----------------------------------------------------------
If request("text1") <> "" AND request("text2") <> "" Then
 '-----------------------------------------------------------
 ' Send the word from the first form field to GetResult( ),
 ' and it will return the estimated total results.
 '-----------------------------------------------------------
 intResult1 = GetResult(request("text1"))

 '-----------------------------------------------------------
 ' Check to make sure the first result is an integer. If not,
 ' Google has returned an error message and the script will
 ' move on.
 '-----------------------------------------------------------
 If isNumeric(intResult1) Then
  intResult2 = GetResult(request("text2"))
 End If

 '-----------------------------------------------------------
 ' Check to make sure the second result is also an integer.
 ' If they're both numeric, the script can display the
 ' results.
 '-----------------------------------------------------------
 If isNumeric(intResult1) AND isNumeric(intResult2) Then
  intResult1 = CDbl(intResult1)
  intResult2 = CDbl(intResult2)
```

```
    '------------------------------------------------------------
    ' Begin writing the results to the page...
    '------------------------------------------------------------
    response.write "<h2>The Results</h2>"
    response.write "And the undisputed champion is...<br>"
    response.write "<ol>"


    '------------------------------------------------------------
    ' Compare the two results to determine which should be
    ' displayed first.
    '------------------------------------------------------------
    If intResult1 > intResult2 Then
      response.write "<li>" & request("text1") & " (<a target=""_blank""
    href=""http://www.google.com/search?hl=en&ie=UTF8&oe=UTF8&q=" & Server.
    URLEncode("""" & request("text1") & """") & """>" & FormatNumber(intResult1,0)
    & "</a>)<br>"
      response.write "<li>" & request("text2") & " (<a target=""_blank""
    href=""http://www.google.com/search?hl=en&ie=UTF8&oe=UTF8&q=" & Server.
    URLEncode("""" & request("text2") & """") & """>" & FormatNumber(intResult2,0)
    & "</a>)<br>"
    Else
      response.write "<li>" & request("text2") & " (<a target=""_blank""
    href=""http://www.google.com/search?hl=en&ie=UTF8&oe=UTF8&q=" & Server.
    URLEncode("""" & request("text2") & """") & """>" & FormatNumber(intResult2,0)
    & "</a>)<br>"
      response.write "<li>" & request("text1") & " (<a target=""_blank""
    href=""http://www.google.com/search?hl=en&ie=UTF8&oe=UTF8&q=" & Server.
    URLEncode("""" & request("text1") & """") & """>" & FormatNumber(intResult1,0)
    & "</a>)<br>"
    End If
    '------------------------------------------------------------
    ' Finish writing the results to the page and include a link
    ' to the page for another round.
    '------------------------------------------------------------
    response.write "</ol>"
    response.write "<a href=""smackdown.asp"">Another Challenge?</a>"
    response.write "<br>"
  Else
    '------------------------------------------------------------
    ' One or both of the results are not numeric. We can assume
    ' this is because the developer's key has reached its
    ' 1,000 query limit for the day. Because the script has
    ' made it to this point, the SOAP response did not return
    ' an error. If it had, GetResult() would have stopped the
    ' script.
    '------------------------------------------------------------
    intResult1 = Replace(intResult1,"key " & strGoogleKey,"key")
    intResult2 = Replace(intResult2,"key " & strGoogleKey,"key")


    '------------------------------------------------------------
    ' Write out the error to the user...
    '------------------------------------------------------------
```

```
    response.write "<h2>It Didn't Work, Error</h2>"
    '----------------------------------------------------------
    ' If the results are the same, we don't need to write out
    ' both of them.
    '----------------------------------------------------------
    If intResult1 = intResult2 Then
     response.write intResult1 & "<br><br>"
    Else
     response.write intResult1 & "<br><br>" & intResult2 & "<br><br>"
    End If
    '----------------------------------------------------------
    ' A link to the script for another round.
    '----------------------------------------------------------
    response.write "<a href=""smackdown.asp"">Another Challenge?</a>"
    response.write "<br>"
   End If
Else
'----------------------------------------------------------
' The form request items "text1" and "text2" are empty,
' which means the form has not been submitted to the page
' yet.
'----------------------------------------------------------
%>
<h2>The Arena</h2>
<div class="clsPost">The setting is the most impressive search engine ever
built: <a href="http://www.google.com/">Google</a>. As a test of its <a
href="http://www.google.com/apis">API</a>, two words or phrases will go head-
to-head in a terabyte tug-of-war. Which one appears in more pages across the
Web?
<h2>The Challengers</h2>
You choose the warring words...
<br><br>
<form name="frmGSmack" action="smackdown.asp" method="post" onSubmit="return
checkForm( );">
<table>
 <tr>
  <td align="right">word/phrase 1</td> <td><input type="text" name="text1"></
td>
 </tr>
 <tr>
  <td align="right">word/phrase 2</td> <td><input type="text" name="text2"></
td>
 </tr>
 <tr>
  <td> </td><td><input type="submit" value="throw down!"></td>
 </tr>
</table>
</form>
<%
End If
'----------------------------------------------------------
' This is the end of the If statement that checks to see
' if the form has been submitted. Both states of the page
```

```
' get the closing tags below.
'----------------------------------------------------------------
%>
</body>
</html>
```

Running the Hack

The hack is run in exactly the same manner as the live version of Google Smackdown (*http://www.onfocus.com/googlesmack/down.asp*) running on Onfocus.com. Point your web browser at it and fill out the form. Figure 2-14 shows a sample Smackdown between negative feelings about Macintosh versus Windows.

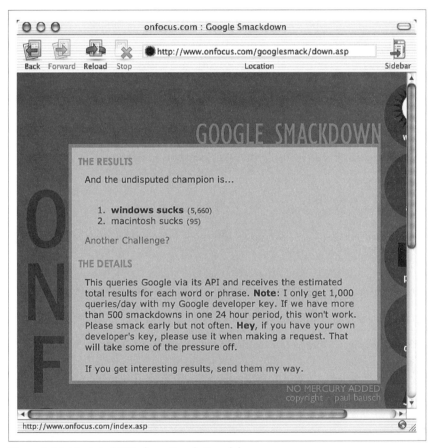

Figure 2-14. Macintosh/Windows Google Smackdown

Scrape Yahoo! Buzz for a Google Search

A proof-of-concept hack scrapes the buzziest items from Yahoo! Buzz and submits them to a Google search.

No web site is an island. Billions of hyperlinks link to billions of documents. Sometimes, however, you want to take information from one site and apply it to another site.

Unless that site has a web service API like Google's, your best bet is scraping. Scraping is where you use an automated program to remove specific bits of information from a web page. Examples of the sorts of elements people scrape include stock quotes, news headlines, prices, and so forth. You name it and someone's probably scraped it.

There's some controversy about scraping. Some sites don't mind it, while others can't stand it. If you decide to scrape a site, do it gently; take the minimum amount of information you need and, whatever you do, don't hog the scrapee's bandwidth.

So, what are we scraping?

Google has a query popularity page called Google Zeitgeist (*http://www.google.com/press/zeitgeist.html*). Unfortunately, the Zeitgeist is updated only once a week and contains only a limited amount of scrapable data. That's where Yahoo! Buzz (*http://buzz.yahoo.com*) comes in. The site is rich with constantly updated information. Its Buzz Index keeps tabs on what's hot in popular culture: celebs, games, movies, television shows, music, and more.

This hack grabs the buzziest of the buzz, the top of the Leaderboard, and searches Google for all it knows on the subject. And to keep things current, only pages indexed by Google within the past few days **[Hack #16]** are considered.

This hack requires additional Perl modules: *Time::JulianDay* (*http://search.cpan.org/search?query=Time%3A%3AJulianDay*) and *LWP::Simple* (*http://search.cpan.org/search?query=LWP%3 A%3ASimple*). It won't run without them.

The Code

Save the following code to a plain text file named *buzzgle.pl*:

```
#!/usr/local/bin/perl
# buzzgle.pl
# Pull the top item from the Yahoo! Buzz Index and query the last
# three day's worth of Google's index for it.
# Usage: perl buzzgle.pl
```

```perl
# Your Google API developer's key.
my $google_key='insert key here';

# Location of the GoogleSearch WSDL file.
my $google_wdsl = "./GoogleSearch.wsdl";

# Number of days back to go in the Google index.
my $days_back = 3;

use strict;

use SOAP::Lite;
use LWP::Simple;
use Time::JulianDay;

# Scrape the top item from the Yahoo! Buzz Index.

# Grab a copy of http://buzz.yahoo.com.

my $buzz_content = get("http://buzz.yahoo.com/")
  or die "Couldn't grab the Yahoo Buzz: $!";

# Find the first item on the Buzz Index list.
my($buzziest) =  $buzz_content =~ m!http://search.yahoo.com/search\?p=.+">(.
+?)<\/a>!i;
die "Couldn't figure out the Yahoo! buzz\n" unless $buzziest;

# Figure out today's Julian date.
my $today = int local_julian_day(time);

# Build the Google query.
my $query = "\"$buzziest\" daterange:" . ($today - $days_back) . "-$today";

print
  "The buzziest item on Yahoo Buzz today is: $buzziest\n",
  "Querying Google for: $query\n",
  "Results:\n\n";

# Create a new SOAP::Lite instance, feeding it GoogleSearch.wsdl.
my $google_search = SOAP::Lite->service("file:$google_wdsl");

# Query Google.
my $results = $google_search ->
    doGoogleSearch(
      $google_key, $query, 0, 10, "false", "",  "false",
      "", "latin1", "latin1"
    );

# No results?
@{$results->{resultElements}} or die "No results";

# Loop through the results.
foreach my $result (@{$results->{'resultElements'}}) {
```

```
my $output =
 join "\n",
 $result->{title} || "no title",
 $result->{URL},
 $result->{snippet} || 'no snippet',
 "\n";
     $output =~ s!<.+?>!!g; # drop all HTML tags
     print $output;
}
```

Running the Hack

The script runs from the command line ["How to Run the Hacks" in the Preface] without need of arguments of any kind. Probably the best thing to do is to direct the output to a pager (a command-line application that allows you to page through long output, usually by hitting the spacebar), like so:

```
% perl buzzgle.pl | more
```

Or you can direct the output to a file for later perusal:

```
% perl buzzgle.pl > buzzgle.txt
```

As with all scraping applications, this code is fragile, subject to breakage if (read: when) HTML formatting of the Yahoo! Buzz page changes. If you find you have to adjust to match Yahoo!'s formatting, you'll have to alter the regular expression match as appropriate:

```
my($buzziest) = $buzz_content =~ m!http://search.yahoo.com/search\?p=.+">(.
+?)<\/a>!i;
```

> Regular expressions and general HTML scraping are beyond the scope of this book. For more information, I suggest you consult O'Reilly's *Perl and LWP* (*http://www.oreilly.com/catalog/perllwp*) or *Mastering Regular Expressions* (*http://www.oreilly.com/catalog/regex*).

The Results

At the time of this writing, Maria Sharapova, the Russian tennis star, is all the rage:

```
% perl buzzgle.pl | less
The buzziest item on Yahoo Buzz today is: Maria Sharapova
Querying Google for: "Maria Sharapova" daterange:2453292-2453295
Results:
Maria Sharapova
http://www.mariaworld.net/
everything about Maria Sharapova: photos, interviews, articles, statistics,
results and much more! ... Maria Sharapova: 2004 Tokyo Champion! ...
Maria Sharapova
http://www.mariaworld.net/photos.htm
```

everything about Maria Sharapova: photos, interviews, articles, statistics,
results and much more! HOME, BIOGRAPHY, PHOTOS, RESULTS, ...
Maria Sharapova Picture Page
http://milano.vinden.nl/
Maria Sharapova Picture Page. Country: Russia. Date of Birth: April 19,
1987. Place of Birth: Nyagan, Russia. Residence: Bradenton, Florida USA.
Height: 1.83 metres ...

Hacking the Hack

Here are some ideas for hacking the hack:

- As it stands, the program returns 10 results. You could change that to one result and immediately open that result instead of returning a list. Bravo, you've just written I'm Feeling Popular, as in Google's I'm Feeling Lucky.

- This version of the program searches the last three days of indexed pages. Because there's a slight lag in indexing news stories, I would index at least the last two days' worth of indexed pages, but you could extend it to seven days or even a month. Simply change my $days_back = 3;, altering the value of the $days_back variable.

- You could create a "Buzz Effect" hack by running the Yahoo! Buzz query with and without the date range limitation. How do the results change between a full search and a search of the last few days?

- Yahoo!'s Buzz has several different sections. This one looks at the Buzz summary, but you could create other ones based on Yahoo!'s other buzz charts (television, *http://buzz.yahoo.com/television/*, for instance).

Compare Google's Results with Other Search
#42 Engines

Compare Google search results with results from other search engines.

True Google fanatics might not like to think so, but there's really more than one search engine. Google's competitors include the likes of Teoma and Yahoo!.

Equally surprising to the average Google fanatic is the fact that Google doesn't index the entire Web. There are, at the time of this writing, over eight billion web pages in the Google index, but that's just a fraction of the Web. You'd be amazed how much nonoverlapping content there is in each search engine. Some queries that bring only a few results on one search engine bring plenty on another search engine.

This hack gives you a program that compares counts for Google and several other search engines, with an easy way to plug in new search engines that you want to include. This version of the hack searches different domains for the query, in addition to getting the full count for the query itself.

 This hack requires the *LWP::Simple* (*http://search.cpan.org/ search?query=LWP%3A%3ASimple*) module to run.

The Code

Save the following code as a CGI script **["How to Run the Hacks" in the Preface]** named *google_compare.cgi* in your web site's *cgi-bin* directory:

```perl
#!/usr/local/bin/perl
# google_compare.cgi
# Compares Google results against those of other search engines.

# Your Google API developer's key.
my $google_key='insert key here';

# Location of the GoogleSearch WSDL file.
my $google_wdsl = "./GoogleSearch.wsdl";

use strict;

use SOAP::Lite;
use LWP::Simple qw(get);
use CGI qw{:standard};

my $googleSearch = SOAP::Lite->service("file:$google_wdsl");

# Set up our browser output.
print "Content-type: text/html\n\n";
print "<html><title>Google Compare Results</title><body>\n";

# Ask and we shell receive.
my $query = param('query');
unless ($query) {
    print "<h1>No query defined.</h1></body></html>\n\n";
    exit; # If there's no query there's no program.
}

# Spit out the original before we encode.
print "<h1>Your original query was '$query'.</h1>\n";

$query =~ s/\s/\+/g ;   #changing the spaces to + signs
$query =~ s/\"/%22/g;  #changing the quotes to %22

# Create some hashes of queries for various search engines.
# We have four types of queries ("plain", "com", "edu", and "org"),
# and three search engines ("Google", "AlltheWeb", and "Altavista").
# Each engine has a name, query, and regular expression used to
```

```
# scrape the results.
my $query_hash = {
   plain => {
      Google => { name => "Google", query => $query, },
      AlltheWeb => {
         name    => "AlltheWeb",
         regexp => '<span class="ofSoMany">(.*)</span>',
         query  => "http://www.alltheweb.com/search?cat=web&q=$query",
      },
      Altavista => {
         name  => "Altavista",
         regexp => 'AltaVista found (.*) results',
         query => "http://www.altavista.com/sites/search/web?q=$query",
      }
   },
   com => {
      Google => { name => "Google", query => "$query site:com", },
      AlltheWeb => {
         name    => "AlltheWeb",
         regexp => '<span class="ofSoMany">(.*)</span>',
         query  => "http://www.alltheweb.com/
search?cat=web&q=$query+domain%3Acom",
      },
      Altavista => {
         name  => "Altavista",
         regexp => 'AltaVista found (.*) results',
         query => "http://www.altavista.com/sites/search/
web?q=$query+domain%3Acom",
      }
   },
   org => {
      Google => { name => "Google", query => "$query site:org", },
      AlltheWeb => {
         name    => "AlltheWeb",
         regexp => '<span class="ofSoMany">(.*)</span>',
         query  => "http://www.alltheweb.com/
search?cat=web&q=$query+domain%3Aorg",
      },
      Altavista => {
         name  => "Altavista",
         regexp => 'AltaVista found (.*) results',
         query => "http://www.altavista.com/sites/search/
web?q=$query+domain%3Aorg",
      }
   },
   net => {
      Google => { name => "Google", query => "$query site:net", },
      AlltheWeb => {
         name    => "AlltheWeb",
         regexp => '<span class="ofSoMany">(.*)</span>',
         query  => "http://www.alltheweb.com/
search?cat=web&q=$query+domain%3Anet",
      },
```

```
      Altavista => {
         name   => "Altavista",
         regexp => 'AltaVista found (.*) results',
         query  => "http://www.altavista.com/sites/search/
web?q=$query+domain%3Anet",
      }
   }
};

# Now we loop through each of our query types
# under the assumption there's a matching
# hash that contains our engines and string.
foreach my $query_type (keys (%$query_hash)) {
   print "<h2>Results for a '$query_type' search:</h2>\n";

   # Now, loop through each engine we have and get/print the results.
   foreach my $engine (values %{$query_hash->{$query_type}}) {
      my $results_count;

      # If this is Google, we use the API and not port 80.
      if ($engine->{name} eq "Google") {
         my $result = $googleSearch->doGoogleSearch(
            $google_key, $engine->{query}, 0, 1,
            "false", "", "false", "", "latin1", "latin1");
         $results_count = $result->{estimatedTotalResultsCount};
         # The Google API doesn't format numbers with commas.
         my $rresults_count = reverse $results_count;
         $rresults_count =~ s/(\d\d\d)(?=\d)(?!\d*\.)/$1,/g;
         $results_count = scalar reverse $rresults_count;
      }

      # It's not Google, so we GET like everyone else.
      elsif ($engine->{name} ne "Google") {
         my $data = get($engine->{query}) or print "ERROR: $!";
         $data =~ /$engine->{regexp}/; $results_count = $1 || 0;
      }

      # and print out the results.
      print "<strong>$engine->{name}</strong>: $results_count<br />\n";
   }
}
```

Running the Hack

This hack runs as a CGI script, called from your web browser as google_
compare.cgi?query=*your query keywords*.

Why?

You might be wondering why you would want to compare result counts
across search engines. It's a good idea to follow what different search

engines offer in terms of results. While you might find that a phrase on one search engine provides only a few results, another engine might return results aplenty. It makes sense to spend your time and energy using the latter for the research at hand.

—*Tara Calishain and Kevin Hemenway*

HACK #43 Scattersearch with Yahoo! and Google

Sometimes, illuminating results can be found when scraping from one site and feeding the results into the API of another. With scattersearching, you can narrow down the most popular related results, as suggested by Yahoo! and Google.

We've combined a scrape of a Yahoo! web page with a Google search **[Hack #41]**, blending scraped data with data generated via a web service API to good effect. In this hack, we're doing something similar, except this time we're taking the results of a Yahoo! search and blending it with a Google search.

Yahoo! has a "Related searches" feature, where you enter a search term and get a list of related terms under the search box, if any are available. This hack scrapes those related terms and performs a Google search for the related terms in the title. It then returns the count for those searches, along with a direct link to the results. Aside from showing how scraped and API-generated data can live together in harmony, this hack is good to use when you're exploring concepts; for example, you might know that something called *Pokemon* exists, but you might not know anything about it. You'll get Yahoo!'s related searches and an idea of how many results each of those searches generates in Google. From there, you can choose the search terms that generate the most results or look the most promising based on your limited knowledge, or you can simply pick a road that appears less traveled.

The Code

Save the following code to a file called *scattersearch.pl*.

Bear in mind that this hack, while using the Google API for the Google portion, involves some scraping of Yahoo!'s search pages and thus is rather brittle. If it stops working at any point, take a gander at the regular expressions for they're almost sure to be the breakage point.

```
#!/usr/bin/perl -w
#
# Scattersearch -- Use the search suggestions from
# Yahoo! to build a series of intitle: searches at Google.
```

```perl
use strict;

use LWP;
use SOAP::Lite;
use CGI qw/:standard/;

# Get our query, else die miserably.
my $query = shift @ARGV; die unless $query;

# Your Google API developer's key.
my $google_key = 'insert key here';

# Location of the GoogleSearch WSDL file.
my $google_wdsl = "./GoogleSearch.wsdl";

# Search Yahoo! for the query.
my $ua  = LWP::UserAgent->new;
my $url = URI->new('http://search.yahoo.com/search');
$url->query_form(rs => "more", p => $query);
my $yahoosearch = $ua->get($url)->content;
$yahoosearch =~ s/[\f\t\n\r]//isg;

# And determine if there were any results.
$yahoosearch =~ m!Also try:(.*?)  !migs;
die "Sorry, there were no results!\n" unless $1;
my $recommended = $1;

# Now, add all our results into
# an array for Google processing.
my @googlequeries;
while ($recommended =~ m!<a href=".*?">(.*?)</a>!mgis) {
    my $searchitem = $1;
    $searchitem =~ s/nobr|<[^>]*>|\///g;
    print "$searchitem\n";
    push (@googlequeries, $searchitem);
}

# Print our header for the results page.
print join "\n",
start_html("ScatterSearch"),
    h1("Your Scattersearch Results"),
    p("Your original search term was '$query'"),
    p("That search had " . scalar(@googlequeries). " recommended terms."),
    p("Here are result numbers from a Google search"),
    CGI::start_ol(  );

# Create our Google object for API searches.
my $gsrch = SOAP::Lite->service("file:$google_wdsl");

# Running the actual Google queries.
foreach my $googlesearch (@googlequeries) {
    my $titlesearch = "allintitle:$googlesearch";
```

```
my $count = $gsrch->doGoogleSearch($google_key, $titlesearch,
                            0, 1, "false", "",  "false",
                            "", "", "");
my $url = $googlesearch; $url =~ s/ /+/g; $url =~ s/\"/%22/g;
print li("There were $count->{estimatedTotalResultsCount} ".
        "results for the recommended search <a href=\"http://www.".
        "google.com/search?q=$url&num=100\">$googlesearch</a>");
}

print CGI::end_ol(  ), end_html;
```

Running the Hack

This script generates an HTML file, ready for you to upload to a publicly accessible web site. If you want to save the output of a search for siamese to a file called *scattersearch.html* in your *Sites* directory, run the following command ["How to Run the Hacks" in the Preface]:

```
% perl scattersearch.pl "siamese" > ~/Sites/scattersearch.html
```

Your final results, as rendered by your browser, will look similar to Figure 2-15.

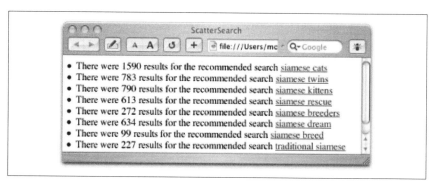

Figure 2-15. Scattersearch results for siamese

You'll have to do a little experimenting to find out which terms have related searches. Broadly speaking, very general search terms are bad; it's better to zero in on terms that people would search for and that would be easy to group together. At the time of this writing, for example, heart has no related search terms, but blood pressure does.

Hacking the Hack

You have two choices: you can either hack the interaction with Yahoo! or expand it to include something in addition to or instead of Yahoo! itself. Let's look at Yahoo! first. If you take a close look at the code, you'll see we're passing an unusual parameter to our Yahoo! search results page:

```
$url->query_form(rs => "more", p => $query);
```

The rs=>"more" part of the search shows the related search terms. Getting the related search this way will show up to 10 results. If you remove that portion of the code, you'll get roughly four related searches when they're available. That might suit you if you want only a few, but perhaps you want dozens and dozens! In that case, replace more with all.

Beware, though: this can generate a lot of related searches, and it can certainly eat up your daily allowance of Google API requests. Tread carefully.

—*Kevin Hemenway and Tara Calishain*

HACK #44 Yahoo! Directory Mindshare in Google

How does link popularity compare in Yahoo!'s searchable subject index versus Google's full-text index? Find out by calculating mindshare!

Yahoo! and Google are two very different animals. Yahoo! indexes only a site's main URL, title, and description, while Google builds full-text indexes of entire sites. Surely there's some interesting cross-pollination when you combine results from the two.

This hack scrapes all the URLs in a specified subcategory of the Yahoo! directory. It then takes each URL and gets its link count from Google. Each link count provides a nice snapshot of how a particular Yahoo! category and its listed sites stack up on the popularity scale.

> What's a *link count*? It's simply the total number of pages in Google's index that link to a specific URL.

There are a couple of ways you can use your knowledge of a subcategory's link count. If you find a subcategory whose URLs have only a few links each in Google, you may have found a subcategory that isn't getting a lot of attention from Yahoo!'s editors. Consider going elsewhere for your research. If you're a webmaster and you're considering paying to have Yahoo! add you to their directory, run this hack on the category in which you want to be listed. Are most of the links really popular? If they are, are you sure your site will stand out and get clicks? Maybe you should choose a different category.

We got this idea from a similar experiment Jon Udell (*http://weblog. infoworld.com/udell/*) did in 2001. He used AltaVista instead of Google; see *http://udell.roninhouse.com/download/mindshare-script.txt*. We appreciate the inspiration, Jon!

The Code

You will need a Google API account (*http://api.google.com*), as well as the *SOAP::Lite* (*http://www.soaplite.com*) and *HTML::LinkExtor* (*http://search. cpan.org/author/GAAS/HTML-Parser/lib/HTML/LinkExtor.pm*) Perl modules to run this hack.

Save the code as *mindshare_calculator.pl*, remembering to replace *insert key here* with your Google API key:

```perl
#!/usr/bin/perl -w

use strict;
use LWP::Simple;
use HTML::LinkExtor;
use SOAP::Lite;

my $google_key  = 'insert key here';
my $google_wdsl = "GoogleSearch.wsdl";
my $yahoo_dir   = shift || "/Computers_and_Internet/Data_Formats/XML__".
                  "eXtensible_Markup_Language_/RSS/News_Aggregators/";

# Download the Yahoo! directory.
my $data = get("http://dir.yahoo.com" . $yahoo_dir) or die $!;

# Create our Google object.
my $google_search = SOAP::Lite->service("file:$google_wdsl");
my %urls; # where we keep our counts and titles.

# Extract all the links and parse 'em.
HTML::LinkExtor->new(\&mindshare)->parse($data);
sub mindshare { # for each link we find...

    my ($tag, %attr) = @_;

    # Continue on only if the tag was a link,
    # and the URL matches Yahoo!'s redirectory.
    return if $tag ne 'a';
    return unless $attr{href} =~ /rds.yahoo/;
    return unless $attr{href} =~ /\*http/;

    # Now get our real URL.
    $attr{href} =~ /\*(http.*)/; my $url = $1;
      $url =~ s/%3A/:/; # turn encoding into legits.

    # And process each URL through Google.
    my $results = $google_search->doGoogleSearch(
                    $google_key, "link:$url", 0, 1,
                    "true", "", "false", "", "", ""
                ); # wheee, that was easy, guvner.
    $urls{$url} = $results->{estimatedTotalResultsCount};
}
```

```
# Now sort and display.
my @sorted_urls = sort { $urls{$b} <=> $urls{$a} } keys %urls;
foreach my $url (@sorted_urls) { print "$urls{$url}: $url\n"; }
```

Running the Hack

The hack has its only configuration—the Yahoo! directory you're interested in—passed as a single argument (in quotes) on the command line ["How to Run the Scripts" in the Preface]. If you don't pass one of your own, a default directory will be used instead.

```
% perl mindshare_calculator.pl "/Entertainment/Humor/Procrastination/"
```

Your results show the URLs in those directories, sorted by total Google links:

```
340: http://www.p45.net/
246: http://www.ishouldbeworking.com/
81: http://www.india.com/
33: http://www.jlc.net/~useless/
23: http://www.geocities.com/SouthBeach/1915/
18: http://www.eskimo.com/~spban/creed.html
13: http://www.black-schaffer.org/scp/
3: http://www.angelfire.com/mi/psociety
2: http://www.geocities.com/wastingstatetime/
```

Hacking the Hack

Yahoo! isn't the only searchable subject index out there, of course. There's also the Open Directory Project (DMOZ, *http://www.dmoz.org*), which is the product of thousands of volunteers busily cataloging and categorizing sites on the Web—the web community's Yahoo!, if you will. This hack works just as well on DMOZ as it does on Yahoo!; they're very similar in structure.

Replace the default Yahoo! directory with its DMOZ equivalent:

```
my $dmoz_dir = shift || "/Reference/Libraries/Library_and_Information_RETURN
Science/Technical_Services/Cataloguing/Metadata/RDF/Applications/RSS/RETURN
News_Readers/";
```

You'll also need to change the download instructions:

```
# Download the Dmoz.org directory.
my $data = get("http://dmoz.org" . $dmoz_dir) or die $!;
```

Next, replace the lines that check whether a URL should be measured for mindshare. When we were scraping Yahoo! in our original script, all directory entries were always prepended with *http://srd.yahoo.com/* and then the URL itself. Thus, to ensure we received a proper URL, we skipped over the link unless it matched that criteria:

```
return unless $attr{href} =~ /srd.yahoo/;
return unless $attr{href} =~ /\*http/;
```

Since DMOZ is an entirely different site, our checks for validity have to change. DMOZ doesn't modify the outgoing URL, so our previous Yahoo! checks have no relevance here. Instead, we'll make sure it's a full-blooded location (i.e., it starts with *http://*) and it doesn't match any of DMOZ's internal page links. Likewise, we'll ignore searches on other engines:

```
return unless $attr{href} =~ /^http/;
return if $attr{href} =~ /dmoz|google|altavista|lycos|yahoo|alltheweb/;
```

Our last change is to modify the bit of code that gets the real URL from Yahoo!'s modified version. Instead of "finding the URL within the URL":

```
# Now get our real URL.
$attr{href} =~ /\*(http.*)/; my $url = $1;
```

we simply assign the URL that *HTML::LinkExtor* has found:

```
# Now get our real URL.
my $url = $attr{href};
```

Can you go even further with this? Sure! You might want to search a more specialized directory, such as the FishHoo! fishing search engine (*http:// www.fishhoo.com*).

You might want to return only the most linked-to URL from the directory, which is quite easy, by piping the results ["How to Run the Hacks" in the Preface] to another common Unix utility:

```
% perl mindshare_calculator.pl | head 1
```

Alternatively, you might want to go ahead and grab the top 10 Google matches for the URL that has the most mindshare. To do so, add the following code to the bottom of the script:

```
print "\nMost popular URLs for the strongest mindshare:\n";
my $most_popular = shift @sorted_urls;
my $results = $google_search->doGoogleSearch(
                $google_key, "$most_popular", 0, 10,
                "true", "", "false", "", "", "" );

foreach my $element (@{$results->{resultElements}}) {
  next if $element->{URL} eq $most_popular;
  print " * $element->{URL}\n";
  print "   \"$element->{title}\"\n\n";
}
```

Then, run the script as usual (the output here uses the default hardcoded directory).

```
% perl mindshare_calculator.pl
27800: http://radio.userland.com/
6670: http://www.oreillynet.com/meerkat/
```

```
5460: http://www.newsisfree.com/
3280: http://ranchero.com/software/netnewswire/
1840: http://www.disobey.com/amphetadesk/
847: http://www.feedreader.com/
797: http://www.serence.com/site.php?page=prod_klipfolio
674: http://bitworking.org/Aggie.html
492: http://www.newzcrawler.com/
387: http://www.sharpreader.net/
112: http://www.awasu.com/
102: http://www.bloglines.com/
67: http://www.blueelephantsoftware.com/
57: http://www.blogtrack.com/
50: http://www.proggle.com/novobot/
```

```
Most popular URLs for the strongest mindshare:
  * http://groups.yahoo.com/group/radio-userland/
    "Yahoo! Groups : radio-userland"

  * http://groups.yahoo.com/group/radio-userland-francophone/message/76
    "Yahoo! Groupes : radio-userland-francophone Messages : Message 76 ... "

  * http://www.fuzzygroup.com/writing/radiouserland_faq.htm
    "Fuzzygroup :: Radio UserLand FAQ"
...
```

—Kevin Hemenway and Tara Calishain

Glean Weblog-Free Google Results

HACK #45

> With so many weblogs being indexed by Google, you might worry about too much emphasis on the hot topic of the moment. In this hack, we'll show you how to remove the weblog factor from your Google results.

Weblogs—those frequently updated, link-heavy personal pages—are quite the fashionable thing these days. There are at least 4,000,000 active weblogs across the Internet, covering almost every possible subject and interest. For humans, they're good reading, but for search engines, they're heavenly bundles of fresh content and links galore.

Some people think that the search engine's delight in weblogs slants search results by placing too much emphasis on too small a group of recent rather than evergreen content. As I write, for example, I am the twelfth most important Ben on the Internet, according to Google. This rank comes solely from my weblog's popularity.

This hack searches Google, discarding any results coming from weblogs. It uses the Google Web Services API (*http://api.google.com*) and the API of Technorati (*http://www.technorati.com/members*), an excellent interface to David Sifry's weblog data-tracking tool. Both APIs require keys, available from the URLs mentioned.

Finally, you'll need a simple HTML page with a form that passes a text query to the parameter q (the query that will run on Google), something like this:

```
<form action="googletech.cgi" method="POST">
Your query: <input type="text" name="q">
<input type="submit" name="Search!" value="Search!">
</form>
```

Save the form as googletech.html.

The Code

Save the following code ["How to Run the Hacks" in the Preface] to a file called *googletech.cgi*.

 You'll need the *XML::Simple* and *SOAP::Lite* Perl modules to run this hack.

```perl
#!/usr/bin/perl -w
# googletech.cgi
# Getting Google results
# without getting weblog results.
use strict;
use SOAP::Lite;
use XML::Simple;
use CGI qw(:standard);
use HTML::Entities ( );
use LWP::Simple qw(!head);

my $technoratikey = "insert technorati key here";
my $googlekey = "insert google key here";

# Set up the query term
# from the CGI input.
my $query = param("q");

# Initialize the SOAP interface and run the Google search.
my $google_wdsl = "http://api.google.com/GoogleSearch.wsdl";
my $service = SOAP::Lite->service->($google_wdsl);

# Start returning the results page;
# do this now to prevent timeouts.
my $cgi = new CGI;

print $cgi->header( );
print $cgi->start_html(-title=>'Blog Free Google Results');
print $cgi->h1('Blog Free Results for '. "$query");
print $cgi->start_ul( );
```

```
# Go through each of the results.
foreach my $element (@{$result->{'resultElements'}}) {

    my $url = HTML::Entities::encode($element->{'URL'});

    # Request the Technorati information for each result.
    my $technorati_result = get("http://api.technorati.com/bloginfo?".
                                "url=$url&key=$technoratikey");

    # Parse this information.
    my $parser = new XML::Simple;
    my $parsed_feed = $parser->XMLin($technorati_result);

    # If Technorati considers this site to be a weblog,
    # go onto the next result. If not, display it, and then go on.
    if ($parsed_feed->{document}{result}{weblog}{name}) { next; }
    else {
        print $cgi-> i('<a href="'.$url.'">'.$element->{title}.'</a>');
        print $cgi-> l("$element->{snippet}");
    }
}
print $cgi -> end_ul( );
print $cgi->end_html;
```

Let's step through the meaningful bits of this code. First comes pulling in the query from Google. Notice the 10 in the doGoogleSearch; this is the number of search results requested from Google. You should try to set this as high as Google will allow whenever you run the script; otherwise, you might find that searching for terms that are extremely popular in the weblogging world does not return any results at all, having been rejected as originating from a blog.

Since we're about to make a web services call for every one of the returned results, which might take a while, we want to start returning the results page now; this helps prevent connection timeouts. As such, we spit out a header using the *CGI* module, and then jump into our loop.

We then get to the final part of our code: actually looping through the search results returned by Google and passing the HTML-encoded URL to the Technorati API as a get request. Technorati will then return its results as an XML document.

Be careful that you do not run out of Technorati requests. As I write this, Technorati is offering 500 free requests a day, which, with this script, is around 50 searches. If you make this script available to your web site audience, you will soon run out of Technorati requests. One possible workaround is forcing the user to enter her own Technorati key. You can get the user's key from the same form that accepts the query. See the "Hacking the Hack" section for a means of doing this.

Parsing this result is a matter of passing it through *XML::Simple*. Since Technorati returns only an XML construct containing name when the site is thought to be a weblog, we can use the presence of this construct as a marker. If the program sees the construct, it skips to the next result. If it doesn't, the site is not thought to be a weblog by Technorati and we display a link to it, along with the title and snippet (when available) returned by Google.

Running the Hack

Point your browser at the form *googletech.html*.

Hacking the Hack

As mentioned previously, this script can burn through your Technorati allowances rather quickly under heavy use. The simplest way of solving this is to force the end user to supply his own Technorati key. First, add a new input to your HTML form for the user's key:

```
Your query: <input type="text" name="key">
```

Then, suck in the user's key as a replacement to your own:

```
# Set up the query term
# from the CGI input.
my $query = param("q");
$technoratikey = param("key");
```

—Ben Hammersley

HACK #46   Spot Trends with Geotargeting

Compare the relative popularity of a trend or fashion in different locations, using only Google and Directi search results.

One of the latest buzzwords on the Internet is *geotargeting*, which is just a fancy name for the process of matching hostnames (e.g., *http://www.oreilly.com*) to addresses (e.g., 208.201.239.36) to country names (e.g., U.S.). The whole thing works because there are people who compile such databases and make them readily available. This information must be compiled by hand or at least semiautomatically because the DNS system that resolves hostnames to addresses does not store it in its distributed database.

While it is possible to add geographic location data to DNS records, it is highly impractical to do so. However, since we know which addresses have been assigned to which businesses, governments, organizations, or educational establishments, we can assume with a high probability that the geographic location of the institution matches that of its hosts, at least for most of them. For example, if the given address belongs to the range of addresses assigned to British Telecom, then it is highly probable that it is used by a host located within the territory of the United Kingdom.

Why go to such lengths when a simple DNS lookup (e.g., nslookup 208.201. 239.36) gives the name of the host, and in that name we can look up the top-level domain (e.g., .pl, .de, or .uk) to find out where this particular host is located? There are four good reasons for this:

- Not all lookups on addresses return hostnames.
- A single address might serve more than one virtual host.
- Some country domains are registered by foreigners and hosted on servers on the other side of the globe.
- .com, .net, .org, .biz, or .info domains tell us nothing about the geographic location of the servers they are hosted on. That's where geotargeting can help.

Geotargeting is by no means perfect. For example, if an international organization such as AOL gets a large chunk of addresses that it uses not only for servers in the U.S., but also in Europe, the European hosts might be reported as being based in the U.S. Fortunately, such aberrations do not constitute a large percentage of addresses.

The first users of geotargeting were advertisers, who thought it would be a neat idea to serve local advertising. In other words, if a user visits a *New York Times* site, the ads they see depend on their physical location. Those in the U.S. might see the ads for the latest Chrysler car, while those in Japan might see ads for i-mode; users from Poland might see ads for "Ekstradycja" (a cult Polish police TV series), and those in India might see ads for the latest Bollywood movie. While such use of geotargeting might be used to maximize the return on the invested dollar, it also goes against the idea behind the Internet, which is a global network. (In other words, if you are entering a global audience, don't try to hide from it by compartmentalizing it.) Another problem with geotargeted ads is that they follow the viewer. Advertisers must love it, but it is annoying to the user; how would you feel if you saw the same ads for your local burger bar everywhere you went in the world?

Another application of geotargeting is to serve content in the local language. The idea is really nice, but it's often poorly implemented and takes a lot of clicking to get to the pages in other languages. The local pages have a habit of returning out of nowhere, especially after you upgrade your web browser. A much more interesting application of geotargeting is the analysis of trends, which is usually done in two ways: analysis of server logs and via analysis of results of querying Google.

Server log analysis is used to determine the geographic location of your visitors. For example, you might discover that your company's site is being visited by a large number of people from Japan. Perhaps that number is so significant that it would justify the rollout of a Japanese version of your site. Or it might be a signal that your company's products are becoming popular in that country and you should spend more marketing dollars there. But if you run a server for U.S. expatriates living in Tokyo, the same information might mean that your site is growing in popularity and you need to add more information in English. This method is based on the list of addresses of hosts that connect to the server, stored in your server's access log. You could write a script that looks up their geographic location to find out where your visitors come from. It is more accurate than looking up top-level domains, although it's a little slower due to the number of DNS lookups that need to be done.

Another interesting use of geotargeting is analysis of the spread of trends. This can be done with a simple script that plugs into the Google API and the IP-to-Country database provided by Directi (*http://ip-to-country.directi.com*). The idea behind trend analysis is simple: perform repetitive queries using the same keywords, but change the language of results and top-level domains for each query. Compare the number of results returned for each language, and you will get a good idea of the spread of the analyzed trend across cultures. Then, compare the number of results returned for each top-level domain, and you will get a good idea of the spread of the analyzed trend across the globe. Finally, look up geographic locations of hosts to better approximate the geographic spread of the analyzed trend.

You might discover some interesting things this way: it could turn out that a particular *.com* domain that serves a significant number of documents and that contained the given query in Japanese is located in Germany. It might be a sign that there is a large Japanese community in Germany that uses that particular *.com* domain for their portal. Shouldn't you be trying to get in touch with them?

The *geospider.pl* script shown in this hack is a sample implementation of this idea. It queries Google and then matches the names of hosts in returned URLs against the IP-to-Country database.

The Code

Save the following code **["How to Run the Hacks" in the Preface]** as *geospider.pl*.

> You will need the *Getopt::Std* and *Net::Google* modules for this script. You'll also need a Google API key (*http://api.google.com*) and the latest *ip-to-country.csv* database (*http://ip-to-country.webhosting.info/downloads/ip-to-country.csv.zip*).

```perl
#!/usr/bin/perl-w
#
# geospider.pl
#
# Geotargeting spider -- queries Google through the Google API, extracts
# hostnames from returned URLs, looks up addresses of hosts, and matches
# addresses of hosts against the IP-to-Country database from Directi:
# ip-to-country.directi.com. For more information about this software:
# http://www.artymiak.com/software or contact jacek@artymiak.com.
#
# This code is free software; you can redistribute it and/or
# modify it under the same terms as Perl itself.
#

use strict;
use Getopt::Std;
use Net::Google;
use constant GOOGLEKEY => 'insert key here';
use Socket;

my $help = <<"EOH";
--------------------------------------------------------------------------
Geotargeting trend analysis spider
--------------------------------------------------------------------------
Options:

    -h    prints this help
    -q    query in utf8, e.g. 'Spidering Hacks'
    -l    language codes, e.g. 'en fr jp'
    -d    domains, e.g. '.com'
    -s    which result should be returned first (count starts from 0), e.g. 0
    -n    how many results should be returned, e.g. 700
--------------------------------------------------------------------------
EOH

# Define our arguments and show the
# help if asked, or if missing query.
```

```
my %args; getopts("hq:l:d:s:n:", \%args);
die $help if exists $args{h};
die $help unless $args{'q'};

# Create the Google object.
my $google = Net::Google->new(key=>GOOGLEKEY);
my $search = $google->search( );

# Language, defaulting to English.
$search->lr(qw($args{l}) || "en");

# What search result to start at, defaulting to 0.
$search->starts_at($args{'s'} || 0);

# How many results, defaulting to 10.
$search->starts_at($args{'n'} || 10);

# Input and output encoding.
$search->ie(qw(utf8)); $search->oe(qw(utf8));

my $querystr; # our final string for searching.
if ($args{d}) { $querystr = "$args{q} .site:$args{d}"; }
else { $querystr = $args{'q'} } # domain specific searching.

# Load in our lookup list from
# http://ip-to-country.directi.com/.
my $file = "ip-to-country.csv";
print STDERR "Trying to open $file... \n";
open (FILE, "<$file") or die "[error] Couldn't open $file: $!\n";

# Now load the whole shebang into memory.
print STDERR "Database opened, loading... \n";
my (%ip_from, %ip_to, %code2, %code3, %country);
my $counter=0; while (<FILE>) {
    chomp; my $line = $_; $line =~ s/"//g; # strip all quotes.
    my ($ip_from, $ip_to, $code2, $code3, $country) = split(/,/, $line);

    # Remove trailing zeros.
    $ip_from =~ s/^0{0,10}//g;
    $ip_to =~ s/^0{0,10}//g;

    # And assign to our permanents.
    $ip_from{$counter} = $ip_from;
    $ip_to{$counter}   = $ip_to;
    $code2{$counter}   = $code2;
    $code3{$counter}   = $code3;
    $country{$counter} = $country;
    $counter++; # move on to next line.
}

$search->query(qq($querystr));
print STDERR "Querying Google with $querystr... \n";
print STDERR "Processing results from Google... \n";
```

```
# For each result from Google, display
# the geographic information we've found.
foreach my $result (@{$search->response( )}) {
    print "-" x 80 . "\n";
    print " Search time: " . $result->searchTime( ) . "s\n";
    print "        Query: $querystr\n";
    print "    Languages: " . ( $args{l} || "en" ) . "\n";
    print "       Domain: " . ( $args{d} || "" ) . "\n";
    print "     Start at: " . ( $args{'s'} || 0 ) . "\n";
    print "Return items: " . ( $args{n} || 10 ) . "\n";
    print "-" x 80 . "\n";

    map {
        print "url: " . $_->URL( ) . "\n";
        my @addresses = get_host($_->URL( ));
        if (scalar @addresses != 0) {
            match_ip(get_host($_->URL( )));
        } else {
            print "address: unknown\n";
            print "country: unknown\n";
            print "code3: unknown\n";
            print "code2: unknown\n";
        } print "-" x 50 . "\n";
    } @{$result->resultElements( )};
}

# Get the IPs for
# matching hostnames.
sub get_host {
    my ($url) = @_;

    # Chop the URL down to just the hostname.
    my $name = substr($url, 7); $name =~ m/\//g;
    $name = substr($name, 0, pos($name) - 1);
    print "host: $name\n";

    # And get the matching IPs.
    my @addresses = gethostbyname($name);
    if (scalar @addresses != 0) {
        @addresses = map { inet_ntoa($_) } @addresses[4 .. $#addresses];
    } else { return undef; }
    return "@addresses";
}

# Check our IP in the
# Directi list in memory.
sub match_ip {
    my (@addresses) = split(/ /, "@_");
    foreach my $address (@addresses) {
        print "address: $address\n";
        my @classes = split(/\./, $address);
        my $p; foreach my $class (@classes) {
            $p .= pack("C", int($class));
```

```
        } $p  = unpack("N", $p);
        my $counter = 0;
        foreach (keys %ip_to) {
            if ($p <= int($ip_to{$counter})) {
                print "country: " . $country{$counter} . "\n";
                print "code3: "    . $code3{$counter}   . "\n";
                print "code2: "    . $code2{$counter}   . "\n";
                last;
            } else { ++$counter; }
        }
    }
}
```

Be sure to replace *insert key here* with your Google API key.

Running the Hack

Here, we're querying to see how much worldly penetration AmphetaDesk, a popular news aggregator, has, according to Google's top search results:

```
% perl geospider.pl -q "amphetadesk"
Trying to open ip-to-country.csv...
Database opened, loading...
Querying Google with amphetadesk...
Processing results from Google...
--------------------------------------------------------------
 Search time: 0.081432s
        Query: amphetadesk
    Languages: en
      Domain:
    Start at: 0
Return items: 10
--------------------------------------------------------------
url: http://www.macupdate.com/info.php/id/9787
host: www.macupdate.com
host: www.macupdate.com
address: 64.5.48.152
country: UNITED STATES
code3: USA
code2: US
---------------------------------------------------
url: http://allmacintosh.forthnet.gr/preview/214706.html
host: allmacintosh.forthnet.gr
host: allmacintosh.forthnet.gr
address: 193.92.150.100
country: GREECE
code3: GRC
code2: GR
---------------------------------------------------
...etc...
```

Hacking the Hack

This script is only a simple tool. You will make it better, no doubt. The first thing you could do is implement a more efficient way to query the IP-to-Country database. Storing data from *ip-to-country.csv* in a database would speed script startup time by several seconds. Also, the answers to address-to-country queries could be obtained much faster.

You might ask if it wouldn't be easier to write a spider that doesn't use the Google API and instead downloads page after page of results returned by Google at *http://www.google.com*. Yes, it is possible, and it is also the quickest way to get your script blacklisted for the breach of the Google's user agreement. Google is not only the best search engine, it is also one of the best-monitored sites on the Internet.

—*Jacek Artymiak*

HACK #47 Bring the Google Calculator to the Command Line

Perform feats of calculation on the command line, powered by the magic of the Google calculator.

Everyone, whether they admit it or not, forgets how to use the Unix dc command-line calculator a few moments after they figure it out for the nth time and stumble through the calculation at hand. And, let's face it, the default desktop (and I mean *computer desktop*) calculator usually doesn't go beyond the basics: add, subtract, multiply, and divide—you'll have some grouping ability with clever use of M+, M-, and MR, if you're lucky.

What if you're interested in more than simple math? I've lived in the U.S. for years now and still don't know a yard from three feet (I know now, thanks to the Google Calculator), let alone converting ounces to grams or stone to kilograms.

This two-line PHP script by Adam Trachtenberg (*http://www.trachtenberg. com*) brings the Google calculator to your command line so that you don't have to skip a beat—or open your browser—when you just need to calculate something quickly.

The Code

The script uses PHP (*http://www.php.net*), better known as a web programming and templating language, on the command line, passing your calculation query to Google, scraping the returned results, and dropping the answer into your virtual lap.

This hack assumes that you have PHP installed on your computer and it lives in the */usr/bin* directory. If PHP is somewhere else on your system, you should alter the path on the first line accordingly (e.g., *#!/usr/local/bin/php4*).

```
#!/usr/bin/php
<?php
preg_match_all('{<b>.+= (.+?)</b>}',
   file_get_contents('http://www.google.com/search?q=' .
      urlencode(join(' ', array_splice($argv, 1)))), $matches);
print str_replace('<font size=-2> </font>', ',',
   "{$matches[1][0]}\n");
?>
```

Save the code to a file called *calc* in your path (I keep such things in a *bin* in my home directory) and make it available to run by typing `chmod +x calc`.

Running the Hack

Invoke your new calculator on the command line **["How to Run the Scripts" in the Preface]** by typing `calc` (or `./calc` if you're in the same directory and don't feel like fiddling about with paths) followed by any Google calculator query that you might run through the regular Google web search interface.

Here are a few examples:

```
% calc "21 * 2"
42
% calc 26 ounces + 1 pint in ounces
42 US fluid ounces
% calc pi
3.14159265
% calc answer to life, the universe and everything
42
```

If your shell gives you a parse error or returns garbage, try placing the calculation inside quotation marks. For example, `calc 21 * 2`, without the double-quotes in the previous example, returns `$int($<b>calc`.

There's absolutely no error checking in this hack, so if you enter something that Google doesn't think is a calculation, you'll likely get garbage or nothing at all. Likewise, remember that if Google changes its HTML output, the regular expression could fail; after all, as we'll point out several times in this book, scraping web pages is a brittle affair. That said, if this were made more robust, it'd no longer be a hack, now would it?

Build a Custom Date Range Search Form

Search only Google pages indexed today, yesterday, the last 7 days, or last 30 days.

Google has a date-based search [Hack #16] but uses Julian dates. Most people can't convert Gregorian to Julian in their heads. But with a conversion formula and a little Perl scripting, you can have a Google search form that offers to let users search Google pages indexed today, yesterday, the last 7 days, or the last 30 days.

The Form

The frontend to the script is a simple HTML form:

```html
<form action="http://path/to/cgi-bin/goofresh.cgi"
method="get">
Search for:<br />
<input type="text" name="query" size="30" />
<p />
Search for pages indexed how many days back?<br />
<select name="days_back">
<option value="0">Today</option>
<option value="1">Yesterday</option>
<option value="7">Last 7 Days</option>
<option value="30">Last 30 Days</option>
</select>
<p />
<input type="submit" value="Search">
</form>
```

The form prompts for two user inputs. The first is a Google query, complete with support for special syntax ["Special Syntax" in Chapter 1] and syntax mixing ["Mixing Syntaxes" in Chapter 1]; after all, we'll just be passing your query along to Google itself. The second input, a pull-down list, prompts for how many days' worth of search the form should perform.

The Code

Note that this script just does a couple of date translations in Perl and redirects the browser to Google, altered query in tow. It's just a regular query as far as Google is concerned, so it doesn't require a developer's API key.

This hack requires an additional module, *Time::JulianDay*, and won't run without it (*http://search.cpan.org/ search?query=Time%3A%3AJulianDay*).

```
#!/usr/local/bin/perl
# goofresh.cgi
```

```
# Searches for recently indexed files on Google.
# Usage: goofresh.cgi is called as a CGI with form input,
# redirecting the browser to Google, altered query in tow.

use CGI qw/:standard/;
use Time::JulianDay;

# Build a URL-escaped query.
(my $query = param('query')) =~ s#(\W)#sprintf("%%%02x", ord($1))#ge;

# How many days back?
my $days_back = int param('days_back') || 0;

# What's the current Julian date?
my $julian_date = int local_julian_day(time);

# Redirect the browser to Google with query in tow.
print redirect(
    'http://www.google.com/search?num=100' .
    "&q=$query" .
    "+daterange%3A" . ($julian_date - $days_back) . "-$julian_date"
);
```

Running the Hack

Point your browser at the location of the form you just created. Enter a query, choose how many days to go back, and click the Search button. You'll be sent on to Google with the appropriate daterange: restriction in tow.

Hacking the Hack

If you don't like the date ranges hardcoded into the form, make up your own and adjust the form accordingly:

```
<form action="http://path/to/cgi-bin/goofresh.cgi"
method="get">
Search for:<br />
<input type="text" name="query" size="30" />
<p />
Search for pages indexed how many days back?<br />
<select name="days_back">
<option value="0">Today</option>
<option value="30">Around 1 Month</option>
<option value="60">Around 2 Months</option>
<option value="90">Around 3 Months</option>
<option value="365">1 Year</option>
</select>
<p />
<input type="submit" value="Search">
</form>
```

Or simply let the user specify how many days to go back in a text field:

```
<form action="http://path/to/cgi-bin/goofresh.cgi"
method="get">
Search for:<br />
<input type="text" name="query" size="30" />
<p />
Search for pages indexed how many days back?<br />
<input type="text" name="days_back" size="4"
maxlength="4" />
<p />
<input type="submit" value="Search">
</form>
```

Search Yesterday's Index

#49   Monitor a set of queries for new finds added to the Google index yesterday.

"Build a Custom Date Range Search Form" **[Hack #48]** is a simple web form-driven CGI script for building date range Google queries. A simple web-based interface is fine when you want to search for only one or two items at a time. But what of performing multiple searches over time, saving the results to your computer for comparative analysis?

A better fit for this task is a client-side application that you run from the comfort of your own computer's desktop. This Perl script feeds specified queries to Google via the Google Web API, limiting results to those indexed yesterday. New finds are appended to a comma-delimited text file per query, suitable for import into Excel or your average database application.

> This hack requires an additional Perl module, *Time::Julian-Day* (*http://search.cpan.org/author/MUIR/*); it just won't work until you have the module installed.

The Queries

First, you'll need to prepare a few queries to feed the script. Try these out via the Google search interface itself first to make sure you're receiving the kind of results you're expecting. Your queries can be anything that you'd be interested in tracking over time: topics of long-lasting or current interest, searches for new directories of information **[Hack #1]** coming online, unique quotes from articles, or other sources that you want to monitor for signs of plagiarism.

Use whatever special syntaxes you like except for link:; as you might remember, link: can't be used in concert with any other special syntax such as daterange:, upon which this hack relies. If you insist on trying anyway (e.g., link:www.yahoo.com daterange:2452421-2452521), Google will simply treat link as yet another query word (e.g., link www.yahoo.com), yielding some unexpected and useless results.

Put each query on its own line. A sample query file will look something like this:

```
"digital archives"
intitle:"state library of"
intitle:directory intitle:resources
"now * * time for all good men * come * * aid * * party"
```

Save the text file somewhere memorable; alongside the script you're about to write is as good a place as any.

The Code

Save the following code as *goonow.pl*. Be sure to replace *insert key here* with your Google API key along the way.

```perl
#!/usr/local/bin/perl -w
# goonow.pl
# Feeds queries specified in a text file to Google, querying
# for recent additions to the Google index.  The script appends
# to CSV files, one per query, creating them if they don't exist.
# usage: perl goonow.pl [query_filename]

# My Google API developer's key.
my $google_key='insert key here';

# Location of the GoogleSearch WSDL file.
my $google_wdsl = "./GoogleSearch.wsdl";

use strict;

use SOAP::Lite;
use Time::JulianDay;

$ARGV[0] or die "usage: perl goonow.pl [query_filename]\n";

my $julian_date = int local_julian_day(time) - 2;

my $google_search  = SOAP::Lite->service("file:$google_wdsl");

open QUERIES, $ARGV[0] or die "Couldn't read $ARGV[0]: $!";

while (my $query = <QUERIES>) {
  chomp $query;
  warn "Searching Google for $query\n";

  $query .= " daterange:$julian_date-$julian_date";
  (my $outfile = $query) =~ s/\W/_/g;
```

```
open (OUT, ">> $outfile.csv")
  or die "Couldn't open $outfile.csv: $!\n";

my $results = $google_search ->
  doGoogleSearch(
    $google_key, $query, 0, 10, "false", "",  "false",
    "", "latin1", "latin1"
  );
foreach (@{$results->{'resultElements'}}) {
  print OUT '"' . join('","', (
    map {
      s!\n!!g; # drop spurious newlines
      s!<.+?>!!g; # drop all HTML tags
      s!"!""!g; # double escape " marks
      $_;
    } @$_{'title','URL','snippet'}
  ) ) . "\"\n";
}
}
```

You'll notice that GooNow checks the day before yesterday's rather than yesterday's additions (my $julian_date = int local_julian_day(time) - 2;). Google indexes some pages very frequently; these show up in yesterday's additions and really bulk up your search results. So if you search for yesterday's results in addition to updated pages, you'll get a lot of noise, pages that Google indexes every day, rather than the fresh content that you're after. Skipping back one more day is a nice hack to get around the noise.

Running the Hack

This script is invoked on the command line ["Running the Hacks" in Preface] like so:

```
$ perl goonow.pl query_filename
```

where *query_filename* is the name of the text file holding all the queries to be fed to the script. The file can be located either in the local directory or elsewhere; if the latter, be sure to include the entire path (e.g., */mydocu~1/ hacks/queries.txt*).

Bear in mind that all output is directed to CSV files, one per query, so don't expect any fascinating output on the screen.

The Results

Here's a quick look at one of the CSV output files created, *intitle_state_ library_of_.csv*:

```
"State Library of Louisiana","http://www.state.lib.la.us/"," ...
Click
here if you have any questions or comments. Copyright <C2><A9>
1998-2001 State Library of Louisiana Last modified: August 07,
```

```
2002. "
"STATE LIBRARY OF NEW SOUTH WALES, SYDNEY
AUSTRALIA","http://www.slnsw.gov.au/", " ... State Library of New
South
Wales Macquarie St, Sydney NSW Australia 2000 Phone: +61 2 9273
1414
Fax: +61 2 9273 1255. Your comments You could win a prize! ...   "
"State Library of Victoria","http://www.slv.vic.gov.au/"," ...
clicking
on our logo. State Library of Victoria Logo with link to homepage
State
Library of Victoria. A world class cultural resource ...   "
...
```

Hacking the Hack

The script keeps appending new finds to the appropriate CSV output file. If you wish to reset the CSV files associated with particular queries, simply delete them, and the script will create them anew.

Or you can make one slight adjustment to have the script create the CSV files anew each time, overwriting the previous version, like so:

```
...
(my $outfile = $query) =~ s/\W/_/g;
open (OUT, "> $outfile.csv")
  or die "Couldn't open $outfile.csv: $!\n";
my $results = $google_search ->
  doGoogleSearch(
    $google_key, $query, 0, 10, "false", "", "false",
    "", "latin1", "latin1"
  );
...
```

Notice the only change in the code is the removal of one of the > characters when the output file is created—i.e., open (OUT, "> $outfile.csv") instead of open (OUT, ">> $outfile.csv").

## CHAPTER THREE

Images
Hacks 50–53

Take a break from all that text and check out Google Images (*http://images.google.com/*), an index of just under 900 million images available on the Web. While sorely lacking in special syntaxes, the Advanced Image Search (*http://images.google.com/advanced_image_search*) does offer some interesting options.

> Of course, any options on the Advanced Image Search page can be expressed via a little URL hacking **["Understand Google URLs" in Chapter 1]**.

Google's Image Search starts with a plain keyword search. Images are indexed under a variety of keywords, some broader than others; be as specific as possible. If you're searching for cats, don't use cat as a keyword unless you don't mind getting results that include "cat scan." Use words that are more uniquely cat related, such as feline or kitten. Narrow down your query as much as possible, using as few words as possible. A query like feline fang, which would get you over 75,800 results on Google, will get you only three results on Google Image Search; in this case, cat fang works better. (Building queries for image searching takes a lot of patience and experimentation.)

Search results include a thumbnail, name, size (both pixels and kilobytes), and the URL where the picture is to be found. Clicking the picture will present a framed page, Google's thumbnail of the image at the top, and the page where the image originally appeared at the bottom. Figure 3-1 shows a typical Google Images result after choosing and clicking one of the images found by your search.

Searching Google Images can be a real crapshoot because it's difficult to build multiple-word queries, and single-word queries lead to thousands of

Figure 3-1. A Google Images search result

results. You do have more options to narrow your search both through the Advanced Image Search interface and through the Google Image Search special syntaxes.

Google Images Advanced Search Interface

The Google Advanced Image Search (*http://images.google.com/advanced_image_search*) allows you to specify the size (expressed in pixels, not kilobytes) of the returned image. You can also specify the kind of pictures that you want (Google Images indexes only JPEG and GIF files), image color (black and white, grayscale, or full color), and any domain to which you wish to restrict your search.

Google Image search also uses three levels of filtering: none, moderate, and strict. Moderate filters only explicit images, while strict filters both images and text. While automatic filtering doesn't guarantee that you won't find any offensive content, it will help. However, sometimes filtering works against you. If you're searching for images related to breast cancer, Google's strict filtering will cut down greatly on your potential number of results. Any time you're using a word that might be considered offensive—even in an innocent context—you'll have to consider turning off the filters or risk missing relevant results. One way to get around the filters is to try alternate words. If you're searching for breast cancer images, try searching for mammograms or Tamoxifen, a drug used to treat breast cancer.

Google Images Search Syntax

Google Images offers a few special syntaxes:

`intitle:`
> Finds keywords in the page title. This is an excellent way to narrow down search results.
>
> `intitle:paramecium`

`filetype:`
> Finds pictures of a particular type: JPEG, GIF, or PNG. Note that searching for `filetype:jpg` and `filetype:jpeg` will get you different results because the filtering is based on file extension, not some deeper understanding of the file type.
>
> `filetype:jpg paramecium`

`inurl:`
> As with any regular Google search, `inurl:` finds the search term in the URL. The results for this one can be confusing. For example, you may search for `inurl:cat` and get the following URL as part of the search result:
>
> *www.example.com/something/somethingelse/something.html*
>
> Hey, where's the cat? Because Google indexes the graphic name as part of the URL, it's probably there. If the page above includes a graphic named *cat.jpg*, that's what Google is finding when you search for `inurl: cat`. It's finding the cat in the name of the picture, not in the URL itself.
>
> `inurl:cat`

`site:`
> As with any other Google web search, `site:` restricts your results to a specified host or domain. Don't use this to restrict results to a certain host unless you're really sure what's there. Instead, use it to restrict results to certain domains. For example, search for `football.site:uk` and then search for `football`.
>
> `site:com` is a good example of how dramatic a difference using `site:` can make.
>
> `site:amazon.com shakespeare`

H A C K
#50

Borrow a Corporate or Product Logo

Add a bit of spice to your presentation or school report by using a corporate, project, product, or service logo.

You have a presentation or proposal to make and want to add a hint of your target audience's branding. Or perhaps you want to spice up a school report on a company, product, or service. You visit their web site and find that every instance of their logo would need some heavy editing to get rid of background clutter, toolbar bits, and so forth.

There are a few ways that Google can help you.

This hack began as a discussion at *http://hacks.oreilly.com/ pub/h/227* and owes a debt to the comments on that page.

Google Images

Point your browser at Google Images (*http://images.google.com*) and search for the company, project, product, or service name—grouped together in double quotes (") if you think this needs to be explicit—and a modifier signifying what sort of image you're after: `logo`, `emblem`, `mascot`, `crest`, `"coat of arms"`, etc. On the whole, `logo` seems to work best. Here are some examples:

```
"microsoft research" logo
"harvard university" crest
"apache software foundation" logo
```

Google Images will usually return a virtual gallery of logos. And, chances are, one of them is an unadulterated version on a plain white or black background. Figure 3-2 shows what turns up if you search for `"microsoft research"` logo.

Save the image—usually a right mouse click (Windows) or Control-click (Macintosh) and Save Picture as... or the like—and drag it right into your PowerPoint or Word document. You can then use the application's basic built-in image editing tools to crop, rotate, or otherwise frame the logo nicely.

While most images produced for the Web wouldn't translate well if you were to print them out, they're usually good enough for a slide presentation, web page mockup, or school project.

For a better version, you might try a Google Web search for `"company/ project/product/service name"` logo filetype:tif. For a logo you can scale and otherwise manipulate, try using filetype:eps or filetype:pdf.

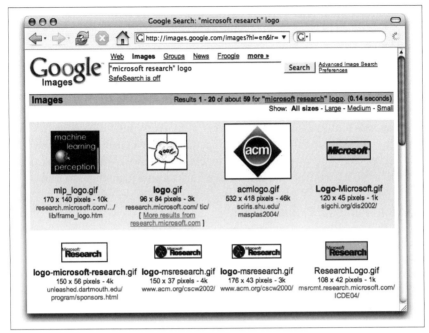

Figure 3-2. Microsoft Research logos turned up by Google Images

Annual Reports

Public companies' annual reports tend to be rather bland affairs emblazoned with a corporate logo and often provided online in PDF form. Perform a Google Web search for "company name" "annual report" filetype: pdf. If you care about print quality, open the PDF in Adobe Illustrator or the like, grab the logo, scale, and add to your own document as needed.

Just remember that scraping a low-resolution GIF or JPG off a web site will work great for screen presentations (Web, PowerPoint, etc.) but will not work for print or slides. When incorporating a low-resolution GIF or JPG into a printed piece, slide, or overhead, the output will look jaggy. Instead, add EPS to the search terms and search Google Web (not Images) to find the company's style guide, which usually includes high-resolution vector logos (.eps, .ai, etc.).

Browse the World Wide Photo Album

HACK #51

Take a random stroll through the world's photo album using some clever Google Image searches (and, optionally, a smidge of programming know-how).

The proliferation of digital cameras and growing popularity of camera phones are turning the Web into a worldwide photo album. It's not only the holiday snaps of your Aunt Minnie or minutiae of your moblogging friend's day that are available to you. You can actually take a stroll through the publicly accessible albums of perfect strangers if you know where to look. Happily, Google has copies, and a couple of hacks know just where to look.

Random Personal Picture Finder

Digital photo files have relatively standard filenames (e.g., *DSC01018.JPG*) by default and are usually uploaded to the Web without being renamed. The Random Personal Picture Finder (*http://www.diddly.com/random*) sports a clever little snippet of JavaScript code that simply generates one of these filenames at random and queries Google Images for it.

The result, shown in Figure 3-3, is something like looking through the world's photo album: people eating, working, posing, and snapping photos of their cats, furniture, or toes. And since it's a normal Google Images search, you can click on any photo to see the story behind it, and the other photos nearby.

Neat, huh?

> Note that people snap pictures of not just their toes (or the toes of others). While an informal series of Shift-Reloads in my browser turned up only a couple of questionable bits of photographic work, you should assume the results are not workplace- or child-safe.

The code behind the scenes, as I mentioned, is really very simple—a swatch of JavaScript (view the source of *http://www.diddly.com/random/random. html* in your browser to see the JavaScript bits for yourself) and list of camera types and their respective filename structures (*http://www.diddly.com/ random/about.html*). You're simply redirected to Google Images with generated search query in tow.

A smidge of Python illustrates just how simple it is to generate a link to some random collection of photos shot with a Canon digital camera:

```
$ python
Python 2.3 (#1, Sep 13 2003, 00:49:11)
[GCC 3.3 20030304 (Apple Computer, Inc. build 1495)] on darwin
```

Figure 3-3. The Random Personal Picture Finder

```
Type "help", "copyright", "credits" or "license" for more information.
>>> from random import randint
>>> linkform = 'http://images.google.com/images?q=IMG_%s.jpg'
>>> print linkform % str(randint(1, 9999)).zfill(4)
http://images.google.com/images?q=IMG_7931.jpg
```

You can easily use this as the basis of a CGI script that acts in the same manner as the Random Personal Picture Finder does.

WebCollage

And if you think the Random Personal Picture Finder is fun, you'll love Jamie Zawinski's WebCollage (*http://www.jwz.org/webcollage/*), a Perl script that finds random pages, strips them of their images, and puts these images together to create a collage. The collage is remixed and added to once a minute, your browser reloading a fresh version every so often (or just hit Shift-Reload on your browser yourself to speed up the process). Figure 3-4 shows a WebCollage snapshot in time.

Click on any one element and you'll be taken to the page that the image is from.

Figure 3-4. A typical WebCollage snapshot of random pictures gleaned through Internet search

You can grab the Perl source (*http://www.jwz.org/webcollage/webcollage*) and generate a page similar to Jamie's like so:

```
$ webcollage -size '800x600' -imagemap ~/public_html/collage
```

where 800x600 is the size and *~/public_html/collage* is the path to and file you'd like to save the image map as.

WebCollage is also included in Zawinski's XScreenSaver (*http://www.jwz.org/xscreensaver*), a screensaver system for computers running the X Windows System (usually some brand of Unix).

 As Jamie notes, he's disabled the Google search in WebCollage (you can just uncomment it in your own downloaded version) because it's not a Google API–based application and so is not in keeping with Google's Terms of Service ["A Note on Spidering and Scraping" in Chapter 9]. You can, however, very easily write a Google-specific API-friendly version.

—*Aaron Swartz*

Google Cartography: Street Art in Your Neighborhood

car·tog·ra·phy n. The art or technique of making maps or charts.

Google Cartography (found here: *http://richard.jones.name/google-hacks/google-cartography/google-cartography.html*) uses Google via the Google Search API [Chapter 9] to build a visual representation of the interconnectivity of streets in an area.

This application takes a starting street and finds streets that intersect with it. Traversing the streets in a breadth-first manner, the application discovers more and more intersections, eventually producing a graph that shows the interconnectivity of streets flowing from the starting street.

Figures 3-5 and 3-6 show maps generated for two of the world's great cities, New York and Melbourne, respectively.

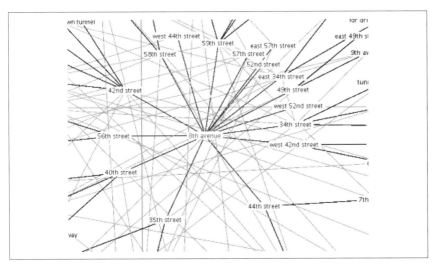

Figure 3-5. New York, U.S., as determined by Google cartography

 If you know the streets in the areas shown, you will be able to find inconsistencies introduced by the text parsing process, explained in more detail in the following section.

The Gory Details

Google Cartography uses the Google API to find web pages that refers to street names. Initial street and region criteria are combined to form a search query, which is then executed by the Google API. Each URL from the

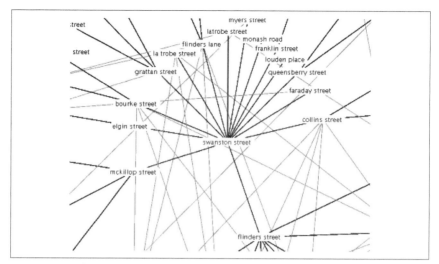

Figure 3-6. Melbourne, Australia, mapped by a little Google cartography

Google results is fetched and the content of the pages converted into text. The text is then processed using pattern matching (programmers, read: regular expressions) designed to capture information relating to the relationship between streets (for example, streets that cross each other or turn into other streets).

For each page a list of vertices is produced, where each vertex represents an intersection between two streets. After the results for the initial street have been processed, the list of vertices will hopefully contain some vertices that intersect with the initial street.

At this point, the mapper performs a breadth-first search through the streets that can be reached from the initial street. Each street traversed during this process is subjected to the same process as the initial street, expanding the list of known street intersections. This process continues until no more streets can be reached from the initial street or until the halting criteria is satisfied (for instance, reaching the maximum amount of Google API key usage).

Once the data collection phase has completed, the application converts the intersection vertices into a graph. Each street becomes a vertex of its own, with outgoing edges connecting to the vertices of intersecting streets. The connectivity of this graph is analyzed (using the Jung graph package at *http://jung.sourceforge.net*) to determine the largest maximal subgraph where all pairs of vertices are reachable from each other. This subgraph almost always contains the starting street; the probability of this not occurring should decrease proportionally to the number of streets traversed (which naturally selects for streets that are in the same subgraph as the starting street).

The largest connected subgraph is then visualized using a Radial Layout algorithm provided by the Prefuse graph visualization framework (*http:// prefuse.sourceforge.net*). The graph is initially centered on the start street but will automatically adjust its focus to center around the most recently selected street.

Ignoring its general lack of usefulness (at the time of this writing), there are several problems with the application worth noting:

- Using regular expressions instead of a custom parser means that parsing mistakes are not uncommon. The online version of the applet has a voting option enabled for particularly error-prone regular expressions, where more than one page must agree on the analysis for it to form part of the final graph. This eliminates some mistakes but at the cost of many valid intersections. In the future, the applet should make this behavior optional.

- Due to the regular expressions used, the application works only with English text and English street-naming conventions. When examining the output, it is also obvious that regional variations of English make a difference. American English, British English, and Australian English often have slightly different ways of referring to street relationships. I've tried to allow for some of the more common variations.

- Google's 10-word limit **["The 10-Word Limit" in Chapter 1]** means an inability to effectively filter out previously traversed street names by packing them into the query prepended by a negative (-) sign. Because the street traversal algorithm deliberately tries streets closest to the initial street, the search results returned on those streets often include pages already processed. These duplicate pages are filtered from further processing but getting search results back for already-processed pages wastes precious Google API key usage juice.

- Some streets are hard to disambiguate. Highly generic street names such as Main Street or High Street can pollute the connectivity graph. So, for example, if Interesting Road is found to intersect with High Street, there may be several High Streets found in the results other than the one coming off Interesting Road—thus producing connectivity via High Street, which is not even indirectly connected to Interesting Road and is therefore highly uninteresting.

Having more specific constraints in the search can help, but that will reduce the overall quantity of results.

Another approach would be to prune connections that have low connectivity with other parts of the graph. This will be the case with streets that come off the "wrong" High Street. Again, this would increase overall quality but at the cost of quantity, with inevitable false positives.

- The pattern matching (using regular expressions) for street name and type is fairly limited. Examples of streets the current pattern matching will not catch are Route N or Highway N and single name streets such as Broadway.

Running the Hack

Point your web browser at *http://richard.jones.name/google-hacks/google-cartography/applet/mapping.html*.

> You will need a recent version of the Java plug-in (1.3.x is not new enough). You can download the JRE which includes the java plug-in from *http://java.sun.com/j2se/1.4.2/download.html*. You'll also need your own Google API key ["Using Your Google API Key" in Chapter 9].

When the "Enter parameters" applet window appears (shown in Figure 3-7), enter your Google API key and adjust the maximums per instructions on the Google Cartography page. Now, type in your starting street and any additional search criteria by which to narrow the search.

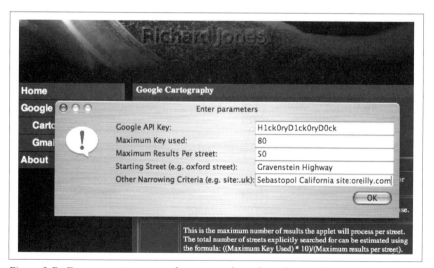

Figure 3-7. Enter a starting point of interest and anything that might narrow down the possibilities

After a little churning, the applet will display a map for your street and region of interest similar to those in Figures 3-5 and 3-6.

Be warned that the applet may use large amounts of bandwidth, depending on the parameters you enter.

—*Richard Jones*

Capture the Map

#53

Put a little Risk into your Googling as you try your hand at world domination.

Capture the Map (*http://www.capturethemap.de*; Flash required) is altogether a little silly, but it's a spot of fun nevertheless. A strategy game similar in flavor to the popular (at least it was when I was growing up) board game of Risk (*http://www.google.com/search?q=risk+board+game*), you attempt near-global domination by taking turns placing pins into a map of the world, claiming more territory than your opponent.

Would that it were that easy?

You don't simply get to place pins into the map; that's where Google comes in. You and your opponent battle it out by supplying queries to be run against the Google index. The first nine results are localized according to where in the world the server hosting the resulting page lives, each represented by a pushpin at a particular latitude and longitude on the map. For example, if you searched for news and one of the first nine results were the BBC News home page, you'd find yourself with a pin in the UK-York, to be precise. A CNN hit would net you a pin in Reston, Virginia.

But simply placing a pin isn't enough to maintain your hold on any particular spot. A well-placed query can replace your pin with that of your opponent. Perhaps he searched for CNN directly and not only knocked your Reston pin out of its spot, but also chalked up three Reston pins of their own. The only way to protect your pins is by collecting several in one spot; for each pin placed, you also claim one of the adjacent squares. Amass a three-by-three grid of squares and you're safe from any further attack.

The game is over when either player is out of pins. The player with a higher sum of placed pins, captured squares, and saved captured squares (three-by-three grids) is the winner.

Figure 3-8 shows a game of Capture the Map underway. Blue (that's me) is in the midst of placing pins, mostly in Reston, VA, thanks to a search for CNN. Notice the dragable magnifying glass over the United States, revealing overlaid details in the form of larger squares showing the number of pins at each spot. A scorecard beneath each player's search box shows number of pins placed, number of squares captured, and number of squares captured and saved.

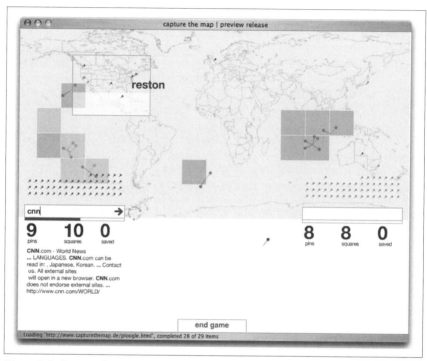

Figure 3-8. Capture the Map turns Google into Risk

Capture the Map is surprisingly addictive, as you try to noodle which search will return the maximum number of results from the same geographical location. You'll likely spend hours just trying to take down your opponent's all-but-three-by-three grid in Melbourne, Australia.

News and Groups
Hacks 54–58

The Internet is a worldwide conversation, and nowhere is that better reflected than in the flow of news coverage by "official" news sources and bloggers alike, as well as the tangled discussions of Usenet news and mailing lists. Google trawls through our conversations, threads them together, tidies them up (just a tad), and reflects them back at us in Google News and Google Groups.

Google News

At the time of this writing, Google News (*http://news.google.com*) culls around 4,500 news sources—from *The Scotsman* to *The China Daily*, *The New York Times* to *The Minneapolis Star Tribune*.

The front page, shown in Figure 4-1, is updated algorithmically without any involvement by puny humans—aside, of course, from those writing the news in the first place—several times a day. The "most relevant news" rises to the top.

Stories are organized into clusters, drawing together coverage and photographs from various news sources around the Web. Click the "all *n* related" link for a list of all stories falling within that cluster. Click "sort by date" to see how the story unfolded across sources over time.

All of this doesn't apply just to the front page, but to all of the newspaper-like sections within: World, U.S., Business, Sci/Tech, Sports, Entertainment, and Health.

Figure 4-1. The Google News front page

For a text-only and PDA/smartphone-friendlier version of Google News, click the Text Version link in the left column or point your browser at *http://news.google.com/ news?ned=tus*. You may notice that it takes a little longer to load; this is because it combines all sections, from Top Stories to Health, into one text-only page.

Google News Search Syntax

When you search Google News, the default is to search for your query keywords anywhere in the news article's headline, story text, source, or URL.

iht will find stories appearing in the International Herald Tribune (*http://www.iht.com*) even if "iht" appears nowhere in the headline, story, or source's proper name.

Google News Search uses basic boolean just like Google's Web Search ["Basic Boolean" in Chapter 1].

Google News supports the following special search syntax:

`intitle:`
> Finds words in an article headline.
>
> > `intitle:beckham`
>
> An `allintitle:` variation finds stories wherein all the words specified appear in an article headline—effectively the same as using `intitle:` before each keyword.
>
> > `allintitle:miners strike benefits`

`intext:`
> Finds search terms in the body of a story.
>
> > `intext:"crude oil"`
>
> An `allintext:` variation finds stories where all your search keywords appear in article text—effectively the same as using `intext:` before each keyword.
>
> > `allintext:US stocks rebound`

`inurl:`
> Looks for particular keywords in a news story's URL:
>
> > `ipod inurl:reuters`

`source:`
> Finds articles from a particular source. Unfortunately, Google News does not offer a list of its over 4,500 sources, so you'll have to guess a little. Also, you need to replace any spaces in the source's name with underscore characters; e.g., *The New York Times* becomes new_york_ times (case insensitive).
>
> > `miners source:international_herald_tribune`
> > `"international space station" source:new_york_times`

`location:`
> Filters articles from sources located in a particular country or state. For country names consisting of more than one word, replace any spaces with underscore characters; e.g., South Africa becomes south_africa (case insensitive). In the case of state names, use official abbreviations like ca for California and id for Idaho.
>
> > `"organic farming" location:france`
> > `election 2004 location:ca`

Advanced News Search

Google Advanced News Search, shown in Figure 4-2, is much like the Advanced Web Search. It provides access to the Google News special syntax from the comfort of a web form. You'll notice a set of fields and pull-down menus associated with Date; use these to search for articles published in the last hour, day, week, month, or between any two days in particular.

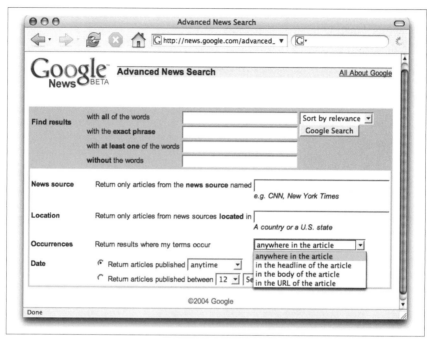

Figure 4-2. *The Google News Advanced Search form*

Fill in the fields, click the Search button, and notice how your query is represented in the search box on the results page.

Making the Most of Google News

The best thing about Google News is its clustering capability. On an ordinary news search engine, a breaking news story can overwhelm search results. For example, in late July 2002, a story broke that hormone replacement therapy might increase the risk of cancer. Suddenly, using a news search engine to find the phrase "breast cancer" was an exercise in futility, because dozens of stories around the same topic were clogging the results page.

That doesn't happen when you search the Google News engine because Google groups similar stories by topic. You'd find a large cluster of stories about hormone replacement therapy, but they'd be in one place, leaving you to find other news about breast cancer.

Some searches cluster easily; they're specialized or tend to spawn limited topics. But other queries (such as "George Bush") spawn lots of results and several different clusters. If you need to search for a famous name or a general topic (such as `crime`, for example) narrow your search results in one of the following ways:

- Add a topic modifier that will significantly narrow your search results, as in: "`George Bush`" `environment crime arson`.

- Limit your search with one of the special syntaxes, for example: `intitle:"George Bush"`.

- Limit your search to a particular source. Be warned that, while this works well for a major breaking news story, you might miss local stories. If you're searching for a major American story, CNN is a good choice (`source:cnn`). If the story you're researching is more international in origin, the BBC works well (`source:bbc_news`).

Receive Google News Alerts

Google Alerts keep tabs on your Google News searches [Hack #59], notifying you if any news stories appear matching your search criteria. They're easy to set up, alter, and delete—and free.

Beyond Google for News Search

After a long dry spell, news search engines have popped up all over the Internet. Here are my top two:

Rocketinfo (http://www.rocketnews.com)
Does not use the most extensive sources in the world, but lesser-known press release outlets (such as PETA) and very technical outlets (e.g., OncoLink, BioSpace, Insurance News Net) are to be found here. Rocketinfo's main drawback is its limited search and sort options.

Yahoo! Daily News (http://dailynews.yahoo.com)
Sports its source list right on the advanced search page. A 30-day index means that sometimes you can find things that have slipped off the other engines. Provides free news alerts for registered Yahoo! users. One drawback is that Yahoo! Daily News has few technical sources, which means stories sometimes appear over and over in search results.

HACK #54 Scrape Google News

Scrape Google News Search results to get at the latest from thousands of aggregated news sources.

Google News, with its thousands of news sources worldwide, is a veritable treasure trove for any news hound. However, because you can't access Google News through the Google API [Chapter 9], you'll have to scrape your results from the HTML of a Google News results page. This hack does just that, gathering up results into a comma-delimited file suitable for loading into a spreadsheet or database. For each news story, it extracts the title, URL, source (i.e., news agency), publication date or age of the news item, and an excerpted description.

Because Google's Terms of Service prohibit the automated access of their search engines except through the Google API, this hack does not actually connect to Google. Instead, it works on a page of results that you've saved from a Google News Search that you've run yourself. Simply save the results page as HTML source using your browser's File → Save As... command.

Make sure the results are listed by date instead of relevance. When results are listed by relevance, some of the descriptions are missing because similar stories are clumped together. You can sort results by date by choosing the "Sort by date" link on the results page or by adding &scoring=d to the end of the results URL. Also, make sure you're getting the maximum number of results by adding &num=100 to the end of the results URL. For example, Figure 4-3 shows results of a query for election 2004, the latest on the 2004 United States Presidential Election—something of great import at the time of this writing.

Figure 4-3. Google News results for election 2004, sorted by date

Bear in mind that scraping web pages is a brittle occupation. A single change in the HTML code underlying the standard Google News results page and you're more than likely to end up with no results.

At the time of this writing, a typical Google News Search result looks a little something like this:

```
<a href="http://www.townhall.com/columnists/phyllisschlafly/ps20041018.
shtml" id=r-1>Show Me State debate spotlights conservative issues</a><br>
<font size=-1><font color=#6f6f6f>Town Hall, DC -</font> <nobr>8
minutes ago</nobr></font><br><font size=-1><b>...</b> The <b>2004</b> <b>
election</b> presents a stark choice to voters on many issues. The second
debate highlighted those differences on taxes, sovereignty <b>...</b> </
font><br>
```

While for most of you this is utter gobbledygook, it is probably of some use to those trying to understand the regular expression matching in the following script.

The Code

Save this code to a file called *news2csv.pl*:

```perl
#!/usr/bin/perl
# news2csv.pl
# Google News Results exported to CSV suitable for import into Excel.
# Usage: perl news2csv.pl < news.html > news.csv

print qq{"title","link","source","date or age", "description"\n};

my %unescape = ('&lt;'=>'<', '&gt;'=>'>', '&amp;'=>'&',
  '&quot;'=>'"', ' '=>' ');
my $unescape_re = join '|' => keys %unescape;

my $results = join '', <>;
$results =~ s/($unescape_re)/$unescape{$1}/migs; # unescape HTML
$results =~ s![\n\r]! !migs; # drop spurious newlines

while ( $results =~ m!<a href="([^"]+)" id="?r-[0-9]+"?>(.+?)</a><br>(.
+?)<nobr>(.+?)</nobr>.*?<br>(.+?)<br>!migs ) {
  my($url, $title, $source, $date_age, $description) =
  ($1||'',$2||'',$3||'',$4||'', $5||'');
  $title =~ s!"!""!g; # double escape " marks
  $description =~ s!"!""!g;
  my $output =
    qq{"$title","$url","$source","$date_age","$description"\n};
  $output =~ s!<.+?>!!g; # drop all HTML tags
  print $output;
}
```

Running the Script

Run the script from the command line ["Running the Hacks" in the the Preface], specifying the Google News results HTML filename and the name of the CSV file that you wish to create or to which you wish to append additional results. For example, using *news.html* as our input and *news.csv* as our output:

```
$ perl news2csv.pl < news.html > news.csv
```

Leaving off the > and CSV filename sends the results to the screen for your perusal.

The Results

The following are some of the 20,300 results returned by a Google News Search for election 2004 and using the HTML page of results shown in Figure 4-3:

```
$ perl news2csv.pl < news.html
"title","link","source","date or age", "description"
"Bush and Kerry on the razor's edge","http://www.dallasnews.com/
sharedcontent/dws/dn/opinion/columnists/mdavis/stories/101304dnedidavis.
97af9.html","Dallas Morning News (subscription),<AO>TX<AO>- ","12 minutes
ago","... But just as the election is a referendum on Mr. Bush, debate
analysis depends on ... Tonight history will write whether the Bush debate
grade for 2004 is generally ...  "
"MINNESOTA: Notes and quotes from battleground Minnesota in ...","http://
www.twincities.com/mld/twincities/news/state/minnesota/9902651.htm","Pioneer
Press (subscription),<AO>MN<AO>- ","16 minutes ago","... the state. Both
sides had assumed Minnesota would easily go Democratic, as it had for every
presidential election since 1972. In ...  "
"MINNESOTA: Notes and quotes from battleground Minnesota in ...","http://
www.duluthsuperior.com/mld/duluthsuperior/news/politics/9902651.htm","Duluth
News Tribune,<AO>MN<AO>- ","19 minutes ago","... the state. Both sides had
assumed Minnesota would easily go Democratic, as it had for every
presidential election since 1972. In ...  "
...
```

 Each listing actually occurs on its own line.

Hacking the Hack

You'll want to leave most of the *news2csv.pl* script alone, since it's been built to make sense out of the Google News formatting. If you don't like the way the program organizes the information that's taken out of the results page, you can change it. Just rearrange the variables on the following line, sorting them in any way that you choose. Be sure to keep a comma between each one.

```
my $output =
  qq{"$title","$url","$source","$date_age","$description"\n};
```

For example, perhaps you want only the URL and title. The line should read:

```
my $output =
  qq{"$url","$title"\n};
```

That \n specifies a new line, and the $ characters specify that $url and $title are variable names; keep them intact.

Of course, now your output won't match the header at the top of the CSV file, by default:

```
print qq{"title","link","source","date or age", "description"\n};
```

As before, simply change this to match, as follows:

```
print qq{"url","title"\n};
```

Visualize Google News

Watch stories aggregated by Google News unfold over time, coverage broaden and fade, and hotspots emerge and fade again into the background.

Newsmap (*http://www.marumushi.com/apps/newsmap*) is a whizbang Flash-based treemap representation (*http://www.cs.umd.edu/hcil/treemap/index. shtml*) of the stories flowing through Google News. The Newsmap home page describes it best:

> Treemaps are traditionally space-constrained visualizations of information. Newsmap's objective takes that goal a step further and provides a tool to divide information into quickly recognizable bands which, when presented together, reveal underlying patterns in news reporting across cultures and within news segments in constant change around the globe.

Point your web browser at the Newsmap page and click the LAUNCH button to begin. Figure 4-4 shows Newsmap in action.

Each color-coded band (you'll have to take our word for its being in color) represents a Google News section: from top to bottom are World, Nation, Business, Technology, Sports, Entertainment, and Health. Notice that I've only selected the first three by checking their associated checkboxes at the bottom-right. Also notice that I've selected news only from the U.K. in the Countries tab across the top.

The colors appear in a gradient from brightest ("less than 10 minutes ago") to darkest ("more than 1 hour ago") such that the latest stories stand right out.

Figure 4-4. Newsmap's Standard banded layout, focusing on U.K. coverage of world, nation, and business news

The more substantial the band and bigger the enclosed headline, the greater the number of related stories. You can easily spot the freshest and most covered stories: they're the big, bright blocks.

Hover your mouse over any story for a brief description drawn from the primary source—the story around which others are clustered—as chosen by Google News.

There's also a Squarified version (Figure 4-5) that I prefer: more so than with the Standard version (Figure 4-4), you are able to see the spread of coverage across all news categories. Switch between the two layouts by clicking the appropriate Layout button near the bottom-right.

Newsmap provides a fascinating bird's-eye view of news as it unfolds on the Web. Here are a couple of my favorite Newsmap settings:

- Select only one news category—World works best—and draw coverage in from two or three countries. Set the layout to Squarified. Now take a gander at the headlines and notice how they differ in title and coverage by country.

- Select only one news category and one country from which to draw sources. Set the layout to Standard. Now, meander back through the archive (bottom-left) day-by-day or hour-by-hour and watch how the

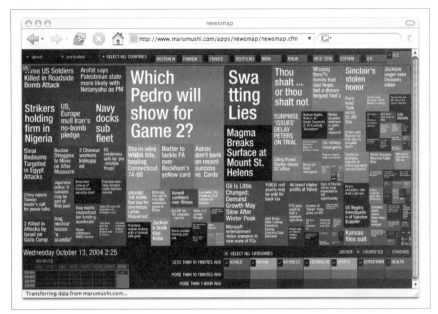

Figure 4-5. Newsmap's Squarified layout, drawing from U.S. coverage of news across all Google News categories

stories unfold over time—bands widen and narrow, hotspots appear and disappear, and the headline changes right along with the primary source.

Google Groups

Usenet groups, text-based discussion groups covering literally hundreds of thousands of topics, have been around since long before the World Wide Web. Deja News used to be *the* repository of Usenet information until it sold off its archive to Google in early 2001. Google filled it out still further and relaunched it as Google Groups (*http://groups.google.com*). Its search interface, shown in Figure 4-6, is rather different from the Google Web Search, as all messages are divided into groups, and the groups themselves are divided into topics called hierarchies.

The Google Groups archive begins in 1981 and covers up to the present day. Just shy of 850 million messages are archived. As you might imagine, that's a pretty big archive, covering literally decades of discussion. Stuck in an ancient computer game? Need help with that sewing machine you bought in 1982? You might be able to find the answers here.

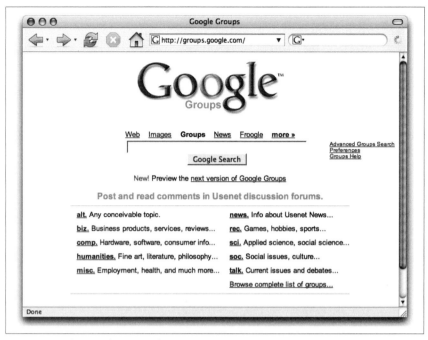

Figure 4-6. The Google Groups home page

Google Groups also allows you to participate in Usenet discussions, handy because not all ISPs provide access to Usenet these days (and even those that do tend to limit the number of newsgroups they carry). See the Google Groups posting FAQ (*http://groups.google.com/googlegroups/posting_faq. html*) for instructions on how to post to a newsgroup. You'll have to start by locating the group to which you want to post and that means using the hierarchy.

10 Seconds of Hierarchy Funk

There are regional and smaller hierarchies, but the main ones are *alt*, *biz*, *comp*, *humanities*, *misc*, *news*, *rec*, *sci*, *soc*, and *talk*. Most web groups are created through a voting process and are put under the hierarchy that's most applicable to the topic.

Browsing Groups

From the main Google Groups page, you can browse through the list of groups by picking a hierarchy from the front page. You'll see that there are subtopics, sub-subtopics, sub-sub-subtopics, and—well, you get the picture. For example, in the *comp* (computers) hierarchy, you'll find the subtopic *comp.sys* or computer systems. Beneath that lie 75 groups and subtopics, including *comp.sys.mac*, a branch of the hierarchy devoted to the Macintosh computer system. There are 24 Mac subtopics, one of which is *comp.sys. mac.hardware*, which has, in turn, three groups beneath it. Once you've drilled down to the most specific group applicable to your interests, Google Groups presents the postings themselves, sorted in reverse chronological order.

This strategy works fine when you want to read a slow (i.e., containing little traffic) or moderated group, but when you want to read a busy, free-for-all group, you may wish to use the Google Groups Search engine. The search on the main page works much like the regular Google search; the differences are the Google Groups tab and the associated group and posting date that accompanies each result.

The Advanced Groups Search (*http://groups.google.com/advanced_group_ search*), however, looks much different. You can restrict your searches to a certain newsgroup or newsgroup topic. For example, you can restrict your search as broadly as the entire *comp* hierarchy (comp* would do it) or as narrowly as a single group such as *comp.robotics.misc*. You can restrict messages to subject and author, or restrict them by message ID.

> Of course, any options on the Advanced Groups Search page can be expressed via a little URL hacking **["Understanding Google URLs" in Chapter 1]**.

Possibly the biggest difference between Google Groups and Google Web Search is the date searching. With Google Web Search, date searching is notoriously inexact; *date* refers to when a page was added to the index rather than when the page was created. Each Google Groups message is stamped with the day that it was actually posted to the newsgroup. Thus, the date searches on Google Groups are accurate and indicative of when content was produced. And, thankfully, they use the more familiar Gregorian dates rather than the Google Web Search's Julian dates **[Hack #16]**.

Google Groups Search Syntax

By default, Google Groups looks for your query keywords anywhere in the posting subject or body, group name, or author name. Groups search uses the same sort of basic Boolean as Google Web Search **["Basic Boolean" in Chapter 1]**.

Google Groups is an archive of conversations. Thus, when you're searching, you'll be more successful if you try looking for conversational and informal language, not the carefully structured language you'll find on Internet sites—well, some Internet sites, anyway.

And, thanks to some special syntax, you can do some precise searching if you know the magic incantations:

`insubject:`
> Searches posting subjects for query words.
>
> ```
> insubject:rocketry
> ```

`group:`
> Restricts your search to a certain group or set of groups (topic). The * (asterisk) wildcard modifies a `group:` syntax to include everything beneath the specified group or topic. `rec.humor*` or `rec.humor.*` (effectively the same) will find results in the group *rec.humor*, as well as *rec.humor.funny*, *rec.humor.jewish*, and so forth.
>
> ```
> group:rec.humor*
> group:alt*
> group:comp.lang.perl.misc
> ```

`author:`
> Specifies the author of a newsgroup post. This can be a full or partial name, even an email address.
>
> ```
> author:fred
> author:"fred flintstone"
> author:flintstone@bedrock.gov
> ```

Mixing syntaxes in Google Groups. Google Groups is much more friendly to syntax mixing ["Mixing Syntax" in Chapter 1] than Google Web Search. You can mix any two or more syntaxes together in a Google Groups Search, as exemplified by the following typical searches:

```
intitle:literature group:humanities* author:john
intitle:hardware group:comp.sys.ibm* pda
```

Some common search scenarios. There are several ways you can mine Google Groups for research information. Remember, though, to view any information that you get here with a certain amount of skepticism. Usenet is just hundreds of thousands of people tossing around links; in that respect, it's just like the Web.

Tech support. Ever used Windows and discovered that there's some program running that you've never heard of? Uncomfortable, isn't it? If you're wondering if HIDSERV is something nefarious, Google Groups can tell you. Just search Google Groups for HIDSERV. You'll find that plenty of people had the same question before you did, and it's been answered.

I find that Google Groups is sometimes more useful than manufacturers' web sites. For example, I was trying to install a set of flight devices for a friend—a joystick, throttle, and rudder pedals. The web site for the manufacturer couldn't help me figure out why they weren't working. I described the problem as best I could in a Google Groups search—using the name of the parts and the manufacturer's brand name—and although it wasn't easy, I was able to find an answer.

Sometimes your problem isn't as serious but it's just as annoying; you might be stuck in a computer game. If the game has been out for more than a few months, your answer is probably in Google Groups. If you want the answer to an entire game, try the magic word *walkthrough*. So if you're looking for a walkthrough for Quake II, try the search "quake ii" walkthrough. (You don't need to restrict your search to newsgroups; walkthrough is a word strongly associated with gamers.)

Finding commentary immediately after an event. With Google Groups, date searching is very precise (unlike date searching Google's Web index), so it's an excellent way to get commentary during or immediately after events.

Barbra Streisand and James Brolin were married on July 1, 1998. Searching for "Barbra Streisand" "James Brolin" between June 30, 1998 and July 3, 1998 leads to over 48 results, including reprinted wire articles, links to news stories, and commentary from fans. Searching for "barbra streisand" "james brolin" without a date specification finds more than 1,800 results.

Usenet is also much older than the Web and is ideal for finding information about an event that occurred before the Web. Coca-Cola released New Coke in April 1985. You can find information about the release on the Web, of course, but finding contemporary commentary would be more difficult. After some playing around with the dates (just because it's been released doesn't mean it's in every store) I found plenty of commentary about New Coke in Google Groups by searching for the phrase "new coke" during the month of May 1985. Information included poll results, taste tests, and speculation on the new formula. Searching later in the summer yields information on Coke re-releasing old Coke under the name "Coca-Cola Classic."

Advanced Groups Search

The Advanced Groups Search, shown in Figure 4-7, is much like the Advanced Web Search and Advanced News Search.

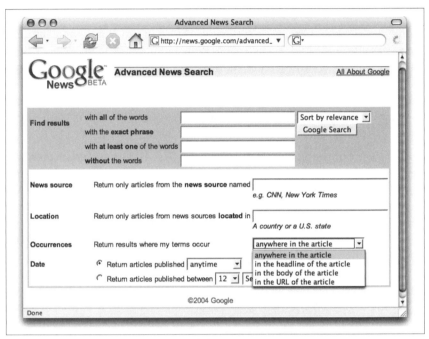

Figure 4-7. The Advanced Groups Search form

Rather than fiddling about with the special syntax detailed earlier, simply fill out the form, hit the Search button, and let Google Groups compose the query for you. You can restrict your search to a specific newsgroup or section of hierarchy (e.g., comp.os.*), particular person, a language, or posts arriving in the past 24 hours, week, month, three months, six months, or year. You can even search for a particular message if you know the message ID. And since Usenet can be just as wooly as the Web, you might decide to turn on SafeSearch.

HACK
#56 Go Deeper into Groups with Google Groups 2
Google Groups 2 merges Usenet news with mailing lists.

Google Groups is a great way to research tech problems or get help with game walkthroughs and other topics of geek discussion. But the first version of Google Groups doesn't for the most part index mailing list archives; the 800-pound gorilla in that space is Yahoo! Groups, which specializes in mailing lists (tens of thousands of them!). Google might just be a challenger yet, however, with the release of Google Groups 2.

Google Groups 2 (*http://groups-beta.google.com*) is in beta, as you might suspect given the URL—at least it is at the time of this writing. That's why we're covering it separately rather than simply doing away with the previous bit on Google Groups.

As you can see in Figure 4-8, Google Groups 2 starts out with a subject index that looks a bit like Yahoo! Groups (or Yahoo!, for that matter). Topics include Arts and Entertainment, Business and Finance, and Computers. As you start browsing and exploring Google Groups 2, you'll notice that it consists of a combination of Usenet newsgroups (in standard Usenet hierarchy: *alt*, *comp*, *news*, etc.).

Figure 4-8. The Google Groups 2 home page

There are a couple of mailing lists in Google Groups 2 made to look like Usenet newsgroups: the obviously unofficial *google.public.bork.bork.bork* is an example. Just because it looks like a Usenet newsgroup, don't assume that it is.

Each newsgroup is accompanied by a brief description so that you don't feel like you're fumbling about in the dark. Email-based groups stand out ever so slightly: while they are also accompanied by a brief description, they are not listed by hierarchy and indicate how many people are subscribed to the list.

 At this point, Google Groups 2 is a new offering, so you won't find many mailing lists that have large numbers of members. Expect that to change over time.

Click on a group and you'll see a list of the latest topics with excerpts on the left and older, though still active, topic titles on the right. Click the "read more >>" link associated with a topic to read individual postings.

For longer discussions, you may want to see the messages in a particular topic laid out in threads so that you can more easily follow who was responding to whom. Click the "view as tree" link just beneath the topic title. The window splits into two frames: on the right is the same screen you just saw, while on the left is a list of all the messages in the discussion, arranged in a tree or threaded style. Click any message in the tree to read its contents in the frame on the right.

Monitor Group Activity

A group's "About:" description provides just enough information for you to decide whether or not to read on, but there's a page of information for each group that you just don't want to miss. Click the "more about this group" link next to the group's description and you'll see a bird's-eye view of the group (Figure 4-9):

- Where in the Usenet hierarchy it fits (if it's a newsgroup)
- Activity level
- Number of members (subscribers or guest members, presumably based on postings)
- Messages per month, with month-by-month details
- Top posters this month and since the group began (or was picked up by Google)

No matter how appealing the topic, a mailing list or newsgroup is going to have a minimum amount of usefulness if there's only a message or so posted each month. Conversely, a mailing list that gets 500 messages a month may be too busy for you to receive individual postings by email. You may well decide to join the list, but read it through the Google Groups site.

About google.public.web-apis

Description:

Join this group

Directory: Usenet: google > public
Activity: Low
Members: 10-100

About: Public - Usenet

Messages per month

	Jan	Feb	Mar	Apr	May	Jun	Jul	Aug	Sep	Oct	Nov	Dec
2002				271	136	70	76	45	46	55	82	39
2003	64	35	60	85	79	53	64	33	46	98	98	52
2004	82	58	99	116	37	42	47	58	94	7		

Top authors

Figure 4-9. A bird's-eye view of a Google Group

There's also the option of subscribing to a public group's messages and topics via Atom (*http://help.blogger.com/bin/answer.py?answer=697&topic=36*), an XML-based syndication format. That way, you can keep tabs on a set of groups alongside all those RSS feeds you're reading.

> Find an RSS/Atom feed reader to suit your needs and platform at *http://www.atomenabled.org/everyone/atomenabled/index.php?c=5*.

Search Group Messages

Confusingly enough, the Google Groups 2 home page has two search boxes, both labeled Search Groups. At the time of this writing, they both return the same results: a set of groups matching your search criteria, followed by individual message results, as shown in Figure 4-10).

Google Groups 2 has an Advanced Search at *http://groups-beta.google.com/advanced_search*. You'll notice that the advanced search here looks much like the advanced search for the older Google Groups; however, you cannot do the date searching that you can do with the Google Groups Advanced Search. You also cannot, at least not at the time of writing, search by language. Bear in mind that Google Groups 2 is still in beta; I expect that there will eventually be at least as much functionality for it as there is for the

Figure 4-10. Search results show groups first, then messages

regular Google Groups. In the meantime, you can take advantage of the existing search form, and try out the same Google Groups Search syntax in Google Groups 2.

Sign In

Sign in (or sign up for a free Google account if you've not already done so) and you'll be able to subscribe to groups and create your own. You'll find a "Sign in" link at the top-right of the Google Groups 2 home page.

To subscribe to a group, simply click the "Subscribe to this group" link associated with any group. As a subscriber, you can receive no email at all and read messages on the Web, a summary of the day's activities, or a single daily digest of all messages. There is currently no option for receiving individual messages as they are posted to your group.

> Google Groups 2 and Gmail **[Chapter 6]** are a perfect combination, allowing you to read mailing lists and newsgroup messages in an email environment without cluttering up your home or work inbox.

Create a new group of your very own by clicking the "Create a new group" link in the sidebar on the left side of the Google Groups 2 home page. You'll be guided through a two-step process:

1. Set up your group. Give it a name (e.g., Google Hacks), email address (e.g., googlehacks@googlegroups.com), and description. Decide whether it should be public (anyone can join, members can post, and the archive is public), announcement only (the archive is public, but only moderators can post), or restricted (membership is invite-only and nothing appears in the directory or shows up in search results).

2. Add members to your group, and Google Groups 2 will invite them by email.

This Must Be the Future

It's not clear when Google is going to make this version of Google Groups the dominant version; it could very well be so by the time you read this. People are used to the old version, and Version 2 still has some user interface issues to work through.

You're sure to see more and bigger mailing lists appearing in the coming months. Email is still the killer app of the Internet, and there's always room for another discussion.

Scrape Google Groups

HACK #57 Pull results from Google Groups searches a comma-delimited file.

It's easy to look at the Internet and say that it's a group of web pages or computers or networks. But look a little deeper and you'll see that the core of the Internet is discussions: mailing lists, online forums, and even web sites, where people hold forth in glorious HTML, waiting for people to drop by, consider their philosophies, make contact, or buy their products and services.

Nowhere is the Internet-as-conversation idea more prevalent than in Usenet newsgroups. Google Groups has an archive of over 800 million messages from years of Usenet traffic. If you're researching a particular time, searching and saving Google Groups message pointers comes in really handy.

Because Google Groups is not searchable by the current version of the Google API, you can't build an automated Google Groups query tool without violating Google's Terms of Service. However, you can scrape the HTML of a page you visit personally and save to your hard drive.

The first thing that you need to do is run a Google Groups Search. See the "Google Groups" section earlier in this chapter for some hints on the best practices for searching this massive message archive.

> This hack works with Google Groups, not Google Groups 2. While any sort of scraping is brittle, we expect Version 2 to change form many times in the very near future and wanted to be sure you had the best chance of success with this hack.

It's best to put pages that you're going to scrape in order of date; that way if you're going to scrape more pages later, it's easy to look at them and check the last date that the search results changed. Let's say that you're trying to keep up with uses of Perl in programming the Google API; your query might look like this:

```
perl group:google.public.web-apis
```

On the right side of the results page is an option to sort either by relevance or date; click the "Sort by date" link. Your results page should look something like Figure 4-11.

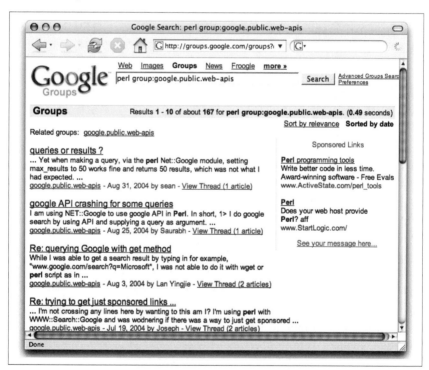

Figure 4-11. The results of a Google Groups Search, sorted by date

Save this page to your hard drive, naming it something memorable, like
groups.html.

 Scraping is brittle at best. A single change in the HTML code
underlying Google Groups pages and the script won't get
very far.

At the time of this writing, a typical Google Groups Search result looks like
this:

```
<a href=/groups?q=perl+group:google.public.web-
apis&hl=en&lr=&c2coff=1&safe=off&scoring=d&selm=bfd91813.0408311406.
21d2bb89%40posting.google.com&rnum=1>queries or results ?</a><font size=-1>
<br> <b>...</b> Yet when making a query, via the <b>perl</b> Net::Google
module, setting max_results to 50 works fine and returns 50 results, which
was not what I had expected. <b>...</b> <br><font color=green><a href=/
groups?hl=en&lr=&c2coff=1&safe=off&group=google.public.web-apis class=a>
google.public.web-apis</a> - Aug 31, 2004 by sean - <a href=/
groups?hl=en&lr=&c2coff=1&safe=off&threadm=bfd91813.0408311406.
21d2bb89%40posting.google.com&rnum=1&prev=/groups%3Fq%3Dperl%2Bgroup:google.
public.web-
apis%26hl%3Den%26lr%3D%26c2coff%3D1%26safe%3Doff%26sa%3DG%26scoring%3Dd
class=a>View Thread (1 article)</a>
```

As with the HTML example given for Google News in "Scrape Google
News" **[Hack #54]**, this might be utter gobbledygook for some of you. Those of
you with an understanding of the code below should see why the regular
expression matching was written in the way it was.

The Code

Save the following code as *groups2csv.pl*:

```perl
#!/usr/bin/perl
# groups2csv.pl
# Google Groups results exported to CSV suitable for import into Excel.
# Usage: perl groups2csv.pl < groups.html > groups.csv

# The CSV Header.
print qq{"title","url","group","date","author","number of articles"\n};

# The base URL for Google Groups.
my $url = "http://groups.google.com";

# Rake in those results.
my($results) = (join '', <>);

# Perform a regular expression match to glean individual results.
```

```
while ( $results =~ m!<a href=(/groups[^\>]+?rnum=[0-9]+)>(.+?)</a>.*?<br>(.
+?)<br>.*?<a href="?/groups.+?class=a>(.+?)</a> - (.+?) by (.+?)\s+.*?\(([0-
9]+) article!mgis ) {
    my($path, $title, $snippet, $group, $date, $author, $articles) =
        ($1||'',$2||'',$3||'',$4||'',$5||'',$6||'',$7||'');
    $title =~ s!"!'"!g; # double escape " marks
    $title =~ s!<.+?>!!g; # drop all HTML tags
    print qq{"$title","$url$path","$group","$date","$author","$articles"\n\
n};
}
```

Running the Hack

Run the script from the command line ["How to Run the Hacks" in the Preface], specifying the Google Groups results filename that you saved earlier and the name of the CSV file that you wish to create or to which you wish to append additional results. For example, use *groups.html* as your input and *groups.csv* as your output:

```
$ perl groups2csv.pl < groups.html > groups.csv
```

Leaving off the > and CSV filename sends the results to the screen for your perusal.

Using >> before the CSV filename appends the current set of results to the CSV file, creating it if it doesn't already exist. This is useful for combining more than one set of results, represented by more than one saved results page:

```
$ perl groups2csv.pl < results_1.html > results.csv
$ perl groups2csv.pl < results_2.html >> results.csv
```

The Results

Scraping the results of a search for perl group:google.public.web-apis for anything mentioning the Perl programming language on the Google API's discussion forum looks like this:

```
$ perl groups2csv.pl < groups.html
"title","url","group","date","author","number of articles"
"queries or results ?","http://groups.google.com/groups?q=perl+group:google.
public.web-apis&hl=en&lr=&c2coff=1&safe=off&scoring=d&selm=bfd91813.
0408311406.21d2bb89%40posting.google.com&rnum=1","google.public.web-
apis","Aug 31, 2004","sean",
"1"
...
"Re: Whats the Difference between using the API and ordinary ... ","http://
groups.google.com/groups?q=perl+group:google.public.web-
apis&hl=en&lr=&c2coff=1&safe=
off&scoring=d&selm=882fdb00.0405052309.44fe831b%40posting.google.
com&rnum=7","google.public.web-apis","May 6, 2004","tonio","4"
...
```

Simplify Google Groups URLs

#58 If the Google Groups URLs are a little too unwieldy, the Google Groups Simplifier will cut them down to size.

Google Groups can produce some rather abominable URLs for individual posts. One message can generate a URL along the likes of this:

```
http://groups.google.com/groups?q=0%27reilly+%22mac+os+x%22
&hl=en&lr=&ie=UTF-8&oe=utf-8&scoring=d
&selm=ujaotqldn50oo4%40corp.supernews.com&rnum=37
```

This is a difficult URL to save and reference—not to mention to email to a colleague.

URL-shortening services generate unique codes for each URL provided, allowing extremely long URLs to be compressed into much shorter, unique URLs. For example, Yahoo! News URLs can be terribly long, but with TinyURL, they can be shortened to something like *http://tinyurl.com/2ph8*.

> These URLs are not private, so don't treat them as such. TinyURL whacking (*http://marnanel.org/writing/tinyurl-whacking*) covers making up TinyURLs to find sites other people have fed into the system.
>
> Don't use these services unless you absolutely have to; they obscure the origin of the URL, making the URLs difficult to track for research. They do come in handy if you have to reference a page cached by Google. For example, here's a URL for a cached version of *http://www.oreilly.com*: *http://216. 239.39.100/search?q=cache:TbOF_622vaYC:www.oreilly.com/ +oreilly&hl=en&ie=UTF-8*. While it's not as long as a typical Google Groups message URL, it's long enough to be difficult to paste into an email and otherwise distribute.

TinyURL (http://www.tinyurl.com)
Shortens URLs to 23 characters. A bookmarklet is available. The service converted the Google Groups URL at the beginning of this hack to *http://tinyurl.com/180q*.

MakeAShorterLink (http://www.makeashorterlink.com)
Shortens URLs to about 40 characters, which, when clicked, take the browser to *gateway* pages with details of where they're about to be sent, after which the browser is redirected to the desired URL. MakeAShorterLink converted that Google Groups URL to *http://makeashorterlink. com/?A2FD145A1*.

Shorl (http://www.shorl.com)

In addition to shortening URLs to about 35 characters, Shorl tracks click-through statistics for the generated URL. These stats can be accessed only by the person who created the Shorl URL using a password generated at the time. Shorl turned the Groups URL above into *http://www.shorl.com/jasomykuprystu*, with the stats page at *http://shorl.com/stat.php?id=jasomykuprystu&pwd=jirafryvukomuha*. Note the embedded password (`pwd=jirafryvukomuha`).

Add-Ons
Hacks 59–70

Google is *of* the Web, but that doesn't mean that it's trapped in your browser. Google has become so much a part of the fabric of our everyday lives that it shows up just about everywhere. Google via email [Hack #64], through instant messaging [Hack #65], from a chat room [Hack #66], on your mobile phone [Hack #67]; you can even take it out for a night on the town in the form of a groovy belt buckle [Hack #70].

This chapter is a tour of some of the more interesting ways in which Google has leapt out of the pages of cyberspace and into what hackers affectionately call *meat space*: everyday life, to you and me.

HACK
#59

Keep Tabs on Your Searches with Google Alerts

Receive alerts in your email Inbox or RSS reader when something you're after makes its way into the Google Web index or a Google News story.

There are two classes of search that one generally runs in Google. One is of the sort that you generally run just the once: you're trying to find information on some topic, a phone number, or that URL you visited yesterday but have since forgotten.

Then there's the search that you'd run every day if you could. You're interested in a particular subject matter and want to know the moment Google finds and indexes something new on the topic.

There are a couple of services available that'll do the trick: the official Google Alerts notifies you of any new web pages or news stories matching your search criteria, while the third-party service GoogleAlert watches only for new web pages but sports a few extra features and delivery options not found in Google's version.

Google's Web index does not consider a page "new" based on the date it was created. Instead, it considers a page new based on the date that it was found and indexed by the Googlebot. For more detail on the difference, see "daterange:" under the "Special Syntax" section in Chapter 1.

Google Alerts

Google Alerts (*http://www.google.com/alerts*), Google's official alert offering, allows you to monitor both Google's Web index and Google News stories. To set up a Google Alert, visit the Google Alerts page. In the Create a Google Alert form (shown in Figure 5-1), type in a search query and choose whether to monitor news, the Web, or both.

Figure 5-1. Monitor Google's Web Index and Google News stories with Google Alerts

You have a choice when it comes to how often you're notified: as it happens, once a day, or once a week. Provide your email address, click the Create Alert button, and you'll receive a confirmation email message a few moments later. Follow the link provided in the email message—thus confirming that your email address is legitimate and that it was you who requested the Google Alert—and you're all set.

Be careful of the update frequency option; monitoring Google News' 4,500 sources for even a slightly common word, phrase, or name and choosing to receive notification "as it happens" can fill your inbox with an avalanche of email.

Each alert that you receive includes your search query, the found page's title, a snippet of content, and the URL (for web index results) or story title, URL, description, and source (for news stories). You can set up to 50 alerts per email address.

While all you need to sign up for Google Alerts is a valid email address, there's also the option to sign into Google for a more hands-on approach to managing your alerts. On the Google Alerts page, click the "sign in to manage your alerts" link.

You'll need to already have or sign up for a free Google account. But membership has its privileges:

- Signing in provides you with a nice overview of your active alerts.
- If you don't sign in to manage your Google Alerts, you can't edit the Google Alerts that you create. All you can do is delete them and create new ones.
- Google Alerts are delivered in HTML format as a default; by signing in, you can switch to text and back again.
- A Google account opens doors to other Google properties such as Google Answers (*http://answers.google.com*), allows you to create your own Google Groups (*http://groups.google.com*) **[Hack #56]**, etc.

GoogleAlert

Before there were Google Alerts, there was GoogleAlert (*http://www.googlealert.com*), a third-party alert service built on the Google API **[Chapter 9]**. Being built on the API, it is kept to only the Google Web index and can't monitor anything like Google News or whatever else Google decides to have the official Google Alerts cover in the near future.

However, GoogleAlert does offer a few features worth checking out. Start by signing up for a trial account, which affords you up to three queries.

Full GoogleAlert accounts aren't free; they range from $4.95 to $19.95 per month, affording you more searches with more extensive delivery options.

GoogleAlert's Advanced Search form, shown in Figure 5-2, is similar to Google's Advanced Search page (*http://www.google.com/advanced_search*), allowing you to build Boolean searches, search for exact phrases, restrict your searches to a particular site or date range, specify the file types that you're interested in, and more—all without having to fiddle with special syntax.

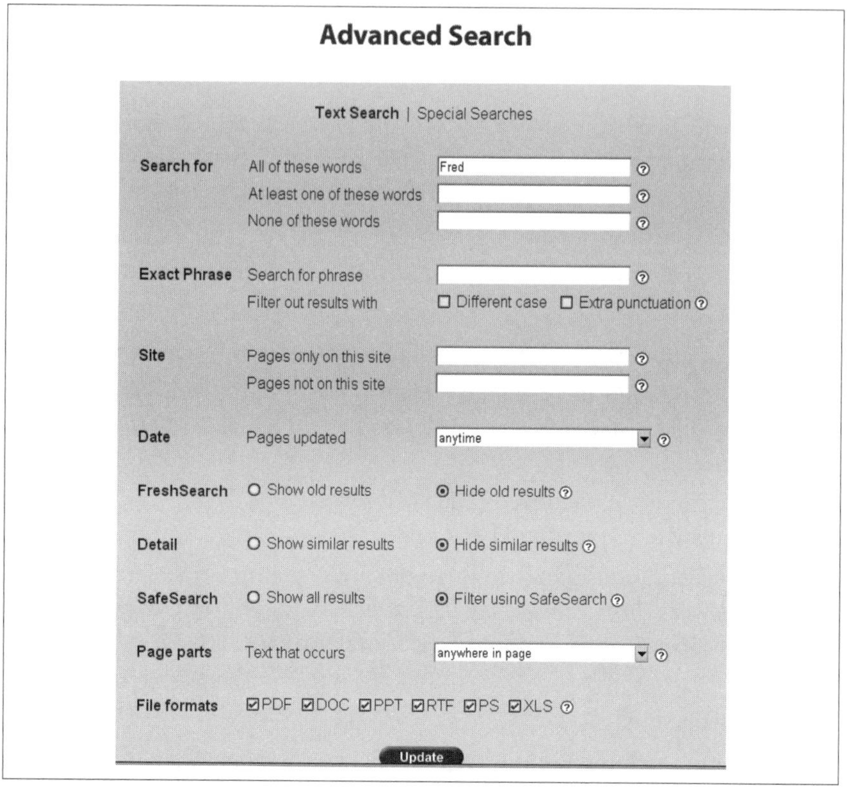

Figure 5-2. GoogleAlert offers search extras like case-sensitivity and delivery via RSS

You can receive your alerts by email, of course. But you can also subscribe to them as a syndicated RSS feed, or have a page on your weblog pinged by TrackBack (*http://www.movabletype.org/trackback/beginners*) notification any time something new comes up.

Monitoring Google's Web index allows me to find search engines or directories of information that I might have missed otherwise. I keep tabs on Google to find pages that don't tend to appear out of thin air all that often: those containing "online museum" or "online reference service", for example.

I tend to use broader search queries when monitoring Google News. While watching the Google Web index for "online database" or "new search engine" might net me thousands of results—and those long after the sites were actually new—online news stories about new online databases and search engines tend to crop up less frequently and provide a higher signal-to-noise ratio.

Add Google to Your Toolbar or Desktop

Google from wherever you are without skipping a beat, thanks to an assortment of browser search boxes, toolbars, and desktop applications.

Just because Google is a web site doesn't mean that you have to deal with it as such. Picture this: you're in the zone, working on that big project, browser windows, spreadsheets, and slides littering your desktop—both figuratively and literally. At some point you need to check a fact, find a statistic, or read a news story. Now, you could open yet another browser window, type google.com, and search the Web, but that's about two steps too many and (done repeatedly) may well disrupt your flow.

Take, for instance, what happened in the midst of writing this hack. Up popped an instant message from a friend with a patent number that he'd stumbled across and that he thought I might find interesting. I could have opened another browser window, browsed to *http://www.google.com*, Googled for "us patent database", and searched for that particular patent. Instead, I pasted that number into the Google Search box built right into my Firefox web browser (shown in Figure 5-3), prefixed it with patent, hit Return, and clicked the quick link to the patent at the U.S. Patent Database ["Quick Links: Google by Numbers" in Chapter 1]. This sort of flow, despite saving only a step or two at most, is so catchy that it has become an integral part of my workflow.

> By *toolbar*, we actually mean one of several add-ons: search boxes built into your web browser (as described earlier), toolbars that attach themselves to your browser and provide search and other capabilities, and search boxes you that you can embed elsewhere into your desktop, taskbar, or toolbars.

This hack is a roundup of some of the Google toolbars that you'll find available from Google itself or from third-party developers (all of them are free for the taking.)

Figure 5-3. *The Firefox built-in search box expands to talk to just about any search engine*

Browser Search Boxes

The open source Mozilla (*http://www.mozilla.org/products/mozilla1.x*), Firefox (*http://www.mozilla.org/products/firefox*), and Netscape (*http://channels. netscape.com/ns/browsers*) browsers, as well as the Mac OS X Safari (*http:// www.apple.com/safari*) and Opera Software's Opera (*http://www.opera.com*) browsers, all sport a search box either in the toolbar itself or a sidebar like the one shown in Figure 5-4. Most often, too, the search box can be configured to redirect your searches to any number of search engines using a drop-down menu or preference setting.

The Mozilla search functionality shown in Figure 5-4 can be reached by various means: typing a search into the address bar and clicking the Search button, selecting View → Sidebar and choosing the Search tab, or highlighting a word in any web page, right-clicking it, and selecting "Search Web for ..."

The Official Google Toolbar

The official Google Toolbar (*http://toolbar.google.com*; Windows only) goes so much further than a simple search box for Google and so is highly recommended for Windows users. It is constantly updated, sometimes with Google slipping in little Easter eggs (read: surprise features) just for fun. Figure 5-5 shows the Google Toolbar in action.

Search the Web, the site you're currently visiting, by country domain, or use any of the various Google properties, including Google Images, Directory,

Figure 5-4. The Mozilla Search sidebar is always within easy reach

Figure 5-5. The official Google Toolbar; don't be fooled by imposters

News, Froogle, and so forth. There are even voting buttons (the happy- and sad-face icons) if you feel like letting Google know what you think of the page you're on. And the official toolbar is the only version that sports PageRank ["The Mysterious PageRank" in Chapter 8] for the page you're currently visiting. Additional features include pop-up blocking, auto-fill for web forms, highlighting of search keywords in resulting pages, and more.

The Mozilla Googlebar

Mozilla/Firefox users (whether on Windows, Mac, or Unix/Linux) can't use the Google Toolbar, but the Googlebar (http://googlebar.mozdev.org) is a rather acceptable substitute. It looks and acts very much like the official version, attempting to match any functionality that it can (see Figure 5-6). It doesn't, however, provide PageRank.

Most people don't care one whit about PageRank. But webmasters and researchers consider PageRank a critical indicator of the importance of a particular web site or individual page. If you're a Mozilla/Firefox user and

Figure 5-6. The Mozilla Googlebar mimics the official offering as much as possible

just can't live without PageRank, PRGooglebar (*http://www.prgooglebar.org*) is a modification of the Googlebar that incorporates PageRank. And then there's also the Google PageRank extension (*http://www.tapouillo.com/firefox_extension*), embedding PageRank into the Mozilla/Firefox status bar.

Desktop Search Boxes

And then there are applications that live not in the browser, but on your desktop, in your taskbar or toolbar, or behind a right-mouse-click.

Gophoria (*http://www.gophoria.com*; Windows only) turns any text, URL, or image into a right-clickable search. Highlight some text, right click, and select "gophoria search" from the context menu.

The official Google Deskbar (*http://toolbar.google.com/deskbar*; Windows only) affords you a quick and simple interface to Google Web Search,

Google Images, Google News, and Froogle. Results show up in a small preview window that looks like the familiar Google results page.

Dave's Quick Search Deskbar (*http://dqsd.net*; Windows only), as you may have guessed from the name, sits in your deskbar or taskbar. But the simple name belies some incredible functionality, not the least of which is special triggers and switches. Enter a query in the box and hit the Enter key on your keyboard to search Google; results pop up in your browser. Feeling lucky? Add an exclamation mark (!) to your query (e.g., "washington post"!) and you'll be taken straight to the top ranked result. The # tacked on to George Bush (tx)# performs a phonebook lookup. & dives into the Google cache. And there are tons more; press F1 for a full list, shown in Figure 5-7.

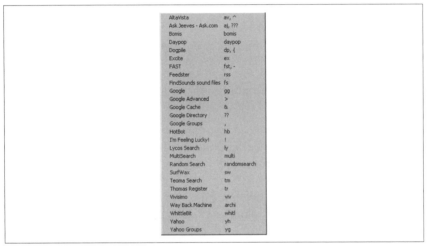

Figure 5-7. Dave's Quick Search Deskbar provides no-nonsense search shortcuts

GGSearch (*http://www.frysianfools.com/ggsearch*; Windows only) is one of the more gorgeous toolbars I've seen, with several themes and skins. There are many search tools here, accessible via a series of menus. It's rather mind-bending to see Google's simple interface sliced and diced into menu item within menu item (Figure 5-8), but it's a flexible, useful tool, nevertheless.

Mac OS X's built-in Search with Google service (Mac only ;-)) puts Google only a three-finger key combo away. Highlight any text in any OS X Service–aware application (e.g., not a Microsoft Office for Mac OS X product) and select Services → Search with Google from the application menu (i.e., Finder if you you're in the Finder, Safari if you're in Safari) or type Command-Shift-L and you'll Google for the highlighted words. The results appear in your browser window.

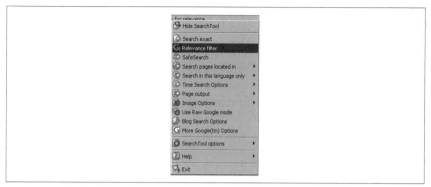

Figure 5-8. GGSearch slices and dices Google's search options

Google Your Desktop

HACK
#61

Google your desktop and the rest of your filesystem, mailbox, and instant messenger conversations—even your browser cache.

Not content just to help you find things on the Internet, Google takes on that teetering pile on your desktop—your computer's desktop, that is.

The Google Desktop (*http://desktop.google.com*) is your own private little Google server. It sits in the background, slogging through your files and folders, indexing your incoming and outgoing email messages, listening in on your instant messenger chats, and browsing the Web right along with you. Just about anything you see and summarily forget, the Google Desktop sees and memorizes: it's like a photographic memory for your computer.

And it operates in real time.

Beyond the initial sweep, that is. When you first install Google Desktop, it makes use of any idle time to meander your filesystem, email application, instant messages, and browser cache. Imbued with a sense of politeness, the indexer shouldn't interfere at all with your use of your computer; it only springs into action when you step away, take a phone call, or doze off for 30 seconds or more. Pick up the mouse or touch the keyboard and the Google Desktop scuttles off into the corner, waiting patiently for its next opportunity to look around.

Its initial inventory taken, the Google Desktop server sits back and waits for something of interest to come along. Send or receive an email message, strike up an AIM conversation with a friend, or get a start on that Power-Point presentation and it'll be noticed and indexed within seconds.

The Google Desktop full-text indexes:

- Text files, Microsoft Word documents, Excel workbooks, and Power-Point presentations living on your hard drive
- Email handled through Outlook or Outlook Express
- AOL Instant Messenger (AIM) conversations
- Web pages browsed in Internet Explorer

Additionally, any other files you have lying about—photographs, MP3s, movies—are indexed by their filename. So while the Google Desktop can't tell a portrait of Uncle Alfred (*uncle_alfred.jpg*) from a song by "Uncle Cracker" (*uncle_cracker__double_wide__who_s_your_uncle.mp3*), it'll file both in a search for uncle.

And the point of all this is to make your computer searchable with the ease, speed, and familiar interface you've come to expect of Google. The Google Desktop has its own home page on your computer, shown in Figure 5-9, whether you're online or not. Type in a search query just like you would at Google proper and click the Search Desktop button to search your personal index. Or click Search the Web to send your query out to Google.

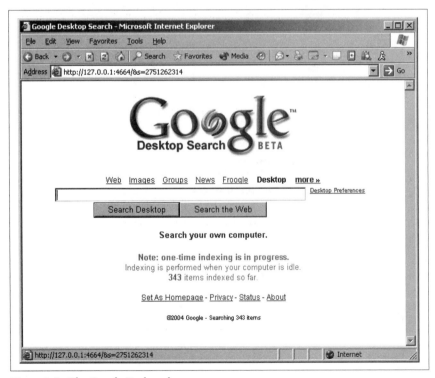

Figure 5-9. The Google Desktop home page

But we're getting a little ahead of ourselves here.

Let's take a few steps back, download and install the Google Desktop, and work our way back to searching again.

Installing the Google Desktop

The Google Desktop is a Windows-only application, requiring Windows XP or Windows 2000 Service Pack 3 or later. The application itself is tiny, but it'll consume about 500 MB of room on your hard drive and works best with 400 MHz of computing horsepower and 128 MB of memory.

Point your browser at *http://desktop.google.com*, download, and run the Google Desktop installer. It'll install the application, embed a little swirly icon in your taskbar, and drop a shortcut onto your desktop. When it's finished installing and setting itself up, your default browser pops open and you're asked to set a few preferences, as shown in Figure 5-10.

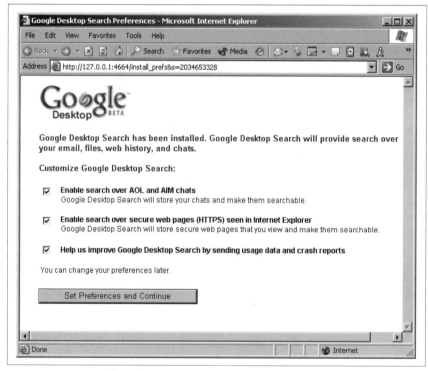

Figure 5-10. Set Google Desktop search preferences

Click the Set Preferences and Continue button and you'll be notified that the Google Desktop is starting its initial indexing sweep. Click the Start Searching button to get to the Google Desktop home page (Figure 5-9).

Searching Your Desktop

From here on out, any time you're looking for something on your computer, rather than invoking Windows search and waiting impatiently while it grinds away (and you grind your teeth) and returns with nothing, double-click the swirly Google Desktop taskbar icon and Google for it. Don't bother combing through an endless array of Inboxes, Outboxes, Sent Mail, and folders or wishing you could remember whether your AIM buddy suggested starving or feeding your cold. Click the swirl.

Figure 5-11 shows the results of a Google Desktop search for hacks. Notice that it found 16 email messages, 2 files, 1 chat, and 1 item in my IE browsing history matching my hacks query. As you can probably guess from the icons to the left of each results, the first three are an AIM chat, HTML file (most likely from my browser's cache), and an email message. These are sorted by date, but you can easily make a switch to relevance by clicking the "Sort by relevance" link at the top-right of the results list.

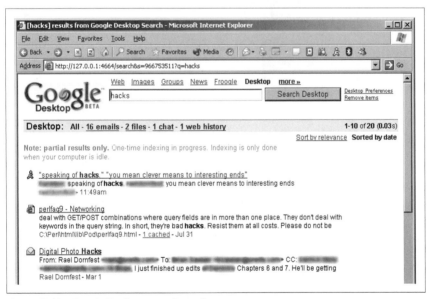

Figure 5-11. Google Desktop search results

Figures 5-12, 5-13, and 5-14 show each of these individual search results as I clicked through them. Note that each is displayed in a manner appropriate to the content.

Click the "Chat with..." link shown in Figure 5-12 to launch an AIM conversation with the person at hand.

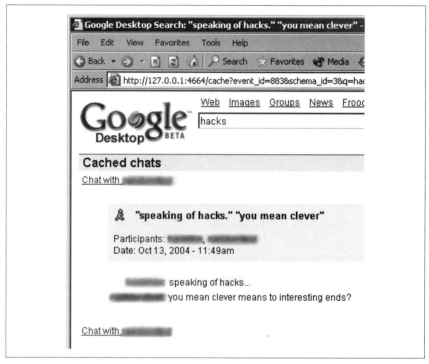

Figure 5-12. An AIM instant message

Cached pages are presented, as shown in Figure 5-13, in much the same manner as they are in the Google cache.

The various Reply, Reply to All, Forward, etc., links associated with an individual message result (Figure 5-14) work: click them and the appropriate action will be taken by Outlook or Outlook Express.

Google Desktop Search Syntax

It just wouldn't be a Google search interface if there weren't special search syntax to go along with it.

The Boolean OR works as expected (e.g., hacks OR snacks), as does negation (e.g., hacks -evil).

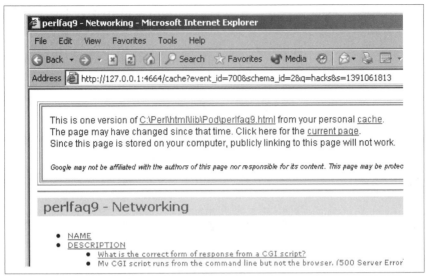

Figure 5-13. A cached web page

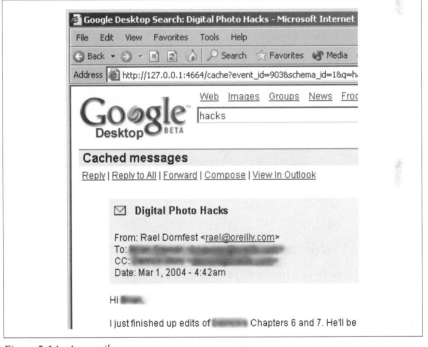

Figure 5-14. An email message

A filetype: operator restricts searches to only a particular type of file: filetype:powerpoint or filetype:ppt (.*ppt* being the PowerPoint file extension) both find only Microsoft PowerPoint files while filetype:word or filetype:doc (.*doc* being the Word file extension) both restrict results to Microsoft Word documents.

Searching the Web

Now you'd think I'd hardly need to cover Googling ... and you'd be right. But there's a little more to googling via the Google Desktop than you might expect. Take a close look at the results of a Google search for hacks shown in Figure 5-15.

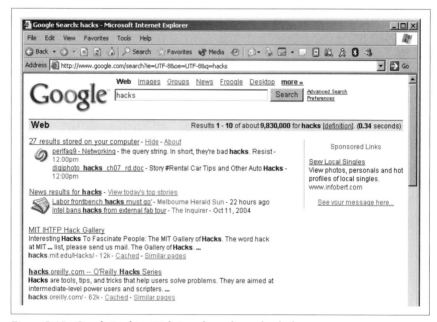

Figure 5-15. Google Desktop Web Search results pack a little extra

Come on back when you're through with that double take.

If you missed it, notice the new quick links **["Quick Links" in Chapter 1]**: "27 results stored on your computer."

Yes, those are the same results (and then some, given my indexer was hard at work) returned in my earlier Google Desktop Search of my local machine. As an added reminder, they're called out by that Google Desktop swirl. Click a local result and you'll end up in just the same place as before: all 27 results, an HTML page, or Microsoft Word document. Click any other quick link or search result and they'll act in the manner that you'd expect from any Google.com results.

Behind the Scenes

Now before you start worrying about the results of a local search—or indeed your local files—being sent off to Google, read on. What's actually going on is that the local Google Desktop server is intercepting any Google Web searches, passing them on to Google.com in your stead, and running the same search against your computer's local index. It's then intercepting the Web search results as they come back from Google, pasting in local finds, and presenting it to you in your browser as a cohesive whole.

All work involving your local data is done on your computer. Neither your filenames nor your files themselves are ever sent on to Google.com.

For more on Google Desktop and privacy, right-click the Google Desktop taskbar swirl, select About, and click the Privacy link.

Twiddling Knobs and Setting Preferences

There are various knobs to twiddle and preferences to set through the Google Desktop browser-based interface and taskbar swirl.

Set various preferences in the Google Desktop Preferences page. Click the Desktop Preferences link on the Google Desktop home page or any results page to bring up the settings shown in Figure 5-16.

Hide your local results from sight when sharing Google Web Search results with a friend or colleague by clicking the Hide link next to any visible Google Desktop quick links. You can also turn Desktop quick link results on and off from the Google Desktop Preferences page.

Click the "Remove results" link next to the Search Desktop button on the top-right of any results page and you'll be able to go through and remove particular items from Google Desktop index, as shown in Figure 5-17. Do note that if you open or view any of these items again, they'll once again be indexed and start showing up in search results.

Search, set preferences, check the status of your index, pause or resume indexing, quit Google Desktop, or browse the "About" docs by right-clicking the Google Desktop taskbar swirl and choosing an item from the menu, shown in Figure 5-18.

When evaluating the Google Desktop as an interface to finding needles in my personal haystack, one thing sticks in my mind: I stumbled across an old email message that I was sure I'd lost.

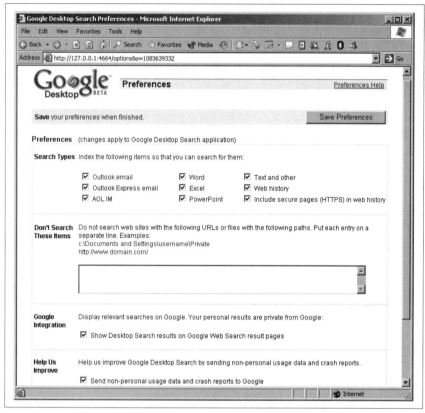

Figure 5-16. Google Desktop Preferences

See Also

- The Google Desktop Proxy (*http://www.projectcomputing.com/resources/ desktopProxy*) takes desktop searching beyond your own desktop. A little proxy server sitting on your computer accepts queries from other machines on the network, passes them to the Google Desktop engine running locally, and forwards the results on.

HACK
#62   Google with Bookmarklets

Create interactive bookmarklets to perform Google functions from the comfort of your own browser.

You probably know what *bookmarks* are. But what are *bookmarklets*? Bookmarklets are like bookmarks but with an extra bit of JavaScript magic added. This makes them more interactive than regular bookmarks; they can perform small functions like opening a window, grabbing highlighted text from

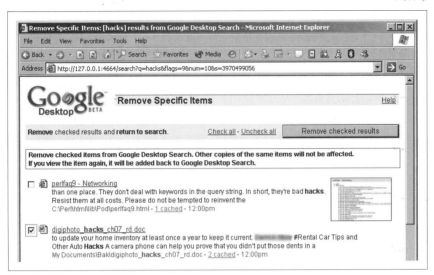

Figure 5-17. Removing items from your Google Desktop index

Figure 5-18. The Google Desktop taskbar menu gets you to knobs to twiddle and preferences to set

a web page, or submitting a query to a search engine. There are several bookmarklets that allow you to perform useful Google functions right from the comfort of your own browser.

If you're using Internet Explorer for Windows, you're in gravy: all these bookmarklets will most likely work as advertised. But if you're using a less-appreciated browser (such as Opera) or operating system (such as Mac OS X), pay attention to the bookmarklet requirements and instructions; there may be special magic needed to get a particular bookmark working, or indeed, you may not be able to use the bookmarklet at all.

Google Translate! (http://www.microcontentnews.com/resources/translator.htm)
> Puts Google's translation tools into a bookmarklet, enabling one-button translation of the current web page.

Google Jump (http://www.angelfire.com/dc/dcbookmarkletlab/Bookmarklets/script002.html)
> Prompts you for search terms, performs a Google search, and takes you straight to the top hit thanks to the magic of Google's I'm Feeling Lucky function.

The Dooyoo Bookmarklets (http://dooyoo-uk.tripod.com/bookmarklets2.html) collection
> Features several bookmarklets for use with different search engines—two for Google. Similar to Google's Browser Buttons, one finds highlighted text and the other finds related pages.

Joe Maller's Translation Bookmarkets (http://www.joemaller.com/translation_bookmarklets.shtml)
> Translate the current page into the specified language via Google or AltaVista.

Bookmarklets for Opera (http://www.philburns.com/bookmarklets.html)
> Includes a Google translation bookmarklet, a Google bookmarklet that restricts searches to the current domain, and a bookmarklet that searches Google Groups. As you might imagine, these bookmarklets were created for use with the Opera browser.

LuckyMarklets (http://www.researchbuzz.org/archives/001414.shtml)
> Tara's bookmarklets taking advantage of the I'm Feeling Lucky feature in Google Web Search, Google News, and Google Images.

Milly's Bookmarklets (http://www.imilly.com/bm.htm)
> An incredible collection of bookmarklets for all things Google: Web Search, Images, Directory, Definitions, Cache, the Google site itself, and many more, Google or otherwise.

H A C K   Google from Word
#63   Add a little Google to Microsoft Word.

You probably use Google a few dozen times a day. If you work a lot within Microsoft Word, using Google usually means switching over to your web browser, checking the results, and then going back to Word. This hack will show you how to display the search results in Word's New Document Task Pane.

This hack uses a plain text *.ini* file to store data and some Visual Basic for Applications (VBA) code that also uses VBScript regular expressions.

> This hack will work only with Word 2003 for Windows.

Using Google from Word requires a bit of setup, but once you've installed the appropriate tools, you can use Google from within any Word macro.

Install the Web Services Toolkit

First, install the free Microsoft Office 2003 Web Services Toolkit 2.01. Search for it on the Microsoft web site (*http://www.microsoft.com/ downloads/*) or Google it.

Create a New Template

Next, create a new template to hold your Google-related macros. The Web Services Toolkit will create some code so that you can work with Google. A separate template will help you keep track of the code. Create a new, blank document and save it as a Document Template named *GoogleTools.dot*.

Install the Google Interface VBA Code

From your new *GoogleTools.dot* template, select Tools → Macro → Visual Basic Editor. The Web Services Toolkit will have added a new item called Web Service References on the Tools menu, as shown in Figure 5-19.

Figure 5-19. Creating a new reference for accessing Google

Select Tools → Web Service References to display the dialog shown in Figure 5-20. Enter `google` in the Keywords field and click the Search button. When the web service is found, check the box next to it, and click the Add button.

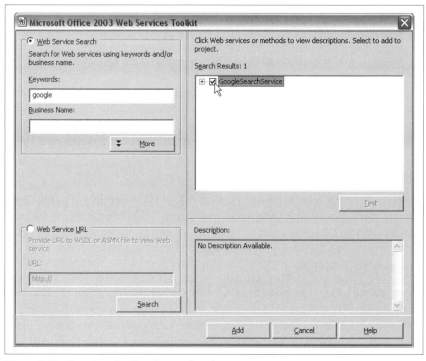

Figure 5-20. Locating the Google search web service

When you click the Add button, you'll notice a flurry of activity on your screen as the Web Services Toolkit installs several new class modules into your template project, as shown in Figure 5-21.

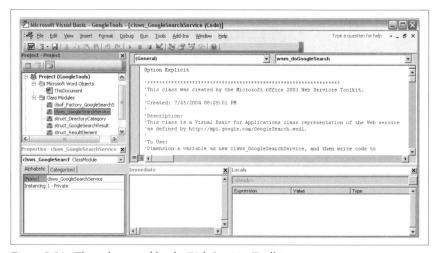

Figure 5-21. The code created by the Web Services Toolkit

The Web Services Toolkit creates the code, but it actually comes from Google using Web Services Description Language (WSDL). The Toolkit interprets this information and generates the VBA code needed to access the web service—in this case, Google.

The Code

With the *GoogleTools.dot* template you created open, select Tools → Macro → Macros and insert the following code, which consists of a procedure named GoogleToTaskPane and a supporting function named StripHTML.

Make sure you replace the value *insert key here* with your Google API developer's key.

```
Sub GoogleToTaskPane( )
Dim vSearchResults As Variant
Dim v As Variant
Dim sResults As String
Dim sEntryName As String
Dim sEntryURL As String
Dim sLogFile As String
Dim sSearchDisplayTitle As String
Dim sSearchURL As String
Dim i As Integer

' Google API variables
Dim sGoogleAPIKey As String
Dim sSearchQuery As String
Dim lStart As Long
Dim lMaxResults As Long
Dim bFilter As Boolean
Dim sRestrict As String
Dim bSafeSearch As Boolean
Dim sLanguageRestrict As String
Dim sInputEncoding As String
Dim sOutputEncoding As String
Dim google_search As New clsws_GoogleSearchService

' Initialize variables
sLogFile = "C:\google_taskpane.ini"
sGoogleAPIKey = "insert your key"
lStart = 1
lMaxResults = 10
bFilter = True
sRestrict = ""
bSafeSearch = False
sLanguageRestrict = ""
```

```
        sInputEncoding = "UTF-8"
        sOutputEncoding = "UTF-8"

        ' Hide the Task Pane
        Application.CommandBars("Task Pane").Visible = False

        ' Remove existing items from New Document Task Pane
        For i = 0 To 9
            sEntryURL = System.PrivateProfileString( _
                    FileName:=sLogFile, _
                    Section:="GoogleTaskPane", _
                    Key:="URLName" & CStr(i))
            sEntryName = System.PrivateProfileString( _
                    FileName:=sLogFile, _
                    Section:="GoogleTaskPane", _
                    Key:="EntryName" & CStr(i))
            If Len(sEntryURL) > 0 Then
                Application.NewDocument.Remove _
                    FileName:=sEntryURL, _
                    Section:=msoBottomSection, _
                    DisplayName:=sEntryName, _
                    Action:=msoOpenFile
            End If
        Next i

        ' Get new search query
        sSearchQuery = InputBox("Enter a Google query:")
        If Len(sSearchQuery) = 0 Then Exit Sub

        ' Get search results
        vSearchResults = google_search.wsm_doGoogleSearch( _
                str_key:=sGoogleAPIKey, _
                str_q:=sSearchQuery, _
                lng_start:=lStart, _
                lng_maxResults:=lMaxResults, _
                bln_filter:=bFilter, _
                str_restrict:=sRestrict, _
                bln_safeSearch:=bSafeSearch, _
                str_lr:=sLanguageRestrict, _
                str_ie:=sInputEncoding, _
                str_oe:=sOutputEncoding).resultElements

        ' Check for no results
        On Error Resume Next
        v = UBound(vSearchResults)
        If Err.Number = 9 Then
            MsgBox "No results found"
            Exit Sub
        ElseIf Err.Number <> 0 Then
            MsgBox "An error has occurred: " & _
                Err.Number & vbCr & _
                Err.Description
            Exit Sub
        End If
```

```
' Add each result to the task pane
' and to the log file
i = 0
For Each v In vSearchResults
    sSearchURL = v.URL
    sSearchDisplayTitle = StripHTML(v.title)
    Application.NewDocument.Add _
        FileName:=sSearchURL, _
        Section:=msoBottomSection, _
        DisplayName:=sSearchDisplayTitle, _
        Action:=msoOpenFile

    System.PrivateProfileString( _
        FileName:=sLogFile, _
        Section:="GoogleTaskPane", _
        Key:="URLName" & CStr(i)) = sSearchURL
    System.PrivateProfileString( _
        FileName:=sLogFile, _
        Section:="GoogleTaskPane", _
        Key:="EntryName" & CStr(i)) = sSearchDisplayTitle
    i = i + 1
Next v

' Show the New Document Task Pane
CommandBars("Menu Bar").Controls("File").Controls("New...").Execute

End Sub

Function StripHTML(str As String) As String
Dim re As Object
Dim k As Long
On Error Resume Next
Set re = GetObject(Class:="VBScript.RegExp")
If Err.Number = 429 Then
    Set re = CreateObject(Class:="VBScript.RegExp")
    Err.Clear
ElseIf Err.Number <> 0 Then
    MsgBox Err.Number & vbCr & Err.Description
End If

' Check for common character entities by ASCII value
For k = 33 To 255
    re.Pattern = "&#" & k & ";"
    str = re.Replace(str, Chr$(k))
Next k

' Remove common HTML tags
re.Pattern = "<[^>]+?>|&[^;]+?;"
re.Global = True
str = re.Replace(str, vbNullString)
StripHTML = str
End Function
```

This hack uses two parts of the Google search results: the URLs and titles. Google formats the search result title as HTML, but you can only put plain text in the Task Pane. The StripHTML function uses a few simple VBScript Regular Expressions to strip out common HTML tags (such as <b>) and replace character entities (such as @) with their ASCII character equivalents.

It can be tricky to remove files from the Task Pane using VBA unless you know their exact name. This macro, however, stores the search results in a plain-text *.ini* file. The next time you do a search, you can easily remove the previous results. The macro uses a file named *C:\google_taskpane.ini*, which is defined in the GoogleToTaskPane procedure.

Running the Hack

After you insert the code, switch back to Word. Next, select Tools → Macro → Macros, choose GoogleToTaskPane, and click the Run button to display the dialog shown in Figure 5-22.

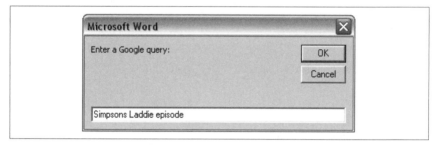

Figure 5-22. Entering a Google search that will display in the Task Pane

Enter your search terms and click the OK button. The New Document Task Pane appears and displays the search results, as shown in Figure 5-23. Hover your mouse over any of the entries to display the URL. Click a URL to open the site in your web browser.

Every time you run a search, the macro removes the previous results from the Task Pane. If you want to remove the previous results without displaying new ones, click the Cancel button in the dialog box shown in Figure 5-22.

> To make sure this handy macro loads automatically when Word starts, put *GoogleTools.dot* into your Startup folder, typically *C:\Documents and Setting\<username>\Application Data\Microsoft\Word\STARTUP*.

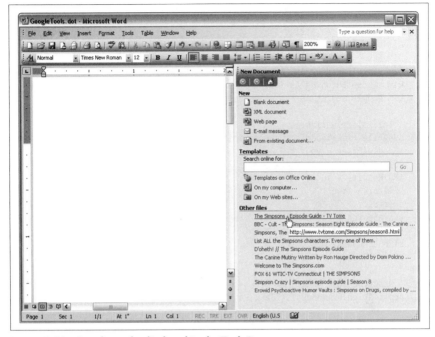

Figure 5-23. Google results displayed in the Task Pane

Hacking the Hack

To take this hack one step further, you can modify it to use the currently selected text as the search text, rather than displaying an input box and entering text.

The following macro, named GoogleSelectionToTaskPane, does a Google search of the currently selected text and displays the results in the Task Pane. The modified code is shown in bold.

```
Sub GoogleSelectionToTaskPane( )
Dim vSearchResults As Variant
Dim v As Variant
Dim sResults As String
Dim sEntryName As String
Dim sEntryURL As String
Dim sLogFile As String
Dim sSearchDisplayTitle As String
Dim sSearchURL As String
Dim i As Integer

' Google API variables
Dim sGoogleAPIKey As String
Dim sSearchQuery As String
Dim lStart As Long
```

```
        Dim lMaxResults As Long
        Dim bFilter As Boolean
        Dim sRestrict As String
        Dim bSafeSearch As Boolean
        Dim sLanguageRestrict As String
        Dim sInputEncoding As String
        Dim sOutputEncoding As String
        Dim google_search As New clsws_GoogleSearchService

        ' Initialize variables
        sLogFile = "C:\google_taskpane.ini"
        sGoogleAPIKey = your_key_here
        lStart = 1
        lMaxResults = 10
        bFilter = True
        sRestrict = ""
        bSafeSearch = False
        sLanguageRestrict = ""
        sInputEncoding = "UTF-8"
        sOutputEncoding = "UTF-8"

        ' Hide the Task Pane
        Application.CommandBars("Task Pane").Visible = False

        ' Remove existing items from New Document Task Pane
        For i = 0 To 9
            sEntryURL = System.PrivateProfileString( _
                    FileName:=sLogFile, _
                    Section:="GoogleTaskPane", _
                    Key:="URLName" & CStr(i))
            sEntryName = System.PrivateProfileString( _
                    FileName:=sLogFile, _
                    Section:="GoogleTaskPane", _
                    Key:="EntryName" & CStr(i))
            If Len(sEntryURL) > 0 Then
                Application.NewDocument.Remove _
                    FileName:=sEntryURL, _
                    Section:=msoBottomSection, _
                    DisplayName:=sEntryName, _
                    Action:=msoOpenFile
            End If
        Next i

        ' Move ends of selection to exclude spaces
        ' and paragraph marks
        Selection.MoveStartWhile cset:=Chr$(32) & Chr$(19), _
            Count:=Selection.Characters.Count
        Selection.MoveEndWhile cset:=Chr$(32) & Chr$(19), _
            Count:=-Selection.Characters.Count

        ' Get selection text for search
        sSearchQuery = Selection.Text
        If Len(sSearchQuery) = 0 Then Exit Sub
```

```
' Get search results
vSearchResults = google_search.wsm_doGoogleSearch( _
        str_key:=sGoogleAPIKey, _
        str_q:=sSearchQuery, _
        lng_start:=lStart, _
        lng_maxResults:=lMaxResults, _
        bln_filter:=bFilter, _
        str_restrict:=sRestrict, _
        bln_safeSearch:=bSafeSearch, _
        str_lr:=sLanguageRestrict, _
        str_ie:=sInputEncoding, _
        str_oe:=sOutputEncoding).resultElements

' Check for no results
On Error Resume Next
v = UBound(vSearchResults)
If Err.Number = 9 Then
    MsgBox "No results found"
    Exit Sub
ElseIf Err.Number <> 0 Then
    MsgBox "An error has occurred: " & _
        Err.Number & vbCr & _
        Err.Description
    Exit Sub
End If

' Add each result to the task pane
' and to the log file
i = 0
For Each v In vSearchResults
    sSearchURL = v.URL
    sSearchDisplayTitle = StripHTML(v.title)
    Application.NewDocument.Add _
        FileName:=sSearchURL, _
        Section:=msoBottomSection, _
        DisplayName:=sSearchDisplayTitle, _
        Action:=msoOpenFile

    System.PrivateProfileString( _
        FileName:=sLogFile, _
        Section:="GoogleTaskPane", _
        Key:="URLName" & CStr(i)) = sSearchURL
    System.PrivateProfileString( _
        FileName:=sLogFile, _
        Section:="GoogleTaskPane", _
        Key:="EntryName" & CStr(i)) = sSearchDisplayTitle
    i = i + 1
Next v

' Show the New Document Task Pane
CommandBars("Menu Bar").Controls("File").Controls("New...").Execute

End Sub
```

To help ensure a good Google search, the following two lines collapse two ends of the selection if they contain spaces or a paragraph mark:

```
Selection.MoveStartWhile cset:=Chr$(32) & Chr$(19), _
    Count:=Selection.Characters.Count
Selection.MoveEndWhile cset:=Chr$(32) & Chr$(19), _
    Count:=-Selection.Characters.Count
```

—Andrew Savikas

HACK #64 Google by Email

Access 10 of Google's search results at a time via email.

Long before the Web existed, there was email. And now, thanks to the Google API, there's Google email. Created by the team at Cape Clear (*http://capescience.capeclear.com/google*), CapeMail queries Google via email. Send email to *google@capeclear.com* with the query in the subject line. You'll receive a message back with the estimated results count and the first 10 results.

Here's an excerpt from a search for Frankenstein:

```
Estimated Total Results Number = 591000

    URL  = "http://www.literature.org/authors/shelley-mary/frankenstein/"
    Title = "Online Literature Library - Mary Shelley - Frankenstein"
    Snippet = "Next Back Contents Home Authors Contact, Frankenstein.
Mary Shelley. Preface; Chapter 1; Chapter 2; Chapter 3; Chapter 4;
Chapter 5; Chapter 6; Chapter 7; Chapter ...  "

    URL  = "http://www.nlm.nih.gov/hmd/frankenstein/frankhome.html"
    Title = "Frankenstein Exhibit Home Page"
    Snippet = "Table of Contents Introduction The Birth of Frankenstein,
The Celluloid Monster. Promise and Peril, Frankenstein: The Modern
Prometheus. ...  "

    URL  = "http://www.sangfroid.com/frank/"
    Title = "Frankenstein, or The Modern Prometheus"
    Snippet = "1818 (this edition 1831) Frankenstein is the world-famous
story of a doctor whose brilliant mind gets the better of him. "

    URL  = "http://www.imdb.com/Title?0021884"
    Title = "Frankenstein (1931)"
    Snippet = "Frankenstein (1931) - Cast, Crew, Reviews, Plot Summary,
Comments, Discussion, Taglines, Trailers, Posters, Photos, Showtimes,
Link to Official Site, Fan Sites. ...  "
```

Like many other Google API applications, you can use CapeMail only 1,000 times per day, since the Google API allows the use of the key only that many times. Don't rely on this to the exclusion of other ways to access Google.

But if you're in a situation where web searching is not quite as easy as sending an email message—you're on the go with a mobile phone or PDA, for example—this is a quick and easy way to interface with Google.

Hacking the Hack

CapeMail comes in handy with the combination of an email application and a way to automate sending messages (Unix's cron, for example). Say you're researching a particular topic—a relatively obscure topic but one that does generate web page results. You could set up your scheduler (or even your email program if able to send timed messages) to fire off a message to Cape-Mail once a day, gather, and archive the search results. Further, you could use your email's filtering rules to divert the CapeMail messages to their own folder for offline browsing. Make sure your search is fairly narrow, though, because CapeMail returns only 10 results at a time.

Google Alerts [Hack #59] are more apropos for this sort of application, but CapeMail was interesting enough to be worth mentioning.

Google by Instant Messenger
#65
Accessing Google with AOL Instant Messenger.

If we're going to step out beyond the Google interface, why even bother to use the Web at all? The Google API makes it possible to access Google's information in many different ways. Googlematic makes it possible to query Google from the comfort of AOL Instant Messenger.

Here's how it works: send a message (a Google query) to the instant messenger buddy *googlematic*. Googlematic will message you back with the top result for your query. Reply with More and you'll get more results formatted as a numbered list, as shown in Figure 5-24.

Message with the number associated with a particular result for further details, as shown in Figure 5-25.

You can find the Googlematic script, further instructions, and links to required modules at *http://interconnected.org/googlematic*.

The Code

Here's all there is to the code:

```
#!/usr/bin/perl -w
# googlematic.pl
# Provides an AIM interface to Google, using the Google SOAP API
```

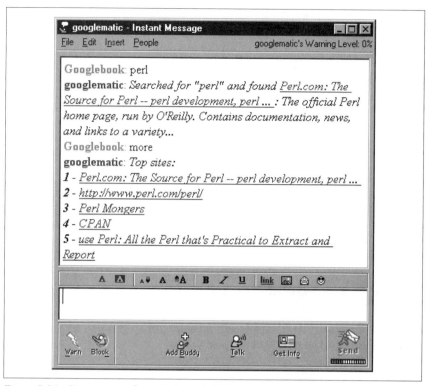

Figure 5-24. Query to googlematic through AOL Instant Messenger

```
# and POE to manage all the activity.
#
# Usage
# ./googlematic.pl &
#
# Requirements
# - Googlematic::IM, Googlematic::Responder, Googlematic::Search,
#   which are all distributed with this script
# - CGI
# - HTML::Entities
# - Net::AOLIM
# - POE
# - SOAP::Lite
# - XML::Parser
#
# Essential configuration (below)
# - AIM username and password (used in Googlematic::IM)
# - Google API Developer Key (used in Googlematic::Search)
#
# Optional configuration (below)
# - Search request throttling (used in Googlematic::Search)
# - Limit of number of user sessions open (used in Googlematic::IM)
```

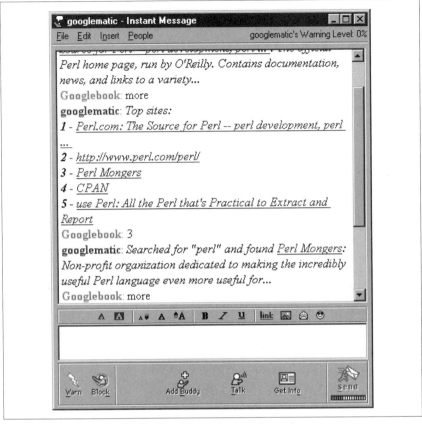

Figure 5-25. Requesting further detail for a googlematic result

```
# - Time limit on a user session (used in Googlematic::Responder)
#
# (c) 2002 Matt Webb <matt@interconnected.org> All rights reserved

use strict;
use POE;

$| = 1;

use Googlematic::IM;
use Googlematic::Search;

# Configuration variables
$Googlematic::CONFIG = {
  aim_username => "xxxxxxx",
  aim_password => "xxxxxxx",
  google_key   => "your key goes here",
  searches_per_hour => "35", # the Google limit is 1000/day
  max_user_sessions => "5",
```

```
    user_session_timeout => "120" # in seconds
};

# There are two POE sessions:
# 1 - Googlematic::IM, known as 'im', takes care of the Instant Messager
#      connection and looks after user sessions (which are created as new
#      POE sessions, and known as Responders).
POE::Session->create(
  package_states => [
    Googlematic::IM => [
      '_start', 'login_aim', 'loop', 'spawner',
      'handler_aim', 'send', '_child', '_stop', 'proxy'
    ]
  ]
);

# 2 - Googlematic::Search, known as 'google', takes care the SOAP::Lite
#      object making the searches on Google. Requests to it are sent from the
#      individual Responders.
POE::Session->create(
  package_states => [
    Googlematic::Search => [
      '_start', 'loop', 'search', 'reset'
    ]
  ]
);

# Run the POE machine.
$poe_kernel->run( );

exit;
```

—*Tara Calishain and Matt Webb*

H A C K   Google from IRC
#66

Performing Google searches from IRC is not only convenient, but also efficient. See how fast you can Google for something on IRC and click on the URL highlighted by your IRC client.

When someone pops into your IRC channel with a question, you can bet your life that 9 times out of 10, he could have easily found the answer on Google. If you think this is the case, you could tell him that, or you could do it slightly more subtly by suggesting a Google search term to an IRC bot, which will then go and look for a result.

Most IRC clients are capable of highlighting URLs in channels. Clicking on a highlighted URL will open your default web browser and load the page. For some people, this is a lot quicker than finding the icon to start your web browser and then typing or pasting the URL. More obviously, a single Google search will present its result to everybody in the channel.

The goal is to have an IRC bot called GoogleBot that responds to the !google command. It will respond by showing the title and URL of the first Google search result. If the size of the page is known, that will also be displayed.

The Code

First, unless you've already done so, you will need to grab a copy of the Google Web APIs Developer's Kit (*http://www.google.com/apis/download. html*) and create a Google account and obtain a license key **[Chapter 9]**. As I write this, the free license key entitles you to 1,000 automated queries per day. This is more than enough for a single IRC channel.

The *googleapi.jar* file included in the kit contains the classes that the bot will use to perform Google searches, so you will need to make sure this is in your classpath when you compile and run the bot (the simplest way is to drop it into the same directory as the bot's code itself).

The GoogleBot is built upon the PircBot Java IRC API (*http://www.jibble. org/pircbot.php*), a framework for writing IRC bots. You'll need to download a copy of the PircBot ZIP file, unzip it, and drop *pircbot.jar* into the current directory, along with the *googleapi.jar*.

 For more on writing Java-based bots with the PircBot Java IRC API, be sure to check out "IRC with Java and PircBot" **[Hack #35]** in *IRC Hacks* (O'Reilly) by Paul Mutton.

Create a file called *GoogleBot.java*:

```
import org.jibble.pircbot.*;
import com.google.soap.search.*;

public class GoogleBot extends PircBot {

    // Change this so it uses your license key!
    private static final String googleKey =
"00000000000000000000000000000000";

    public GoogleBot(String name) {
        setName(name);
    }

    public void onMessage(String channel, String sender, String login,
            String hostname, String message) {
```

```
                message = message.toLowerCase( ).trim( );
                if (message.startsWith("!google ")) {
                    String searchTerms = message.substring(8);

                    String result = null;
                    try {
                        GoogleSearch search = new GoogleSearch( );
                        search.setKey(googleKey);
                        search.setQueryString(searchTerms);
                        search.setMaxResults(1);
                        GoogleSearchResult searchResult = search.doSearch( );
                        GoogleSearchResultElement[] elements =
                                searchResult.getResultElements( );
                        if (elements.length == 1) {
                            GoogleSearchResultElement element = elements[0];
                            // Remove all HTML tags from the title.
                            String title = element.getTitle( ).replaceAll("<.*?>",
"");

                            result = element.getURL( ) + " (" + title + ")";
                            if (!element.getCachedSize( ).equals("0")) {
                                result = result + " - " + element.getCachedSize( );
                            }
                        }
                    }
                    catch (GoogleSearchFault e) {
                        // Something went wrong. Say why.
                        result = "Unable to perform your search: " + e;
                    }

                    if (result == null) {
                        // No results were found for the search terms.
                        result = "I could not find anything on Google.";
                    }

                    // Send the result to the channel.
                    sendMessage(channel, sender + ": " + result);
                }
            }
        }

    }
```

Your license key will be a simple string, so you can store that in the Google-
Bot class as googleKey.

You now need to tell the bot which channels to join. If you want, you can
tell the bot to join more than one channel, but remember, you are limited in
the number of Google searches that you can do per day.

Create the file *GoogleBotMain.java*:

```
    public class GoogleBotMain {

        public static void main(String[] args) throws Exception {
```

```
        GoogleBot bot = new GoogleBot("GoogleBot");
        bot.setVerbose(true);
        bot.connect("irc.freenode.net");
        bot.joinChannel("#irchacks");
    }

}
```

Running the Hack

When you compile the bot, remember to include both *pircbot.jar* and *googleapi.jar* in the classpath:

```
C:\java\GoogleBot> javac -classpath .;pircbot.jar;googleapi.jar *.java
```

You can then run the bot like so:

```
C:\java\GoogleBot> java -classpath .;pircbot.jar;googleapi.jar GoogleBotMain
```

The bot will then start up and connect to the IRC server.

The Results

Figure 5-26 shows GoogleBot running in an IRC channel and responding with the URL, title, and size of each of the results of a Google search.

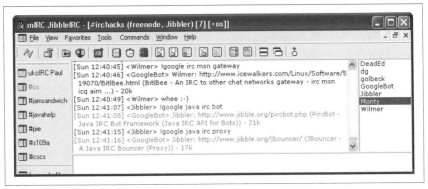

Figure 5-26. The GoogleBot performing an IRC-related search

Performing a Google search is a popular task for bots to do. Take this into account if you run your bot in a busy channel, because there might already be a bot there that lets users search Google.

—Paul Mutton

HACK #67   Google on the Go

Being on the go and away from your laptop or desktop doesn't mean leaving
Google behind.

As the saying goes, "You can't take it with you." Unless, that is, you're talking about Google. Just because you've left your laptop at home or at the
office, that doesn't necessarily mean leaving the Web and Google behind. So
long as you have your trusty cell phone or network-enabled PDA in your
pocket, so too do you have Google.

Whether you have the top-of-the-line Treo 600, Blackberry, or Sidekick with
integrated web browser; base-model cell phone that your carrier gave you
for free; or anything in between, chances are that you're able to Google on
the go.

Google caters to the "on the go" crowd with its Google wireless interfaces: a
simpler, lighter, gentler PDA- and smartphone-friendly version of Google, a
WAP (read: wireless Web) flavor for cell phones with limited web access,
and an SMS gateway for messaging your query to and receiving an almost
instantaneous response from Google. There's even a mobile interface to
Google's Froogle (*http://froogle.google.com*) product search.

Google by PDA or Smartphone

Google PDA Search (*http://www.google.com/palm*) brings all the power of
Google to the PDA in your palm, hiptop on your belt, or cell phone in your
pocket.

> Don't be fooled by the *palm* in the Google PDA Search URL,
> which is an artifact of Palm's majority mindshare at the time.
> The interface will work with your Pocket PC, Zaurus, Treo,
> or any other mobile device that benefits from lighter web
> pages.

Settle that "in like Flynn" versus "in like Flint" dinner-table argument without leaving your seat. Find quickie reviews and commentary on that Dust-
meister 2000 vacuum *before* making the purchase. Figure out where you've
seen that bit-part actor before without having to wait for the credits.

Your modern PDA and the smarter so-called *smartphones* sport a full-
fledged web browser on which you can surf all the Web has to offer in living color—albeit substantially smaller. You find the usual Address Bar, Back
and Forward buttons, Bookmarks or Favorites, and point-and-click (or
point-and-tap, as the case may be) hyperlinks. While the onboard browser

might just be able to handle the regular Google.com web pages, the Google PDA Search provides simpler, smaller, no-nonsense, plain HTML Pages. And results pages pack in fewer results for faster loading.

Just point your mobile browser at *http://google.com/palm*, enter your search terms, click the Google Search button, and up come your results, as shown in Figure 5-27.

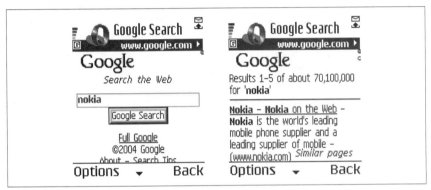

Figure 5-27. Google PDA Search (left) and results (right) on a Nokia smartphone

You have the full range of Google search syntax **[Chapter 1]** and complete web index available to you, although it might be more than a little challenging to enter those quotes, colons, parentheses, and minus signs.

Google by Cell Phone

If you have a garden-variety cell phone—of the sort your mobile provider either gives away free with signup or charges on the order of $40 for—you may yet find you have a built-in browser...of a sort. Don't expect anything nearly as fast, colorful, or feature-filled as your computer's web browser. This is a text-only world, limited in both display and interactivity.

That all said, you have the wealth—if not the Technicolor—of the Web right in your very pocket.

Step one, however, is to find the browser in the first place. It's usually hidden in plain sight, cleverly hidden behind some (possibly meaningless) moniker such as WAP, Web, Internet, Services, Downloads, or a brand name such as mMode or T-Zones. If nothing of the sort leaps out at you, look for an icon sporting your cell phone provider's logo, take a stroll through the menus, dig out your manual, or give your provider a ring (usually 611 on your cell phone).

Texting Sure Ain't QWERTY

Whether you're a 70-word-per-minute touch typist or you hunt and peck your way through the QWERTY keyboard, you're initially going to find texting a pokey chore. Rather than the array of letters, numbers, symbols, and shift keys on your computer keyboard, everything you do on your cell phone is confined to twelve keys: 0–9, *, and #. Frankly, it's an annoying system to learn, but once you get used to it, it's not too painful to use; some folks actually become rather adept at it, rivaling their regular keyboarding speeds.

Look closely at your phone and you'll notice each button also holds either a set of three to four alphabetic characters or obscure symbols not unlike those you'd expect to find on the UFO landing in your back yard. Like your regular phone, the 1 button is devoid of letters while 2 holds ABC, 3 DEF, and so on to 9 WXYZ.

When you're in web-browsing mode on your phone, you can tap the 2 button once to type an A, twice in quick succession for a B, and thrice for a C. Four times nets you a 2. Keep going and you'll make it back through A, B, C, and 2 again—on some phones encountering strange and wonderful foreign letters along the way. Do this for each and every letter in the word you're trying to spell out, spelling the word "google" like so: 4666 666455533. Notice the gap between the 666 and 666? What you're after is two "o"s in a row, but typing 666666 will get you either a single "o" or an "ø" since your phone doesn't know when you want to move on to the next letter. To type two of the same characters one after another, either wait a second or so after tapping in the first "o" or jiggle your phone's joystick to the right or down.

When it comes to special characters like the dot (.) and slash (/) common in web addresses, you'll turn to the 1 button. A period or dot is a single tap. The slash is usually 15. For those of you keeping score at home, that'll leave you with 92714666 6664555331 11111111111111196555 for *wap.google.com/wml*.

The texting equivalent of the spacebar is the 0 button.

What of digits? Surely you don't need to type 17 or so 1s—scrolling through all the symbols associated with the 1 button ([.,-?!'@:;/()])—just to get back around to the 1 you wanted in the first place. Thankfully, all it takes is holding down the button for a second or so to jump right to the numeral. So instead of tapping through WXYZ to get to 9, hold down that 9 key for a moment or so and you're there.

There are more efficient input techniques, such as *T9* ("Text on 9 keys") and other predictive text systems, but they're not as useful for entering possibly obscure words like those in web addresses and Google searches.

Browser in hand, point it at *wap.google.com/wml*, tap in a search (without tripping over your fingers), and click the Search button or link (as shown in Figure 5-28, left). A few moments later, your first set of results show up (as shown in Figure 5-28, center). Scroll to the bottom of the results and click the Next link (shown in Figure 5-28, right) to move on to the next page of results.

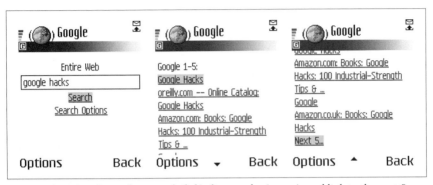

Figure 5-28. Google wireless search (left), first results (center), and link to the next 5 results (right)

Click any of the results to visit the page in question, just as you would in a normal browser. You'll notice immediately that the pages you visit by clicking a result link are dumbed down—similar to Google's wireless search itself—to suit the needs of your mobile's display abilities.

Truth be told, you're not visiting the resulting page directly at all. What you see on your screen and in Figure 5-29 is courtesy of the Google WAP proxy, a service turning HTML pages into WAP/WML (think of it as HTML for wireless devices) on the fly. Click another link on the resulting page and you'll continue browsing via the Google proxy, Google essentially turning all the Web into a mobile Web.

In fact, you can actually surf rather than search the Web using the Google WAP proxy. Find your mobile browser's Options menu and click the Go to URL link. In the resulting page, enter any web site URL into the Go to URL box and click the Go button to visit a mobile version of that page.

> The Options menu is chock-full of additional options provided by the Google WAP site: search the full Web, the mobile Web (sites Google has found to be optimized for mobile devices), language **["Language Tools" in Chapter 1]**, and Help documentation.

Figure 5-29. An ordinary web page as seen through the lens of the Google WAP proxy

Google by SMS

As a *New York Times* article ("All Thumbs, Without the Stigma"; *http://tech2.
nytimes.com/mem/technology/techreview.html?res=9E00E6DE163FF931A2575
BC0A9629C8B63*) suggested recently, the thumb is the power digit. While the
thumboard of choice for executives tends to be the Blackberry mobile email
device (*http://www.blackberry.com/*), for the rest of the world (and many of the
kids in your neighborhood), it's the cell phone and Short Message Service
(SMS).

SMS messages are quick-and-dirty text messages (think mobile instant messaging) tapped into a cell phone and sent over the airwaves to another cell
phone for around 5 to 10 cents apiece.

But SMS isn't just for person-to-person messaging. In the UK, BBC Radio
provides so-called *shortcodes* (really just short telephone numbers) to which
you can SMS your requests to the DJ's automated request-tracking system.
You can SMS bus and rail systems for travel schedules. Your airline will SMS
you updates on the status of your flight. And now you can talk to Google via
SMS as well.

Google SMS (*http://www.google.com/sms/*) provides an SMS gateway for querying the Google Web index, looking up phone numbers [Hack #6], seeking out
definitions [Hack #10], and comparative shopping in the Froogle product catalog service (*http://froogle.google.com*).

Simply send an SMS message to U.S. shortcode 46645 (read: GOOGL), as
shown later in Figure 5-30, with one of the following forms of query:

Web Search

Search the Google Web by prefixing your query with a G (upper- or low-ercase). You'll receive the top two results in return, formatted as text snippets, hopefully containing some information of use to you.

```
g capital of south africa
G answer to life the universe and everything
```

Google Local Business Listing

Consult Google Local's business listings by passing it a business name or type and city, state combination, or Zip Code.

```
vegetarian restaurant Jackson MS
southern cooking 95472
scooters.New York NY
```

 The Google SMS documentation suggests using a period (.) between your query and city name or zip code to be sure that you're triggering a Google Local Search.

Residential Phone Number

Find a residential phone number with some combination of first or last name, city, state, Zip Code, or area code.

```
augustus gloop Chicago il
violet beauregard 95472
mike teevee ny
```

 As with any Google Phonebook **[Hack #6]** query, you'll find only listed numbers in your results.

Froogle Prices

Check the current prices of items for sale online through Froogle (*http://froogle.google.com/*). To trigger a Froogle lookup, prefix your query with an F (upper- or lowercase), price, or prices (the latter two will also work at the end of the query).

```
g nokia 6230 cellphone
price bmw 2002
ugg boots prices
```

Definition

Rather than scratching your head trying to understand just what Ms. Austen means by *disapprobation*, ask Google for a definition **[Hack #10]**. Prefix the word or phrase of interest with a D (upper- or lowercase) or the word define.

```
D disapprobation
define osteichthyes
```

Calculation

Perform feats of calculation and conversion using the Google Calculator [Hack #47].

```
(2*2)+3
12 ounces in grams
```

Zip Code

Pass Google SMS a U.S. Zip Code to find out where one might find it in the country.

```
95472
```

> Google SMS is sure to sport more features by the time you read this. Be sure to consult the "Google SMS: How to Use" page at *http://www.google.com/sms/howtouse.html* for the latest or—for the real thumb jockeys among you—subscribe your email address to an announcement list from the Google SMS home page.

You'll receive your results as one or more SMS messages labeled, appropriately enough, (1of3, 2of3, etc.), as shown in Figure 5-30. Notice that there are no URLs or links in the responses: what's the point when you can't click on them?

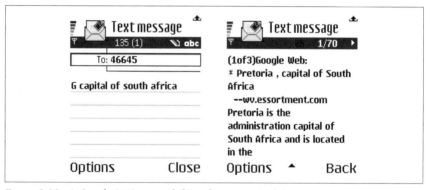

Figure 5-30. A Google SMS query (left) and response (right)

> While the cost of sending an SMS messages (typically between 5 and 10 cents apiece) is usually borne by the sender, automated messages like those sent by Google SMS are usually charged to you, the receiver. Unless you have an unlimited SMS plan, all that googling can add up. Be sure to check out what's included in your mobile plan, check your phone bill, or call your mobile operator before you spend a lot of time (and money) on this service.

Froogle on the Go

If you wish you could compare prices at that "One Day Sale" on kitchen gadgets without leaving the store, Wireless Froogle (*http://froogle.google.com*) is as much a part of the shopping experience as that credit card.

Point your mobile browser at *wml.froogle.com*, tap in the name of the product you're about to take to the checkout (Figure 5-31, left), and up pops a list of prices as advertised by online vendors (Figure 5-31, right).

Figure 5-31. Wireless Froogle Search (left) and results (right)

You'll find everything from cellular phones to yogurt makers, abacuses to faux yak fur coats on Froogle.

At the time of this writing, Wireless Froogle is nowhere near as complete as one might hope. You can't constrain your results by price, group them by store, or sort them in any way. Results don't link to anywhere. That said, it is a still a handy price-check tool as you're standing in that checkout line.

$49.99 for a pashmina—lemme at it! Sometimes instant gratification is worth it; sometimes paying only $49.99 for silk is well worth the wait.

HACK Visit the Google Labs
#68

Google Labs, as the name suggests, sports Google's experiments, fun little hacks, and inspirational uses of the Google engine and database.

Be sure not to miss Google Labs (*http://labs.google.com*). The whole point of this part of Google's site is that things will appear, vanish, change, and basically do whatever they want. So, while the site might be different by the time you read this, it's still worth covering, because you might find one of the tools here useful in sparking ideas.

At the time of this writing, there are a number of experiments running at the lab, some of which are covered in depth elsewhere in this book:

Google Desktop Search (http://desktop.google.com)
    Covered in "Google Your Desktop" [Hack #61].

Google SMS (http://sms.google.com)
    Covered in "Google on the Go" [Hack #67].

Site-Flavored Google Search Box (http://www.google.com/services/siteflavored. html)
    Tailor a Google search box to return results of a particular slant (e.g., kids' content, computers: hacking, etc).

Google Groups 2 (http://groups-beta.google.com)
    Covered in "Go Deeper into Groups with Google Groups 2" [Hack #56].

Google Personalized Web Search (http://labs.google.com/personalized)
    Tailor your Google results to suit your interests—essentially an individualized version of Site-Flavored Google Search.

Froogle Wireless (http://labs.google.com/frooglewml.html)
    Covered in "Google on the Go" [Hack #67].

Google Deskbar (http://toolbar.google.com/deskbar)
    Covered in "Add Google to Your Toolbar or Desktop" [Hack #60].

Google Compute (http://toolbar.google.com/dc/offerdc.html)
    An add-in to the Google Toolbar [Hack #60], Google Compute borrows a few cycles from your computer as it sits idle and applies this computing energy to solve difficult scientific problems around the world.

Google Sets (http://labs1.google.com/sets)
    Enter a few terms, and Google will try to come up with an appropriate set of phrases. For example, enter Amazon and Borders, and Google will come up with Borders, Amazon, Barnes & Noble, Buy.com, Media Play, SunCoast, Samgoody, etc. It doesn't always work like you'd expect. Enter vegan and vegetarian and you'll get veal, Valentine's Day, Tasmania; it goes a bit far afield. Clicking any item in the group list will launch a regular Google search.

Google WebQuotes (http://labs.google.com/cgi-bin/webquotes/)
    Many times, you can learn the most about a web page by what other web pages say about it. Google WebQuotes takes advantage of this fact by providing a preview of what other sites are saying about a particular link before you actually meander over to the site itself.

    From the Google WebQuotes home page, specify how many WebQuotes you'd like for a particular search (the default is three, a number that I find works well) and enter a search term. Google WebQuotes returns the top 10 sites (or, if you suffix the resultant URL with &num=100, the top 100 sites) with as many WebQuotes for each page as you specified. Note, however, that not every page has a WebQuote.

This comes in rather handy when you're doing some general research and want to know immediately whether the search result is relevant. When you're searching for famous people, you can get some useful information on them this way, too—and all without leaving the search results page!

HACK #69 Find Out What Google Thinks ___ Is

What does Google think of you, your friends, your neighborhood, or your favorite movie?

If you've ever wondered what people think of your home town, your favorite band, your favorite snack food, or even you, Googlism (*http://www. googlism.com*) may provide you with something useful.

The Interface

The interface is dirt simple. Enter your query and check the appropriate radio button to specify whether you're looking for a *who*, a *what*, a *where*, or a *when*. Figure 5-32 shows a representative results page for Clive Sinclair, inventor of the Sinclair ZX-80 personal computer (*http://www.nvg.ntnu.no/ sinclair/computers/zx80/zx80.htm*). You can also use the tabs to see what other objects people are searching for and what searches are the most popular. A word of warning: some of these are not safe for work.

What You Get Back

Googlism will respond with a list of things Google believes about the query at hand, be it a person, place, thing, or moment in time. For example, a search for Perl and "What" returns, along with a laundry list of others:

```
Perl is a fairly straightforward
Perl is aesthetically pleasing
Perl is just plain fun
```

These are among the more humorous results for Steve Jobs and "Who":

```
steve jobs is my new idol
steve jobs is at it again
steve jobs is apple's focus group
```

To figure out what page any particular statement comes from, simply copy and paste it into a plain old Google search. That last statement, for instance, came from an article titled "Innovation: How Apple does it" at *http://www. gulker.com/ra/appleinnovation.html*.

Figure 5-32. Googlism results for Clive Sinclair

Practical Uses

For the most part, this is a party hack—a good party hack. It's a fun way to aggregate related statements into a silly (and occasionally profound) list.

But that's just for the most part. Googlism also works as a handy ready-reference application, allowing you to quickly find answers to simple or simply asked questions. Just ask them of Googlism in a way that can end with the word is. For example, to discover the capital of Virginia, enter The capital of Virginia. To learn why the sky is blue, try The reason the sky is blue. Sometimes this doesn't work very well; try the oldest person in the world and you'll immediately be confronted with a variety of contradictory information. You'd have to visit each page represented by a result and see which answer, if any, best suits your research needs.

Expanding the Application

This application is a lot of fun, but it could be expanded. The trick is to determine how web page creators generate statements.

For example, when initially describing an acronym, many writers use the words "stands for". So you could add a Googlism that searches for your keyword and the phrase "stands for." Do a Google search for "SETI stands for" and "DDR stands for" and you'll see what I mean.

When referring to animals, plants, and even stones, the phrase "are found" is often used, so you could add a Googlism that located things. Do a Google search for sapphires are found and jaguars are found and see what you find.

See if you can think of any phrases that are in common usage, and then check those phrases in Google too see how many results each phrase has. You might get some ideas for a topic-specific Googlism tool yourself.

HACK #70 The Search Engine Belt Buckle

Take the Web out for a night on the town.

It was a late August Saturday night in Seattle. We decided not only to hit the dance floor, but to boogie down in a whole new way. All the cats in town were wearing big belt buckles then, so we thought, hey, here's our chance to strut our latest hack: the Search Engine Belt Buckle.

What in Blazes Is a Search Engine Belt Buckle?

The Search Engine Belt Buckle is a repurposed PDA, shown in Figure 5-33, that displays a scrolling list of 24 hours' worth of all the bizarre and banal things that people are looking for on the Web—right there just above or below your navel, depending on local custom or personal preference.

Just to give you some idea of the sort of thing that you're in for, here is a smattering of queries scrolling across my belt buckle's screen at the time of this writing:

- "olympic nude athletes"
- "leaving the scene of an accident"
- "night diaper bondage"
- "food"
- "used juicer"
- "homeopathic sinus remedies"

The Search Engine Belt Buckle has enough battery power to last for about two to three hours, plenty of time for gettin' down and attracting (or warding off) the ladies (or the gents), as the case may be. If there's WiFi in the area, it'll stream live queries, but since that's always an unknown, we have a few hours of search queries on hand at all times.

Figure 5-33. The author, sporting the Search Engine Belt Buckle

Step 1: The Video

As our source, we used SearchSpy (*http://www.dogpile.com/info.dogpl/searchspy*), a groovy scrolling list of search terms submitted to the Dogpile (*http://www.dogpile.com*) meta-search engine. We captured a good 24 hours' worth to keep in the cache.

Capture SearchSpy results by pointing your browser at either *http://www.dogpile.com/info.dogpl/searchspy/results.htm?filter=1* for "family-friendly real-time searches" or *http://www.dogpile.com/info.dogpl/searchspy/results.htm?filter=0* for "unedited real-time Web searches. Consider yourself warned."

Shoot the footage. Grab and install a copy of Windows Media Encoder 9 (*http://www.microsoft.com/windows/windowsmedia/9series/encoder/default.aspx*; free). In the New Session wizard, shown in Figure 5-34, click "Capture screen" and the OK button.

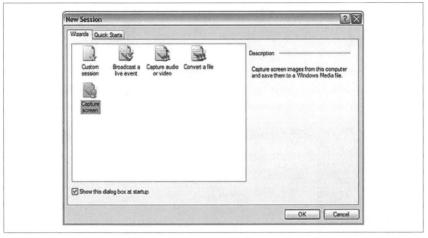

Figure 5-34. Windows Media Encoder's Wizard walks you through screen capture setup

Yes, we could have grabbed the XML from the Flash SWF file (bear in mind that the XML would need to be updated every so often for the latest results, something that's not possible if you don't have an Internet connection in the disco) and built a custom app to do all the display work, but we wanted to make this approachable for the typical reader—an odd definition of *typical*, I grant you, given that we're making a search engine belt buckle. By using a garden-variety video file, we can display it on a broader spectrum of systems and mediums.

In the next menu choose "Region of the screen" and click the Next button.

Click the "Use selection button" and drag an outline around the scrolling search results, indicated by the rectangle in Figure 5-35.

Pick a name for the file and click Next. Choose an encoding method; we picked Medium (Figure 5-36) because all we're displaying here is text on a belt buckle. Click the Next button to continue.

Give the video a title, author, and so forth. Click the Finish button when you're done.

Windows Media Encoder is now recording all those scrolling searches in real time. Capture a good 24 hours' worth of scrolling search terms to keep in the cache, as it were. When you think you've got enough, click the Encoder's application icon on your Windows taskbar and stop the recording.

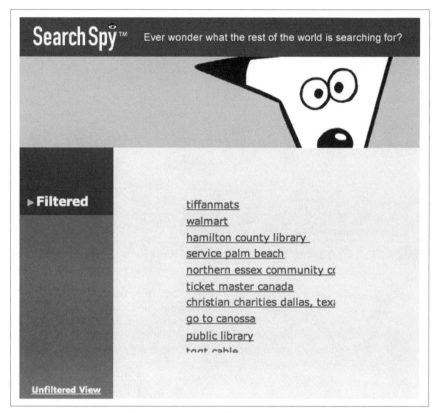

Figure 5-35. Drag an outline around the scrolling search results

To give you some idea of the sort of thing you should expect to see scrolling across your belt buckle, take a gander at the 10-minute sample at *http://www.engadget.com/common/videos/pt/search.wmv* (Windows Media).

Encode for Pocket PC. Before you throw this video at your Pocket PC, you'll want to recode it to play full screen in the Pocket PC version of Windows Media Player.

Close the Windows Media Encoder and start it back up again. In the starting Wizard, click "Convert a file," click Browse, and choose the video file you just recorded. Click the Next button and choose Pocket PC.

In the Encoding Options window, select "Pocket PC widescreen video (CBR)" from the Video pull-down menu (see Figure 5-37); this will encode the video as 320×240. Click Finish and go get a cup of coffee as it churns through the job of re-encoding.

Figure 5-36. Medium encoding is good enough for scrolling text

Figure 5-37. Re-encode the video to fill the Pocket PC's screen

When the re-encoding is done, move that file over to the Pocket PC. While you can do so over the USB cable with Active Sync or even send it through the ether over Bluetooth, the simplest method is to put it onto an SD card (using a card reader plugged into your computer) and pop the card into your Pocket PC.

Get the settings just right. Find the file in your Pocket PC's File Explorer, click it to start it playing (as shown in Figure 5-38, and click the Stop button.

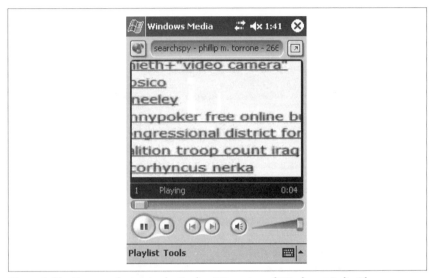

Figure 5-38. Footage playing in the Pocket PC version of Windows Media Player

Tap Tools → Settings → Audio & Video. From the "While using another program" pull-down menu, choose "Continue playback" and select "Always" from the "Play video in full screen" menu. These settings are shown in Figure 5-39. Tap the OK circle at the top-right.

Tap Tools → Repeat to have the video play again and again, uninterrupted.

Now we need to turn off the Power Management nonsense—necessary for day-to-day Pocket PC usage, but not optimal for making sure our belt buckle is always on. Tap the Start Menu → Settings → System → Power → Advanced tab. Uncheck the "Turn off device is not used for" checkbox, as shown in Figure 5-40.

Tap the "Adjust backlight settings to conserve power" link and uncheck the "Turn off backlight if device is not used for" checkbox (Figure 5-41). This will keep the device on (and you looking groovy) until you press the power button or run out of juice—the Pocket PC or your dancin' feet, whichever comes first.

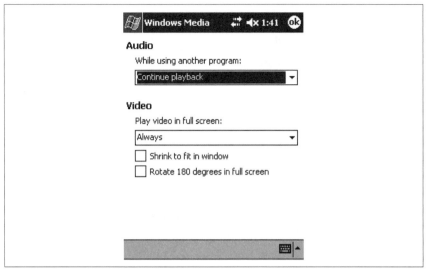

Figure 5-39. Setting Audio and Video play options

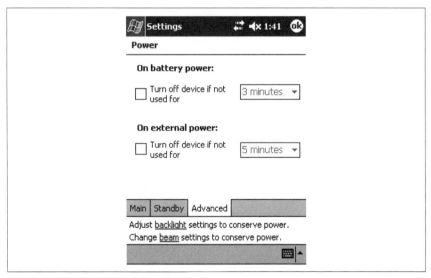

Figure 5-40. Keep your belt buckle groovin'

Tap the OK circle at top-right to finish.

Tap the Start Menu, followed by the Windows Media Player icon. Tap Play and your search video will play as long as you want it to, rotated to the right for optimal belt buckle viewing (Figure 5-42).

If you want, you can also adjust the brightness (the Brightness tab in the Backlight settings window), depending on the vibe.

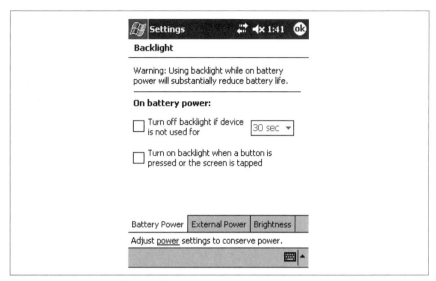

Figure 5-41. *Keep your belt buckle glowin'*

Figure 5-42. *Playback is oriented to the right for optimal viewing*

All of this works just as well with any other hip video you might like to strap on to your midriff. And you can always edit the video, alter color, add effects and transitions, and so forth. How about a collage of digital photos from the Google Images gallery **[Hack #51]**?

Making the Belt Buckle

Now, of course, you can stop here. You don't really *need* to make this into a belt buckle. It's rather mesmerizing in and of itself and is an entertaining addition to your desk at the office (assuming you chose Filtered mode, that is).

That said, we just couldn't resist the temptation to make a big, bad belt buckle. So we grabbed a few supplies (belt, shiny beads, black electrical tape, Velcro, and a hot glue gun, shown in Figure 5-43) from around the house, and we were off.

Figure 5-43. You'll find all you need lying about the house or at your corner craft shop

First, we wrapped the Pocket PC in black electrical tape, leaving only the screen and useful buttons showing, as shown in Figure 5-44.

For some flash, we hot-glued shiny beads (from here on out called *studs*) to the tape around the edges in Figure 5-45.

To attach the buckle to the belt, we stuck one side of a strip of adhesive Velcro to the back of the Pocket PC, the other side to the unadorned buckle of a simple black belt we had in our closet, as shown in Figure 5-46.

Put on your dancin' shoes, disco shirt, some natty slacks, Search Engine Belt Buckle (Figure 5-47), and enjoy a night out on the town.

—*Phillip Torrone*

Figure 5-44. "Disappear" that Pocket PC with a roll of black electrical tape

Figure 5-45. Glue on some flash

Figure 5-46. Velcro the buckle to the belt

Figure 5-47. The finished product, a snazzy Search Engine Belt Buckle

## CHAPTER SIX

Gmail
Hacks 71–80

Google's Gmail web-based email service (*http://www.gmail.com*) isn't your ordinary web mail service. Maybe you're attracted to the slick, interactive, real application–like JavaScript-powered web interface. Or the command-line jockey in you likes the Pine-like keyboard shortcuts (Pine is a text-only email application, typically found on Unix systems). Or is it the sheer volume of storage—one gigabyte, at the time of this writing—that's made you question your relationship with your existing web mail service and its puny 50 megabyte allotment. Most are enticed by the promise (and delivery, mind you) of a Google-like search interface to their email.

 There was a day when a simple off-by-one (technically, an off-by-999 error) caused quite a stir among early Gmail users. Logging into your Gmail account, you were met with the double take–worthy: "You are currently using 16 MB (0%) of your 1000000 MB." I'll see your gigabyte and raise you a terabyte.

Whatever your reasons for trying, switching to, or lusting after a Gmail account, you're sure to be delighted both by its proper and "improper" uses—the latter being the focus of this chapter.

As with all things Google, the official interface to Gmail is only one of many. Thanks to some clever screen scraping, analysis of the data model and format underlying the candy-coated JavaScript frontend, and some good old tinkerer's enthusiasm, you can use Gmail as everything from a filesystem [Hack #78 and Hack #79] to a backup server [Hack #80] to a mobile email account for Gmail on the go [Hack #77].

Gmail Search Syntax

Gmail offers a rich search syntax for routing through your email message archive—as if you'd expect, or indeed stand for, any less.

from:
> Digs through the headers of your email message archive in search of mail sent by someone matching the keyword that you provide.
>
>   from:rael@oreilly.com

to:
> The yang to from:'s yin, to: finds all messages sent to someone matching a provided keyword. (Don't forget plus-addressing **[Hack #72.]**)
>
>   to:engineers@example.com
>   to:raelity+shopping@gmail.com

subject:
> Matches messages with a particular subject.
>
>   subject:"meeting notes"

label:
> Looks for messages with a particular label applied.
>
>   label:knitting

has:attachment
> The has: syntax has only one possible value (at least at the time of this writing): attachment. has:attachment in a query returns only messages having one or more attachments.
>
>   has:attachment

filename:
> Finds messages with an attachment filename matching a provided pattern. Used with just a file extension (e.g., pdf or txt), filename: turns up all messages with attachments of a particular type.
>
>   filename:meeting_notes.txt
>   filename:pdf

in:
> Returns a list of messages in a particular collection (read: folder). Acceptable values for in: are inbox, trash, spam, and anywhere (trash and spam are not included in searches unless explicitly included using in: trash, in:spam, or in:anywhere). Oddly enough, sent isn't a usable value for in:.
>
>   in:inbox
>   in:anywhere

`is:`

> Acceptable values for `is:` are `starred`, `unread`, and `read`, which return starred, unread, and read messages, respectively.
>
> `is:read`

`cc:`

> Finds messages carbon copied to particular recipients.
>
> `cc:tara@example.com`

`bcc:`

> Finds outgoing messages blind carbon copied to particular recipients. Note that `bcc:` won't work on any incoming mail since there's no way to tell who was on the bcc line.
>
> `bcc:tara@example.com`

`before:`

> Matches messages sent or received before a particular date, specified in yyyy/mm/dd format. Unfortunately, partial dates—year only or year and month—don't find anything at all.
>
> `before:2004/10/02`

`after:`

> Match messages sent or received *on or after* a particular date, specified in yyyy/mm/dd format.
>
> `after:2004/11/21`

Phrase Searches

Enclose phrases in double-quotes (") to have Gmail search treat them as a unit to be matched exactly (case isn't taken into account). The following query finds only accounting department reports:

```
Subject:"accounting department report"
```

Basic Boolean

The only Boolean operator supported by Gmail search is `OR` (uppercase is required). In the absence of the `OR` operator, `AND` is implicit.

The Boolean `OR` operator works in Gmail searches just as it does in Google Web searches: specify that any one word or phrase is acceptable by putting an `OR` between each, such as this query, which finds all messages from the boss or with their subjects marked as urgent:

```
from:boss@example.com OR subject:urgent
```

Negation

The negation operator (-) also works as it does in Google Web Search, excluding messages matching the negated keyword or operator:keyword pair. So, the following query turns up all messages to my Example Co. *not* sent from the company's special offers department:

```
to:@examplecom -from:offers@
```

Grouping

Parentheses are used a little strangely in Gmail queries. When enclosing a set of words, they specify that all of those words must be found to be considered a match. So, the following matches messages sent to both Sam and Mira:

```
to:(sam mira)
```

Throwing in an OR allows optional matches while being explicit about groups of options—while we humans tend to be able to parse precedence without need of parentheses, search engines need a little more help. The following query finds all messages sent to Sam about rockets or helicopters:

```
to:sam subject:(rockets OR helicopters)
```

Mixing Syntax

Gmail's various search operators tend to play well together. While the tendency is to start out with minimal search criteria and keep whittling down, with a large number of email messages, crafting your searches can start to take a lot of work. Take a chance and provide as much information as you know about the message you're after and back off bit by bit if you don't find it. The following query, for instance, is one that I just couldn't pull off in my computer's email client:

```
from:Duncan before:2004/10/01 subject:today "World Cup" lunch
```

Additional Resources

As with all Hacks books, what you find here is just a taste of what's most likely available by the time this book ends up in your hands. Here are a few more resources you might visit:

- The Gmail documentation (*http://gmail.google.com/support*) is chock-full of tips, tricks, keyboard shortcuts, search syntax, and more.
- Gmail Gems (*http://gmailgems.blogspot.com*) "reveals the tips and tricks of Gmail masters."

- Justin Blanton's "Getting More Out of Gmail" (*http://justinblanton.com/ archives/2004/06/20/getting_more_out_of_gmail*) provided much grist and many pointers for this chapter.

- GmailForums (*http://www.gmailforums.com*), as the name suggests, is a place to discuss all things Gmail.

- Mark Lyon, author of Google Email Loader **[Hack #74** has collected a good list of apps and hacks (*http://www.marklyon.org/gmail/gmailapps.htm*).

- And, of course, you can always Google for gmail hacks and gmail hacking.

> Remember that all of these are hacks and, as such, have no quality of service guarantees; if they break, they break. About all you can do is go back to the hack's home page and see if there's a new version available.

HACK #71   Glean a Gmail Invite

Ask a friend, acquaintance, or stranger; swap, auction, or finagle. A Gmail invite is hard to come by—but not that hard.

Gmail is one hot property and Gmail accounts are not available to just any-one. Yes, it's a free web mail service, but free doesn't necessarily mean freely available—much to the chagrin of those just itching to give it a whirl. You have to be invited, either by a Googler (someone working at Google) or a friend willing to spend one of their occasionally available Gmail invites on you.

Hmm... scarce commodity, high demand... sounds like a market to me.

And that's precisely what's happened. Gmail accounts are meted out to close friends, traded for wares and services, auctioned off, donated, and oth-erwise trafficked in a marketplace of sorts.

So, where do I glean myself a Gmail invite?

Ask a friend
> Chances are one of your alpha-geek friends has a Gmail account. Ask nicely and be prepared to offer a latte or three.

Ask an acquaintance
> Email acquaintances with Gmail accounts are easy to spot: just look for the *@gmail.com* email address. Set up a filter in your email application to highlight any incoming Gmail and rifle off a response the moment you see one pop up. Your ingenuity and bravado are sure to be admired—and hopefully rewarded.

Request one of a stranger

The isnoop.net Gmail invite spooler (*http://isnoop.net/gmailomatic.php*) offers "a place for people with Gmail invites and those who want them to come together with minimal effort and fuss."

eBay for one

Yes, I know it seems silly, but Gmail invites are going for between $0.30 and $3.00 on eBay.

Swap something

Gmail swap (*http://www.gmailswap.com*) is a virtual swap meet for Gmail invites where people offer everything from CDs to kisses for an invite. If you've an invite or three to trade, ask for a joke, picture, or "anything Disney" and bring your sense of humor.

Join the military

Gmail for the Troops (*http://www.gmailforthetroops.com*) and Gmail 4 Troops (*http://www.gmail4troops.com*) are sites dedicated to garnering Gmail accounts for troops currently serving to keep in touch with their loved ones at home.

Google for it

Try searching Google for "have * Gmail invites" (wow, that full-word wildcard really comes in handy!). Often webloggers who have Gmail invites available will post about it on their weblog. Even if you've found an old entry, you've found someone with a Gmail account—and Google periodically refreshes the number of invites a user has available.

By the time you read this, Gmail may well be freely available. If so, think of this hack as a moment in time when Gmail was the geek equivalent of a collector's plush toy.

—Rael Dornfest and Justin Blanton

HACK #72 Create and Use Custom Addresses

Make up an unlimited number of arbitrary email addresses to use when signing up for something, making a purchase online, or tracking a conversation.

Those who've been exposed to the power of a little something called *plus-addressing* never look back, using it anywhere and everywhere they can. And, for something so useful, there's really not much to it.

Simply append a plus sign (+) and some meaningful string of letters or numbers (meaningful to you, that is) to the first part of your email address—the part before the "at" sign (@)—and you have a way of tagging a particular conversation, an address used to sign up for a service or buy something online, or create a throwaway address you have no intention of paying attention to again.

Say your email address is *raelity@gmail.com.* A plus-addressed version might be *raelity+shopping@gmail.com.* And you don't have to stop there; you can create subtags and sub-subtags such as *raelity+shopping+amazon@gmail.com* and *raelity+shopping+amazon+books@gmail.com* for even more granularity.

And the magic of it is that all plus-addressed email still arrives at the same email address: yours, sans the plus bit. At that point you can filter, sort, highlight, or trash email sent to that particular address as you see fit.

Plus-addressing means never having to say you only have one email address again.

And you'll be glad to know that Gmail supports plus-addressing, affording you some rather powerful email handling, routing, and filtering functionality.

Some of my favorite uses of plus-addressing are:

Tagging a conversation
  Keep track of a particular email conversation—no matter how long it lasts—by copying yourself (i.e., putting yourself in the Cc: field) with a plus-address (e.g., *raelity+conundrum@gmail.com* or *raelity+tag+conundrum@gmail.com*). That way, so long as you're copied on any ongoing conversation, you'll know just where it all started (and, hopefully, eventually ended).

Inviting people to a party
  This is just a variation on the previous theme of tagging a conversation. Invite people to a party and copy yourself with a plus-address (e.g., *raelity+scavengerhunt@gmail.com* or *raelity+rsvp+scavengerhunt@gmail.com*) to label and track RSVPs.

Signing up for services
  Just about every online service has you provide an email address in order to sign up. If you never want to hear by mail from these people again (aside from the initial—and often required—confirmation email, that is), assign a plus-address to each service (e.g., *raelity+morningtimes@gmail.com* or *raelity+service+morningtimes@gmail.com*) and, when you've had quite enough of their follow-up messages, announcements, and special offers, set up a filter (*http://gmail.google.com/support/bin/answer.py?answer=6579&query=filter&topic=&type=f*) to direct them right into the Trash.

Buying things online

Buying things online usually involves some amount of email traffic: purchase confirmation, shipping notification, tracking, and problems. By assigning a plus address to each vendor (e.g., *raelity+amazon@gmail. com* or *raelity+shopping+amazon@gmail.com*), you can group all of your online transactions with that vendor.

> While there usually isn't anything you can do about vendors and service providers sharing your email address with others, at the very least, you can keep tabs on the offending party.

Subscribing to mailing lists

There comes a time in any subscriber's life when she wants to disambiguate email pouring in from various mailing lists from more important mail. Give every mailing list its own plus-address (e.g., *raelity+xmlsomething@gmail.com* or *raelity+mailinglist+xmlsomething@gmail.com*) and you can label or siphon incoming mailing list posts into your Archive.

Import Your Contacts into Gmail

H A C K
#73

Data entry's a drag. Export your contacts from an existing web mail service, desktop email application, or database, and import them into your Gmail address book.

Possibly the most annoying aspect of moving into any new web mail home is bringing all your family, friends, and business contacts along with you. The average end user has almost been trained not to expect any sort of import utility, instead sighing and settling in for an evening of data entry.

Gmail, as with most post-1990s web mail applications worth their salt, provides the facility for importing all those contacts in just a few clicks; just how many depends on where you're exporting them from. Gmail accepts only one format: comma-separated values (CSV). Thankfully, CSV is about as low a common denominator as you could wish for; Yahoo! Address Book, Outlook, Outlook Express, Mac OS X Address Book (with a little help from a free application), Excel, and many other applications, web or otherwise, speak CSV.

> Gmail's Help documentation on the subject of importing contacts is sure to keep up with the needs of its users, so keep an eye on "How do I import addresses into my Contacts list?" (*http://gmail.google.com/support/bin/answer. py?answer=8301*).

Anatomy of a Contacts CSV

First, a quick tour of a typical contacts CSV file as consumed by Gmail's import tool.

CSV files, as the name suggests, are little more than garden-variety text files in which data is listed one record per line, each field separated by (you guessed it!) a comma. The simplest of all *contacts.csv* files might then look something like this:

```
name,email
Rael Dornfest,rael@oreilly.com
Tara Calishain,tara@researchbuzz.com
...
```

The first line lists field names, in this case name and email address. Each line thereafter is a single person or entity (business, organization, etc.) in your contacts list with a corresponding name and email address.

Gmail accepts various formats of contact entry, recognizing some of the more common fields such as name, email address, phone, birthday, etc. Here's a slightly more detailed *contacts.csv*:

```
first name,last name,email address,phone
Rael,Dornfest,rael@oreilly.com,(212) 555-1212
Tara,Calishain,tara@researchbuzz.com, (212) 555-1213
...
```

Notice that name is split into first and last name fields, email is called email address, and there's a phone field too.

Unless you're going to be using Gmail as your main contacts database—and I can't quite see why you would—you don't need to import any more than name and email address (something akin to the first *contacts.csv* example) to find it useful.

> In fact, at the time of this writing, Gmail does little with fields beyond name and email address but shove them into a Notes field.

Feed CSV to Gmail

Assuming that you have a CSV file to work with (if you don't, read on to the sections below for some guidance), importing is a snap.

From the main Gmail screen in your web browser, click the Contacts link (Figure 6-1) found at the bottom of the menu on the left side of the page.

The Contacts page opens, listing all of (or none of, if you don't yet have any) your existing Gmail contacts. These may have been entered by hand,

@gmail.com | Contacts | Settings | Help | Sign out

Figure 6-1. Clicking the Contacts link gets you to your Gmail contacts

gleaned from incoming and outgoing mail, or imported at some earlier date. Click the Import Contacts link link at the top right of the page.

Click the Browse... (or equivalent) button when prompted to do so, as shown in Figure 6-2 and find your CSV file on your computer's hard drive. (Just what this looks like depends on your operating system and browser, but essentially you're just choosing a file much like you would from any application.) Click the Import Contacts button and—Bob's your uncle (that's "tada!" for my American readers)—you should see a confirmation that all went to plan and you've imported some number of contacts into your Gmail address book.

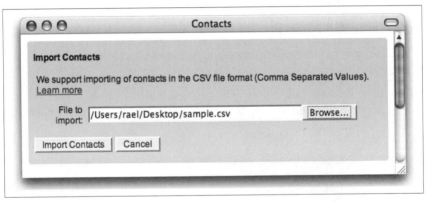

Figure 6-2. Finding that CSV file

Click the Return to Contacts link and you'll see your now fully stocked contacts list. Figure 6-3 shows mine, after importing the second sample CSV at the beginning of this hack.

Delete any number of contacts by clicking their associated checkboxes and clicking the Delete Selected button. Edit a contact by clicking the appropriate [edit] link. Or type in a contact or three by hand using the Add Contact link.

Now, any time you start typing a known contact's name into the To, Cc, or Bcc field of a new message, Gmail will autocomplete it for you. No need to remember that cousin Adam is *adamg@ozziesurfers.co.au* or Auntie Joan is *joan42@tepidmail.com*.

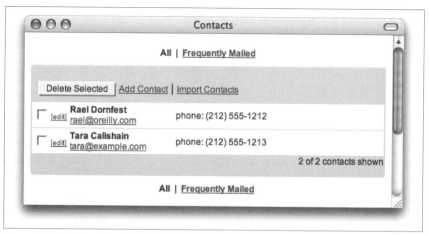

Figure 6-3. Feeding that CSV file to Gmail

Out of Outlook (Express)

Both Outlook Express and Outlook in Windows can export their address books as CSV.

In Outlook Express, select File → Export → Address Book..., choose Text File (Comma Separated Values) as your output format (see Figure 6-4), and click the Export button.

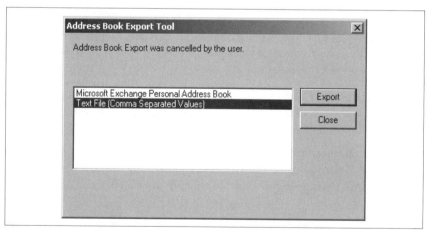

Figure 6-4. Export your Outlook Express Address Book as CSV

In Outlook, select File → Import and Export..., choose "Export to a file" and click Next, select Comma Separated Values (Windows) as your output format, and click Next again. An Export Wizard will then guide you the rest of the way to saving your contacts as a CSV file.

Feed either to Gmail as described earlier.

Hopping out of Hotmail

There are a couple ways to hop out of Hotmail with your contacts in tow. The first goes by way of Outlook Express or Outlook and the second using a touch of copy-and-paste, as suggested by the Gmail team in their online Help documentation.

By way of Outlook (Express). As described earlier, both Outlook Express and Outlook are able to export to CSV. Both are also able to subscribe to Hotmail accounts and synchronize contacts therewith. Putting two and two together, you can use Outlook (Express) as an intermediary as follows.

Set up a new account in Outlook Express or Outlook, choosing HTTP as the server type and Hotmail as the mail service provider, as shown in Figure 6-5.

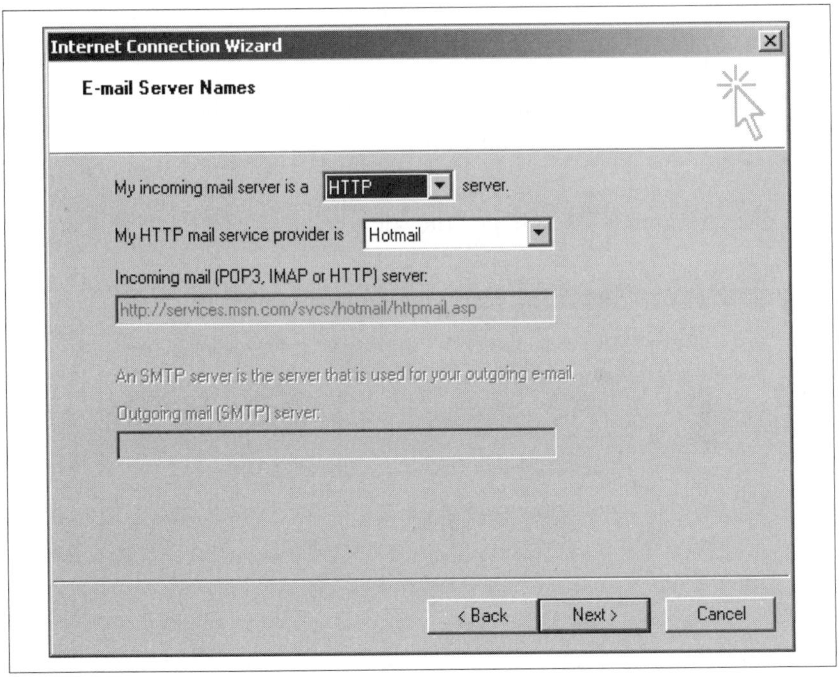

Figure 6-5. Setting up a Hotmail email account in Outlook Express

In Outlook Express, click the Addresses icon in the toolbar to open your Address Book. Select Tools → Synchronize Now (Figure 6-6) to synchronize your contacts between Outlook Express and Hotmail, thus bringing your Hotmail contacts to your computer.

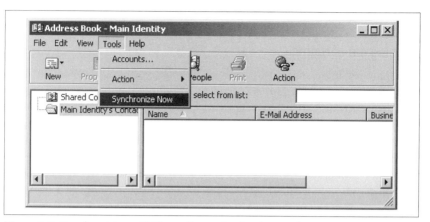

Figure 6-6. *Synchronizing with Hotmail to grab a local copy of your contacts*

After a few moments of synchronization, your local Address Book will be up to date and you can export those contacts to CSV as described earlier in the "Out of Outlook (Express)" section.

By way of copy-and-paste. This is one of those ugly methods that you can't quite knock because it just plain works.

Log into Hotmail in your web browser of choice and select the Contacts tab, as shown in Figure 6-7. Click the Print View link in the Hotmail toolbar.

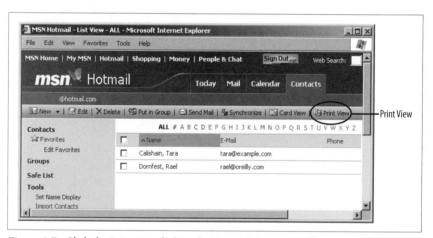

Figure 6-7. *Click the Print View link in the Hotmail Contacts toolbar*

In the Print View window that pops up, highlight everything (click and drag your mouse) from Name at the top left to the bottom most row in your list of contacts. Press Control-C or select Edit → Copy to copy the contacts, as shown in Figure 6-8.

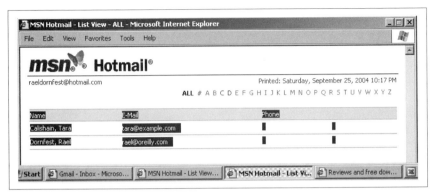

Figure 6-8. Copying your contacts

Open Microsoft Excel, start a new workbook, select the A1 cell, and type Control-V or select Edit → Paste to paste in your contacts list. Your workbook should look something like Figure 6-9.

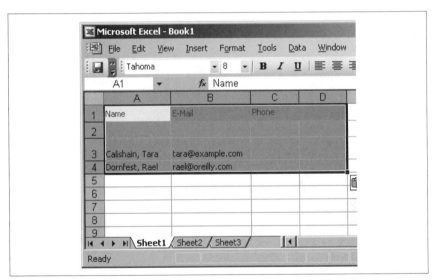

Figure 6-9. Pasting your contacts into an Excel workbook

Save the workbook as "CSV (Comma delimited)" (never mind the couple warnings about incompatibilities that Excel throws at you) and give the resulting CSV file to Gmail's import tool.

> This turns into an unholy mess under Mac OS X. Contacts are not nicely spread across columns, leaving you with a row of contacts, empty cells, and some odd characters in any CSV file that you attempt to create.

Yumping from Yahoo!

Yahoo! Address Book exports directly to CSV.

Log into Yahoo! and visit your Address Book (the Addresses tab). Click the Import/Export link on the top right (Figure 6-10).

Figure 6-10. Using the Yahoo! Address Book's Import/Export feature

On the Export section of the resulting page, click the Yahoo! CSV Export Now button (Figure 6-11).

> **Yahoo! CSV:**   Export Now |

Figure 6-11. Exporting as Yahoo! CSV

Your browser will most likely prompt you for a place to save the CSV file on your computer's hard drive, as shown in Figure 6-12.

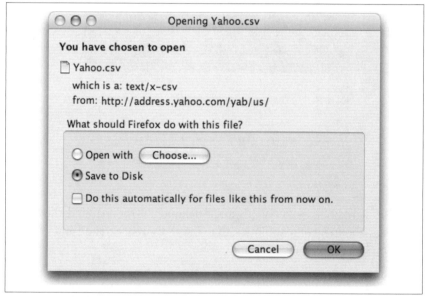

Figure 6-12. Saving the exported CSV file to your hard drive

Now, go ahead and import that CSV using the Gmail import tool, described earlier.

> I do apologize for the bad "Yumping" pun, but "Yahoo!" doesn't leave you much room for alliterated action verbs: yodeling? yanking?

Moving from .Mac

The Mac OS X Address Book only exports to something called vCard, which is understood by many contacts applications, but not by Gmail.

Thankfully, someone's written a magical little app to help. AddressBookToCSV (*http://homepage.mac.com/kenferry/software.html#AddressBookToCSV*; freeware) slurps up all of your contacts—name and email address only, which is nicer to my mind than uploading a slew of data unnecessary for your Gmailing needs—out of Address Book and spits them into a CSV file that you can feed to Gmail. Download the app, mount the *.dmg* on your desktop, and run it right from there, as shown in Figure 6-13. (If you'll likely use it again and again, go ahead and drag it into your *Applications/Utilities* folder.)

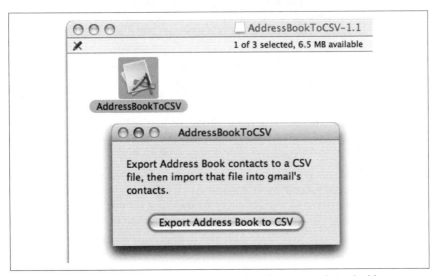

Figure 6-13. AddressBookToCSV exports Address Book names and email addresses to CSV

When prompted to do so, choose a place to save the *contacts.csv* file and click the Save button. Close the application using Command-Q (it doesn't do so by itself when done).

Feed *contacts.csv* to Gmail as usual.

Hand-Crafting a CSV

If your contacts exist in some form with no obvious path to CSV, you can always export them in any way you can, arriving at some point at either a plain-text file that you can manipulate by hand—tedious, but possible—or something Excel can read. If you can get to Excel, you can get to CSV; massage the data into a form similar to that discussed at the top of this hack, select File → Save As... and save as "CSV (Comma delimited)."

Last-Ditch Effort

If, for whatever reason, you can't massage your contacts into CSV form or use Gmail's Import Contacts tool, there is a (admittedly grotty) way to get all your contacts to Gmail using email itself.

Send out a single email message (preferably one that announces your intention) to (on the To: line) your Gmail account (or one that forwards to your Gmail account), copying all your contacts on the Cc: line.

 You should probably batch these such that there's some semblance of privacy, with your family not seeing all of your business associates' addresses and vice versa. Send a separate message for contacts of a sensitive nature.

When you receive that message at Gmail, open it and choose "Reply to all." Write something explanatory again and send it off.

Gmail automatically adds to your contact list the names and email addresses of the people you send email to from Gmail, so you've just added all of those people to your Gmail address book.

 Again, this is a rather annoying way (annoying to your friends, family, and business contacts) to get your contacts list to Gmail, so it should be regarded as a last-ditch effort.

—Rael Dornfest and Justin Blanton

Import Mail into Gmail

HACK #74

Moving to Gmail doesn't have to mean starting from scratch. Forward mail in bulk from your computer or other web mail service to your Gmail account.

The most enticing feature of Gmail is probably its ability to perform Google-style searches on your own inbox. The one gigabyte of free space is intriguing, but it's not much when you consider that you have far more than that available to you on even your most outdated PC. And I'd warrant that not even its snazzy JavaScripted user interface is enough to tear you away from your existing web mail service, uprooting yourself and starting over.

Gmail doesn't currently provide any way to import your existing email archive (web mail service or desktop mailbox). While you already might have considered forwarding all that mail to your Gmail account, just how to do so—even just the few hundred "important" messages—is quite a trick.

Not so, thanks to hacks like the Google Mail Loader for forwarding desktop mail and web mail intermediaries YPOPs! for Yahoo! Mail and MSN email and GetMail for Hotmail.

Forward Desktop Mail

The Google Mail Loader (*http://www.marklyon.org/gmail*; GNU Public License) is a point-and-click application that reads your existing mail files on your computer and forwards the messages on to Gmail—one every two seconds, so as not to overload or otherwise annoy the Gmail servers. It does so without deleting mail from your local computer; what's sent to Gmail is a copy of each and every message. You can even set it to drop uploaded messages into your Gmail Inbox or Sent Mail folder.

GML is cross-platform and understands multiple mailbox formats:

- Mbox (used by Netscape, Mozilla, Thunderbird, and many other email applications)
- MailDir (Qmail and others)
- MMDF (Mutt)
- MH (NMH)
- Babyl (Emacs RMAIL).
- Microsoft Outlook, via a utility such as PST Reader (*http://www. mailnavigator.com/reading_ms_outlook_pst_files.html*), which converts Outlook's PST files to Mbox format

Installing the hack. Download the Windows or Linux/Mac OS X, source-only version (*http://www.marklyon.org/gmail/download.htm*). The Windows version is definitely the simplest version to set up and use, requiring no prerequisites and other bits and pieces.

The source version assumes you have the Python scripting language and the Python Mega Widgets (*http://pmw.sourceforge.net*) toolkit installed.

The ins and outs of installing GML and all the prerequisites from source is beyond the scope of this book. If you need help, consult the documentation for Python (*http://www. python.org*) and Python Mega Widgets (*http://pmw. sourceforge.net*), or ask your local technical guru or system administrator.

If, on the other hand, you have Python on your system and don't much care whether the Google Mail Loader is a desktop or command-line application, skip ahead to the "Hacking the hack" section.

Running the hack. Since Google Mail Loader works directly with your email application's mailboxes, you'll need to figure out where they live before you can go much further. Consult your email app's preferences or documentation or just dig around—both on your hard drive and by googling for `"outlook express" mailbox files location`, replacing `"outlook express"` with the name of your email program.

You'll also need to make sure that your mailbox files are in a format that Google Mail Loader can read, as listed in the beginning of this hack. If there's any conversion to do, do so now. For instance, use PST Reader (*http://www. mailnavigator.com/reading_ms_outlook_pst_files.html*) to turn Outlook and Outlook Express PST files into DBX format.

With mailbox files in hand, launch Google Mail Loader by double-clicking *gmlw.exe* on Windows or typing `python gmlw.py` on the Unix or Mac OS X command line. Figure 6-14 shows Google Mail Loader running under Linux.

Work your way down the settings on the left half of the GML window:

1. The default SMTP server (that's the sendmail server, the one used to send your messages to Gmail) of *gsmtp57.google.com* works for most users. If, for some reason, you are required by your local network administrator or Internet service provider to use their outgoing mail server, replace the default with the appropriate address. If your outgoing mail server requires authentication, click the Requires Authentication checkbox and fill in your username and password.

2. Click the Find button and point GML at your mailbox file. If your email application uses MailDir format, select any file inside your MailDir directory.

3. From the File Type pull-down menu, choose your mailbox type (Figure 6-15). There are two versions of Mbox format: one stricter about the format of files and therefore more accurate, while the other is more lenient and works better on some Mbox files.

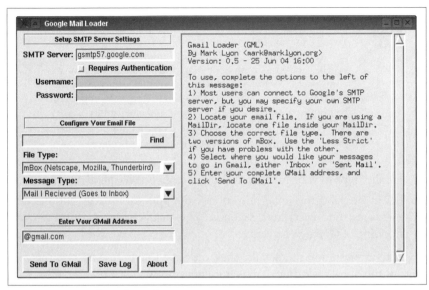

Figure 6-14. Google Mail Loader

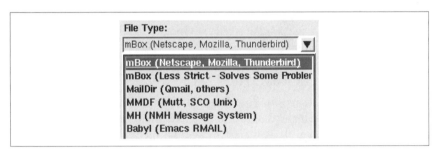

Figure 6-15. Select your mailbox file type

 For some of the history, read Jamie Zawinski's "mail summary files" at *http://www.jwz.org/doc/mailsum.html*.

If you don't know what format your mail application uses, try googling for mail format pine, replacing pine with your mail app's name. (Pine uses Mbox, by the by.)

4. GML is able to upload both your incoming and outgoing mail. Choose Mail I Received from the Message Type pull-down menu, and messages will be dropped into your Gmail Inbox and appear to be from the original sender, just as they did in your email application's mailbox. If you choose Mail I Sent, the messages will be relabeled as coming from your Gmail address and appear in your Gmail Sent Mail folder.

Gmail automatically labels incoming messages as Inbox. There's no way, unfortunately, for an external application to change this behavior, so messages imported as Mail I Sent will be labeled as both Sent Mail and Inbox and appear in both places. Mind you, there is only actual one copy of the message stored and sent mail is relabeled so as to appear to be from your Gmail address, not your old email address.

If you Archive the copy you see in your Gmail Inbox, it will then appear only in Sent Mail (and Archive, of course).

5. Finally, type in your full Gmail address (e.g., *hank@gmail.com*).

6. Click the Send to Gmail button and the application will start sending messages, one every two seconds. The delay is necessary to prevent flooding of Google's servers.

If you're interested in the details, click the Save Log button to save the contents of the output window to a file for later review.

There are, as with any hack of this sort, some issues worth noting:

- The timestamp of imported messages in your Gmail Inbox will be that of when the message was received by Google. Inside the message itself, however, the original date is still preserved. You can search for parts of dates to retrieve matching messages: Aug 94, for instance, will find all messages from August of 1994.

- The count of messages in your Inbox will not match the number GML reports as sent. This is due to the fact that the number GML reports is the number of new threads, not individual messages. Gmail automatically groups related messages as they arrive.

- Some people, especially users of Mozilla or Firefox, report problems with their Mbox files being corrupt. I have tracked down a Python script (*http://www.marklyon.org/gmail/cleanmbox.py*) that'll clean up most of these problems.

- Importing mail from Outlook is a bit spotty. I recommend one of two things: import your Outlook mail into Outlook Express and then into the open source Thunderbird mail application (*http://www.mozilla.org/products/thunderbird/*), or use PST Reader or the like to convert your Outlook mail to Mbox.

Hacking the hack. If you're a command-line jockey or don't particularly relish installing the various prerequisites (Tk, Python Mega Widgets) necessary to get the graphical version of Google Mail Loader running, there's also a text-only version available at *http://www.marklyon.org/gmail/old/default.htm*.

The only requirement for the command-line GML is Python (*http://www.python.org*).

Here's a sample session with the older GML on the Mac OS X command line:

```
$ python gml.py
Mbox & Maildir to Google Mail Loader (GML) by Mark Lyon <mark@marklyon.org>

Usage: gml.exe [mbox or maildir] [mbox file or maildir path] [gmail address]
[Optional SMTP Server]
Exmpl: gml.exe mbox "c:\mail\Inbox" marklyon@gmail.com
Exmpl: gml.exe maildir "c:\mail\Inbox" marklyon@gmail.com gsmtp171.google.
com

$ python gml.py mbox ~/Library/Mail/Mailboxes/1999.mbox/mbox
'hank+gml@gmail.com'

Mbox & Maildir to Google Mail Loader (GML) by Mark Lyon <mark@marklyon.org>

    1 Forwarded a message from  : someone@example.com

Done. Stats: 1 success 0 error 0 skipped.
```

Migrate from an Existing Web Mail Service

Despite attempts by your existing web mail service to entice you to stay, Gmail beckons with its one gigabyte of storage, powerful search, rich web interface, and chance of grabbing a better email address than raelity973@. That said, you're loathe to leave behind the last year or three's email.

Well, you can indeed take it with you, thanks to some nice donateware Web-to-POP mail utilities. These intermediaries operate in one of two ways:

- The utility sits between your desktop email application and web mail service, allowing you to download all of your mail to your computer, after which you can use the Google Mail Loader to feed it all to Gmail.

- The utility combines these two steps into one, grabbing all of your web mail and forwarding it on in bulk to your Gmail account.

While there are no doubt any number of these utilities, two we stumbled across were GetMail and YPOPs!

Of course, you may just opt to pay for POP mail access to your web mail service, download all your mail like you would any other, and use the Google Mail Loader from there. If, however, you've gone this long without paying for POP service, chances are you're not going to do so now just to move out of the service.

Hop from Hotmail/MSN. GetMail (*http://www.e-eeasy.com/GetMail.aspx*; donate-ware) is a two-in-one for Hotmail and MSN that runs under Windows.

Move any messages that you want to send across to your Gmail account to your Hotmail Inbox (if you've previously filed them elsewhere) and mark them as unread.

Launch GetMail (shown in Figure 6-16), provide it with your Hotmail/MSN account name and password, and type your full Gmail address into the Forward To box. Check whatever options you prefer; I'd uncheck the Delete checkbox. Now click Check for New Mail to set GetMail in motion and go get a cup of coffee while it moves all those messages across for you. You can even leave it running, transferring your Hotmail messages to Gmail on an ongoing basis.

Yank your Yahoo! Mail. YPOPs! (*http://yahoopops.sourceforge.net/*; donatew-are) is a POP mail proxy, sitting between your preferred email application and Yahoo! Mail. It is available for Windows, Mac OS X, Linux, and Solaris. The Windows version self-installs while the others require that you compile from source code and so are a little more difficult for the uninitiated to get up and running.

Move any messages you want to download and carry across to Gmail into your Yahoo! Mail Inbox and mark them as unread.

On Windows, run YPOPs! after installation. A little icon appears in your Windows taskbar; double-click it to get to the settings, shown in Figure 6-17.

While you can go ahead and make a few changes in the settings, YPOPs! runs right out of the box without any further configuration.

Now, simply set up a POP mail account like any other, only pointing to YPOPs! running locally as your mail server—both incoming and outgoing. The YPOPs! site has details on configuring most email clients at *http://yahoopops.sourceforge.net/modules.php?op=modload&name=Sections&file=index&req=listarticles&secid=1*.

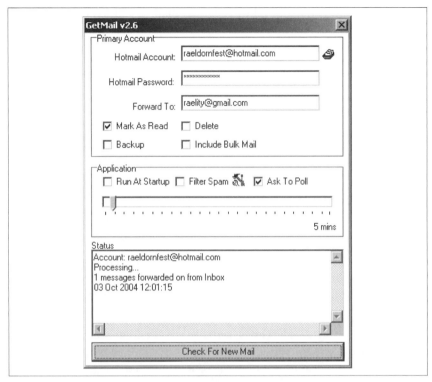

Figure 6-16. GetMail can download Hotmail/MSN messages and forward them on to Gmail

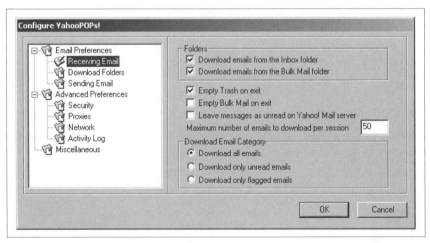

Figure 6-17. YPOPs! proxies POP mail requests

Once you have downloaded all of your web mail to your computer, use the Google Email Loader to send all the contents of your local inbox to Gmail.

See Also

- GmailerXP (*http://gmailerxp.sourceforge.net*; donateware) is the be-all and end-all of Gmail/Windows integration, providing a full-featured frontend to your Gmail email, importing and uploading legacy messages to Gmail, new mail notification, and so on.

—Mark Lyon, Justin Blanton, and Rael Dornfest

Export Your Gmail

#75

Back up or export your Gmail messages to your computer for safe-keeping or offline reading.

You're nicely settled in to your new Gmail account and may even have brought over all of your email [Hack #74 since time began. You're mailing up a storm, taking full advantage of the one gigabyte of storage space you're allotted.

What, now, if you decide Gmail actually isn't for you and you'd like to move out again, either to another Web mail service or back to the more traditional email application running on your computer? Or perhaps you just want a local archive of your Gmail for safe-keeping or offline trawling when you're on a plane and desperately need a copy of that meeting report.

A nifty little archiving script packaged with the libgmail (*http://libgmail. sourceforge.net*) Python interface to Gmail [Hack #80 is just the ticket. It logs into your Gmail account for you, looks around, prompts you to select a collection of messages to archive, and downloads them to your laptop or desktop.

Installing the Hack

There's really nothing to do beyond downloading (*http://sourceforge.net/ project/showfiles.php?group_id=113492*, or click the Downloads link on the libgmail home page) and unstuffing the libgmail archive (*http://libgmail. sourceforge.net*).

> The only requirement for libgmail is Python (*http://www. python.org*).

Running the Hack

Among libgmail's demo applications is *archive.py*, a script that logs into Gmail, downloads your email messages, and saves them on your computer's hard drive in a format (Mbox) suitable for importing into many an email program:

On the command line (whether that be the Windows DOS-alike, Mac OS X's Terminal, or Unix shell), run the archive script like so:

```
$ python demos/archive.py
```

You'll be prompted for your Gmail account name and password, after which libgmail will log you in:

```
Gmail account name: raelity
Password:

Please wait, logging in...
Log in successful.
```

There we are. At this point you can choose to archive just what's in your inbox (0), all messages (2), starred, drafts, sent, or a particular set of labeled messages (6 and 7 in my case). Choose the associated number and hit the return key on your keyboard:

```
WARNING:root:Live Javascript and constants file versions differ.
Select folder or label to archive: (Ctrl-C to exit)
Note: *All* pages of results will be archived.
    0. inbox
    1. starred
    2. all
    3. drafts
    4. sent
    5. spam
    6. foo
    7. Peeps
Choice: 2
```

Libgmail begins slurping your messages out of Gmail, one by one, and downloading them to an archive file in the current directory on your computer.

As is stated by he program at the outset, "*All* pages of results will be archived," meaning that all messages in the collection you've chosen will be downloaded, not just those that fit on a single page when you're looking at that collection through the standard Gmail web browser interface.

```
ff602fe48d89bc3 1 \<b\>Hello from Hotmail\</b\>
    ff602fe48d89bc3 1 Hello from Hotmail

ff5fb9c2829c165 1 Hello Gmail via Gmail Loader
    ff5fb9c2829c165 1 Hello Gmail via Gmail Loader

ff5691f7170cb62 1 Hello Gmail via Gmail Loader
    ff5691f7170cb62 1 Hello Gmail via Gmail Loader

ff3f4310237b607 1 Howdy gmail-lite
    ff3f4310237b607 1 Howdy gmail-lite

ff39c1fc71abbf1 1 Hello from Gmail mobile
    ff39c1fc71abbf1 1 Hello from Gmail mobile

...

fbd0c388dd1684e 1 Hello, Gmail
    fbd0c388dd1684e 1 Hello, Gmail

fbd0c1db3bcffe2 1 Gmail is different. Here's what you need to know.
    fbd0c1db3bcffe2 1 Gmail is different. Here's what you need to know.

Select folder or label to archive: (Ctrl-C to exit)
Note: *All* pages of results will be archived.
    0. inbox
    1. starred
    2. all
    3. drafts
    4. sent
    5. spam
    6. foo
    7. Peeps
Choice: ^C

Done.
```

And we're done. Choose another collection to download and archive if you wish; otherwise, press Control-C on your keyboard to stop the *archive.py* script.

Now, if you look in the directory from which you invoked *archive.py*, you should see a new Mbox-format archive (the one I just created is *archive-all-1096849647.72.mbox*) of your chosen collection of messages, suitable for importing into many an email program:

```
jane:~/Desktop/libgmail-0.0.8 rael$ ls
ANNOUNCE                          constants.pyc
CHANGELOG                         demos
README                            libgmail.py
archive-all-1096849647.72.mbox    lib
```

See Also

- gmail.py (*http://www.holovaty.com/blog/archive/2004/06/18/1751*) is a simple Python interface to Gmail, focusing on exporting raw messages for backup and import.

Take a Walk on the Lighter Side

Gmail with grace from any web browser, whether JavaScript-disabled, not yet supported, text-only, or on a PDA or mobile phone.

Being a child of Google, Gmail hides all of its complexity behind a rich, deep, feature-packed yet user-friendly web mail interface, assuming you have the right browser—one of recent vintage—for the job. But what to do if your IT department hasn't upgraded your version of the Internet Explorer browser since Windows 95, you're quite happy with the text-only Lynx browser, you're running the latest nightly build of browser XYZ, which Gmail simply doesn't like, or you're trying to reach your mail from a PDA or smartphone?

Gmail-lite (home page: *http://sourceforge.net/projects/gmail-lite*, Source-Forge project page: *http://sourceforge.net/projects/gmail-lite*; GNU Public License), as the name suggests, puts a plain HTML face on Gmail. It is a PHP application that proxies your interactions with Gmail, allowing you to surf using whatever browser you have at hand or just plain prefer just plain prefer, while keeping Gmail happy with its end of the conversation.

The authors of gmail-lite have done a fantastic job, affording you a plain HTML interface to just about every bit of functionality Gmail provides through its more interactive JavaScript-based frontend.

Installing the Hack

You have to marvel at the wonders of PHP-based applications and their simple installation. Assuming you have the prerequisites taken care of, it's just a matter of downloading, unpacking, and enjoying. I installed gmail-lite both on my local Mac OS X laptop and under my hosted ISP account in seconds each.

Gmail-lite assumes you have PHP installed on a web server. It relies upon the libgmailer library (*http://gmail-lite. sourceforge.net*), included for your convenience in the gmail-lite distribution. You also need the curl library (*http://www. php.net/curl*) with SSL support (*http://www.openssl.org*) since gmail-lite always talks to Gmail over a secure channel.

Download gmail-lite (*http://sourceforge.net/projects/gmail-lite*) and unpack the distribution (0.56 at the time of this writing, but yours is sure to be a later version) somewhere under your web server's document root, where the rest of your web site lives (ask your system administrator or service provider if you're not sure where this is):

```
$ tar -xvzf gmail-lite-0.56.tar.gz
gmail-lite-0.56/
gmail-lite-0.56/compose.php
gmail-lite-0.56/config.php
gmail-lite-0.56/debug.php
gmail-lite-0.56/diagnose.php
gmail-lite-0.56/dl.php
gmail-lite-0.56/docs.html
gmail-lite-0.56/index.php
gmail-lite-0.56/INSTALL
gmail-lite-0.56/libgmailer.php
gmail-lite-0.56/logout.php
gmail-lite-0.56/main.php
gmail-lite-0.56/star.gif
$ mv gmail-lite-0.56 gmail-lite
```

 That last command simply renames the directory to something that will be a little friendlier and easier to remember when it comes to visiting in my browser.

To verify that everything went to plan, point your web browser at *diagnose.php* using the URL corresponding to the *gmail-lite* directory on your web site—e.g., *http://www.example.com/~rael/gmail-lite/diagnose.php*. The resulting page should look like Figure 6-18.

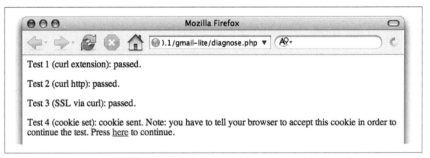

Figure 6-18. The diagnose.php script makes sure that everything is installed as expected

If *diagnose.php* does indicate that something's gone wrong, consult the installation and troubleshooting documentation in the *INSTALL* text file in your *gmail-lite* folder.

Running the Hack

Point your computer's web browser at the URL corresponding to the *gmail-mobile* directory on your web site—e.g., *http://www.example.com/~rael/gmail-lite* (or just click the "Press here..." link on the *diagnose.php* page).

> Depending on your setup, you may actually need to tack `/index.php` on to that URL, but most PHP-enabled servers know to look for and serve up *index.php* as a default when no filename is specified and there's no static *index.html* in sight. The gmail-lite package includes just such an *index.php* file.

Figure 6-19 shows the plain HTML login screen as it will appear in a typical browser window. Enter your Gmail login (e.g., *username*@gmail.com) and password, alter the time zone if you feel so inclined, and click the "sign-in" button.

Figure 6-19. A gloriously plain HTML Gmail login page in a typical browser window

You're greeted with a summary page with links to your Gmail Inbox, Sent, Trash, and Spam folders, Starred messages, and personal labels—shown in Figure 6-20 as it appears in a smartphone XHTML web browser.

Click the Inbox link and you'll be presented with a simple list of your incoming messages, as shown on a Pocket PC in Figure 6-21. At the top is a quick-link toolbar and pull-down menus for switching views, exploring labeled mail, and searching your Gmail messages ["Gmail Search Syntax" earlier in this chapter]. (Click the Get button after making your selections or entering a

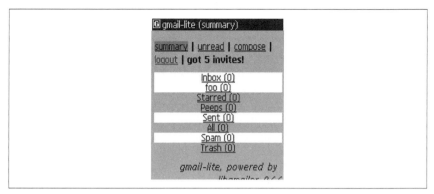

Figure 6-20. A summary of the state of your Gmail account as it appears in a smartphone XHTML browser

search query.) At the bottom are actions you can apply to any number of checked messages (check the associated checkbox to the right of a message subject to act upon it), including archive/unarchive, label, star/unstar, mark as read/unread, mark/unmark as spam, and trash/untrash. (Click the Do button to apply any action.)

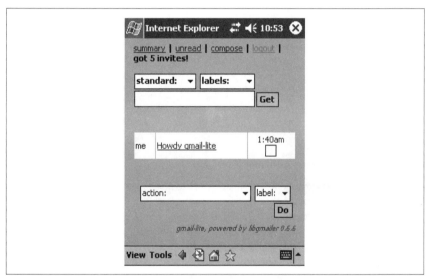

Figure 6-21. Your Gmail inbox, as seen through a Pocket PC

Select any email message to open it. Figure 6-22 shows a typical email message viewed in the text-only Lynx browser. The layout of individual message pages is much like that of the Inbox (or any folder) view. As you can see in the figure, I'm about to take a look at all my "foo"-labeled messages.

```
                                                            gmail-lite (inbox)

           summary | unread | compose | logout | got 5 invites!

           [standard:__]  labels:  _____ Get
                          foo (0)
                          Peeps (0)
       me Howdy gmail-lite 5:40
       [ ]

       [action:_____] [label:] Do

              gmail-lite, powered by libgmailer 0.6.6







    (Choice list) Hit return and use arrow keys and return to select option.

    H)elp O)ptions P)rint G)o M)ain screen Q)uit /=search [delete]=history list
```

Figure 6-22. An individual message in the Lynx text-only browser

So, there you have it: a plain old HTML interface to about anything you can do through Gmail proper. (In all likelihood, by the time you read this, Gmail will have built its own plain HTML version without all the browser and JavaScript requirements. Still, this is a great hack and worth fiddling about with.)

> The gmail-lite author does caution that "GMail is a still in beta, and GMailer (along with gmail-lite) is, I would say, an 'alpha hack' of a beta software. So don't expect it to work all the time, and do not build critical mission applications upon it" (*http://gmail-lite.sourceforge.net/*).

See Also

- If you're wanting to Gmail from a mobile phone with only a very basic WAP browser on board, you can still Gmail on the go with gmail-mobile **[Hack #77**. And be sure to check out "Google on the Go" **[Hack #67]** for taking Google search along too.

Gmail on the Go

#77   You can take it with you ... Gmail on your mobile phone, that is.

Web mail means never having to say you're sorry that you left your laptop at home. While I can't quite fathom it myself—I keep a lot I need beyond basic email on my laptop—there are those that wander the world sans the very core of the mobile office. They're happy to use OP's (other people's). "Where there's a web browser, there's a way" is their credo, and for those who can swing it, more power to them.

Where this falls down for me are the between times: dashing to a meeting without the latest agenda in hand (it's in my email inbox, but my laptop's in my bag and there's no wireless network in sight), meandering a foreign city and wanting to keep in touch with the folks back home but without having to lug around a laptop, and other moments such as these.

The browser experience on even the smartest of smartphones has a way to go. And most folks don't have any more of the Internet on their phones than a basic text-only WAP view of the world **[Hack #67.** While WAP works to some degree, web mail services don't tend to spend much time, if any at all, on providing a WAP interface to your email.

But there's always a workaround ...

Gmail-mobile (*http://sourceforge.net/projects/gmail-mobile*; GNU Public License) is a PHP (*http://www.php.net*) application that sits on your web site, between your mobile phone's WAP browser and Gmail, brokering requests on your behalf and returning a mobile-appropriate view of your Gmail mail.

> This hack assumes you have an account that allows WAP access to the wild, woolly Web from your mobile phone. Check with your mobile operator about your data plan, and don't forget to ask what you're charged per megabyte, because even the lightest of interactions can add up over time.

You can catch a quick status update, read, and even reply to your Gmail—and there are more features promised.

Installing the Hack

Installing gmail-mobile is a piece of cake; I installed it under both Mac OS X and Linux in a matter of seconds each.

Gmail-mobile assumes you have PHP installed on a web server running on port 80 (the WAP, and indeed web, default). You also need the curl library (*http://www.php.net/ curl*), which gmail-mobile uses to talk to Gmail over the Web and the libgmailer (*http://gmail-lite.sourceforge.net*) **[Hack #80** library, included for your convenience in the gmail-mobile distribution.

Download gmail-mobile (*http://sourceforge.net/projects/gmail-mobile*) and unpack the distribution (0.11 at the time of this writing, but yours is sure to be a later version) somewhere under your web server's document root, where the rest of your web site lives (ask your system administrator or service provider if you're not sure where this is):

```
$ tar -xvzf gmail-mobile-0.11.tar.gz
gmail-mobile-0.11/
gmail-mobile-0.11/AUTHORS
gmail-mobile-0.11/COPYING
gmail-mobile-0.11/INSTALL
gmail-mobile-0.11/README
gmail-mobile-0.11/TODO
gmail-mobile-0.11/compose.php
gmail-mobile-0.11/config.php
gmail-mobile-0.11/index.php
gmail-mobile-0.11/libgmailer.php
gmail-mobile-0.11/logout.php
gmail-mobile-0.11/main.php
gmail-mobile-0.11/star.gif
$ mv gmail-mobile-0.11 gmail-mobile
```

That last bit renamed the gmail-mobile directory to something a little easier to type on my mobile phone's keypad.

And you're done. No, really, I was surprised too at just how easy it was.

By default, gmail-mobile uses browser cookies to maintain state between requests to Gmail's servers. If you have PHP Session (*http://www.php.net/ session*) installed, you can choose to use it instead of cookies. Just comment out the appropriate line in the *config.php* file in your newly unpacked *gmail-mobile* directory. Here, I've left things as they were, using the cookie default:

```
<?php

    require_once("libgmailer.php");

    /** Session handling method. You must at least choose (uncomment) one.
**/
```

```
/**** have PHP Session installed, prefer to use cookie to store session
**/
//$config_session = (GM_USE_PHPSESSION | GM_USE_COOKIE);
/**** have PHP Session installed, prefer NOT to use cookie **/
//$config_session = (GM_USE_PHPSESSION | !GM_USE_COOKIE);
/**** do not have PHP Session installed **/
$config_session = (!GM_USE_PHPSESSION | GM_USE_COOKIE);

?>
```

Running the Hack

With the easy part out of the way (isn't it wonderful when installation and configuration is the easy part?) you're ready to break out your mobile phone's browser and muddle through typing on that minute keypad.

Before trying this out from your mobile phone (and to remove one variable in case something doesn't work as expected), point your computer's web browser at a URL corresponding to the *gmail-mobile* directory on your web site—e.g., *http://www.example.com/~rael/gmail-mobile*.

> You may actually need to tack /index.php on to that URL, but most PHP-enabled servers know to look for and serve up *index.php* as a default when no filename is specified and there's no static *index.html* in sight. The gmail-mobile package includes just such an *index.php* file.

Your browser will respond in one of two ways. Either it'll serve up the raw WML source delivered by gmail-mobile, as shown in Figure 6-23, or it'll throw up its hands in confusion and prompt you to save the source as a file on your hard drive. If the source (displayed in your browser or saved and opened using something like TextEdit on Mac OS X or Notepad on Windows) looks something like Figure 6-23 and doesn't seem to report any PHP or other errors, you're ready to switch to your mobile phone.

Launch your mobile phone's WAP browser [Hack #67] and key in the appropriate URL to reach the *gmail-mobile* directory on your web site, as above.

After a few moments of churning (WAP is lightweight, but most mobile bandwidth is on the light side too), you should be greeted with a login screen (Figure 6-24, left). Key in your Gmail login (*username*@gmail.com) and password, alter the time zone if you feel so inclined, and click OK. Just where you find OK will vary from phone to phone, WAP browser to WAP browser. I found it under the left soft key → Service options → OK on my Nokia Series 60 phone, as shown in Figure 6-24, right.

Figure 6-23. Raw Gmail Mobile WAP as viewed through a regular browser

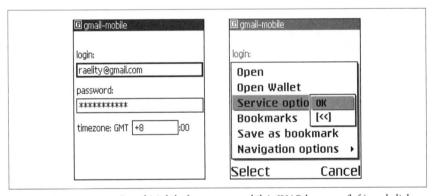

Figure 6-24. Log in to Gmail Mobile from your mobile's WAP browser (left) and click
OK (right)

A few more moments of churning and you should see a summary view of
your Gmail account (Figure 6-25, left). To visit any of the folders, navigate
over the appropriate link and select it, much as you would links in a regular
browser—albeit with esoteric keystrokes rather than a mouse. Figure 6-25,
right, shows my rather empty inbox.

Visit any message (Figure 6-26, left, shows a sample email message) in any of
your mailboxes by selecting its link. Compose a new message by selecting
the Compose link; reply using the Reply link at the bottom of a message.
Figure 6-26, right, shows the composition window in action.

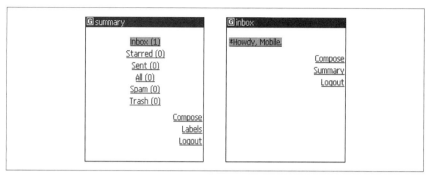

Figure 6-25. Take a gander at a summary of the state of your Gmail (left) and visit your inbox (right)

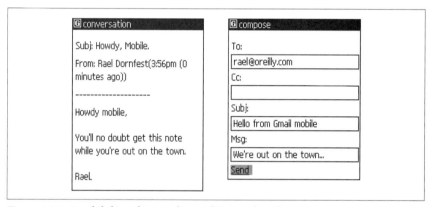

Figure 6-26. Read (left) and respond to (right) Gmail mail on the go

While you can't (at least, at the time of this writing) create, alter, or delete Gmail labels, you can see what they are (Figure 6-27, left) by following the Labels link on the Summary screen (Figure 6-27, left). Figure 6-27, right, shows all of my messages labeled "Peeps."

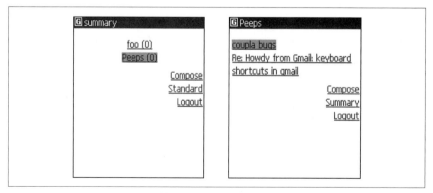

Figure 6-27. Browse your Gmail labels (left) and visit labeled messages (right)

It's not the spiffy tricked-out Gmail interface that you've come to expect, but it's a great way to take your Gmail with you—and, quite frankly, it's better than some of the mobile email applications that I've come across.

See Also

- The gmail-mobile project has on its to-do list just about anything you're currently wishing for, including search, archive, delete, forward, label, mark as spam, and working with the Gmail address book [Hack #73]. Keep an eye on the project page (*http://sourceforge.net/projects/gmail-mobile*) for the latest news and distributions.

  If you're new to mobile browsing, you might want to take a gander at "Google on the Go" [Hack #67].

HACK #78 Use Gmail as a Linux Filesystem

Repurpose your gig of Gmail as a networked filesystem.

What I wouldn't give for a spare gig of networked filesystem on which to stash a backup of my work in progress or as an intermediary between two firewalled systems (thus not directly reachable from one to the other).

GmailFS (*http://richard.jones.name/google-hacks/gmail-filesystem/gmail-filesystem.html*) puts your gigabyte of Gmail storage to work for just such a purpose. It provides a mountable Linux filesystem repurposing your Gmail account as its storage medium.

GmailFS is a Python application that uses the FUSE (*http://sourceforge.net/projects/avf*) userland filesystem infrastructure to help provide a filesystem and the libgmail (*http://libgmail.sourceforge.net*) [Hack #80] library to communicate with Gmail.

GmailFS supports most file operations, such as read, write, open, close, stat, symlink, link, unlink, truncate, and rename. This means that you can use the lion's share of your favorite Unix command-line tools (cp, ls, mv, rm, ln, grep, et al) to operate on files stored on Google's Gmail servers.

So, what might you store on and do with the Gmail filesystem? About anything that you would with any other (possibly unreliable) networked filesystem built on a cool hack or three. Figure 6-28 shows the Firefox web browser launched from an executable stored as a message in my Gmail account.

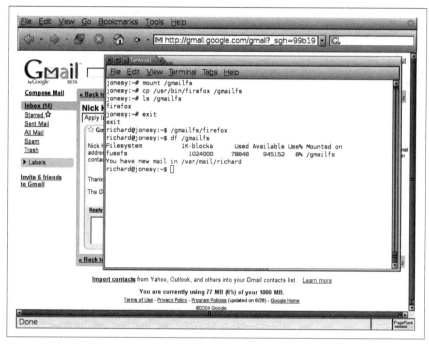

Figure 6-28. Reading my Gmail via the Firefox web browser launched from an executable stored on the selfsame Gmail account

This is my first foray into Python and I'm sure the code is far from elegant. That said, the language has a reputation as an excellent choice for rapid prototyping—and this was borne out in my experience. The first working version of GmailFS took about two days of coding with an additional day and a half spent on performance tuning and bug fixing. Given that this includes the learning curve of the language itself, the reputation seems well deserved.

A special mention should go to libgmail and FUSE, as both greatly contributed to the short development time.

(I'm particularly concerned with my attempts to manipulate mutable byte arrays. I'm sure that there must be a less clumsy way of doing it than the nasty list → array → string path that I'm currently using.)

So, do be careful using the GmailFS and certainly don't use it for anything important.

Implementation Details

All meta-information in the GmailFS is stored in the subjects of emails sent by the Gmail user to themselves.

 This was not as good an idea as I'd first thought. I thought I could speed things up by grabbing the message summary without having to download the entire message, as Gmail elides subjects (abbreviates them and adds ellipses) to fit them on the screen, but it turned out that I needed to get the full message anyway. (Yes, the message bodies are empty, but it does add considerable latency to operations such as listing the contents of a large directory.)

The actual file data is stored in attachments. Files can span several attachments, allowing file sizes greater than the maximum Gmail attachment. File size should be limited only by the amount of free space in your Gmail account.

There are three types of important structures in the GmailFS:

- Directory and file entry structures hold the parent path and name of files or directories. Symlink information is also kept here. These structures have a reference to the file's or directory's *inode* (a data structure holding information about where and how the file or directory is stored).

- Inode structures hold the kind of information usually found in a Unix inode, such as mode, uid, gid, size, etc.

- Data block structures are one of three types of messages GmailFS uses to store information related to the filesystem. The subject of the messages holding these structures contains a reference to the file's inode as well as the current block number.

- As GmailFS can store files longer than the maximum Gmail attachment size, it uses block numbers to refer to the slice of the original file that this data block message refers to. For example, if you have a blocksize of 5 MB and a file 22 MB long, you will have five blocks (5 MB, 5 MB, 5 MB, 5 MB, and 2 MB); the block numbers for these will be 0, 1, 2, 3, and 4, respectively.

All subject lines contain an *fsname* (filesystem name) field that serves two purposes.

- Prevents the injection of spurious data into the filesystem by external attackers. As such, the fsname should be chosen with the same care that you would exercise in choosing a password.

- Allows multiple filesystems to be stored on a single Gmail account. By mounting with different fsname options set, the user can create distinct filesystems.

Installing the Hack

This isn't for the uninitiated. I haven't provided newbie-focused step-by-step installation instructions, because if you aren't able to take care of some of these details yourself, you probably shouldn't be mucking about in this hack. If you're out of your depth, sit back, relax, and read on for edification's sake.

Before you begin, make sure you have Python 2.3 and the python2.3-dev packages installed.

Install Version 1.3 of FUSE (*http://sourceforge.net/projects/avf*). Some Linux distributions (such as Debian) make this available as a package. If your distro doesn't, you'll need to download the source (*http://sourceforge.net/ project/showfiles.php?group_id=21636*) and make and install it manually.

Next you'll need the Python FUSE bindings (*http://richard.jones.name/ google-hacks/gmail-filesystem/fuse-python.tar.gz*). Download and extract *fuse-python.tar.gz* and follow the instructions in *fuse-python/INSTALL*.

> The Python FUSE bindings are also available from FUSE's CVS page (*http://sourceforge.net/cvs/?group_id=21636*), but if you grab CVS, remember that the Python bindings don't work with the rest of CVS at the moment (at the time of this writing); you still need to use FUSE 1.3.

Grab libgmail (*http://sourceforge.net/project/showfiles.php?group_id=113492*) [Hack #80]. After unarchiving the package, copy *libgmail.py* and *constants.py* to somewhere Python can find them (*/usr/local/lib/python2.3/site-packages* works for Debian; others may vary).

Finally, download GmailFS (*http://richard.jones.name/google-hacks/gmail- filesystem/gmailfs.tar.gz*) itself and unarchive it. Copy *gmailfs.py* to somewhere easily accessible (*/usr/local/bin/gmailfs.py*, for example) and *mount. gmailfs* (a modified version of mount.fuse distributed with FUSE 1.3) to */sbin/ mount.gmailfs*.

If you have an older version of Python interfering with the running of GmailFS and would rather have it using a newer version, alter the first line of *gmailfs.py* to point at *#!/path/to/newer/python2.3* rather than the #!/usr/bin/env python default.

Take a moment to enjoy just how much you know about such things and move on when you're ready.

Running the Hack

All that remains is to mount your Gmail filesystem.

You can do so via fstab or on the command line using mount. To use fstab, create an */etc/fstab* entry that looks something like this:

```
/usr/local/bin/gmailfs.py /path/of/mount/point gmailfs \
noauto,username=gmailuser,password=gmailpass,fsname=zOlRRa
```

Replace *gmailuser* and *gmailpass* with your Gmail username and password, respectively. The value you pass to fsname is one you'd like to dub this Gmail filesystem.

It is important to choose a hard-to-guess name here. If others can guess the fsname, they can corrupt your Gmail filesystem by injecting spurious messages into your inbox (read: sending you mail).

To mount the filesystem from the command line, use the following command:

```
# mount -t gmailfs /usr/local/bin/gmailfs.py /path/of/mount/point \
-o username=gmailuser,password=gmailpass,fsname=zOlRRa
```

Again, replace *gmailuser*, *gmailpass*, and *zOlRRa* with your Gmail username, Gmail password, and preferred filesystem name.

At the time of this writing, both of these command-line invocations have serious security issues. If you run a multiuser system, others can easily see your Gmail username and password. If this is a problem for you, your only option at present is to modify *gmailfs.py* itself, changing DefaultUsername, DefaultPassword, and DefaultFsname as appropriate.

A future version of GmailFS (perhaps already out by the time you read this) will load these values from configuration files in your home directory.

Figure 6-28 shows my mounted *gmailfs* filesystem in action.

Things You Should Know

There are a few things you should know as you start strolling about and storing things on your Gmail filesystem:

- GmailFS also has a blocksize option, the default being 5 MB. Files smaller than the minimum blocksize will only use the amount of space required to store the file, *not the full blocksize*. Note that any files created during a previous mount with a different blocksize will retain their original blocksize until deleted. For most applications you will make best use of your bandwidth by keeping the blocksize as large as possible.

- When you delete files, GmailFS will place the files in the trash. The libgmail library does not currently support purging items from the trash, so you will have to do this manually through the regular Gmail web interface.

- To avoid seeing the messages created for your Gmail filesystem in your inbox, you probably want to create a filter (*http://gmail.google.com/support/bin/answer.py?answer=6579&query=filter&topic=&type=f*) to automatically archive GmailFS messages as they arrive in your inbox. The best approach is probably to search for the `fsname` value; it'll be in the subject of all your GmailFS messages.

Outstanding Issues

At the time of this writing, there are some outstanding issues with GmailFS that you should be aware of:

- I don't recommend storing your only copy of anything important on GmailFS for the following two reasons:

    — GmailFS is currently a 0.2 release and should be treated as such. You can depend on its being undependable.

    — There's no cryptography involved, so your files will all be stored in plain text on Google's Gmail servers. This will no doubt make some of you nervous.

- Performance is acceptable for uploading and downloading very large files (obviously dependent on your having decent bandwidth). However, operations such as listing the contents of a large directory, which requires many round trips, are extremely slow. The poor performance here is largely independent of bandwidth and is related to having to grab entire messages instead of being able to use message summaries.

- I haven't done any testing where GmailFS opens the same file multiple times and performs subsequent operations on the file. I suspect it will behave badly.

If all of this doesn't dissuade you from giving GmailFS a whirl, have at it and enjoy. Just be sure to visit the GmailFS page (*http://richard.jones.name/google-hacks/gmail-filesystem/gmail-filesystem.html*) to find out what's new and grab the latest instructions and code.

See Also

- Gmcp (*http://mindtrick.net/archives/2004/08/gmail_as_an_online_backup_system_gmcp.php*) is a small Perl utility to employ Gmail as a backup service.
- There's also a PHP (*http://ilia.ws/archives/15_Gmail_as_an_online_backup_system.html*) backup utility.
- Gmail Drive Shell Extension (*http://www.viksoe.dk/code/gmail.htm*; Windows only) wraps up the GmailFS into a virtual filesystem visible as just another drive in Windows Explorer.
- "Use Gmail as a Windows Drive" [Hack #79].

—*Richard Jones*

HACK #79   Use Gmail as a Windows Drive

Drop a gig of Gmail storage on your Windows desktop and treat it just about like any other drive.

If "Use Gmail as a Linux Filesystem" [Hack #78] had you Windows users salivating over the prospect of adding a gigabyte of networked storage to your computer, do we have a find for you. GMail Drive (http://www.viksoe.dk/code/gmail.htm) drops the gigabyte of storage allotted your Gmail account right on to your very desktop. It looks and feels just like a regular hard drive—albeit a tad slower (more than a tad if you're on dialup) being networked rather than local.

And it's as simple as one might hope, being a Windows application: none of the odd libraries to install, fstab entries (whatever those are) to edit, and fuss of the Linux version you paged past just a moment ago.

Point your browser at *http://www.viksoe.dk/code/gmail.htm*, scroll down to the Download Files section, and grab a copy of GMail Drive. The download should take only a few seconds. Unzip the installer and double-click the Setup icon. A few moments later, you should see a brand-spanking-new Gmail Drive under My Computer in Windows Explorer.

Click the link and you'll be prompted to log in, as shown in Figure 6-29.

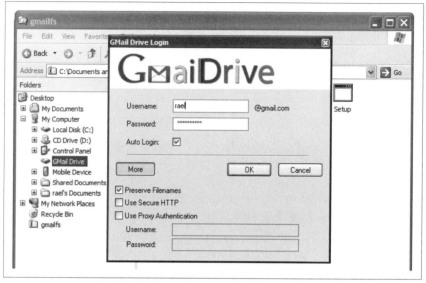

Figure 6-29. GMail Drive prompting for Gmail login

You'll notice GMail Drive provides other options (just click the More button in the Login window), including secure HTTP for encrypted interaction with your remote "drive."

Enter your Gmail username and password and click the OK button to log in. A few seconds later, your drive will be ready to use. Drag-and-drop files merrily to and fro, between your local drive and GMail Drive.

Right-click the GMail Drive icon to log out, check properties (used space, free space), or to log back in. You'll notice the Login option is actually "Login As..." This means you can mount the GMail Account of a friend or family member as easily as you can your own. Transfer that home movie to the grandparents' computer, share your forays into music remixing with your friends, or move files between your home and office computers without need of toting about an external hard drive or shelling out for a 1 gig USB drive.

See Also

- "Use Gmail as a Linux Filesystem" **[Hack #78]**.

HACK #80 Program Gmail

Try your hand at writing an alternative interface to Gmail using the freely available Python, Perl, PHP, Java, and .NET libraries and API frameworks.

The relatively simple and lightweight data interface to Gmail stems from the separation between user interface (client-side JavaScript) and data model. This has spawned myriad frontends (graphical and otherwise), libraries, and unofficial "API" implementations in Python, Perl, PHP, Java, and .NET.

For a glimpse of the Gmail engine and protocol underlying the official Gmail interface and the lion's share of the unofficial APIs and libraries written to the service, take a gander at Johnvey Hwang's "About the Gmail engine and protocol" (*http://johnvey.com/features/gmailapi/*; scroll down).

Programmatic access to Gmail is accomplished by screen-scraping either the web interface or its underlying data format. While the data format is pretty simple and isn't expected to change dramatically, there's no telling what Google might do that could adversely affect the various programmatic interfaces to their service. Thus, it goes without saying that such hackery comes with no quality of service guarantee. In other words, expect breakages. And if you do notice something's gone wrong, visit the home page of your chosen programmatic interface for the latest version of the code, news, and further information.

Rather than taking you step by step through the same code in each of the five languages and frameworks, I provide a walk through in Python. The APIs are all rather similar, which shouldn't come as any great surprise since they are all built upon the Gmail "API" used by the candy-coated JavaScript-powered Gmail Web interface.

Python

The libgmail (*http://libgmail.sourceforge.net*; GNU Public License 2.0/PSF) Python binding for Gmail provides a nice, clean interface (as you'd expect from Python) to your Gmail account.

Libgmail bundles a lovely set of useful example applications, usable right out of the box:

archive.py
  Downloads your Gmail messages to your computer for archiving, importing, or moving purposes.

gmailsmtp.py

Proxies SMTP requests, allowing you to use Gmail to send email from the comfort of your preferred email application; a related script, *sendmsg.py*, sends a single email message via Gmail from the command line—not unlike using the Unix `mail` command.

gmailpopd.py

Proxies a standard POP interface to mail from your preferred email application.

gmailftpd.py

Pretends to be an FTP server, allowing you to download (only) messages labeled "ftp" via a standard FTP application.

Installing the hack. Installation is just a matter of downloading and unpacking the library (*http://sourceforge.net/project/showfiles.php?group_id=113492*, or click the Downloads link on the libgmail home page) and putting it someplace findable by Python.

The code. Libgmail sports much functionality, each with its own rather self-explanatory function name: getMessagesByQuery, getQuotaInfo, getLabelNames, getMessagesByLabel, getRawMessage, and getUnreadMsgCount. Leaf through *libgmail.py* for the kind of details only a programmer could love.

Here's a snippet of sample code showing off login, folder selection, and strolling through email—thread by thread, message by message:

```
#!/usr/bin/python

# libgmail_example.py
# A simple example of the libgmail Python binding for Gmail in action
# http://libgmail.sourceforge.net/
#
# Usage: python gmail_in_python.py

import libgmail

# Login
gmail = libgmail.GmailAccount('raelity@gmail.com', '12bucklemyshoe')
gmail.login()

# Select a folder, label, or starred messages--in this case, the Inbox
folder = gmail.getMessagesByFolder('inbox')

# Stroll through threads in the Inbox
for thread in folder:
    print thread.id, len(thread), thread.subject

    # Stroll through messages in each thread
```

```
for msg in thread:
    print "  ", msg.id, msg.number, msg.subject
```

Replace *raelity@gmail.com* and *12bucklemyshoe* with your Gmail email address and password. Instead of *inbox*, you can use any of Gmail's standard folder names or your custom labels—e.g., *starred*, *sent*, or *friends*.

Save the code to a file called *gmail_in_python.py*.

Running the hack. Run the *gmail_in_python.py* script on the command line, like so:

```
$ python libgmail_example.pl
WARNING:root:Live Javascript and constants file versions differ.
ff602fe48d89bc3 1 Hello from Hotmail
    ff602fe48d89bc3 1 Hello from Hotmail
ff5fb9c2829c165 1 Hello Gmail via Gmail Loader
    ff5fb9c2829c165 1 Hello Gmail via Gmail Loader
ff5691f7170cb62 1 Hello Gmail via Gmail Loader
    ff5691f7170cb62 1 Hello Gmail via Gmail Loader
ff3f4310237b607 1 Howdy gmail-lite
    ff3f4310237b607 1 Howdy gmail-lite
```

Hacking the hack. Swap in a call to getMessagesByQuery and you now have a command line right to the Gmail search engine:

```
#folder = gmail.getMessagesByFolder('inbox')
folder = gmail.getMessagesByQuery('from:rael subject:Howdy')
```

Here are the results of this little switch:

```
$ python libgmail_example.pl
WARNING:root:Live Javascript and constants file versions differ.
ff3f4310237b607 1 Howdy gmail-lite
    ff3f4310237b607 1 Howdy gmail-lite
```

See also. gmail.py (*http://www.holovaty.com/blog/archive/2004/06/18/1751*) is a simple Python interface to Gmail, focusing on exporting raw messages for backup and import.

Perl

Mail::Webmail::Gmail (*http://search.cpan.org/~mincus/Mail-Webmail-Gmail-1.00/lib/Mail/Webmail/Gmail.pm*) provides Perl hackers a programmatic interface to Gmail. You'll find full POD documentation and more sample code than you can shake a stick it in the module and online at the aforementioned URL.

A Comprehensive Perl Archive Network (CPAN) search for gmail (*http://search.cpan.org/search?query=gmail&mode=all*) at the time of this writing finds three more Perl Gmail libraries: *Mail::Webmail::Gmail*, *WWW::GMail*, and *WWW::Scraper::Gmail*.

PHP

GMailer or libgmailer (*http://gmail-lite.sourceforge.net*; GNU Public License) is a PHP library for interacting with Gmail by way of the curl library (*http://www.php.net/curl*) with SSL support (*http://www.openssl.org*). It is the engine underlying gmail-lite [Hack #76], an HTML-only interface to Gmail.

For full libgmailer documentation and plenty of sample code, leaf through the online documentation (*http://gmail-lite.sourceforge.net/docs.html*).

Java

G4j or GMail API for Java (*http://g4j.sourceforge.net*; GNU Public License) is a Java interface to Gmail. The API comes with GMailer for Java, a basic GUI frontend to Gmail built on top of G4j.

Full documentation in Javadoc HTML is available online (*http://g4j.sourceforge.net/doc*).

.NET

The Gmail Agent API (*http://johnvey.com/features/gmailapi*; GNU Public License) is a .NET foundation for programming to Gmail. A full package of source for the API itself; the Gmail Agent Applet, a proof of concept Windows frontend to Gmail; and associated Windows Installer projects are available for download.

There's also full documentation available in both HTML format (*http://johnvey.com/features/gmailapi/docs*) and as Windows Help.

Ads

Hacks 81–85

You've probably noticed Google's advertising—or perhaps you haven't. But it's there, on the periphery of every Google results page. Then again, no one can blame you for overlooking the ads, since they're small, text-only, and rather unobtrusive. Nonetheless, they're effective. It turns out that hiding straightforward, content-like ads in plain sight is rather a relief in today's Web of flashy (and, indeed, flash*ing*) in-your-face advertising. Visitors have learned to tune out traditional billboard-like ads and hone in on textual content—and Google's AdWords™.

But simply grabbing eyeballs isn't quite enough. It's the *click-through*—clicking an ad and following it to the advertiser and its products—that counts. This is where Google's AdWords really shine. They're not simply rotating, flip-of-the-coin ads; they're every bit as relevant as the results of your search are. Query Google for "volvo safety" and alongside the Volvo safety reports and crash tests you'll see Car Safety ads from CARFAX (*http:// www.carfax.com*) and Volvo Auctions from CHEAPCarFinder.com (*http:// www.cheapcarfinder.com*). Try pirates and you'll be served (at least at the time of this writing) a Walmart ad. What's Walmart got to do with pirates, you ask? Not much, it seems, but they purchased the AdWord and must have had some reason for doing so. Click the link and Walmart's product search turns up a Gameboy game, as well as VHS and DVD versions of Disney's *Pirates of the Caribbean*. If Google has nothing relevant to show, it'll show no ads at all.

Google AdSense

AdSense™ (*http://www.google.com/adsense*) is Google's advertising service, intended to deliver just such advertising magic to your web site. With more than 150,000 advertisers signed up, there are sure to be ads targeting your readers, be your site about baseball, computers, or rare spoon collecting.

Google AdWords

On the flipside of the AdSense coin, you'll find Google AdWords (*http://adwords.google.com*), the fount from which those ads are drawn. AdWords is an advertiser base 150,000 strong, from mom-and-pops to Fortune 500s, all looking to make their presence known and wares available alongside Google search results.

And in true Google style, AdWords is different from just about every advertising service you've ever seen. There's virtually no price barrier; anyone with a few marketing dollars in their pocket can buy a few keywords. It's so simple that even the most inexperienced marketer can get a leg up. That said, there's a lot to AdWords, and its simplicity can be deceptive.

> This book, being focused on cool hacks, tools, and techniques, doesn't attempt a comprehensive introduction to Google's advertising programs. For a comprehensive introduction and detailed treatment, pick up a copy of *Google: The Missing Manual* (*http://www.oreilly.com/catalog/googletmm*; O'Reilly) by Sarah Milstein and Rael Dornfest.

HACK
#81   Get the Most out of AdWords

Guest commentary by Andrew Goodman of Traffick on how to write great AdWords.

AdWords (*https://adwords.google.com*) is just about the sort of advertising program that you might expect to roll out of the big brains at Google. The designers of the advertising system have innovated thoroughly to provide precise targeting at low cost with less work—it really is a good deal. The flipside is that it takes a fair bit of savvy to get a campaign to the point where it stops failing and starts working.

For larger advertisers, AdWords Select is a no-brainer. Within a couple of weeks, a larger advertiser will have enough data to decide whether to significantly expand their ad program on AdWords Select or perhaps to upgrade to a premium sponsor account.

I'm going to assume that you have a basic familiarity with how cost-per-click advertising works. AdWords Select ads currently appear next to search results on Google.com (and some international versions of the search engine) and near search results on AOL and a few other major search destinations. There are a great many quirks and foibles to this form of advertising. My focus here will be on some techniques that can turn a mediocre, nonperforming campaign into one that actually makes money for the advertiser while conforming to Google's rules and guidelines.

One thing I should make crystal clear is that advertising with Google bears no relationship to having your web site's pages indexed in Google's search engine. The search engine remains totally independent of the advertising program. Ad results never appear within search results.

I'm going to offer four key tips for maximizing AdWords Select campaign performance, but before I do, I'll start with four basic assumptions:

- High click-through rates (CTRs) save you money, so that should be one of your main goals as an AdWords Select advertiser. Google has set up the keyword bidding system to reward high-CTR advertisers. Why? It's simple. If 2 ads are each shown 100 times, the ad that is clicked on 8 times generates revenue for Google twice as often as the ad that is clicked on 4 times over the same stretch of 100 search queries served. So if your CTR is 4% and your competitor's is only 2%, Google factors this into your bid. Your bid is calculated as if it were "worth" twice as much as your competitor's bid.

- Very low CTRs are bad. Google disables keywords that fall below a minimum CTR threshold ("0.5% normalized to ad position," which is to say, 0.5% for position 1, and a more forgiving threshold for ads as they fall further down the page). Entire campaigns will be gradually disabled if they fall below 0.5% CTR on the whole.

- Editorial disapprovals are a fact of life in this venue. Your ad copy or keyword selections may violate Google's editorial guidelines from time to time. Again, it's very difficult to run a successful campaign when large parts of it are disabled. You need to treat this as a normal part of the process rather than giving up or getting flustered.

- The AdWords Select system is set up like an advertising laboratory; that is to say, it makes experimenting with keyword variations and small variations in ad copy a snap. No guru can prejudge for you what will be your "magical ad copy secrets," and it would be irresponsible to do so, because Google offers such detailed real-time reporting that can tell you very quickly what does and does not catch people's attention.

Now on to four tips to get those CTRs up and to keep your campaign from straying out of bounds.

Matching Can Make a Dramatic Difference

You'll likely want to organize your campaign's keywords and phrases into several distinct *ad groups* (made easy by Google's interface). This will help you more closely match keywords to the actual words that appear in the title of your ad. Writing slightly different ads to closely correspond to the words in each group of keywords that you've put together is a great way to improve your click-through rates. You'd think that an ad title (say, "Deluxe Topsoil in Bulk") would match equally well to a range of keywords that mean essentially the same thing. That is, you'd think this ad title would create about the same CTR with the phrase "bulk topsoil" as it would with a similar phrase (e.g., "fancy dirt wholesaler"). Not so. Exact matches tend to get significantly higher CTRs. Being diligent about matching your keywords reasonably closely to your ad titles will help you outperform your less diligent competition.

If you have several specific product lines, you should consider better matching different groups of key phrases to an ad written expressly for each product line. If your clients like your store because you offer certain specialized wine varieties, for example, have an ad group with "ice wine" and related keywords in it, with "ice wine" in the ad title. Don't expect the same generic ad to cover all your varieties. Someone searching for an "ice wine" expert will be thrilled to find a retailer who specializes in this area. They probably won't click on or buy from a retailer who just talks about wine in general. Search engine users are passionate about particulars, and their queries are highly granular. Take advantage of this passion and granularity.

The other benefit of getting more granular and matching keywords to ad copy is that you don't pay for clicks from unqualified buyers, so your sales conversion rate is likely to be much higher.

Copywriting Tweaks Generally Improve Clarity and Directness

By and large, I don't run across major copywriting secrets. Psychological tricks to entice more people to click, after all, may wind up attracting unqualified buyers. But there are times when the text of an ad falls outside the zone of "what works reasonably well." In such cases, excessively low CTRs kill any chance your web site might have had to close the sale.

Consider using the Goldilocks method to diagnose poor-performing ads. Many ads lean too far to the "too cold" side of the equation. Overly technical jargon may be unintelligible and uninteresting even to specialists, especially given that this is still an emotional medium and that people are looking at search results first and glancing at ad results as a second thought.

The following example is too cold:

```
Faster DWMGT Apps
Build GMUI modules 3X more secure than KLT. V. 2.0 rated as
"best pligtonferg" by WRSS Mag.
```

No one clicks. Campaign limps along. Web site remains world's best-kept secret.

So then a hotshot (the owner's nephew) grabs the reins and tries to put some juice into this thing. Unfortunately, this new creative genius has been awake for the better part of a week, attending raves, placing second in a snowboarding competition, and tending to his various piercings. His agency work for a major Fortune 500 client's television spots once received rave reviews. Of course, those were rave reviews from industry pundits and his best friends, because the actual ROI on the big client's TV branding campaign was untrackable.

The hotshot's copy reads:

```
Reemar's App Kicks!
Reemar ProblemSolver 2.0 is the real slim shady. Don't trust
your Corporate security to the drones at BigCorp.
```

Unfortunately, in a nonvisual medium with only a few words to work with, the true genius of this ad is never fully appreciated. Viewers don't click and may be offended by the ad and annoyed with Google.

The simple solution is something unglamorous but clear, such as:

```
Easy & Powerful Firewall
Reemar ProblemSolver 2.0 outperforms BigCorp
Exacerbator 3 to 1 in industry tests.
```

You can't say it all in a short ad. This gets enough specific (and true) info out there to be of interest to the target audience. Once they click, there will be more than enough info on your web site. In short, your ads should be clear. How's that for a major copywriting revelation?

The nice thing is, if you're bent on finding out for yourself, you can test the performance of all three styles quickly and cheaply, so you don't have to spend all week agonizing about this.

Be Inquisitive and Proactive with Editorial Policies (But Don't Whine)

Editorial oversight is a big task for Google AdWords staff—a task that often gets them in hot water with advertisers, who don't like to be reined in. For the most part, the rules are in the long-term best interest of this advertising medium, because they're aimed at maintaining consumer confidence in the quality of what appears on the page when that consumer types something into a search engine. Human error, however, may mean that your campaign is being treated unfairly because of a misunderstanding. Or maybe a rule is ambiguous and you just don't understand it.

Reply to the editorial disapproval messages (they generally come from *adwords-support@google.com*). Ask questions until you are satisfied that the rule makes sense as it applies to your business. The more Google knows about your business, in turn, the more they can work with you to help you improve your results, so don't hesitate to give a bit of brief background in your notes to them. The main thing is, don't let your campaign just sit there disabled because you're confused or angry about being *disapproved*. Make needed changes, make the appropriate polite inquiries, and move on.

Avoid the Trap of "Insider Thinking" and Pursue the Advantage of Granular Thinking

Using lists of specialized keywords will likely help you to reach interested consumers at a lower cost per click and convert more sales than using more general industry keywords. Running your ad on keywords from specialized vocabularies is a sound strategy.

A less successful strategy, though, is to get lost in your own highly specialized social stratum when considering how to pitch your company. Remember that this medium revolves around consumer search engine behavior. You won't win new customers by generating a list of different ways of stating terminology that only management, competitors, or partners might actually use, unless your ad campaign is just being run for vanity's sake.

Break things down into granular pieces and use industry jargon where it might attract a target consumer, but when you find yourself listing phrases that only your competitors might know or buzzwords that came up at the last interminable management meeting, stop! You've started down the path of insider thinking! By doing so, you may have forgotten about the customer and about the role market research must play in this type of campaign.

It sounds simple to say it, but in your AdWords Select keyword selection, you aren't describing your business. You're trying to use phrases that consumers would use when trying to describe a problem they're having, a specific item they're searching for, or a topic that they're interested in. Mission statements from above versus what customers and prospects actually type into search engines. Big difference. (At this point, if you haven't yet done so, you'd better go back and read over *The Cluetrain Manifesto* to get yourself right out of this top-down mode of thinking.)

One way to find out about what consumers are looking for is to use Wordtracker (*http://www.wordtracker.com*) or other keyword research tools (such as the one that Google offers as part of the AdWords Select interface, a keyword research tool that Google promises it's working on). However, these tools are not in themselves enough for every business; because more businesses are using these keyphrase search frequency reports, the frequently searched terms eventually become picked over by competing advertisers—just what you want to avoid if you're trying to sneak along with good response rates at a low cost per click.

You'll need to brainstorm as well. In the future, there will be more sophisticated software-driven market research available in this area. Search technology companies such as Ask Jeeves Enterprise Solutions are already collecting data about the hundreds of thousands of customer questions typed into the search boxes on major corporate sites, for example. This kind of market research is under-used by the vast majority of companies today.

There are currently many low-cost opportunities for pay-per-click advertisers. As more and larger advertisers enter the space, prices will rise, but with a bit of creativity, granular thinking, and diligent testing, the smaller advertiser will always have a fighting chance on AdWords Select. Good luck!

—Andrew Goodman

HACK #82 Generate Google AdWords

You've written the copy and you've planned the budget. Now, what keywords are you going to use for your ad?

You've read about it and you've thought about it and you're ready to buy one of Google's AdWords. You've even got your copy together and you feel pretty confident about it. You've only got one problem now: figuring out your keywords, the search words that will trigger your AdWord to appear.

You're probably buying into the AdWords program on a budget, and you definitely want to make every penny count. Choosing the right keywords means that your ad will have a higher click-through rate. Thankfully, the Google AdWords program allows you to do a lot of tweaking, so if your first choices don't work, experiment, test, and test some more!

Choosing AdWords

So where do you get the search keywords for your ad? There are four places that might help you find them:

Log files
> Examine your site's log files. How are people finding your site now? What words are they using? What search engines are they using? Are the words they're using too general to be used for AdWords? If you look at your log files, you can get an idea of how people who are interested in your content are finding your site. (If they weren't interested in your content, why would they visit?)

Examine your own site

If you have an internal search engine, check its logs. What are people searching for once they get to your site? Are there any common misspellings that you could use as an AdWord? Are there any common phrases that you could use?

Brainstorm

What do people think of when they look at your site? What keywords do you want them to think of? Brainstorm about the product that's most closely associated with your site. What words come up?

Imagine someone goes to a store and asks about your products. How are they going to ask? What words would they use? Consider all the different ways someone could look for or ask about your product or service, and then consider if there's a set of words or a phrase that pops up over and over again.

Glossaries

If you've brainstormed until wax dribbles out your ears but you're no closer to coming up with words relevant to your site or product, visit some online glossaries to jog your brain. The Glossarist (*http://www. glossarist.com*) links to hundreds of glossaries on hundreds of different subjects. Check and see if they have a glossary relevant to your product or service, and see if you can pull some words from there.

Exploring Your Competitors' AdWords

Once you've got a reasonable list of potential keywords for your ad, take them and run them in the Google search engine. Google rotates advertisements based on the spending cap for each campaign, so even after running a search three or four times, you may see different advertisements each time. Use the AdWords scraper to save these ads to a file and review them later.

If you find a potential keyword that apparently contains no advertisements, make a note. When you're ready to buy an AdWord, you'll have to check its frequency; it might not be searched often enough to be a lucrative keyword for you. But if it is, you've found a potential advertising spot with no other ads competing for searchers' attentions.

Scrape Google AdWords

#83   Scrape the AdWords from a saved Google results page into a form suitable for importing into a spreadsheet or database.

Google's AdWords—the text ads that appear to the right of the regular search results—are delivered on a cost-per-click basis, and purchasers of the

AdWords are allowed to set a ceiling on the amount of money that they spend on their ad. This means that, even if you run a search for the same query word multiple times, you won't necessarily get the same set of ads each time.

If you're considering using Google AdWords to run ads, you might want to gather up and save the ads that are running for the query words that interest you. Google AdWords is not included in the functionality provided by the Google API, so you're left to a little scraping to get at that data.

Be sure to read "A Note on Spidering and Scraping" in Chapter 9 for some understanding of what scraping means.

This hack will let you scrape the AdWords from a saved Google results page and export them to a comma-separated (CSV) file, which you can then import into Excel or your favorite spreadsheet program.

This hack requires a Perl module called *HTML::TokeParser* (*http://search.cpan.org/search?query=htmL%3A%3Atokeparser &mode=all*). You'll need to install it before the hack will run.

The Code

Save this code to a text file named *adwords.pl*:

```perl
#!/usr/bin/perl

# usage: perl adwords.pl results.html
#
use strict;
use HTML::TokeParser;

die "I need at least one file: $!\n"
unless @ARGV;


my @Ads;
for my $file (@ARGV){
    # skip if the file doesn't exist
    # you could add more file testing here.
    # errors go to STDERR so they won't
    # pollute our csv file

    unless (-e $file) {
    warn "What??: $file -- $! \n-- skipping --\n";
    next;
    }
```

```perl
    # now parse the file
    my $p = HTML::TokeParser->new($file);
    while(my $token = $p->get_token) {
    next unless $token->[0] eq 'S'
        and $token->[1] eq 'a'
        and $token->[2]{id} =~ /^aw\d$/;
    my $link = $token->[2]{href};
    my $ad;
    if($link =~ /pagead/) {
        my($url) = $link =~ /adurl=([^\&]+)/;
        $ad->{href} = $url;
    } elsif($link =~ m{^/url\?}) {
        my($url) = $link =~ /\&q=([^&]+)/;
        $url =~ s/%3F/\?/;
        $url =~ s/%3D/=/g;
        $url =~ s/%25/%/g;
        $ad->{href} = $url;
    }
    $ad->{adwords} = $p->get_trimmed_text('/a');
    $ad->{desc} = $p->get_trimmed_text('/font');
    ($ad->{url}) = $ad->{desc} =~ /([\S]+)$/;
    push(@Ads,$ad);

    }
}

print quoted( qw( AdWords HREF Description URL Interest ) );
for my $ad (@Ads) {
    print quoted( @$ad{qw( adwords href desc url )} );
}


sub quoted {
    return join( ",", map { "\"$_\"" } @_ )."\n";
}
```

How It Works

Call this script on the command line ["How to Run the Hacks" in the Preface], providing the name of the saved Google results page and a file in which to put the
CSV results:

```
% perl adwords.pl input.html > output.csv
```

input.html is the name of the Google results page that you've saved. *output.
csv* is the name of the comma-delimited file to which you want to save your
results. You can also provide multiple input files on the command line if
you'd like:

```
% perl adwords.pl input.html input2.html > output.csv
```

The Results

The results will appear in a comma-delimited format that looks like this:

```
"AdWords","HREF","Description","URL","Interest"
"Free Blogging Site","http://www.1sound.com/ix",
" The ultimate blog spot Start your journal now ","www.1sound.com/ix","40"
"New Webaga Blog","http://www.webaga.com/blog.php",
" Fully customizable. Fairly inexpensive. ","www.webaga.com","24"
"Blog this","http://edebates.e-thepeople.org/a-national/article/10245/
view&",
" Will online diarists rule the Net strewn with failed dotcoms? ",
"e-thePeople.org","26"
"Ford - Ford Cars","http://quickquote.forddirect.com/FordDirect.jsp",
" Build a Ford online here and get a price quote from your local dealer! ",
"www.forddirect.com","40"
"See Ford Dealer's Invoice","http://buyingadvice.com/search/",
" Save $1,400 in hidden dealership profits on your next new car. ",
"buyingadvice.com","28"
"New Ford Dealer Prices","http://www.pricequotes.com/",
" Compare Low Price Quotes on a New Ford from Local Dealers and Save! ",
"www.pricequotes.com","25"
```

 Each line is prematurely broken in this code listing for the purposes of publication.

You'll see that the hack returns the AdWords headline, the link URL, the description in the ad, the URL on the ad (this is the URL that appears in the ad text, while the HREF is what the URL links to), and the Interest, which is the size of the Interest bar on the text ad. The Interest bar gives an idea of how many click-throughs an ad has had, showing how popular it is.

—Tim Allwine and Tara Calishain

H A C K   Determine the Worth of AdWords Words

#84   Harness the Google AdWords marketplace to guesstimate the value of a keyword or phrase in online advertising.

Google AdWords create what can only be termed an advertising marketplace.

You can choose to pay more to acquire more prominence on a results page, or pay less and still see your fair share of eyeballs and clicks until your daily budget is spent. By offering to pay a little more for each click-through, you'll move yourself up a spot or two in that list of 8 to 10 Sponsored Links on Google results pages.

Surely, then, you could just be sure to pay enough to keep your ad in the top spot? Not so, actually.

In addition to the cost-per-click (CPC) you're prepared to pay, AdWords pays close attention to the click-through-rate (CTR), the proportion of how many times your ad is shown versus how many times people actually click on it. By carefully balancing the price and effectiveness of ads, Google makes sure the top spots belong to the most relevant and targeted ads, not just those with the deepest pockets.

Now, this might appear at first blush to be a game of poker, and to a certain extent it is. That said, the AdWords Traffic Estimator (see Figure 7-7, later in this hack) is like a silent partner, advising you on your bets (sorry, *bids*) and guestimating your average position (1.0 is the top spot, 2.0 is the second, and so forth) in that list of ads.

The AdWords Traffic Estimator is an incredibly useful tool for experienced online advertisers and newbies alike.

And—of particular interest to us hacker types—it has the nice side effect of harnessing the Google AdWords marketplace to place a very real (albeit esti-mated) price on the relative value of individual words or phrases. It is on this alternate use of the estimator that this hack is focused.

We'll do this two ways: by hand—clicking through the AdWords site, fill-ing in forms, copying, and pasting—and then programmatically—turning keywords or phrases into a comma-separated (CSV) file suitable for import into just about any spreadsheet or database application that you might be running.

> Why do this manually when you can have your computer do all the work for you? First, the whole AdWords process is rather well done and educative. Second, the script auto-mates what is supposed to be the actions of a human on his way to signing up for AdWords and so employs a set of hacks and scrapes and, as such, is brittle and could well not work by the time you read this.

By Hand

It's quite a journey from the AdWords home page to the AdWords Traffic Generator, so we'll walk you through how to get there with the bare mini-mum of work.

Point your Web browser at the home page (*http://adwords.google.com*) and click the "Click to begin" button (Figure 7-1).

Unless you're actually interested in specifying language or location target-ing, go ahead and skip on past the "Choose your language and location tar-geting" page, shown in Figure 7-2, by clicking the Save & Continue button.

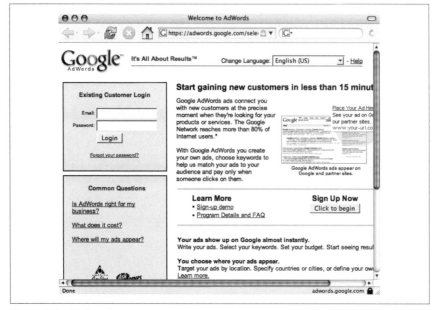

Figure 7-1. Click to begin

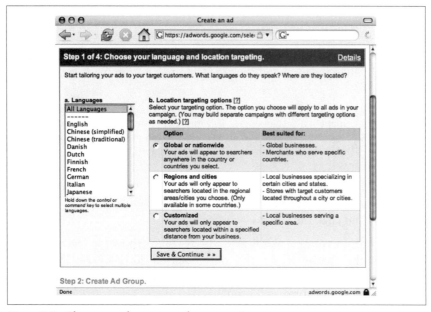

Figure 7-2. Choose your language and geo-targeting

You do need to pick a country or set of countries on the page shown in Figure 7-3. Again, unless you're actually interested in choosing specific

countries, just click the Add button to select All Countries and the Save &
Continue button to move on.

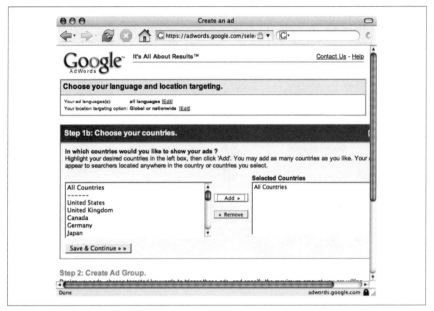

Figure 7-3. Choose your countries

On the "Create ads" page shown in Figure 7-4, you need to create a placeholder ad. Fill in the form and click the Continue button when you're done.

> As an aside, notice that I've spelled Google with two too
> many "o"s: Goooogle. It turns out—for perfectly under-
> standable reasons—that only Google can use the word Goo-
> gle (or Goooogle) in their AdWords program.

Now for the interesting part: choosing keywords or phrases to evaluate.
Type in some number of keywords or phrases into the box shown in
Figure 7-5 and click the Save Keywords button.

AdWords drops your keywords into a pretty table, shown in Figure 7-6, and
gives you the chance to specify your preferred currency and how much
you'd pay for a single click. Adjust these if you wish and, when you're ready,
click the Calculate Estimates button.

Finally, we get to the payoff, shown in Figure 7-7: the table is filled in with
reasonable guesstimates of average CPC, cost per day if you adjust for the
number of clicks per day shown, and expected average position of your ad in
the list of Sponsored Links on a results page in which your ad appears.

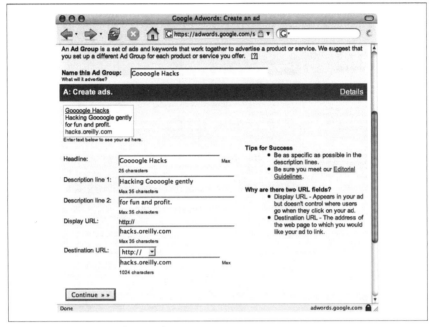

Figure 7-4. Create an ad, any ad

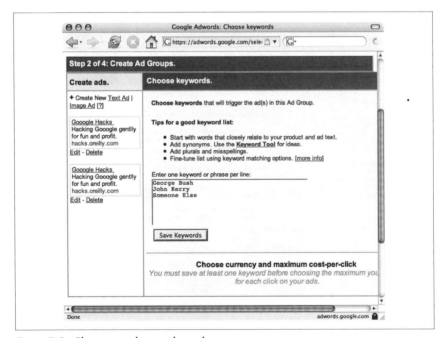

Figure 7-5. Choose your keywords or phrases

Determine the Worth of AdWords Words

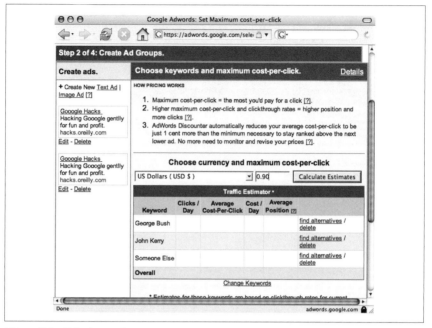

Figure 7-6. Calculate estimates

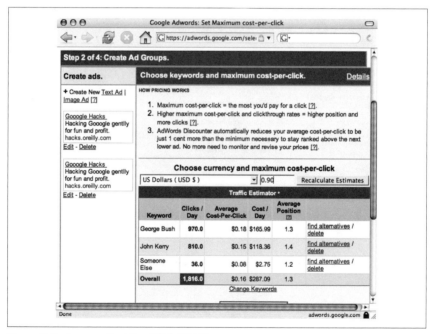

Figure 7-7. Average Cost-Per-Click (CPC)

For our purpose at hand, it's the average CPC numbers that we were after—and here you have them.

At any time, you can change the currency and maximum cost you'd be willing to consider paying per click. Click the Recalculate Estimates button to update the table. You can also change keywords by clicking the Change Keywords button and altering the keywords and phrases that you entered in Figure 7-5.

You'll find another handy tool behind the "find alternatives" links associated with each keyword. As shown in Figure 7-8, AdWords is remarkably good at finding related keywords and phrases for you. Select any number by clicking their checkboxes and click the "Ad these keywords" button at the bottom of the screen. Otherwise, click the Cancel button to leave things as they are.

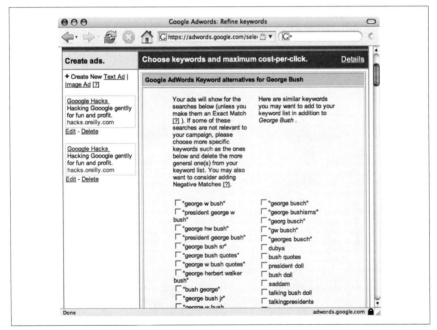

Figure 7-8. Find alternative keywords

Now that you have your keywords or phrases and their respective worth in tabular format, you can simply highlight them with your mouse, as shown in Figure 7-9, and copy them as you would any other text (Control-C on Windows, Command-C on Macintosh).

Paste what you've copied into a text file or spreadsheet (Figure 7-10) and rearrange and clean up as you see fit. At this point you have data you can

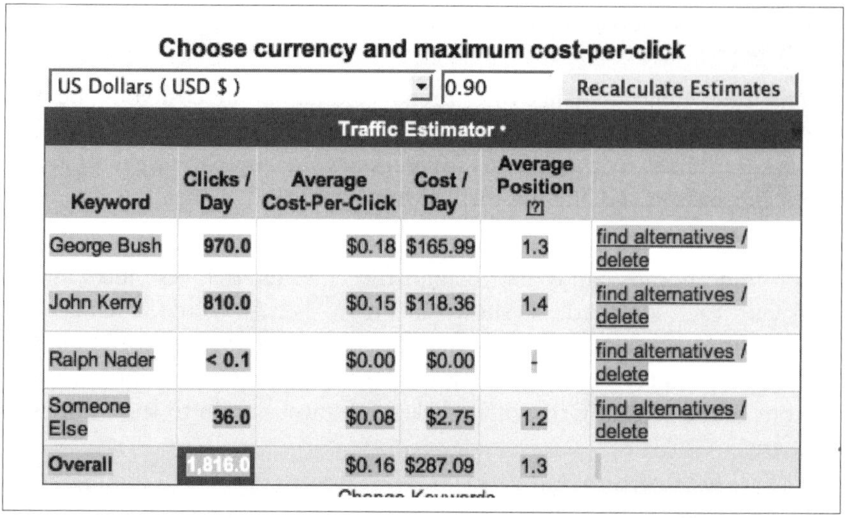

Choose currency and maximum cost-per-click

US Dollars (USD $)   ▾ 0.90   Recalculate Estimates

		Traffic Estimator •			
Keyword	Clicks / Day	Average Cost-Per-Click	Cost / Day	Average Position [?]	
George Bush	970.0	$0.18	$165.99	1.3	find alternatives / delete
John Kerry	810.0	$0.15	$118.36	1.4	find alternatives / delete
Ralph Nader	< 0.1	$0.00	$0.00	-	find alternatives / delete
Someone Else	36.0	$0.08	$2.75	1.2	find alternatives / delete
Overall	1,816.0	$0.16	$287.09	1.3	

Figure 7-9. Copy estimated Cost-Per-Clicks

work with, save as a CSV and import into your preferred database for further analysis, or paste into an email message as a gentle nudge to your marketing department.

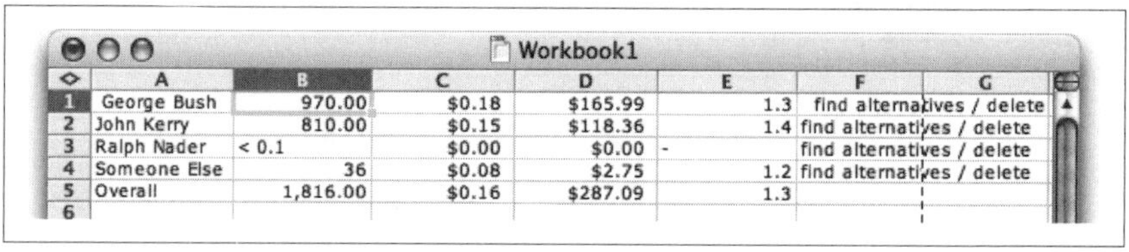

	A	B	C	D	E	F	G	
1	George Bush	970.00	$0.18	$165.99		1.3	find alternatives / delete	
2	John Kerry	810.00	$0.15	$118.36		1.4	find alternatives / delete	
3	Ralph Nader	< 0.1	$0.00	$0.00	-		find alternatives / delete	
4	Someone Else	36	$0.08	$2.75		1.2	find alternatives / delete	
5	Overall	1,816.00	$0.16	$287.09		1.3		
6								

Figure 7-10. Paste estimates into Excel

Programmatically

Doing things by hand is certainly good enough if you only do so once in a while. Let's say, however, that you want to keep an eye on the relative costs of AdWords words that you're interested in buying into at some point—much as you would monitor individual stocks by building a portfolio and checking in on a regular basis or having your online brokerage email you alerts. Google, at least at the time of this writing, offers no such service: the focus of their interface is on the ads you're building right now and those you're running and maintaining on an ongoing basis.

So, let's build such a service on our own.

The code. This script mimics the activity of someone manually going through the AdWords site, filling in forms, clicking buttons, and eventually copying CPC estimates and pasting them into to the screen or a CSV file. In other words, the code does just what we did by hand a scant moment ago.

You'll need to pick up and install a few prerequisite Perl modules along the way: *Crypt::SSLeay* for talking to the Google AdWords site on a secure channel (required by AdWords), *WWW::Mechanize* for automating your interaction with the Google AdWords site, *HTML::TableContentParser* for gleaning results from HTML tables, and *Text::CSV* for spitting out results in CSV format. (See "Program Google in Perl" [Hack #92] for guidance on installing Perl modules.)

The only one of these prerequisites that might cause you a little extra work is *Crypt::SSLeay* on Windows. ActiveState, makers of Active Perl for Windows, does not (at least not at the time of this writing) have permission to distribute the module as a PPM due to Canadian laws around cryptographic software. Check their "Status of the ActiveState PPM Repositories" page (*http://aspn.activestate.com/ASPN/ Downloads/ActivePerl/PPM/Repository*) for details and alternate installation instructions.

Save the following code as *adwords_worth.pl*:

```perl
#!/usr/bin/perl -w

# adwords_worth.pl
# Automate gleaning Google AdWords estimated cost-per-clicks (CPCs)
# Usage: perl adwords_worth.pl <keyword1> <keyword2> [..]
#        perl adwords_worth.pl < keywords.txt

use strict;
use WWW::Mechanize;
use HTML::TableContentParser;
use Text::CSV;

=head1 NAME

adwords_worth - Returns estimated Google AdWords cost-per-clicks (CPCs)
of provided keywords in comma-separated (CSV) format.

=cut

# Fill up keywords.
my $keyword_string;
if( not @ARGV ) {
    # You piped in a file
    local $/ = undef;
```

```
        $keyword_string = <STDIN>;
    } else {
        # Keywords are specified on command line
        $keyword_string = join( "\n", @ARGV );
    }
    $keyword_string =~ s/\s+/\n/g;
    die "No keywords specified!" unless $keyword_string =~ /\w+/;

    =head1 SYNOPSIS

    adwords_worth.pl keyword1 [..]
    adwords_worth.pl < keywords.txt

    =cut

    # Set up WWW::Mechanize to die on errors.
    my $agent = WWW::Mechanize->new( autocheck => 1 );

    # Get initial page.
    print STDERR "Fetching the Adwords initial page... ";
    $agent->get('https://adwords.google.com/');
    $agent->form_number(3);
    $agent->click('start');
    print STDERR "ok\n";

    print STDERR "Visiting the Language and Targeting page... ";
    # On Language and Targeting page.
    # Defaults are okay for now.
    $agent->click('save');
    print STDERR "ok\n";

    # On country selector.
    # Right now default value is "All Countries".
    print STDERR "Visiting the Country selector... ";
    $agent->click('save');
    print STDERR "ok\n";

    # On Create Ad page.
    # Fill in placeholder values, since it doesn't matter.
    # CAVEAT: All creative lines must be spelled correctly.
    # See: Adwords editorial guidelines.
    print STDERR "Creating a placeholder ad... ";
    $agent->current_form->value( 'adGroupName',        'groupname' );
    $agent->current_form->value( 'creative.line1',     'Spelling' );
    $agent->current_form->value( 'creative.line2',     'Spelling' );
    $agent->current_form->value( 'creative.line3',     'Spelling' );
    $agent->current_form->value( 'creative.visibleUrl', 'a.com' );
    $agent->current_form->value( 'creative.destUrl',   'a.com' );
    $agent->click('save');
    print STDERR "ok\n";

    # On Keywords page.
    print STDERR "Plugging in your keywords... ";
```

```perl
$agent->current_form->value( 'keywords', $keyword_string );
$agent->click('save');
print STDERR "ok\n";

# On Price Table Page, but no values are in the table.
print STDERR "Recalculating keyword values... ";
$agent->click('recalculate');
print STDERR "ok\n";

# Now on Price Table page, and the table now has values.
print STDERR "Gleaning keyword values and building you a CSV...\n\n";
my $p       = HTML::TableContentParser->new();
my $tables = $p->parse( $agent->content() );

# Table with the values is has its class attribute set to report.
my @report_tables =
  grep { exists $_->{class} and $_->{class} eq 'report' } @$tables;

# Assuming that Google on has on report table per page.
my $table = $report_tables[0];

# Make CSV object out here instead of having loop make X of them.
my $csv = Text::CSV->new();

# Get the rows of cells out of $table's convoluted structure.
# TODO naming of variables here is odd, but check out Dumper(\@row_cell_
objs).
my @row_cell_objs = grep { $_->{cells} } @{ $table->{rows} };
my @data_cells    = map  { $_->{cells} } @row_cell_objs;

foreach my $row ( $table->{headers}, @data_cells ) {
    # Just being safe here with references.
    if( ref $row eq 'ARRAY' ) {
        # Eliminate title cell and cells in rightmost column.
        # They contain only links.
        my @table_cells =
          grep { not exists $_->{class} or $_->{class} ne 'rightcolumn' }
@$row;
        my @data = map { $_->{data} } @table_cells;

        foreach (@data) {
            # Remove HTML tags and surrounding whitespace.
            s/<[^>]*>//g;
            s/^\s+//;
            s/\s+$//;
            s/\&lt;/</g;
            # Number of clicks contains commas, but we don't want those.
            tr/,//d;
        }

        # Make a CSV line and print it.
        if( $csv->combine(@data) ) {
            print $csv->string, "\n";
```

```
        } else {
            my $err = $csv->error_input;
            print "combine() failed on argument: ", $err, "\n";
        }
    } else {
        print "Row is not an array of cells!\n";
    }
}
print STDERR "Done.\n";

=head1 AUTHOR

Leland Johnson <easyasy2k@gmail.com>

=cut
```

Running the hack. You can invoke the script in two ways. The first is to pass keywords or phrases on the command line ["How to Run the Hacks" in the Preface] to be passed onto and priced by AdWords:

```
$ perl adwords_worth.pl adword "another adword" "one more"
```

> Be sure to wrap phrases in quotes; otherwise, they'll be seen as individual words.

The second way is to maintain a text file of keywords and phrases, one per line (without any enclosing quotes), and feed that file to the script:

```
$ perl adwords_worth.pl < adwords.txt
```

Both of these invocations produce output as CSV, printing them to the screen. To capture them in a *.csv* file, redirect the output like so:

```
$ perl adwords_worth.pl < adwords.txt > adwords.csv
```

The script also keeps you apprised of just where it is in the process with status messages printed to the screen—lest you think it's gone off into wilderness, never to return.

The results. Here's a sample run using the same keywords/phrases used in the "By Hand" walkthrough.

> The estimated worth may well have changed between the versions—and, indeed, any two invocations of the script. We told you AdWords was a real market; and if it weren't, this little experiment wouldn't be anywhere near as interesting.

```
$ perl adwords_worth.pl "George Bush" "John Kerry" "Ralph Nader" "Someone
Else"
Fetching the Adwords initial page... ok
Visiting the Language and Targeting page... ok
Visiting the Country selector... ok
Creating a placeholder ad... ok
Plugging in your keywords... ok
Recalculating keyword values... ok
Gleaning keyword values and building you a CSV...

"Keyword","Clicks /Day","AverageCost-Per-Click","Cost /Day","AveragePosition
[?]"
"George Bush","910.0","$0.21","$189.88","1.3"
"John Kerry","810.0","$0.18","$138.36","1.4"
"Ralph Nader","< 0.1","$0.00","$0.00","-"
"Someone Else","33.0","$0.09","$2.67","1.2"
"Overall","1771.0","$0.19","$334.62","1.3"
```

Hacking the hack. There are any number of ways you could slice and dice this hack:

- Add functionality to set your preferred maximum CPC by adding `$agent->current_form->value( 'price', 1.25 );` just before `$agent-> click('recalculate');` on the pricing page. Or further alter the script to take this value on the command line.

- Make the script more interactive, allowing you to retrieve estimated CPC, alter your keyword list, and go back for recalculation—all without the overhead of logging back in and meandering through the same screens each time.

- Automate things still further such that you can set up campaigns and ads right from the command line or another application. (This is something we weren't inclined to get into, but thought a mention worthwhile.)

 Automating and scraping is a brittle process ["A Note on Spidering and Scraping" in Chapter 9] and, as such, is subject to breakage, lockouts, or simply being asked to stop.

—*Leland Johnson and Rael Dornfest*

Serve Backup Ads

#85   Use AdSense's built-in (and rather thoughtful) ability to serve ads from alternate URLs when there are no targeted ads to offer.

There's a time and place for public service announcements. You just might not think your web site is the place and certainly not if it happens more than occasionally. When you signed up for AdSense (while you're no doubt a good citizen who pays their public radio and television dues), your intent was to reap a revenue stream from all the hard work that you've put into your content.

Yet there are times when a new section of your site hasn't yet been noticed and indexed by Google, AdSense has nothing appropriately targeted in its inventory, or there's a temporary outage of some kind. The net result is that you'll be running public service ads for the Red Cross or the like rather than revenue-generating, targeted advertising. Google AdSense doesn't get paid and so doesn't pay you for click-throughs on public service advertisements.

Now, you can either simply be OK with this coming up every so often—I know I am—or you can make use of a backup system Google AdSense provides: alternate ad URLs.

Point your browser at Google AdSense (*http://www.google.com/adsense*) and click the Ad Settings tab at the top of the page. Then, scroll down until you see "Alternate ad URL or color," as shown in Figure 7-11.

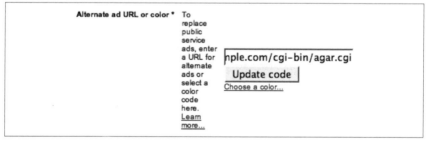

Figure 7-11. Provide an alternate URL for ads when AdSense has only public service advertisements to offer your site

Google AdSense suggests (*https://google.com/adsense/faq#basics10*) four backup options:

Image
   Paste in the URL of an image somewhere on the Web, ad or not, static or dynamically generated. This can be an alternate image that you've created and are serving from your own site, one produced on-the-fly by another advertising service, or any other image that either has some

revenue stream associated with it or simply tickles your fancy. For example, to serve up a static image named *advert1.jpg* residing on your web site, you'd provide a URL like *http://www.example.com/images/advert1.jpg*.

Clickable image

Provide the URL of an HTML page somewhere out on the Web that contains only a snippet of markup for a hyperlinked image. For example, you might have a file on your site called *adsense_alternate.html* that contains the following line:

```
<a href="http://www.example.com/storefront/"><img src="http://www.example.com/images/advert2.jpg border="0" /></a>
```

 That's all the file should have in it, mind you; leave off all the opening `<html><head></head><body>` and closing `</body></html>` bits and everything else you usually pack into your pages.

The URL you'd provide as an alternate would then be a pointer to that partial page, something like *http://www.example.com/adsense_alternate.html*.

HTML color code

If you have nothing to display as an alternative and are dead set against running public service ads, blank out the space where the AdSense ad would have gone by, providing the hexadecimal HTML color code of your page's background or that particular bit of real estate. For example, if your page had a background color of #160B35, a lovely dark blue that I use on my own site, you'd type that color code right into the "Alternate ad URL or color" field.

Collapse your ad

Google provides an HTML file you can download to and serve from your own web site that calls a bit of JavaScript to collapse your ad so that it doesn't show in the event you'd otherwise have seen a public service ad. For instructions and a link to download the file, visit *https://google.com/adsense/faq#basics13*.

Whichever you choose, when you click the "Update code" button, a smidgeon of JavaScript (the third line in Figure 7-12) will be added to the AdSense code that you paste into your web page. This additional line provides all AdSense needs to serve up your alternate ad choice when it has no targeted ad to run on your site.

Then again, there is a fifth alternative...

Your AdSense code	Copy-and-paste this HTML code into your web pages

```
<script type="text/javascript"><!--
google_ad_client = "pub-7123696386042886";
google_alternate_ad_url =
"http://www.example.com/cgi-bin/agar.cgi";
google_ad_width = 728;
google_ad_height = 90;
google_ad_format = "728x90_as";
google_ad_channel ="";
//--></script>
<script type="text/javascript"
   src="http://pagead2.googlesyndication.com/pagead/show_ads.js">
</script>
```

Figure 7-12. An alternate ad URL embedded in Google AdSense JavaScript code

Amazon/Google Ad Replacement (AGAR; *http://www.bestdealsdiscounts. com/agar*; GNU Public License) is a Perl script that supplements your Google AdSense ads with product advertisement drawn from Amazon's Web Services (AWS; *http://webservices.amazon.com*) and Associates (*http:// associates.amazon.com*) programs. Not only does it supplement AdSense, but it also mimics it in appearance, supports all the AdSense ad sizes, and allows you to customize your color scheme to match what you've chosen for AdSense.

> For AGAR to be useful (and financially rewarding), you'll need to have signed up as an Amazon Associate (*http:// associates.amazon.com*) through which you make money on purchases resulting from click-throughs on your site.

Download AGAR and get it running as a CGI script **["How to Run the Hacks" in the Preface]**. There's not much at all you need to change in the script itself, save replacing the default Amazon Associates ID with your own:

```
my $associate_id = "insert your amazon associates id here";
```

> If you're in the United Kingdom rather than the United States, you'll also want to change the locale in my $locale = "us"; to uk and my $uk_associate_id = "coolstufftoown"; to your U.K. Amazon Associates ID. If you're neither in the U. S. nor the U.K., there is some further adjustment necessary, but we leave that as an exercise for the reader.

Point your browser directly at the CGI script to test it out and you should see an ad banner, as shown in Figure 7-13, easily confused for an AdSense ad at first blush, but clearly linked to Amazon products.

The product category is chosen at random by default (go ahead and reload the page a few times to see this in action), but this can be customized either

Figure 7-13. An AGAR-generated AdSense-like Amazon banner ad

by altering the settings baked into the script itself or embedding settings into the agar.cgi URL. For example, instead of just pointing at agar.cgi, try agar.cgi??input_mode=kitchen&input_id=491864&ad_format=125x125_as. This produces a 125 by 125 pixel ad drawing from Amazon's "kitchen" category.

While the concept of mode and id, as expressed in the preceding URL is beyond the scope of this book, suffice it to say that you need to pass matching textual and numerical *browse IDs*. You'll find a detailed description of browse nodes and IDs in the Amazon Web Services documentation and a list of some of the text/number pairs in the AGAR code itself—look for %browse_ids =.

For an introduction to Amazon Web Services and all other things Amazon, pick up this book's cousin, *Amazon Hacks* (*http://www.oreilly.com/catalog/amazonhks*; O'Reilly) by Paul Bausch.

(If I may, I'd like to end with a pitch to at least consider letting the AdSense public service advertisements run. Sorry, I just couldn't help myself.)

## CHAPTER EIGHT

Webmastering
Hacks 86–91

When the Web was younger, the search engine field was wide open. There were lots of major search engines, including AltaVista, Excite, HotBot, and Webcrawler. This proliferation of search engines had both advantages and disadvantages. One disadvantage was that you had to make sure you submitted your query to several different places, while an advantage was that you had several inflows of traffic spawned from search engines.

As the number of search engines has dwindled, Google's index (and influence) has grown. You no longer have to worry so much about submitting to different places, but you do have to be aware of Google at all times.

Google's Importance to Webmasters

But isn't Google just a search engine web site like any other? Actually, its reach is far greater than that. Google partners with other sites to use the Google index results, including the likes of heavyweight properties AOL and Yahoo!, not to mention the multitude of sites out there making use of the Google API. So when you think about potential visitors from Google search results, you have to think beyond traditional search site borders.

Google's perception of your site has become increasingly more important, which means that you're going to have to be sure that your site abides by the Google rules or risks not being picked up. If you're very concerned about search-engine traffic, you're going to have to make sure that your site is optimized for luring in Google spiders and being indexed effectively. And if you're concerned that Google should *not* index some parts of your site, you need to understand the ins and outs of configuring your *robots.txt* file to reflect your preferences.

The Mysterious PageRank

You might hear a lot of people talk about Google's PageRank, bragging about attaining the misty heights of rank 7 or 8 or speaking reverently of sites that have achieved 9 or 10. PageRanks range from 0 (sites that have been penalized or not ranked) to 10 (reserved for only the most popular sites, such as Yahoo! and Google itself). The only place where you can actually see the PageRank of a given URL is the Google Toolbar **[Hack #60]**, though you can get some idea of popularity from the Google Directory. Listings in the Google Directory contain a green bar next to them, providing a good idea of a listing's popularity without giving an exact number.

Google has never provided the entire formula for their PageRank, so all you will find in this book is conjecture. It wouldn't surprise me to learn that the formula is changing all the time; as millions of people try myriad methods to increase their page ranking, Google has to take these efforts into account and (sometimes) react against them.

Why is PageRank so important? Because Google uses that as one aspect of determining how a given URL will rank among millions of possible search results. But that's only one aspect. The other aspects are determined via Google's ranking algorithm.

The Equally Mysterious Ranking Algorithm

If you thought Google was tight-lipped about how it determines PageRank, it's an absolute oyster when it comes to the ranking algorithm, the way that Google determines the order of search results. This book can give you some ideas, but again, these ideas are conjecture, and again, the algorithm is constantly changing. Your best bet is to create a content-rich web site and update it often. Google appreciates good content.

Of course, being listed in Google's index is not the only way to tell visitors about your site. You also have the option to advertise on Google.

Keeping Up with Google's Changes

With Google having such a leading position in the search engine world and so many webmasters looking to Google for traffic, you might guess that there's a lot of discussion about Google in various places around the Web. And you'd be right! My favorite place for Google news and gossip is Webmaster World (*http://www.webmasterworld.com*). It's not often that the terms civilized and *online forums* go together, but they do in this case. Discourse on this site is friendly, informative, and generally flame-free. I have learned a lot from this site.

There are also a few weblogs focused on Google and searching in general:

- Google Weblog (*http://google.blogspace.com*) keeps on top of everything Google, from the newest search syntax to Google's holiday logos (*http://www.google.com/holidaylogos.html*).

- Google Blog (*http://www.google.com/googleblog*) is the official Google weblog and features announcements, pointers, and behind-the-scenes commentary from the Googleplex.

- John Battelle's Searchblog (*http://battellemedia.com*) covers search in all forms.

In a Word: Relax

One of the things that I have learned is that a lot of people spend a lot of time worrying about how Google works, and further, they worry about how they can get the highest possible ranking.

I can appreciate their concern because search engine traffic means a lot to an online business. But the rest of us should just relax. As long as we concentrate on content that's good for visitors (and not just spiders), Google's ranking algorithms will appreciate our sites.

HACK #86 A Webmaster's Introduction to Google

Steps to take for optimal Google indexing of your site.

The cornerstone of any good search engine is highly relevant results. Google's unprecedented success has been due to its uncanny ability to match quality information with a user's search terms. The core of Google's search results are based on a patented algorithm called PageRank.

There is an entire industry focused on getting sites listed near the top of search engines. Google has proven to be the toughest search engine for a site to do well on. Even so, it isn't all that difficult for a new web site to get listed and begin receiving some traffic from Google.

Learning the ins and outs of getting your site listed by a search engine can be a daunting task. There is a vast array of information about search engines on the Web, and not all of it is useful or proper. This discussion of getting your site into the Google database focuses on long-term techniques for successfully promoting your site through Google, helping to avoid some of the common misconceptions and problems that a new site owner might face.

Search Engine Basics

When you type a term into a search site, the engine looks up potential matches in its database and presents the best web page matches first. How those web pages get into the database, and consequently, how you can get yours in there too, is a three-step process:

1. A search engine visits a site with an automated program called a *spider* (sometimes called a *robot*). A spider is just a program similar to a web browser that downloads a site's pages. It doesn't actually display the page anywhere; it just downloads the page data.

2. After the spider has acquired the page, the search engine passes the page to a program called an indexer, which is another robotic program that extracts most of the visible portions of the page. The indexer also analyzes the page for keywords, the title, links, and other important information contained in the code.

3. The search engine adds your site to its database and makes it available to searchers. The greatest difference between search engines is in this final step where ranking or result position under a particular keyword is determined.

Submitting Your Site to Google

The first step is to get your pages listed in the database, and there are two ways to go about it. The first is direct submission of your site's URL to Google via its add URL or submission page. To counter programmed robots, search engines routinely move submission pages around on their sites. You can find Google's submission page linked from their Help pages or Webmaster Info pages (*http://www.google.com/addurl.html*).

Just visit Google's add URL page and enter the main index page for your site into the submission form, and press submit. Google's spider (called Google-Bot) will visit your page usually within four weeks. The spider will traverse all pages on your site and add them to its index. Within eight weeks, you should be able to find your site listed in Google.

The second way to get your site listed is to let Google find you based on links that may be pointing to your site. Once GoogleBot finds a link to your site from a page it already has in its index, it will visit your site.

Google has been updating its database on a monthly basis for three years. It sends its spider out in crawler mode once a month, too. Crawler mode is a special mode when a spider traverses or *crawls* the entire Web. As it runs into links to pages, it indexes those pages in a never-ending attempt to download all the pages it can. Once your pages are listed in Google, they are revisited and updated on a monthly basis. If you frequently update your content, Google may index your search terms more often.

Once you are indexed and listed in Google, the next natural question for a site owner is, "How can I rank better under my applicable search terms?"

The Search Engine Optimization Template

This is my general recipe for the ubiquitous Google. It is generic enough that it works well everywhere. It's as close as I have come to a "one-size-fits-all" SEO (that's Search Engine Optimization) template.

Use your targeted keyword phrase:

- In META keywords. It's not necessary for Google, but a good habit. Keep your META keywords short (128 characters max, or 10 keywords).
- In META description. Keep keyword close to the left but in a full sentence.
- In the title at the far left but possibly not as the first word.
- In the top portion of the page in the first sentence of the first full paragraph (plain text: no bold, no italic, no style).
- In an H3 or larger heading.
- In bold—second paragraph if possible and anywhere but the first usage on page.
- In italic—anywhere but the first usage.
- In subscript/superscript.
- In URL (directory name, filename, or domain name). Do not duplicate the keyword in the URL.
- In an image filename used on the page.
- In ALT tag of that previous image mentioned.
- In the title attribute of that image.
- In link text to another site.
- In an internal link's text.
- In title attribute of all links targeted in and out of page.
- In the filename of your external CSS (Cascading Style Sheet) or JavaScript file.
- In an inbound link on site (preferably from your home page).
- In an inbound link from off site (if possible).
- In a link to a site that has a PageRank of 8 or better.

Other search engine optimization things to consider include:

- Use "last modified" headers if you can.

- Validate that HTML. Some feel Google's parser has become stricter at parsing instead of milder. It will miss an entire page because of a few simple errors—we have tested this in depth.

- Use an HTML template throughout your site. Google can spot the template and parse it off. (Of course, this also means they are pretty good a spotting duplicate content.)

- Keep the page as *.html* or *.htm* extension. Any dynamic extension is a risk.

- Keep the HTML below 20K; 5 to 15K is the ideal range.

- Keep the ratio of text to HTML very high. Text should outweigh HTML by significant amounts.

- Double-check your page in Netscape, Opera, and Internet Explorer. Use Lynx if you have it.

- Use only raw HREFs for links. Keep JavaScript far, far away from links. The simpler the link code the better.

- The traffic comes when you figure out that 1 referral a day to 10 pages is better than 10 referrals a day to 1 page.

- Don't assume that keywords in your site's navigation template will be worth anything at all. Google looks for full sentences and paragraphs. Keywords just lying around orphaned on the page are not worth as much as when used in a sentence.

—Brett Tabke

Get Inside the PageRank Algorithm

Delve into the inner workings of the Google PageRank algorithm and how it affects results.

PageRank is the algorithm used by the Google search engine, originally formulated by Sergey Brin and Larry Page in their paper "The Anatomy of a Large-Scale Hypertextual Web Search Engine."

It is based on the premise, prevalent in the world of academia, that the importance of a research paper can be judged by the number of citations the paper has from other research papers. Brin and Page have simply transferred this premise to its Web equivalent: the importance of a web page can be judged by the number of hyperlinks pointing to it from other web pages.

So What Is the Algorithm?

It may look daunting to non-mathematicians, but the PageRank algorithm is in fact elegantly simple and is calculated as follows:

$$PR(A) = (1 - d) + d \left(\frac{PR(T1)}{C(T1)} + \dots + \frac{PR(Tn)}{C(Tn)} \right)$$

- PR(A) is the PageRank of a page A.
- PR(T1) is the PageRank of a page T1.
- C(T1) is the number of outgoing links from the page T1.
- d is a damping factor in the range 0 < d < 1, usually set to 0.85.

The PageRank of a web page is therefore calculated as a sum of the PageRanks of all pages linking to it (its incoming links), divided by the number of links on each of those pages (its outgoing links).

And What Does This Mean?

From a search engine marketer's point of view, this means there are two ways in which PageRank can affect the position of your page on Google:

- The number of incoming links. Obviously, the more of these, the better. But there is another thing the algorithm tells us: no incoming link can have a negative effect on the PageRank of the page it points at. At worst, it can simply have no effect at all.
- The number of outgoing links on the page that points to your page. The fewer of these, the better. This is interesting: it means that, given two pages of equal PageRank linking to you, one with 5 outgoing links and the other with 10, you will get twice the increase in PageRank from the page with only 5 outgoing links.

At this point, we take a step back and ask ourselves just how important PageRank is to the position of your page in the Google search results.

The next thing that we can observe about the PageRank algorithm is that it has nothing whatsoever to do with relevance to the search terms queried. It is simply a single (admittedly important) part of the entire Google relevance ranking algorithm.

Perhaps a good way to look at PageRank is as a multiplying factor applied to the Google search results after all other computations have been completed. The Google algorithm first calculates the relevance of pages in its index to the search terms, and then multiplies this relevance by the PageRank to produce a final list. The higher your PageRank, therefore, the higher up the results you will be, but there are still many other factors related to the positioning of words on the page that must be considered first.

So What's the Use of the PageRank Calculator?

If no incoming link has a negative effect, surely I should just get as many as possible, regardless of the number of outgoing links on its page?

Well, not entirely. The PageRank algorithm is cleverly balanced. Just like the conservation of energy in physics with every reaction, PageRank is also conserved with every calculation. For instance, if a page with a starting PageRank of 4 has two outgoing links on it, we know that the amount of PageRank it passes on is divided equally between all of its outgoing links. In this case, $4 / 2 = 2$ units of PageRank is passed on to each of 2 separate pages, and $2 + 2 = 4$—so the total PageRank is preserved!

> There are scenarios in which you may find that total PageRank is not conserved after a calculation. PageRank itself is supposed to represent a probability distribution, with the individual PageRank of a page representing the likelihood of a *random surfer* chancing upon it.

On a much larger scale, supposing Google's index contains a billion pages, each with a PageRank of 1, the total PageRank across all pages is equal to a billion. Moreover, each time we recalculate PageRank, no matter what changes in PageRank may occur between individual pages, the total PageRank across all one billion pages will still add up to a billion.

First, this means that, although we may not be able to change the total PageRank across all pages, by strategic linking of pages within our site, we can affect the distribution of PageRank between pages. For instance, we may want most of our visitors to come into the site through our home page. We would therefore want our home page to have a higher PageRank relative to other pages within the site. We should also recall that all the PageRank of a page is passed on and divided equally between each outgoing link on a page. We would therefore want to keep as much combined PageRank as possible within our own site without passing it onto external sites and losing its benefit. This means we would want any page with lots of external links (i.e., links to other people's web sites) to have a lower PageRank relative to other pages within the site to minimize the amount of PageRank that is *leaked* to external sites. Also, bear in mind our earlier statement, that PageRank is simply a multiplying factor applied once Google's other calculations regarding relevance have already been calculated. We would therefore want our more keyword-rich pages to also have a higher relative PageRank.

Second, if we assume that every new page in Google's index begins its life with a PageRank of 1, there is a way we can increase the combined Page-Rank of pages within our site—by increasing the number of pages! A site with 10 pages will start life with a combined PageRank of 10, which is then redistributed through its hyperlinks. A site with 12 pages will therefore start with a combined PageRank of 12. We can thus improve the Page-Rank of our site as a whole by creating new content (i.e., more pages), and then control the distribution of that combined PageRank through strategic interlinking between the pages.

And this is the purpose of the PageRank Calculator—to create a model of the site on a small scale including the links between pages, and see what effect the model has on the distribution of PageRank.

How Does the PageRank Calculator Work?

To get a better idea of the realities of PageRank, visit the PageRank Calculator (*http://www.markhorrell.com/seo/pagerank.asp*).

It's simple, really. Start by typing in the number of interlinking pages that you wish to analyze and hit Submit. I have confined this number to just 20 pages to ease server resources. Even so, this should give a reasonable indication of how strategic linking can affect the PageRank distribution.

Next, for ease of reference once the calculation has been performed, provide a label for each page (e.g., Home Page, Links Page, Contact Us Page, etc.), and again hit Submit.

Finally, use the list boxes to select which pages each page links to. You can use Ctrl and Shift to highlight multiple selections.

You can also use this screen to change the initial PageRanks of each page. For instance, if one of your pages is supposed to represent Yahoo!, you may wish to raise its initial PageRank to, say, 3. However, in actuality, starting PageRank is irrelevant to its final computed value. In other words, even if one page were to start with a PageRank of 100, after many iterations of the equation, the final computed PageRank will converge to the same value as it would had it started with a PageRank of only 1!

You can play around with the damping factor d, which defaults to 0.85, as this is the value quoted in Brin and Page's research paper.

—*Mark Horrell*

26 Steps to 15K a Day

Hot and cold running content is what draws visitors in to your web site.

Too often, getting visitors from search engines is boiled down to a succession of tweaks that may or may not work. But as I show in this hack, solid content thoughtfully put together can make more of an impact than a decade's worth of fiddling with META tags and building the perfect title page.

Following these 26 steps from A to Z will ensure a successful site, bringing in plenty of visitors from Google.

A. Prep Work

Prepare work and begin building content. Long before the domain name is settled on, start putting together notes to build at least a 100-page site. That's 100 pages of "real content," not including link, resource, about, and copyright pages—necessary but not content-rich pages.

Can't think of 100 pages' worth of content? Consider articles about your business or industry, Q&A pages, or back issues of an online newsletter.

B. Choose a Brandable Domain Name

Choose a domain name that's easily brandable. You want *Google.com* and not *Mykeyword.com*.

Keyword domains are out; branding and name recognition are in. Big time in. Keywords in a domain name have never meant less to search engines. Learn the lesson of Goto.com becoming Overture.com and understand why they changed it. It's one of the most powerful gut check calls I've ever seen on the Internet. It took resolve and nerve to blow away several years of branding. (That's a whole 'nother article, but learn the lesson as it applies to all of us.)

C. Site Design

The simpler your site design, the better. As a rule of thumb: text content should outweigh HTML content. The pages should be validated and usable in everything from Lynx to leading browsers. In other words, keep it close to HTML 3.2 if you can. Spiders are not to the point they really like eating HTML 4.0 and the mess that it can bring. Stay away from heavy Flash, Java, or JavaScript.

Go external with scripting languages if you must have them, though there's little reason to have them that I can see. They will rarely help a site and stand to hurt it greatly due to many factors that most people don't appreciate (the search engines' distaste for JavaScript is just one of them). Arrange the site in a logical manner with directory names hitting the top keywords that you wish to emphasize. You can also go the other route and just throw everything in the top level of the directory (this is rather controversial, but it's been producing good long-term results across many engines). Don't clutter and don't spam your site with frivolous links such as "best viewed in ..." or other things such as counters. Keep it clean and professional to the best of your ability.

Learn the lesson of Google itself: simple is retro cool. Simple is what surfers want.

Speed isn't everything; it's almost the only thing. Your site should respond almost instantly to a request. If your site has three to four seconds' delay until "something happens" in the browser, you are in trouble. That three to four seconds of response time may vary in sites destined to be viewed in other countries than your native one. The site should respond locally within three to four seconds (maximum) to any request. Longer than that, and you'll lose 10% of your audience for each additional second. That 10% could be the difference between success and not.

D. Page Size

The smaller the page size, the better. Keep it under 15K, including images, if you can. The smaller the better. Keep it under 12K if you can. The smaller the better. Keep it under 10K if you can; I trust you are getting the idea here. Over 5K and under 10K. It's tough to do, but it's worth the effort. Remember, 80% of your surfers will be at 56K or even less.

E. Content

Build one page of content (between 200 and 500 words) per day and put it online.

If you aren't sure what you need for content, start with the Overture keyword suggestor (*http://inventory.overture.com/d/searchinventory/suggestion/*) and find the core set of keywords for your topic area. Those are your subject starters.

F. Keyword Density and Keyword Positioning

This is simple, old-fashioned Search Engine Optimization (SEO) from the ground up.

Use the keyword once in title, once in description tag, once in a heading, once in the URL, once in bold, once in italic, once high on the page, and make sure the density is between 5% and 20% (don't fret about it). Use good sentences and spellcheck them! Spellchecking is becoming more important as search engines are moving to autocorrection during searches. There is no longer a reason to look like you can't spell.

G. Outbound Links

From every page, link to one or two high-ranking sites under the keyword that you're trying to emphasize. Use your keyword in the link text (this is ultra important for the future).

H. Cross-Links

Cross-links are links *within* the same site.

Link to on-topic quality content across your site. If a page is about food, make sure it links to the apples and veggies page. With Google, on-topic cross-linking is very important for sharing your PageRank value across your site. You do not want an *all-star* page that outperforms the rest of your site. You want 50 pages that produce 1 referral each a day, not 1 page that produces 50 referrals a day. If you do find a page that drastically outproduces the rest of the site with Google, you need to offload some of that PageRank value to other pages by cross-linking heavily. It's the old share-the-wealth thing.

I. Put It Online

Don't go with virtual hosting; go with a standalone IP address.

Make sure the site is *crawlable* by a spider. All pages should be linked to more than one other page on your site, and not more than two levels deep from the top directory. Link the topic vertically as much as possible back to the top directory. A menu that is present on every page should link to your site's main *topic index* pages (the doorways and logical navigation system down into real content). Don't put your site online before it is ready. It's worse to put a *nothing* site online than no site at all. You want it to be fleshed out from the start.

Go for a listing in the Open Directory Project (ODP), *http://dmoz.org/add. html*). Getting accepted to the ODP will probably get your pages listed in the Google Directory.

J. Submit

Submit your main URL to Google, F*, AltaVista, WiseNut, Teoma, DirectHit, and Hotbot. Now comes the hard part: forget about submissions for the next six months. That's right, submit and forget.

K. Logging and Tracking

Get a quality logger/tracker that can do justice to inbound referrals based on log files. Don't use a graphic counter; you need a program that's going to provide much more information than that. If your host doesn't support referrers, back up and get a new host. You can't run a modern site without full referrals available 24/7/365 in real time.

L. Spiderings

Watch for spiders from search engines—one reason you need a good logger and tracker! Make sure that spiders crawling the full site can do so easily. If not, double-check your linking system to make sure that the spider can find its way throughout the site. Don't fret if it takes two spiderings to get your whole site done by Google or F*. Other search engines are potluck; if you haven't been added within six months, it's doubtful that you will be added at all.

M. Topic Directories

Almost every keyword sector has an authority hub on its topic. Find it (Google Directory can be very helpful here because you can view sites based on how popular they are) and submit within the guidelines.

N. Links

Look around your keyword section in the Google Directory; this is best done *after* getting an Open Directory Project listing—or two. Find sites that have link pages or freely exchange links. Simply request a swap. Put a page of on-topic, in-context links on your site as a collection spot. Don't worry if you can't get people to swap links; move on. Try to swap links with one fresh site a day. A simple personal email is enough. Stay low-key about it and don't worry if site Z won't link to you. Eventually it will.

O. Content

Add one page of quality content per day. Timely, topical articles are always the best. Try to stay away from too much weblogging personal materials and look more for *article* topics that a general audience will like. Hone your writing skills and read up on the right style of *web speak* that tends to work with the fast and furious web crowd: lots of text breaks—short sentences—lots of dashes—something that reads quickly.

Most web users don't actually read; they scan. This is why it is so important to keep key pages to a minimum. If people see a huge overblown page, a portion of them will hit the Back button before trying to decipher it. They've got better things to do than waste 15 seconds (a stretch) at understanding your whizbang menu system. Because some big support site can run Flash-heavy pages is no indication that you can. You don't have the pull factor that they do.

Use headers and bold standout text liberally on your pages as logical separators. I call them *scanner stoppers* where the eye will logically come to rest on the page.

P. Gimmicks

Stay far away from any *fads of the day* or anything that appears spammy, unethical, or tricky. Plant yourself firmly on the high ground in the middle of the road.

Q. Linkbacks

When *you* receive requests for links, check sites out before linking back to them. Check them through Google for their PageRank value. Look for directory listings. Don't link back to junk just because they asked. Make sure it is a site similar to yours and on-topic. Linking to *bad neighborhoods*, as Google calls them, can actually cost you PageRank points.

R. Rounding Out Your Offerings

Use options such as "email a friend," forums, and mailing lists to round out your site's offerings. Hit the top forums in your market and read, read, read until your eyes hurt. Stay away from *affiliate fades* that insert content onto your site such as banners and pop-up windows.

S. Beware of Flyer and Brochure Syndrome

If you have an economical site or online version of bricks and mortar, be careful not to turn your site into a brochure. These don't work at all. Think about what people want. They aren't coming to your site to view *your content*, they are coming to your site looking for *their content*. Talk as little about your products and yourself as possible in articles (sounds counterintuitive, doesn't it?).

T. Keep Building One Page of Content Per Day

Head back to the Overture suggestion tool (*http://inventory.overture.com/d/searchinventory/suggestion/*) to get ideas for fresh pages.

U. Study Those Logs

After a month or two, you will start to see a few referrals from places you've gotten listed. Look for the keywords people are using. See any bizarre combinations? Why are people using those to find your site? If there is something you have overlooked, then build a page around that topic. Engineer your site to feed the search engine what it wants. If your site is about oranges, but your referrals are all about orange citrus fruit, then get busy building articles around citrus and fruit instead of the generic oranges. The search engines will tell you exactly what they want to be fed. Listen closely! There is gold in referral logs; it's just a matter of panning for it.

V. Timely Topics

Nothing breeds success like success. Stay abreast of developments in your topic of interest. If big site Z is coming out with product A at the end of the year, build a page and have it ready in October so that search engines get it by December.

W. Friends and Family

Networking is critical to the success of a site. This is where all that time you spend in forums will pay off. Here's the catch-22 about forums: lurking is almost useless. The value of a forum is in the interaction with your fellow colleagues and cohorts. You learn from the interaction, not by just reading. Networking will pay off in linkbacks, tips, and email exchanges, and will generally put you *in the loop* of your keyword sector.

X. Notes, Notes, Notes

If you build one page per day, you will find that brainstorm-like inspiration will hit you in the head at some magic point. Whether it is in the shower (dry off first), driving down the road (please pull over), or just parked at your desk, write it down! Ten minutes of work later, you will have forgotten all about that great idea you just had. Write it down and get detailed about what you are thinking. When the inspirational juices are no longer flowing, come back to those content ideas. It sounds simple, but it's a lifesaver when the ideas stop coming.

Y. Submission Check at Six Months

After six months, walk back through your submissions and see if you have been listed in all the search engines that you submitted to. If not, resubmit and forget again. Try those freebie directories again, too.

Z. Keep Building Those Pages of Quality Content!

Starting to see a theme here? Google loves content, lots of quality content. The content that you generate should be based around a variety of keywords. At the end of a year's time, you should have around 400 pages of content. That will get you good placement under a wide range of keywords, generate reciprocal links, and overall position your site to stand on its own two feet.

Do these 26 things, and I guarantee you that in one year's time you will call your site a success. It will be drawing between 500 and 2,000 referrals a day from search engines. If you build a good site and achieve an average of four to five pageviews per visitors, you should be in the 10K–15K page views per day range in one year's time. What you do with that traffic is up to you!

—Brett Tabke

H A C K

#89

Be a Good Search Engine Citizen
Five don'ts and one do for getting your site indexed by Google.

A high ranking in Google can mean a great deal of traffic. Because of that, there are lots of people spending lots of time trying to figure out the infallible way to get a high ranking from Google. Add this. Remove that. Get a link from this. Don't post a link to that.

Submitting your site to Google to be indexed is simple enough. Google's got a site submission form (*http://www.google.com/addurl.html*), though they say that, if your site has at least a few inbound links (other sites that link to you), they should find you that way. In fact, Google encourages URL submitters to get listed on The Open Directory Project (ODP, *http://www.dmoz.org*) or Yahoo! (*http://www.yahoo.com*).

Nobody knows the secret of achieving high PageRank without effort. Google uses a variety of elements, including page popularity, to determine PageRank. PageRank is one of the factors determining how high up a page appears in search results. But there are several things that you should not be doing and one big thing that you absolutely should.

Does breaking one of these rules mean that you're automatically going to be thrown out of Google's index? No, there are over four billion pages in

Google's index at this writing, and it's unlikely that they'll find out about your violation immediately. But there's a good chance that they'll find out eventually. Is it worth it having your site removed from the most popular search engine on the Internet?

Thou Shalt Not:

Cloak. Cloaking is when your web site is set up such that search engine spiders get different pages from those that human surfers get. How does the web site know which are the spiders and which are the humans? By identifying the spider's User Agent or IP—the latter being the more reliable method.

An Internet Protocol (IP) address is the computer address from which a spider comes. Everything that connects to the Internet has an IP address. Sometimes the IP address is always the same, as with web sites. Sometimes the IP address changes; that's called a *dynamic address*. (If you use a dial-up modem, chances are good that every time you log onto the Internet your IP address is different. That's a dynamic IP address.)

A *User Agent* is a way a program that surfs the Web identifies itself. Internet browsers like Mozilla use User Agents, as do search engine spiders. There are literally dozens of different kinds of User Agents; see the Web Robots Database (*http://www.robotstxt.org/wc/active.html*) for an extensive list.

Advocates of cloaking claim that cloaking is useful to absolutely optimize content for spiders. Anti-cloaking critics claim that cloaking is an easy way to misrepresent site content—feeding a spider a page that's designed to get the site hits for pudding cups when actually it's all about baseball bats. You can get more details about cloaking and different perspectives on it at *http://pandecta.com/*, *http://www.apromotionguide.com/cloaking.html*, and *http://www.webopedia.com/TERM/C/cloaking.html*.

Hide text. Text is hidden by putting words or links in a web page that are the same color as the page's background—putting white words on a white background, for example. This is also called *fontmatching*. Why would you do this? Because a search engine spider could read the words you've hidden on the page while a human visitor couldn't. Again, doing this and getting caught could get you banned from Google's index, so don't.

That goes for other page content tricks too, such as *title stacking* (putting multiple copies of a title tag on one page), putting keywords in comment tags, *keyword stuffing* (putting multiple copies of keywords in very small font on page), putting keywords not relevant to your site in your META tags, and so on. Google doesn't provide an exhaustive list of these types of tricks on their site, but any attempt to circumvent or fool their ranking system is likely to be frowned upon. Their attitude is more like: "You can do anything you want to with your pages, and we can do anything we want to with our index—such as excluding your pages."

Use doorway pages. Sometimes, *doorway pages* are called *gateway pages*. These are pages that are aimed specifically at one topic, which don't have a lot of their own original content and which lead to the main page of a site (thus the name *doorway pages*).

For example, say you have a page devoted to cooking. You create doorway pages for several genres of cooking—French cooking, Chinese cooking, vegetarian cooking, etc. The pages contain terms and META tags relevant to each genre, but most of the text is a copy of all the other doorway pages, and all it does is point to your main site.

Doorway pages are illegal in Google and annoying to the Google user, so don't do it. You can learn more about doorway pages at *http://search enginewatch.com/webmasters/bridge.html* or *http://www.searchengine guide.com/whalen/2002/0530_jw1.html*.

Check your link rank with automated queries. Using automated queries (except for the sanctioned Google API) is against Google's Terms of Service anyway. Using an automated query to check your PageRank every 12 seconds is triple-bad; it's not what the search engine was built for and Google probably considers it a waste of their time and resources.

Link to "bad neighborhoods". *Bad neighborhoods* are those sites that exist only to propagate links. Because link popularity is one aspect of how Google determines PageRank, some sites have set up *link farms*—sites that exist only for the purpose of building site popularity with bunches of links. The links are not topical, like a specialty subject index, and they're not well-reviewed, like Yahoo!; they're just a pile of links. Another example of a *bad neighborhood* is a general FFA page. FFA stands for *free for all*; it's a page where anyone can add their link. Linking to pages like that is grounds for a penalty from Google.

Now, what happens if a page like that links to *you*? Will Google penalize your page? No. Google accepts that you have no control over who links to your site.

Thou Shalt:

Create great content. All the HTML contortions in the world will do you little good if you have lousy, old, or limited content. If you create great content and promote it without playing search engine games, you will get noticed and you will get links. Remember Sturgeon's Law: "Ninety percent of everything is crud." Why not make your web site an exception?

What Happens If You Reform?

Maybe you have a site that is not exactly the work of a good search engine citizen. Maybe you have 500 doorway pages, 10 title tags per page, and enough hidden text to make an O'Reilly Pocket Guide. But maybe now you want to reform. You want to have a clean lovely site and leave the doorway pages to *Better Homes and Gardens*. Are you doomed? Will Google ban your site for the rest of its life?

No. The first thing you need to do is clean up your site—remove all traces of rule breaking. Next, send a note about your site changes and the URL to *help@google.com*. Note that Google really doesn't have the resources to answer every email about why they did or didn't index a site—otherwise, they'd be answering emails all day—and there's no guarantee that they will reindex your kinder, gentler site. But they will look at your message.

What Happens If You Spot Google Abusers in the Index?

What if some other site that you come across in your Google searching is abusing Google's spider and PageRank mechanism? You have two options. You can send an email to *spamreport@google.com* or fill out the form at *http://www.google.com/contact/spamreport.html*. (I'd fill out the form; it reports the abuse in a standard format that Google is used to seeing.)

HACK #90   Clean Up for a Google Visit

Before you submit your site to Google, make sure that you've cleaned it up to make the most of your indexing.

You clean up your house when you have important guests over, right? If you want visitors, Google's crawler is one of the most important guests that your site will ever have. A high Google ranking can lead to incredible numbers of referrals, both from Google's main site and from sites that have search powered by Google.

To make the most of your listing, step back and look at your site. By making some adjustments, you can make your site both more Google-friendly and more visitor-friendly.

If you must use a splash page, have a text link from it.   If I had a dollar for every time I went to the front page of a site and saw no way to navigate besides a Flash movie, I'd be able to nap for a living. Google doesn't index Flash files, so unless you have some kind of text link on your splash page (a "Skip This Movie" link, for example, that leads into the heart of your site), you're not giving Google's crawler anything to work with. You're also making it difficult for surfers who don't have Flash or are visually impaired.

Make sure your internal links work. Sounds like a no-brainer, doesn't it? Make sure your internal page links work so the Google crawler can get to all your site's pages. You'll also want to make sure that your visitors can navigate.

Check your title tags. There are few things sadder than getting a page of search results and finding "Insert Your Title Here" as the title for some of them, although not quite as bad is getting results for the same domain and seeing the *exact same* title tag over and over and over and over.

Look. Google makes it possible to search just the title tags in its index. Further, the title tags are easy to read on Google's search results and are an easy way for a surfer to quickly get an idea of what a page is all about. If you're not making the most of your title tag, you're missing out on a lot of attention to your site.

The perfect title tag, to me, says something specific about the page it heads, and is readable to both spiders and surfers. That means you don't stuff it with as many keywords as you can. Make it a readable sentence, or—and I've found this useful for some pages—make it a question.

Check your META tags. Google sometimes relies on META tags for a site description when there's a lot of navigation code that wouldn't make sense to a human searcher. I'm not crazy about META tags, but I'd make sure that at least the front page of my web site had a description and keyword META tag set, especially if my site relied heavily on code-based navigation (like from JavaScript).

Check your ALT tags. Do you use a lot of graphics on your pages? Do you have ALT tags for them so that visually impaired surfers and the Google spider can figure out what those graphics are? If you have a splash page with nothing but graphics on it, do you have ALT tags on all those graphics so that a Google spider can get some idea of the content? ALT tags are perhaps the most neglected aspect of a web site. Make sure yours are set up.

By the way, just because ALT tags are a good idea, don't go crazy. You don't have to explain in your ALT tags that a list bullet is a list bullet. You can just mark it with an asterisk.

Check your frames. If you use frames, you might be missing out on some indexing. Google recommends you that read Danny Sullivan's article, "Search Engines and Frames," at *http://www.searchenginewatch.com/ webmasters/frames.html.* Be sure that Google can either handle your frame setup or that you've created an alternative way for Google to visit, such as using the NOFRAMES tag.

Consider your dynamic pages. Google says they "limit the number and amount of dynamic pages" they index. Are you using dynamic pages? Do you have to?

Consider how often you update your content. There is some evidence that Google indexes popular pages with frequently updated content more often. How often do you update the content on your front page?

Make sure you have a robots.txt file if you need one. If you want Google to index your site in a particular way, make sure you've got a *robots.txt* file for the Google spider to refer to. You can learn more about *robots.txt* in general at *http://www.robotstxt.org/wc/norobots.html.*

If you don't want Google to cache your pages, you can add a line to every page that you don't want cached. Add this line to the <HEAD> section of your page:

```
<META NAME="ROBOTS" CONTENT="NOARCHIVE">
```

This will tell all robots that archive content, including engines like Daypop and Gigablast, not to cache your page. If you want to exclude just the Google spider from caching your page, use this line:

```
<META NAME="GOOGLEBOT" CONTENT="NOARCHIVE">
```

HACK #91 Remove Your Materials from Google
Remove your content from Google's various web properties.

Some people are more than thrilled to have Google index their sites. Other folks don't want the GoogleBot anywhere near them. If you fall into the latter category and the bot's already done its worst, there are several things you can do to remove your materials from Google's index. Each part of Google—Web Search, Google Images, and Google Groups—has its own set of methodologies.

Google Web Search

Here are several tips to avoid being listed.

Making sure your pages never get there to begin with. While you can take steps to remove your content from the Google index after the fact, it's always much easier to make sure the content is never found and indexed in the first place.

Google's crawler obeys the *robot exclusion protocol*, a set of instructions you put on your web site that tells the crawler how to behave when it comes to your content. You can implement these instructions in two ways: via a META tag that you put on each page (handy when you want to restrict access to only certain pages or certain types of content) or via a *robots.txt* file that you insert in your root directory (handy when you want to block some spiders completely or want to restrict access to kinds or directories of content). You can get more information about the robots exclusion protocol and how to implement it at *http://www.robotstxt.org/*.

Removing your pages after they're indexed. There are several things you can have removed from Google's results.

 These instructions are for keeping your site out of Google's index only. For information on keeping your site out of all major search engines, you'll have to work with the robots exclusion protocol.

Removing the whole site
Use the robots exclusion protocol, probably with *robots.txt*.

Removing individual pages
Use the following META tag in the HEAD section of each page you want to remove:

```
<META NAME="GOOGLEBOT" CONTENT="NOINDEX, NOFOLLOW">
```

Removing snippets
A *snippet* is the little excerpt of a page that Google displays on its search result. To remove snippets, use the following META tag in the HEAD section of each page for which you want to prevent snippets:

```
<META NAME="GOOGLEBOT" CONTENT="NOSNIPPET">
```

Removing cached pages
To prevent Google from keeping cached versions of your pages in its index, use the following META tag in the HEAD section of each page for which you want to prevent caching:

```
<META NAME="GOOGLEBOT" CONTENT="NOARCHIVE">
```

Removing that content now. Once you implement these changes, the next time GoogleBot crawls your web site (usually within a few weeks), it will remove or limit your content according to your META tags and *robots.txt* file. If you want your materials removed right away, you can use the automatic remover at *http://services.google.com:8882/urlconsole/controller.* You'll have to sign in with an account (requires an email address and a password). Using the remover, you can request that Google crawl your newly created *robots. txt* file, or you can enter the URL of a page that contains exclusionary META tags.

> Make sure that you have your exclusion tags all set up before you use this service. Going to all the trouble of getting Google to pay attention to a *robots.txt* file or exclusion rules that you've not yet set up will simply be a waste of your time.

Reporting pages with inappropriate content. While you may like your own content fine, you might find that, even if you have filtering activated, you're getting search results with explicit content. Or you might find a site with a misleading title tag and content completely unrelated to your search.

You have two options for reporting these sites to Google. Bear in mind that there's no guarantee that Google will remove the sites from the index, but they will investigate them. At the bottom of each page of search results, you'll see a "Dissatisfied? Help Us Improve" link; follow it to a form for reporting inappropriate sites. You can also send the URL of explicit sites that show up on a SafeSearch but probably shouldn't to *safesearch@google. com.* If you have more general complaints about a search result, you can send an email to *search-quality@google.com.*

Google Images

Google's Image database of materials is separate from that of the main search index. To remove items from Google Images, use *robots.txt* to specify that the GoogleBot Image crawler should stay away from your site. Add these lines to your *robots.txt* file:

```
User-agent: Googlebot-Image
Disallow: /
```

You can use the automatic remover mentioned in the web search section to have Google remove the images from its index database quickly.

There may be cases where someone has put images on their server for which you own the copyright. In other words, you don't have access to their server to add a *robots.txt* file, but you need to stop Google from indexing your content there. In this case, you need to contact Google directly. Google has instructions for situations just like this at *http://www.google.com/remove.html;*

look at Option 2, "If you do not have any access to the server that hosts your image."

Google Groups

Like the Google Web Index, you have the option to both prevent material from being archived on Google and to remove it after the fact.

Preventing your material from being archived. To prevent your material from being archived on Google, add the following line to the headers of your Usenet posts:

```
X-No-Archive: yes
```

If you do not have the options to edit the headers of your post, make that line the first line in your post itself.

Removing materials after the fact. If you want materials removed after the fact, you have a couple of options:

- If the materials that you want removed were posted under an address to which you still have access, you can use the automatic removal tool mentioned earlier in this hack.
- If the materials that you want removed were posted under an address to which you no longer have access, you'll need to send an email to *groups-support@google.com* with the following information:
  — Your full name and contact information, including a verifiable email address.
  — The complete Google Groups URL or message ID for each message you want removed.
  — A statement that says, "I swear under penalty of civil or criminal laws that I am the person who posted each of the foregoing messages or am authorized to request removal by the person who posted those messages."
  — Your electronic signature.

Google Phonebook

You migt not want to have your contact information made available via the phonebook searches on Google. You'll have to follow one of two procedures, depending on whether the listing you want removed is for a business or for a residential number.

If you want to remove a business phone number, you'll need to send a request on your business letterhead to:

Google PhoneBook Removal
1600 Amphitheatre Parkway
Mountain View, CA 94043

Be sure to include a phone number so that Google can reach you to verify your request.

Removing a residential phone number is much simpler. Fill out the form at *http://www.google.com/help/pbremoval.html*. The form asks for your name, city and state, phone number, email address, and reason for removal, a multiple choice: incorrect number, privacy issue, or "other."

Programming Google
Hacks 92–100

When search engines first appeared on the scene, they were more open to being spidered, scraped, and aggregated. Sites like Excite and AltaVista didn't worry too much about the odd surfer using Perl to grab a slice of a page or meta-search engines including their results in aggregated search results. Sure, egregious data suckers might get shut out, but the search engines weren't worried about sharing their information on a smaller scale.

Google never took that stance. Instead, they have regularly prohibited meta-search engines from using their content without a license, and they try their best to block unidentified web agents like Perl's *LWP::Simple* module or even wget on the command line. Google has even been known to block IP address ranges for running automated queries.

Google had every right to do this; after all, it was their search technology, database, and computer power. Unfortunately, however, these policies meant that casual researchers and Google nuts, like you and I, didn't have the ability to play with their rich dataset in any automated way.

Google changed all that with the release of the Google Web API (*http://api. google.com/*) in the spring of 2002. The Google Web API doesn't allow you to do every kind of search possible—for example, it doesn't support the phonebook: **[Hack #6]** syntax—but it does make available Google's eight-billion-page web database so that developers can create their own interfaces and use Google search results to their liking.

 API stands for "Application Programming Interface," a doorway for programmatic access to a particular resource or application, in this case, the Google index.

So how can you participate in all this Google API goodness?

You have to register for a *developer's key*, a login of sorts to the Google API. Each key affords its owner 1,000 Google Web API queries per day, after which you're out of luck until the next day. Even if you don't plan on writing any applications, having a key at your disposal is still useful. There are various third-party applications built on the Google API that you might want to visit and try out; some of these ask that you use your own key and allotted 1,000 queries.

Signing Up and Google's Terms

Signing up for a Google Web API developer's key is simple. First, create a Google account. The only requirements are a valid email address and a made-up password.

 Not only will you be able to use the Google Web API, but also participate in Google Answers (*http://answers.google.com/answers/main*), volunteer to translate Google into other languages for the Google in Your Language program (*https://services.google.com/tc/Welcome.html*), and post to Usenet through Google Groups **[Chapter 4]**.

You will, of course, have to agree to Google's Terms and Conditions (*http://www.google.com/apis/download.html*) before you can proceed. In broad strokes, this says:

- Google exercises no editorial control over the sites that appear in its index. The Google API might return some results that you might find offensive.

- The Google API may be used for personal, non-commercial use only. It may not be used to sell a product or service or to drive traffic to a site for the sake of advertising sales.

- You can't noodle with Google's intellectual property marks that appear within the API.

- Google does not accept any liability for the use of their API. This is a beta program.

- You may indicate that the program you create uses the Google API, but not if the application(s) "(1) tarnish, infringe, or dilute Google's trademarks, (2) violate any applicable law, and (3) infringe any third-party rights." Any other use of Google's trademark or logo requires written consent.

Once you've entered your email address, created a password, and agreed to the Terms of Service, Google sends you an email message to confirm the legitimacy of your email address. The message includes a link for final activation of the account. Click the link to activate your account, and Google will email you your very own license key.

You have signed in and generated a key; you're all set! What now? If you don't intend to do any programming, just stop here. Put your key in a safe place and keep it on hand to use with any cool third-party Google API–based services that you come across.

The Google Web APIs Developer's Kit

If you are interested in doing some programming, download the Google Web APIs Developer's Kit (*http://www.google.com/apis/download.html*). While not strictly necessary to any Google API programming that you might do, the kit contains much that is useful:

- A cross-platform WSDL file (see below)
- A Java wrapper library abstracting away some of the SOAP plumbing
- A sample .NET application
- Documentation, including JavaDoc and SOAP XML samples

Simply click the download link, unzip the file, and take a look at the *README.txt* file to get underway.

Using Your Google API Key

Every time you send a request to the Google server in a program, you have to send your key along with it. Google checks the key and determines whether it's valid and you're still within your daily 1,000 query limit; if so, Google processes the request.

All the programs in this book, regardless of language and platform, provide a place to plug in your key. The key itself is just a string of random-looking characters (e.g., 12BuCK13mY5hOE/34KNOcK@ttH3DoOR).

If you're going to be making your hack available online for others to use, you might well consider asking visitors to sign up for and use their own Google API key—at least optionally. A thousand queries per day really isn't that much, and should your hack become popular, you'll more than likely have a few unhappy visitors for whom it just doesn't work when you've used up your quota. You can see an example of this in action on Tara's GoogleJack! Page (*http://www.researchbuzz.org/archives/001418.shtml*): notice the spot in the GoogleJack! form for Google API Key.

A Perl hack usually includes a line like the following:

```
...
# Your Google API developer's key.
my $google_key='insert key here';
...
```

The Java *GoogleAPIDemo* included in the Google Web APIs Developer's Kit is invoked on the command line, like so:

```
% java -cp googleapi.jar com.google.soap.search.GoogleAPIDemo
insert_key_here search ostrich
```

In both cases, *insert key here* or *insert_key_here* should be substituted with your own Google Web API key. For example, I would plug my made-up key into the Perl script as follows:

```
...
# Your Google API developer's key.
my $google_key='12BuCK13mY5hOE/34KNOcK@ttH3DoOR';
...
```

What's WSDL?

Pronounced "whiz-dill," WSDL stands for Web Services Description Language, an XML format for describing web services. The most useful bit of the Google Web API Developer's Kit is *GoogleSearch.wsdl*, a WSDL file describing the Google API's available services, method names, and expected arguments to your programming language of choice.

Most of the hacks in this book assume that the *GoogleSearch.wsdl* file is in the same directory as the scripts that you're writing since this is probably the simplest setup. If you prefer to keep it elsewhere, be sure to alter the path in the script at hand. A Perl hack usually specifies the location of the WSDL file, like so:

```
...
# Location of the GoogleSearch WSDL file.
my $google_wdsl = "./GoogleSearch.wsdl";
...
```

I like to keep such files together in a *library* directory and so would make the following adjustment to the previous code snippet:

```
...
# Location of the GoogleSearch WSDL file.
my $google_wdsl = "/home/me/lib/GoogleSearch.wsdl";
...
```

Understanding the Google API Query

The core of a Google application is the query. Without the query, there's no Google data, and without that, you don't have much of an application. Because of its importance, it's worth taking a little time to look into the anatomy of a typical query.

Query Essentials

The command in a typical Perl-based Google API application that sends a query to Google looks like this:

```
my $results = $google_search ->
  doGoogleSearch(
    key, query, start, maxResults,
    filter, restrict, safeSearch, lr,
    ie, oe
  );
```

Usually, the items within the parentheses are variables, numbers, or Boolean values (true or false). In the previous example, I've included the names of the arguments themselves rather than sample values so that you can see their definitions here:

key

This is where you put your Google API developer's key. Without a key, the query won't go very far.

query

This is your query, composed of keywords, phrases, and special syntaxes.

start

Also known as the *offset*, this integer value specifies at what result to start counting when determining which 10 results to return. If this number were 16, the Google API would return results 16–25; if 300, results 300–309 (assuming, of course, that your query found that many results). This is known as a *zero-based index*, since counting starts at 0, not 1. The first result is result 0, and the 999th, 998. It's a little odd, admittedly, but you get used to it quickly—especially if you go on to do a lot of programming. Acceptable values are 0 to 999 because Google only returns up to a thousand results for a query.

maxResults

This integer specifies the number of results that you would like the API to return. The API returns results in batches of up to ten, so acceptable values are 1 through 10.

filter

You might think that the *filter* option concerns the SafeSearch filter for adult content. It doesn't. This Boolean value (true or false) specifies whether your results go through automatic query filtering, removing near-duplicate content (titles and snippets that are very similar) and multiple (more than two) results from the same host or site. With filtering enabled, only the first two results from each host are included in the result set.

restrict

No, *restrict* doesn't have anything to do with SafeSearch either. It allows for restricting your search to one of Google's topical searches or to a specific country. Google has four topic restricts: U.S. Government (unclesam), Linux (linux), Macintosh (mac), and FreeBSD (bsd). You'll find the complete country list in the Google Web API documentation. To leave your search unrestricted, leave this option blank (usually signified by empty quotation marks, "").

safeSearch

Now here's the SafeSearch filtering option. This Boolean (true or false) specifies whether results returned will be filtered for questionable (read: adult) content.

lr

This stands for *language restrict* and it's a bit tricky. Google has a list of languages in its API documentation to which you can restrict search results, or you can simply leave this option blank and have no language restrictions.

There are several ways that you can restrict to language. First, you can simply include a language code. If you want to restrict results to English, for example, use lang_en. But you can also restrict results to more than one language, separating each language code with a | (pipe), signifying OR. lang_en|lang_de, then, constrains results to only those "in English or German."

You can omit languages from results by prepending them with a - (minus sign). -lang_en returns all results but those in English.

ie

This stands for *input encoding*, allowing you to specify the character encoding used in the query that you're feeding the API. Google's documentation says, "Clients should encode all request data in UTF-8 and should expect results to be in UTF-8." In the first iteration of Google's API program, the Google API documentation offered a table of encoding options (latin1, cyrillic, etc.) but now everything is UTF-8. In fact, specifying anything other than UTF-8 is summarily ignored.

oe

This stands for *output encoding*. As with input encoding, everything's UTF-8.

A Sample

Enough with the placeholders; what does an actual query look like?

Take, for example, a query that uses variables for the key and the query, requests 10 results starting at result number 100 (actually the 101st result), and specifies filtering and SafeSearch be turned on. That query in Perl would look like this:

```
my $results = $google_search ->
  doGoogleSearch(
    $google_key, $query, 100, 10,
    "true", "", "true", "",
    "utf8", "utf8"
  );
```

Note that the key and query could just as easily have been passed along as quote-delimited strings:

```
my $results = $google_search ->
  doGoogleSearch(
    "12BuCK13mY5hOE/34KNOcK@ttH3DoOR", "+paleontology +dentistry" , 100, 10,
    "true", "", "true", "",
    "utf8", "utf8"
  );
```

While things appear a little more complex when you start fiddling with the language and topic restrictions, the core query remains mostly unchanged; only the values of the options change.

Intersecting Country, Language, and Topic Restrictions

Sometimes you might want to restrict your results to a particular language in a particular country, or a particular language, particular country, and particular topic. Now here's where things start looking a little on the odd side.

The rules are as follows:

- Omit something by prepending it with a - (minus sign).
- Separate restrictions with a . (period, or full stop); spaces are not allowed.
- Specify an OR relationship between two restrictions with a | (pipe).
- Group restrictions with parentheses. You can have parentheses within parentheses—*nested parentheses*—for fine-grained control over grouping in your queries.

Let's say you want a query to return results in French, draw only from Canadian sites, and focus only within the Linux topic. Your query would look something like this:

```
my $results = $google_search ->
  doGoogleSearch(
    $google_key, $query, 100, 10,
    "true", "linux.countryCA", "true", "lang_fr",
    "utf8", "utf8"
  );
```

For results from Canada or from France, you would use:

```
"linux.(countryCA|countryFR)"
```

Or maybe you want results in French, but from anywhere but France:

```
"linux.(-countryFR)"
```

For a comprehensive list of restricts, see Section 2.4, "Restricts," of *APIs_Reference.html*, part of the Google API documentation

Putting Query Elements to Use

You might use the different elements of the query as follows:

Using SafeSearch
> If you're building a program that's for family-friendly use, you'll probably want to have SafeSearch turned on as a matter of course. But you can also use it to compare safe and unsafe results. "SafeSearch Certify URLs" [Hack #35] does just that. You could create a program that takes a word from a web form and checks its counts in filtered and unfiltered searches, providing a *naughty rating* for the word based on the counts.

Setting search result numbers
> Whether you request 1 or 10 results, you're still using one of your developer key's daily dose of a thousand Google Web API queries. Wouldn't it then make sense to always request 10? Not necessarily; if you're using only the top result—to bounce the browser to another page, generate a random query string for a password, or whatever—you might as well add even the minutest amount of speed to your application by not requesting results that you're just going to throw out or ignore.

Searching different topics
> With four different specialty topics available for searching through the Google API, dozens of different languages, and dozens of different countries, there are thousands of combinations of topic/language/country restriction that you would work through.

Consider an *open source country* application. You could create a list of keywords very specific to open source (such as linux, perl, etc.) and create a program that cycles through a series of queries that restricts your search to an open source topic (such as linux) and a particular country. So you might discover that perl was mentioned in France in the linux topic 15 times, in Germany 20 times, and so on.

You could also concentrate less on the program itself and more on an interface to access these variables. How about a form with pull-down menus that allows you to restrict your searches by continent (instead of country)? You could specify which continent in a variable that's passed to the query. Or how about an interface that lets the user specify a topic and cycles through a list of countries and languages, pulling result counts for each one?

Understanding the Google API Response

While the Google API grants you programmatic access to Google's Web index, it doesn't provide all the functionality available through the Google.com web site's search interface.

Can Do

The Google API, in addition to simple keyword queries, supports the following ["Special Syntaxes" in Chapter 1]:

```
site:
daterange:
intitle:
inurl:
allintext:
allinlinks:
filetype:
info:
link:
related:
cache:
```

Can't Do

The Google API does not support these special syntaxes:

```
phonebook:
rphonebook:
bphonebook:
stocks:
```

While queries of this sort provide no individual results, aggregate result data is sometimes returned and can prove rather useful. googly.php **[Hack #96]**, for instance, displays the number of results (estimatedTotalResultsCount).

The 10-Result Limit

While searches through the standard Google.com home page can be tuned **["Setting Preferences" in Chapter 1]** to return 10, 20, 30, 50, or 100 results per page, the Google Web API limits the number to 10 per query. This doesn't mean, mind you, that the rest are not available to you, but it takes a wee bit of creative programming entailing looping through results, 10 at a time **[Hack #95]**.

What's in the Results

The Google API provides both aggregate and per-result data in its result set.

Aggregate data. The aggregate data, information on the query itself and on the kinds and number of results that query turned up, consists of:

<documentFiltering>
> A Boolean (true/false) value specifying whether or not results were filtered for very similar results or those that come from the same web host.

<searchComments>
> Any commentary (e.g., a note about stop words being removed) Google might throw in that would usually be displayed just beneath the search box on a typical Google results page.

<estimatedTotalResultsCount>
> An estimate of how many results might be found for your search in the Google index. This number may vary from invocation to invocation, moment to moment—thus the "estimated" proviso.

<estimateIsExact>
> Google may sometimes be sure of its estimatedTotalResultsCount, in which case estimateIsExact will be set to true.

<resultElements>
> The individual results themselves, returned as an array.

<searchQuery>
> Your Google query, right back at you.

<startIndex>
> The index of the first result in the current array of results. Assuming your query asked for a start of 0, the first result will have a startIndex of 1. If you asked for a start of 25, startIndex would be 26. Yes, I know it's confusing that start is zero-based, while startIndex is one-based, but that's the way the cookie crumbles, I'm afraid.

`<endIndex>`
The index of the last result in the current array of results. This is always whatever you set as start + maxResults in your query, unless the total is greater than the number of estimatedTotalResultsCount, in which case it is simply estimatedTotalResultsCount.

`<searchTips>`
May provide suggestions on better using Google, suitable for displaying to the end user.

`<directoryCategories>`
A list of directory categories, if any, associated with the query

`<searchTime>`
The time spent by the Google server (in seconds) on your search.

Individual search result data. The "guts" of a search result—the URLs, page titles, and snippets—are returned in a `<resultElements>` list. Each result consists of the following elements:

`<summary>`
The Google Directory summary, if available.

`<URL>`
The search result's URL, consistently starts with http://.

`<snippet>`
A brief excerpt of the page with query terms highlighted in bold (HTML `<b>` `</b>` tags).

`<title>`
The page title in HTML.

`<cachedSize>`
The size in kilobytes (K) of the Google-cached version of the page, if available.

`<relatedInformationPresent>`
If set to 1, means a related: search on the current result's URL will turn up something of use.

`<hostName>`
When you set filter to true in your query, only two results from the same hostname are included in your set of results. In the second of these results, hostName is set to the host from which the result came.

`<directoryTitle>`
The title under which this result appears in the Google Directory (*http:// directory.google.com*, a.k.a. the Open Directory Project) if it is in the directory at all.

`<directoryCategory>`
The Google Directory category, if any, in which you'll find this result. `<directoryCategory>` consists of `<fullViewableName>`, the name given to the category itself, and `<specialEncoding>`, any special encoding assigned to the directory category at hand.

You no doubt notice the conspicuous absence of PageRank. Google does not make PageRank available through anything but the official Google Toolbar [Hack #60]. You can get a general idea of a page's popularity by looking over the *popularity bars* in the Google Directory.

A Note on Spidering and Scraping

Some small share of the hacks in this book involve *spidering*, or meandering through sites and scraping data from their web pages to be used outside of their intended context. Given that we have the Google API at our disposal, why then do we resort at times to spidering and scraping?

The main reason is simply that you can't gain access to everything Google through the API. While it nicely serves the purposes of searching the Web programmatically, the API (at the time of this writing) doesn't go any further than Google's main web search index. And it's even limited in what you can pull from the index. You can't do a phonebook search, trawl Google News, leaf through Google Catalogs, or interact in any way with any of Google's other specialty search properties.

So, while Google provides a good start in its API, there are more often than not situations in which you can't get to the Google data that you're most interested in. Not to mention combining what you can get through the Google API with data from other sites without such a convenience. That's where spidering and scraping comes in.

That said, there are a few things that you need to keep in mind when resorting to scraping:

Scrapers are brittle
The shelf life of a scraper is only as long as the page it is scraping remains formatted in about the same manner. When the page changes, your scraper can—and most likely will—break.

Tread lightly
Tread lightly, taking only as much as you need and no more. If all you need is the data from the page that you already have open in your browser, save the source and scrape that.

Maximize your effectiveness

Make the most out of every page you scrape. Rather than hitting Google again and again for the next 10 results and the next 10, set your preferences **["Setting Preferences" in Chapter 1]** so that you get all you can on a single page. For instance, set your preferred number of results to 100 rather than the default 10.

Mind the terms of service

It might be tempting to go one step further and create programs that automate retrieving and scraping, but you're more likely to tread on the toes of the site owner (Google or otherwise) and be asked to leave or simply locked out.

So use the API whenever you can, scrape only when you absolutely must, and mind your p's and q's when fiddling about with other people's data.

Program Google in Perl

#92   This simple script illustrates the basics of programming the Google Web API with Perl and lays the groundwork for the lion's share of hacks to come.

The vast majority of hacks in this book are written in Perl. While the specifics vary from hack to hack, much of the busy work of querying the Google API and looping over the results remain essentially the same. This hack is utterly basic, providing a foundation on which to build more complex and interesting applications. If you haven't done anything of this sort before, this hack is a good starting point for experimentation. It simply submits a query to Google and prints out the results.

The Code

Type the following code into your preferred plain-text editor—be it Notepad, TextEdit, or a command-line editor like vi or Emacs—and save it to a file named *googly.pl*. Remember to replace *insert key here* with your Google API key, as explained in "Using Your Google API Key" earlier in this chapter.

In addition to the Google API Developer's Kit, you'll need the *SOAP::Lite* Perl module installed **[Hack #93]** before running this hack.

```
#!/usr/local/bin/perl
# googly.pl
# A typical Google Web API Perl script.
# Usage: perl googly.pl <query>
```

```perl
# Your Google API developer's key.
my $google_key='insert key here';

# Location of the GoogleSearch WSDL file.
my $google_wdsl = "./GoogleSearch.wsdl";

use strict;

# Use the SOAP::Lite Perl module.
use SOAP::Lite;

# Take the query from the command line.
my $query = shift @ARGV or die "Usage: perl googly.pl <query>\n";

# Create a new SOAP::Lite instance, feeding it GoogleSearch.wsdl.
my $google_search = SOAP::Lite->service("file:$google_wdsl");

# Query Google.
my $results = $google_search ->
    doGoogleSearch(
      $google_key, $query, 0, 10, "false", "",  "false",
      "", "latin1", "latin1"
    );

# No results?
@{$results->{resultElements}} or exit;

# Loop through the results.
foreach my $result (@{$results->{resultElements}}) {
 # Print out the main bits of each result
 print
  join "\n",
  $result->{title} || "no title",
  $result->{URL},
  $result->{snippet} || 'no snippet',
  "\n";
}
```

Running the Hack

Run this script from the command line ["How to Run the Hacks" in the Preface], passing it any Google search that you want to run like so:

```
$ perl googly.pl "query keywords"
```

The Results

Here's a sample run. The first attempt doesn't specify a query and so triggers a usage message and doesn't go any further. The second searches for
learning perl and prints out the results.

```
% perl googly.pl
Usage: perl googly.pl <query>
```

```
% perl googly.pl "learning perl"
oreilly.com -- Online Catalog: Learning
Perl, 3rd Edition
http://www.oreilly.com/catalog/lperl3/
... learning perl, 3rd Edition Making Easy Things Easy and Hard Things
Possible By Randal L. Schwartz, Tom Phoenix 3rd Edition July
2001 0-596-00132-0
...
Amazon.com: buying info: learning perl (2nd Edition)
http://www.amazon.com/exec/obidos/ASIN/1565922840
... learning perl takes common programming idioms and expresses them
in "perlish"<br> terms. ... (learning perl,
Programming Perl, Perl Cookbook).
```

Install the SOAP::Lite Perl Module

Install the SOAP::Lite Perl module, backbone of the vast majority of hacks in this book.

The *SOAP::Lite* (*http://www.soaplite.com*) Perl module is the de facto standard for interfacing with SOAP-based web services from Perl. As such, it is used extensively throughout this book and in hacks that you might stumble across online.

While teaching you how to install Perl modules is beyond the scope of this book, we've included these instructions to bootstrap your Google hacking without need of wandering off in search of a Perl book.

It's unfortunately rather common for Internet service providers (ISPs) not to make *SOAP::Lite* available to their users. In many cases, ISPs are rather restrictive in general about what modules they make available and scripts they allow users to execute. Others are more accommodating and more than willing to install Perl modules on request. Before taking up your time and brainpower installing *SOAP::Lite* yourself, ask your service provider if it's already there or if it can be installed for you.

Probably the easiest way to install *SOAP::Lite* is via another Perl module, CPAN, included with just about every modern Perl distribution. The CPAN module automates the installation of Perl modules, fetching components and any prerequisites from the Comprehensive Perl Archive Network (thus the name, CPAN) and building the whole kit-and-kaboodle on the fly.

CPAN installs modules into standard system-wide locations and, therefore, assumes you're running as the root user. If you have no more than regular user access, you'll have to install *SOAP::Lite* and its prerequisites by hand **["Unix Instal-laion by Hand" in the next section]**.

Unix and Mac OS X Installation via CPAN

Assuming you have the CPAN module, have root access, and are connected to the Internet, installation should be no more complicated than:

```
% su
Password:
# perl -MCPAN -e shell
cpan shell -- CPAN exploration and modules installation (v1.52)
ReadLine support available (try ``install Bundle::CPAN'')
cpan> install SOAP::Lite
```

Or, if you prefer one-liners:

```
% sudo perl -MCPAN -e 'install SOAP::Lite'
```

In either case, go grab yourself a cup of coffee, meander the garden, read the paper, and check back once in a while. Your terminal's sure to be riddled with incomprehensible gobbledygook that you can, for the most part, summarily ignore. You may be asked a question or three; in most cases, simply hitting return to accept the default answer will do the trick.

Unix Installation by Hand

If CPAN installation didn't quite work as expected, you can of course install *SOAP::Lite* by hand. Download the latest version from SOAPLite. com (*http://www.soaplite.com/*), unpack, and build it like so:

```
% tar xvzf SOAP-Lite-latest.tar.gz
SOAP-Lite-0.55
SOAP-Lite-0.55/Changes
...
SOAP-Lite-0.55/t/37-mod_xmlrpc.t
SOAP-Lite-0.55/t/TEST.pl
% cd SOAP-Lite-0.XX
% perl Makefile.PL
We are about to install SOAP::Lite and for your convenience will
provide you with list of modules and prerequisites, so you'll be able
to choose only modules you need for your configuration.
XMLRPC::Lite, UDDI::Lite, and XML::Parser::Lite are included by default.
Installed transports can be used for both SOAP::Lite and XMLRPC::Lite.
Client HTTP support (SOAP::Transport::HTTP::Client)        [yes]
Client HTTPS support (SOAP::Transport::HTTPS::Client...    [no]
...
SSL support for TCP transport (SOAP::Transport::TCP)       [no]
Compression support for HTTP transport (SOAP::Transport... [no]
Do you want to proceed with this configuration? [yes]
During "make test" phase we may run tests with several SOAP servers
that may take long and may fail due to server/connectivity problems.
Do you want to perform these tests in addition to core tests? [no]
Checking if your kit is complete...
Looks good
```

```
...
% make
mkdir blib
mkdir blib/lib
...
% make test
PERL_DL_NONLAZY=1 /usr/bin/perl -Iblib/arch -Iblib/lib
-I/System/Library/Perl/darwin -I/System/Library/Perl -e 'use
Test::Harness qw(&runtests $verbose); $verbose=0; runtests @ARGV;'
t/01-core.t t/02-payload.t t/03-server.t t/04-attach.t t/05-customxml.t
t/06-modules.t t/07-xmlrpc_payload.t t/08-schema.t t/01-core...........
...
# sudo make install
Password:
Installing /Library/Perl/XMLRPC/Lite.pm
Installing /Library/Perl/XMLRPC/Test.pm
...
```

If, during the perl Makefile.PL phase, you run into any warnings about installing prerequisites, install each in turn before attempting to install *SOAP::Lite* again. A typical prerequisite warning looks something like this:

```
Checking if your kit is complete...
Looks good
Warning: prerequisite HTTP::Daemon failed to load: Can't locate
HTTP/Daemon.pm in @INC (@INC contains: /System/Library/Perl/darwin
/System/Library/Perl /Library/Perl/darwin /Library/Perl /Library/Perl
/Network/Library/Perl/darwin /Network/Library/Perl
/Network/Library/Perl .) at (eval 8) line 3.
```

If you have little more than user access to the system and still insist on installing *SOAP::Lite* yourself, you'll have to install it and all its prerequisites somewhere in your home directory. ~/lib, a *lib* directory in your home directory, is as good a place as any. Inform Perl of your preference like so:

```
% perl Makefile.PL LIB=/home/login/lib
```

Replace */home/login/lib* with an appropriate path.

Windows Installation via PPM

If you're running Perl under Windows, chances are its ActiveState's Active-Perl (*http://www.activestate.com/Products/ActivePerl/*). Thankfully, Active-Perl's outfitted with a CPAN-like module installation utility. The Programmer's Package Manager (PPM, *http://aspn.activestate.com/ASPN/Downloads/ActivePerl/PPM/*) grabs nicely packaged module bundles from the ActiveState archive and drops them into place on your Windows system with little need of help from you.

Simply launch PPM from inside a DOS terminal window and tell it to install the *SOAP::Lite* bundle.

```
C:\>ppm
PPM interactive shell (2.1.6) - type 'help' for available commands.
PPM> install SOAP::Lite
```

If you're running a reasonably recent build, you're probably in for a pleasant surprise:

```
C:\>ppm
PPM interactive shell (2.1.6) - type 'help' for available commands.
PPM> install SOAP::Lite
Version 0.55 of 'SOAP-Lite' is already installed.
```

A Note About Expat

There's a little something called Expat (*http://expat.sourceforge.net*) that, more often than not, is the one hiccup in the installation process—particularly when installing using the CPAN module or by hand. Expat is an XML parser library written in the C programming language and underlying many of the XML modules that you might use. Fortunately, you'll probably find it installed by default on the system you're using, but if it isn't there, you won't get very far.

The easiest way to install Expat under Mac OS X or Unix/Linux goes a little something like this:

```
$ curl -O http://easynews.dl.sourceforge.net/sourceforge/expat/expat-X.XX.X.
tar.gz
$ tar -xvzf xpat-X.XX.X.tar.gz
...
$ cd expat-X.XX.X
$ ./configure
$ make
$ sudo make install
```

HACK #94   Program Google with the Net::Google Perl Module

A crisp, clean, object-oriented alternative to programming Google with Perl and the SOAP::Lite module.

An alternative, more object-oriented Perl interface to the Google API is Aaron Straup Cope's *Net::Google* (*http://search.cpan.org/search?query=net+google&mode=module*). While not fundamentally different from using *SOAP::Lite* [Hack #93] as we do throughout this book, constructing Google API queries and dealing with the results is a little cleaner.

There are three main Google API interfaces defined by the module: search( ), spelling(), and cache( ) for talking to the Google Web search engine, spellchecker, and Google cache, respectively.

To provide a side-by-side comparison to *googly.pl* [Hack #92], the typical *SOAP::Lite*–based way to talk to the Google API, we've provided a script identical in function and almost so in structure.

The Code

Save the following script as *net_googly.pl*. Replace *insert key here* with your Google API key as you type in the code.

> Mind you, you'll still need *SOAP::Lite* and a couple of other prerequisites to use *Net::Google*.

```perl
#!/usr/local/bin/perl
# net_googly.pl
# A typical Google API script using the Net::Google Perl module.
# Usage: perl net_googly.pl <query>

use strict;

# Use the Net::Google Perl module.
use Net::Google;

# Your Google API developer's key.
use constant GOOGLE_API_KEY => 'insert key here';

# Take the query from the command line.
my $query = shift @ARGV or die "Usage: perl net_googly.pl <query>\n";

# Create a new Net::Google instance.
my $google = Net::Google->new(key => GOOGLE_API_KEY);

# And create a new Net::Google search instance.
my $search = $google->search();

# Build a Google query.
$search->query($query);
$search->starts_at(0);
$search->max_results(10);
$search->filter(0);

# Query Google.
$search->results();

# Loop through the results.
foreach my $result ( @{$search->results()} ) {
```

```
# Print out the main bits of each result.
print
  join "\n",
  $result->title() || "no title",
  $result->URL(),
  $result->snippet() || 'no snippet',
  "\n";
}
```

Notice that the code is all but identical to that of *googly.pl* [Hack #92]. The only real changes (called out in bold) are cleaner object-oriented method calls for setting query parameters and dealing with the results. So, rather than passing a set of parameters to a *SOAP::Lite* service call like this:

```
doGoogleSearch(
      $google_key, $query, 0, 10, "false", "",  "false",
      "", "latin1", "latin1"
);
```

Set these parameters individually like this:

```
$search->query($query);
$search->starts_at(0);
$search->max_results(10);
$search->filter(0);
```

Not much difference, but definitely cleaner.

Running the Hack

Invoke the hack on the command line in just the same manner you did in "Program Google in Perl" [Hack #92]:

```
$ perl net_googly.pl "query keywords"
```

The results will be just the same.

Loop Around the 10-Result Limit

#95   If you want more than 10 results, you'll have to loop.

The Google API returns only 10 results per query, plenty for some queries, but for most applications, 10 results barely scratches the surface. If you want more than 10 results, you're going to have to loop, querying for the next set of 10 each time. The first query returns the top 10. The next, 11 through 20. And so forth.

This hack builds on the basic Perl script *googly.pl* [Hack #92] that we showed you in the previous hack. To get at more than the top 10 results, no matter the programming language you're using, you'll have to create a loop.

Bear in mind that each and every query counts against your daily allotment. Loop three times and you've used up three queries. Ten, and you're down 10. While this doesn't seem like much given your quota of 1,000 queries a day, you'd be surprised how quickly you can reach the bottom of the cookie jar without knowing where they all went.

The Code

Save the following code to a text file named *looply.pl*. Again, remember to replace *insert key here* with your Google API key, as explained in "Using Your Google API Key" earlier in this chapter.

In addition to the Google API Developer's Kit, you'll need the *SOAP::Lite* Perl module [Hack #93] installed before running this hack.

The alterations to the previous hack needed to support looping through more than the first 10 results are called out in bold.

```
#!/usr/local/bin/perl
# looply.pl
# A typical Google Web API Perl script.
# Usage: perl looply.pl <query>

# Your Google API developer's key.
my $google_key='insert key here';

# Location of the GoogleSearch WSDL file.
my $google_wdsl = "./GoogleSearch.wsdl";

# Number of times to loop, retrieving 10 results at a time.
my $loops = 3; # 3 loops x 10 results per loop = top 30 results

use strict;

# Use the SOAP::Lite Perl module.
use SOAP::Lite;

# Take the query from the command line.
my $query = shift @ARGV or die "Usage: perl looply.pl <query>\n";

# Create a new SOAP::Lite instance, feeding it GoogleSearch.wsdl.

my $google_search = SOAP::Lite->service("file:$google_wdsl");

# Keep track of result number.
my $number = 0;
```

```
for (my $offset = 0; $offset <= ($loops-1)*10; $offset += 10) {
# Query Google.
my $results = $google_search ->
 doGoogleSearch(
   $google_key, $query, $offset, 10, "false", "", "false",
   "", "latin1", "latin1"
 );

# No sense continuing unless there are more results.
last unless @{$results->{resultElements}};

# Loop through the results.
foreach my $result (@{$results->{'resultElements'}}) {

# Print out the main bits of each result.
print
 join "\n",
 ++$number,
 $result->{title} || "no title",
 $result->{URL},
 $result->{snippet} || 'no snippet',
 "\n";

}
}
```

Notice that the script tells Google which set of 10 results it's after by passing an offset ($offset). The offset is increased by 10 each time ($offset += 10).

Running the Script

Run this script from the command line ["How to Run the Hacks" in the Preface], passing it your Google search:

```
$ perl looply.pl "query keywords"
```

The Results

Here's a sample run. The first attempt doesn't specify a query and so triggers a usage message and doesn't go any further. The second searches for learning perl and prints out the results. Output is just the same as for the *googly.pl* script in the prior hack, but now the number of results you net is limited only by your specified loop count (in this case 3, netting 3 × 10 or 30 results).

```
$ perl googly.pl
Usage: perl looply.pl <query>
% perl looply.pl "learning perl"
1
oreilly.com -- Online Catalog: Learning Perl, 3rd Edition
```

```
http://www.oreilly.com/catalog/lperl3/
... Learning Perl, 3rd Edition Making Easy Things
Easy and Hard Things Possible By Randal<br> L. Schwartz, Tom Phoenix
3rd Edition July 2001 0-596-00132-0, Order Number ...

...
29
Intro to Perl for CGI
http://hotwired.lycos.com/webmonkey/98/47/index2a.html
... Some people feel that the benefits of learning
Perl scripting are few.<br> But ... part. That's right.
Learning Perl is just like being a cop. ...
30
WebDeveloper.com ®: Where Web Developers and Designers Learn How ...
http://www.webdeveloper.com/reviews/book6.html
... Registration CreditCard Processing Compare Prices.
Learning Perl. Learning<br> Perl, 2nd Edition.
Publisher: O'Reilly Author: Randal Schwartz ...
```

Hacking the Hack

Alter the value assigned to the $loops variable to change the number of results. For instance, to loop 9 times and grab the top 90 results, change things like so:

```
# Number of times to loop, retrieving 10 results at a time.
my $loops = 9; # 9 loops x 10 results per loop = top 90 results
```

Program Google in PHP

HACK
#96

A simple example of programming the Google Web API with PHP and the NuSOAP module.

PHP (*http://www.php.net/*), a recursive acronym for PHP Hypertext Processing, has seen wide use as the HTML-embedded scripting language for web development. Add to that the NuSOAP PHP module for creating and consuming SOAP-based web services (*http://dietrich.ganx4.com/nusoap*) and you have a powerful combination.

This hack illustrates basic use of PHP and NuSOAP in concert to interact with the Google Web API.

The Code

Save the following code as a plain text file named *googly.php* somewhere on your web site where PHP is able to run. Don't forget to replace *insert key here* with your Google API key.

```
<!--
# googly.php
```

```
# A typical Google Web API php script.
# Usage: Point your browser at googly.php\
-->
<html>
<head>
 <title>googly.php</title>
</head>
<body>

<h1>Googly</h1>

<form method="GET">

Query: <input name="query" value="<? print $HTTP_GET_VARS['query'] ?>">
<input type="submit" name="Search">

</form>

<?

# Run the search only if you're provided a query to work with.
if ($HTTP_GET_VARS['query']) {

  # Use the NuSOAP php library.
  require_once('nusoap.php');

  # Set parameters.
  $parameters = array(
    'key'=>'insert key here',
    'q' => $HTTP_GET_VARS['query'],
    'start' => 0,
    'maxResults' => 10,
    'filter' => false,
    'restrict' => '',
    'safeSearch' => false,
    'lr' => '',
    'ie' => 'latin',
    'oe' => 'latin'
  );

  # Create a new SOAP client, feeding it GoogleSearch.wsdl on Google's site.
  $soapclient = new soapclient("http://api.google.com/search/beta2");

  # Query Google.
  $results = $soapclient->call('doGoogleSearch',$parameters, 'urn:
GoogleSearch', 'urn:GoogleSearch');

  # Results?
  if ( is_array($results['resultElements']) ) {
    print "<p>Your Google query for '" . $HTTP_GET_VARS['query'] . "' found
"
      . $results['estimatedTotalResultsCount'] . " results, the top ten of
which are:</p>";
```

```
    foreach ( $results['resultElements'] as $result ) {
      print
        "<p><a href='" . $result['URL'] . "'>" .
        ( $result['title'] ? $result['title'] : 'no title' ) .
        "</a><br />" . $result['URL'] . "<br />" .
        ( $result['snippet'] ? $result['snippet'] : 'no snippet' ) .
        "</p>";
    }
  }

  # No results.
  else {
    print "Your Google query for '" . $HTTP_GET_VARS['query'] . "' returned
no results";
  }

}
?>

</body>
</html>
```

Running the Hack

Point your web browser at your *googly.php*, fill in a query, and click the
Search button. Figure 9-1 shows the results of a search for php.

See Also

- An alternate is the Services_Google package (*http://pear.php.net/
  package/Services_Google*), a PHP 5 interface to the Google API.

HACK #97 **Program Google in Java**

Programming the Google Web API in Java is a snap, thanks to the
functionality packed into the Google Web API Developer's Kit.

Thanks to the Java Archive (JAR) file included in the Google Web API
Developer's Kit, programming the Google API in Java couldn't be simpler.
The *googleapi.jar* archive includes *com.google.soap.search*, a nice, clean
wrapper around the underlying Google SOAP, along with the Apache Software Foundation's open source Crimson (*http://xml.apache.org/crimson*)
XML parser and Apache SOAP (*http://xml.apache.org/soap/*) stack, among
others.

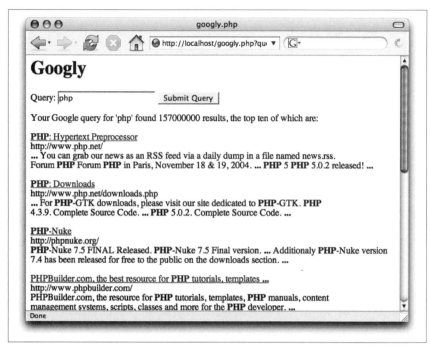

Figure 9-1. Google results by way of googly.php

In addition to the *googleapi.jar* file included in the Google API Developer's Kit, you'll need a copy of the Java 2 Platform, Standard Edition (J2SE, *http://java.sun.com/downloads/*) to compile and run this hack.

The Code

Save the following code to a file called *Googly.java*:

```
// Googly.java
// Bring in the Google SOAP wrapper.
import com.google.soap.search.*;
import java.io.*;
public class Googly {
  // Your Google API developer's key.
  private static String googleKey = "insert key here";
  public static void main(String[] args) {
    // Make sure there's a Google query on the command line.
    if (args.length != 1) {
      System.err.println("Usage: java [-classpath classpath] Googly <query>
");
      System.exit(1);
    }
    // Create a new GoogleSearch object.
```

```
GoogleSearch s = new GoogleSearch( );
try {

    s.setKey(googleKey);
    s.setQueryString(args[0]); // Google query from the command-line
    s.setMaxResults(10);
    // Query Google.
    GoogleSearchResult r = s.doSearch( );
    // Gather the results.
    GoogleSearchResultElement[] re = r.getResultElements( );

    // Output.
    for ( int i = 0; i < re.length; i++ ) {
    System.out.println(re[i].getTitle( ));
    System.out.println(re[i].getURL( ));
    System.out.println(re[i].getSnippet( ) + "\n");
    }

    // Anything go wrong?
    } catch (GoogleSearchFault f) {
      System.out.println("GoogleSearchFault: " + f.toString( ));
    }
  }

}
```

Be sure to drop in your own Google developer's key in place of *insert key here*, like so:

```
// Your Google API developer's key.
private static String googleKey = "12BuCK13mY5hOE/34KNOcK@ttH3DoOR";
```

Compiling the Code

To successfully compile the Googly application, you'll need that *googleapi.jar* archive. I chose to keep it in the same directory as my *Googly.java* source file; if you put it elsewhere, adjust the path after -classpath accordingly.

```
% javac -classpath googleapi.jar Googly.java
```

This should leave you with a brand new *Googly.class* file, ready to run.

Running the Hack

Run Googly on the command line ["How to Run the Hacks" in the Preface], passing it your Google query, like so under Unix and Mac OS X:

```
% java -classpath .:googleapi.jar Googly "query words"
```

and like so under Windows (notice the ; instead of : in the classpath):

```
java -classpath .;googleapi.jar Googly "query words"
```

The Results

```
% java -classpath .:googleapi.jar Googly "Learning Java"
oreilly.com -- Online Catalog: Learning Java
http://www.oreilly.com/catalog/learnjava/
For programmers either just migrating to Java or already working
steadily in the forefront of Java development, Learning Java gives
a clear, systematic   ...
oreilly.com -- Online Catalog:   Learning    Java  , 2nd Edition
http://www.oreilly.com/catalog/learnjava2/
This new edition of Learning Java has been expanded and updated for
Java 2 Standard Edition SDK 1.4. It comprehensively addresses ...
...
Java Programming...From the Grounds Up / Web Developer
http://www.webdeveloper.com/java/java_programming_grounds_up.html
... WebDeveloper.com. Java Programming... From the Grounds Up. by
Mark C. Reynolds ... Java Classes and Methods. Java utilizes the
basic object technology found in C++. ...
```

HACK #98   Program Google in Python

Programming the Google Web API with Python is simple and clean, as these
scripts and interactive examples demonstrate.

Programming to the Google Web API from Python is a piece of cake, thanks
to Mark Pilgrim's PyGoogle wrapper module (*http://pygoogle.sourceforge.
net/*)—now maintained by Brian Landers. PyGoogle abstracts away much of
the underlying SOAP, XML, and request/response layers, leaving you free to
spend your time with the data itself.

PyGoogle Installation

Download a copy of PyGoogle (*http://sourceforge.net/project/showfiles.
php?group_id=99616*) and follow the installation instructions (*http://
pygoogle.sourceforge.net/dist/readme.txt*). Assuming all goes to plan, this
should be nothing more complex than:

```
% python setup.py install
```

Alternatively, if you want to give this a whirl without installing PyGoogle or
don't have permissions to install it globally on your system, simply put the
included *SOAP.py* and *google.py* files into the same directory as the *googly.
py* script itself.

The Code

Save this code to a text file called *googly.py*. Be sure to replace *insert key
here* with your own Google API key.

```
#!/usr/bin/python
# googly.py
# A typical Google Web API Python script using Mark Pilgrim's
# PyGoogle Google Web API wrapper
# [http://diveintomark.org/projects/pygoogle/].
# Usage: python googly.py <query>

import sys, string, codecs

# Use the PyGoogle module.
import google

# Grab the query from the command line
if sys.argv[1:]:
  query = sys.argv[1]
else:
  sys.exit('Usage: python googly.py <query>')

# Your Google API developer's key.
google.LICENSE_KEY = 'insert key here'

# Query Google.
data = google.doGoogleSearch(query)

# Teach standard output to deal with utf-8 encoding in the results.
sys.stdout = codecs.lookup('utf-8')[-1](sys.stdout)

# Output.
for result in data.results:
  print string.join( (result.title, result.URL, result.snippet), "\n"), "\n"
```

Running the Hack

Invoke the script on the command line ["How to Run the Hacks" in the Preface] as follows:

```
% python googly.py "query words"
```

The Results

Here's a sample run, searching for "learning python":

```
% python googly.py "learning python"
oreilly.com -- Online Catalog: <b>Learning</b>
<b>Python</b>
http://www.oreilly.com/catalog/lpython/
<b>Learning</b> <b>Python</b> is an
introduction to the increasingly popular interpreted programming
language that's portable, powerful, and remarkably easy to use in both
<b>...</b>
...
Book Review: <b>Learning</b> <b>Python</b>
```

```
http://www2.linuxjournal.com/lj-issues/issue66/3541.html
<b>...</b> Issue 66: Book Review: <b>Learning</b>
<b>Python</b> <b>...</b> Enter
<b>Learning</b> <b>Python</b>. My executive summary
is that this is the right book for me and probably for many others
as well. <b>...</b>
```

Hacking the Hack

Python has a marvelous interface for working interactively with the interpreter. It's a good place to experiment with modules such as PyGoogle, querying the Google API on the fly and digging through the data structures it returns.

Here's a sample interactive PyGoogle session demonstrating the use of the doGoogleSearch, doGetCachedPage, and doSpellingSuggestion functions:

```
% python
Python 2.2 (#1, 07/14/02, 23:25:09)
[GCC Apple cpp-precomp 6.14] on darwin
Type "help", "copyright", "credits" or "license" for more information.
>>> import google
>>> google.LICENSE_KEY = 'insert key here'
>>> data = google.doGoogleSearch("Learning Python")
>>> dir(data.meta)
['__doc__', '__init__', '__module__', 'directoryCategories',
'documentFiltering', 'endIndex', 'estimateIsExact',
'estimatedTotalResultsCount', 'searchComments', 'searchQuery',
'searchTime', 'searchTips', 'startIndex']
>>> data.meta.estimatedTotalResultsCount
115000
>>> data.meta.directoryCategories
[{u'specialEncoding': '', u'fullViewableName': "Top/Business/Industries/
Publishing/Publishers/Nonfiction/Business/O'Reilly_and_Associates/
Technical_Books/Python"}]
>>> dir(data.results[5])
['URL', '__doc__', '__init__', '__module__', 'cachedSize',
'directoryCategory', 'directoryTitle', 'hostName',
'relatedInformationPresent', 'snippet', 'summary', 'title']
>>> data.results[0].title
'oreilly.com -- Online Catalog: <b>Learning</b> <b>Python'
>>> data.results[0].URL
'http://www.oreilly.com/catalog/lpython/'
>>> google.doGetCachedPage(data.results[0].URL)
'<meta http-equiv="Content-Type" content="text/html; charset=ISO-8859-1">\n
<BASE HREF="http://www.oreilly.com/catalog/lpython/"><table border=1
...
>>> google.doSpellingSuggestion('lurn piethon')
'learn python'
```

Program Google in C# and .NET

#99

Create GUI and console Google search applications with C# and the .NET framework.

The Google Web APIs Developer's Kit includes a sample C# Visual Studio .NET (*http://msdn.microsoft.com/vstudio/*) project for a simple GUI Google search application (take a look in the *dotnet/CSharp* folder). The functional bits that you would probably find most interesting are in the *Form1.cs* code.

This hack provides basic code for a simple console Google search application similar in function (and, in the case of Java [Hack #97], form, too) to those in Perl [Hack #92], Python [Hack #98], et al.

> Compiling and running this hack requires that you have the .NET Framework (*http://msdn.microsoft.com/netframework/downloads/updates/default.aspx*) installed.

The Code

Type this code and save it to a text file called *googly.cs*:

```
// googly.cs
// A Google Web API C# console application.
// Usage: googly.exe <query>
// Copyright (c) 2002, Chris Sells.
// No warranties extended. Use at your own risk.
using System;
class Googly {
  static void Main(string[] args) {
    // Your Google API developer's key.
    string googleKey = "insert key here";
    // Take the query from the command line.
    if( args.Length != 1 ) {
      Console.WriteLine("Usage: google.exe <query>");
      return;
    }
    string query = args[0];
    // Create a Google SOAP client proxy, generated by:
    // c:\> wsdl.exe http://api.google.com/GoogleSearch.wsdl
    GoogleSearchService googleSearch = new GoogleSearchService( );
    // Query Google.
    GoogleSearchResult results = googleSearch.doGoogleSearch(googleKey,
query, 0, 10, false, "", false, "", "latin1", "latin1");
    // No results?
    if( results.resultElements == null ) return;
    // Loop through results.
    foreach( ResultElement result in results.resultElements ) {
      Console.WriteLine( );
```

```
            Console.WriteLine(result.title);
            Console.WriteLine(result.URL);
            Console.WriteLine(result.snippet);
            Console.WriteLine(  );
        }
    }
}
```

Remember to insert your Google developer's key in place of *insert key here,* like so:

```
// Your Google API developer's key.
string googleKey = "12BuCK13mY5hOE/34KNOcK@ttH3DoOR";
```

Compiling the Code

Before compiling the C# code itself, you must create a Google SOAP client proxy. The proxy is a wodge of code custom-built to the specifications of the *GoogleSearch.wsdl* file, an XML-based description of the Google Web Service, all its methods, parameters, and return values. Fortunately, you don't have to do this by hand; the .NET Framework kit includes an application, *wsdl.exe*, that does all the coding for you.

 This is a remarkable bit of magic if you think about it: the lion's share of interfacing to a web service auto-generated from a description thereof.

Call *wsdl.exe* with the location of your *GoogleSearch.wsdl* file like so:

```
C:\GOOGLY.NET>wsdl.exe GoogleSearch.wsdl
```

If you don't happen to have the WSDL file handy, don't fret. You can point *wsdl.exe* at its location on Google's web site:

```
C:\GOOGLY.NET\CS>wsdl.exe http://api.google.com/GoogleSearch.wsdl
Microsoft (R) Web Services Description Language Utility
[Microsoft (R) .NET Framework, Version 1.0.3705.0]
Copyright (C) Microsoft Corporation 1998-2001. All rights reserved.
Writing file 'C:\GOOGLY.NET\CS\GoogleSearchService.cs'.
```

The end result is a *GoogleSearchService.cs* file that looks something like this:

```
//------------------------------------------------------------------------
// <autogenerated>
//     This code was generated by a tool.
//     Runtime Version: 1.0.3705.288
//
//     Changes to this file may cause incorrect behavior and will be lost if
//     the code is regenerated.
// </autogenerated>
//------------------------------------------------------------------------
//
```

```
// This source code was auto-generated by wsdl, Version=1.0.3705.288.
//
using System.Diagnostics;
using System.Xml.Serialization;
using System;
using System.Web.Services.Protocols;
using System.ComponentModel;
using System.Web.Services;
...
    public System.IAsyncResult BegindoGoogleSearch(string key,
    string q, int start, int maxResults, bool filter, string restrict,
    bool safeSearch, string lr, string ie, string oe,
    System.AsyncCallback callback, object asyncState) {
        return this.BeginInvoke("doGoogleSearch", new object[] {
                        key,
                        q,
                        start,
                        maxResults,
                        filter,
                        restrict,
                        safeSearch,
                        lr,
                        ie,
                        oe}, callback, asyncState);
    }
...
```

Now on to *googly.cs* itself:

```
C:\GOOGLY.NET\CS>csc /out:googly.exe *.cs
Microsoft (R) Visual C# .NET Compiler version 7.00.9466
for Microsoft (R) .NET Framework version 1.0.3705
Copyright (C) Microsoft Corporation 2001. All rights reserved.
```

Running the Hack

Run Googly on the command line ["How to Run the Hacks" in the Preface], passing it
your Google query:

```
C:\GOOGLY.NET\CS>googly.exe "query words"
```

 The DOS command window isn't the best at displaying and
allowing scrollback of lots of output. To send the results of
your Google query to a file for perusal in your favorite text
editor, append > results.txt.

The Results

Here's a sample run:

```
% googly.exe "WSDL while you work"
Axis/Radio interop, actual and potential
```

```
http://www.intertwingly.net/stories/2002/02/08/
axisradioInteropActualAndPotential.html <b>...</b> But
<b>you</b> might find more exciting services here
<b>...</b> Instead, we should <b>work</b>
together and<br> continuously strive to <b>...</b>
<b>While</b> <b>WSDL</b> is certainly far from
perfect and has many <b>...</b>
...
Simplified <b>WSDL</b>
http://capescience.capeclear.com/articles/simplifiedWSDL/
<b>...</b> So how does it <b>work</b>?
<b>...</b> If <b>you</b> would like to edit
<b>WSDL</b> <b>while</b> still avoiding<br> all
those XML tags, check out the <b>WSDL</b> Editor in
CapeStudio. <b>...</b>
```

—Chris Sells and Rael Dornfest

Program Google in VB.NET

HACK #100

Create GUI and console Google search applications with Visual Basic and the .NET framework.

Along with the functionally identical C# version [Hack #99], the Google Web APIs Developer's Kit (*dotnet/Visual Basic* folder) includes a sample Google search in Visual Basic. While you can probably glean just about all you need from the *Google Demo Form.vb* code, this hack provides basic code for a simple console Google search application without the possible opacity of a full-blown Visual Studio .NET project.

Compiling and running this hack requires that you have the .NET Framework (*http://msdn.microsoft.com/netframework/ downloads/updates/default.aspx*) installed.

The Code

Save the following code to a text file called *googly.vb*:

```vb
' googly.vb
' A Google Web API VB.NET console application.
' Usage: googly.exe <query>
' Copyright (c) 2002, Chris Sells.
' No warranties extended. Use at your own risk.
Imports System
Module Googly
  Sub Main(ByVal args As String( ))
    ' Your Google API developer's key.
    Dim googleKey As String = "insert key here"
```

```
' Take the query from the command line.
If args.Length <> 1 Then
  Console.WriteLine("Usage: google.exe <query>")
  Return
End If
Dim query As String = args(0)
' Create a Google SOAP client proxy, generated by:
' c:\> wsdl.exe /l:vb http://api.google.com/GoogleSearch.wsdl
Dim googleSearch As GoogleSearchService = New GoogleSearchService( )
' Query Google.
Dim results As GoogleSearchResult = googleSearch.
doGoogleSearch(googleKey, query, 0, 10, False, "", False, "", "latin1",
"latin1")
  ' No results?
  If results.resultElements Is Nothing Then Return
  ' Loop through results.
  Dim result As ResultElement
  For Each result In results.resultElements
    Console.WriteLine( )
    Console.WriteLine(result.title)
    Console.WriteLine(result.URL)
    Console.WriteLine(result.snippet)
    Console.WriteLine( )
  Next
  End Sub
End Module
```

You'll need to replace *insert key here* with your Google API key. Your code should look something like this:

```
' Your Google API developer's key.
Dim googleKey As String = "12BuCK13mY5hOE/34KNOcK@ttH3DoOR"
```

Compiling the Code

Not surprisingly, compiling the code for the VB and .NET application is very similar to compiling the code in C# and .NET [Hack #99].

Before compiling the VB application code itself, you must create a Google SOAP client proxy. The proxy is a wodge of code custom-built to the specifications of the *GoogleSearch.wsdl* file, an XML-based description of the Google Web Service, all its methods, parameters, and return values. Fortunately, you don't have to do this by hand; the .NET Framework kit includes an application, *wsdl.exe,* to do all the coding for you.

Call *wsdl.exe* with the location of your *GoogleSearch.wsdl* file and specify that you'd like VB proxy code:

```
C:\GOOGLY.NET\VB>wsdl.exe /l:vb GoogleSearch.wsdl
```

If you don't happen to have the WSDL file handy, don't fret. You can point *wsdl.exe* at its location on Google's web site:

```
C:\GOOGLY.NET\VB>wsdl.exe /l:vb http://api.google.com/GoogleSearch.wsdl
Microsoft (R) Web Services Description Language Utility
[Microsoft (R) .NET Framework, Version 1.0.3705.0]
Copyright (C) Microsoft Corporation 1998-2001. All rights reserved.
Writing file 'C:\GOOGLY.NET\VB\GoogleSearchService.vb'.
```

What you get is a *GoogleSearchService.vb* file with all that underlying Google SOAP-handling ready to go:

```
'------------------------------------------------------------------------
' <autogenerated>
'     This code was generated by a tool.
'     Runtime Version: 1.0.3705.288
'
'     Changes to this file may cause incorrect behavior and will be lost if
'     the code is regenerated.
' </autogenerated>
'------------------------------------------------------------------------
Option Strict Off
Option Explicit On
Imports System
Imports System.ComponentModel
Imports System.Diagnostics
Imports System.Web.Services
Imports System.Web.Services.Protocols
Imports System.Xml.Serialization
...
    Public Function BegindoGoogleSearch(ByVal key As String, ByVal q As
String, ByVal start As Integer, ByVal maxResults As Integer, ByVal
filter As Boolean, ByVal restrict As String, ByVal safeSearch As
Boolean, ByVal lr As String, ByVal ie As String, ByVal oe As String,
ByVal callback As System.AsyncCallback, ByVal asyncState As Object) As
System.IAsyncResult
        Return Me.BeginInvoke("doGoogleSearch", New Object(  ) {key, q,
start, maxResults, filter, restrict, safeSearch, lr, ie, oe}, callback,
asyncState) End Function

    '<remarks/>
    Public Function EnddoGoogleSearch(ByVal asyncResult As System.
IAsyncResult) As GoogleSearchResult
        Dim results(  ) As Object = Me.EndInvoke(asyncResult)
        Return CType(results(0),GoogleSearchResult)
    End Function
End Class
...
```

Now to compile that *googly.vb*:

```
C:\GOOGLY.NET\VB>vbc /out:googly.exe *.vb
Microsoft (R) Visual Basic .NET Compiler version 7.00.9466
for Microsoft (R) .NET Framework version 1.00.3705
Copyright (C) Microsoft Corporation 1987-2001. All rights reserved.
```

Running the Hack

Run Googly on the command line ["How to Run the Hacks" in the Preface], passing it your Google query:

```
C:\GOOGLY.NET\VB>googly.exe "query words"
```

> The DOS command window isn't the best at displaying and allowing scrollback of lots of output. To send the results of your Google query to a file for perusal in your favorite text editor, append > results.txt

The Results

Functionally identical to its C# counterpart [Hack #99], the Visual Basic hack should turn up about the same results—Google index willing.

—Chris Sells and Rael Dornfest

Index

We'd like to hear your suggestions for improving our indexes. Send email to *index@oreilly.com*.

---

product search with Froogle, 20
proper names, 118
properties, 17
prototyping with Python, 332
proximity searches, 144–147
PST Reader, 312
public service announcements and
        AdSense, 366–369
Python
    as a language for rapid
        prototyping, 332
    Mega Widgets toolkit, 311
    programming Gmail interface
        with, 339–341
    web site, 147

Q

query, permuting, 112–115
query word combinations, 66
query words (see search terms)

R

Radial Layout algorithm, 205
Radio Userland web site, 64
Random Personal Picture Finder web
        site, 200
random results, 108–112
Random Yahoo! Link web site, 108
ranking algorithm, 371
recipes, using Google, 99–102
removing material from
        Google, 390–394
repeating search terms in queries, 68
ResearchBuzz web site, xv
residential phone numbers via SMS, 277
results
    category, 24
    comparing with other search
        engines, 166–170
    excluding weblogs, 177–180
    Google box, 90–96
    interpreting, 22–28
    limiting to a specified
        depth, 126–128
    metadata, 24
    page summary, 24
    random, 108–112
    restricting to top-level, 118–123

returning comma-separated
        output, 131
setting for researchers, 26
setting number per page, 26
summarizing by types of
        domains, 129–132
tweaking with URLs, 27
visually displayed, 36–40
results, search
    visual display (TouchGraph), 36
results, tracking counts over
        time, 102–106
reverse phone number lookup, 45
Richards, Peter, xvi
robots.txt file, 370
Rocketinfo web site, 213
RSS/Atom feed reader web site, 227

S

SafeSearch filtering, 17, 26, 135–139
Savikas, Andrew, xx, 264
Scattersearch application, 170–173
Schwartz, Randal L., 87
scraping, 406
    Google AdWords, 350–353
    Google Groups, 229–232
    Yahoo! Buzz application, 163–166
screen scraping, 87
search
    comparing results over fifty-year
        spans, 74
search engine basics, 373
Search Engine Belt Buckle, 283–291
search engine optimization (see
        webmastering and Google)
search form application, 189–191
search forms
    creating your own, 77–80
Search Grid web site, 66
search language, 26
search results by date, 17
search terms
    10-word limit, 6
    combinations, 66
    favoring obscure keywords, 7
    location in document, 17
    multiple iterations of, 68
    permuting, 112–115
    popularity comparsion
        application, 155